SEMEIA 83/84

SLAVERY IN TEXT AND INTERPRETATION

Guest Editors: Allen Dwight Callahan,
Richard A. Horsley, and Abraham Smith

Board Editor: David Jobling

© 1998
by the Society of Biblical Literature

Published Quarterly by
THE SOCIETY OF BIBLICAL LITERATURE
825 HOUSTON MILL ROAD
Atlanta, GA 30329

Printed in the United States of America
on acid free paper

Contents

Contributors to this Issue v

Introduction: The Slavery of New Testament Studies
    Allen Dwight Callahan, Richard A. Horsley, and Abraham Smith... 1

PART I: "Filled with Bitterness"

1. The Slave Systems of Classical Antiquity and Their Reluctant Recognition by Modern Scholars
    Richard A. Horsley 19

2. Servants of God(s) and Servants of Kings in Israel and the Ancient Near East
    Dexter E. Callender, Jr. 67

3. ʿEbd/doulos: Terms and Social Status in the Meeting of Hebrew Biblical and Hellenistic Roman Culture
    Benjamin G. Wright, III 83

4. The Depiction of Slavery in the Ancient Novel
    Lawrence M. Wills 113

5. Slave Resistance in Classical Antiquity
    Allen Dwight Callahan and Richard A. Horsley 133

6. Paul and Slavery: A Critical Alternative to Recent Readings
    Richard A. Horsley 153

PART II: "The Darkest Days of the World"

7. "Somebody Done Hoodoo'd the Hoodoo Man": Language, Power, Resistance, and the Effective History of Pauline Texts in American Slavery
    Clarice J. Martin 203

8. "Brother Saul": An Amvivalent Witness to Freedom
    Allen Dwight Callahan 235

9. Putting "Paul" Back Together Again: William Wells Brown's
   Clotel and Black Abolitionist Approaches to Paul
   Abraham Smith 251

10. Paul, Slavery and Freedom:
    Personal and Socio-Historical Reflections
    Orlando Patterson 263

RESPONSES

11. Reading our Heritage: A Response
    Antoinette Clark Wire 283

12. Paul and Slavery: A Response
    Stanley K. Stowers 295

CONTRIBUTORS TO THIS ISSUE

Allen Callahan
Harvard University
45 Francis Ave.
Cambridge, MA 02138

Dexter E. Callender, Jr.
Department of Religious Studies
University of Miami
P.O. Box 248264
Coral Gables, FL 33124-4672

Richard A. Horsley
University of Massachusetts, Boston
19 Park Lane
Jamaica Plain, MA 02130

Clarice Martin
Philosophy and Religion Department
Colgate University
103 Hascall Hall
13 Oak Drive
Hamilton, NY 13346

Orlando Patterson
Department of Social Studies
Harvard University
William James Hall
33 Kirkland St.
Cambridge, MA 02138

Abraham Smith
Andover Newton Theological School
210 Herrick Rd.
Newton Centre, MA 02459

Stanley K. Stowers
Department of Religious Studies
Brown University
Box 1927
Providence, RI 02912

Lawrence M. Wills
Episcopal Divinity School
12 Fairview Ave.
Cambridge, MA 02138

Antoinette C. Wire
San Francisco Theological Seminary
2617 Le Conte
Berkeley, CA 94709

Benjamin G. Wright, III
Department of Religious Studies
Lehigh University
Maginnes Hall
9 W Packer Ave.
Bethlehem, PA 18015

Introduction:
The Slavery of New Testament Studies

Allen Dwight Callahan
Harvard University

Richard A. Horsley
University of Massachusetts Boston

Abraham Smith
Andover Newton Theological School

It was slavery that first made possible the division of labor between agriculture and industry on a considerable scale.... Without slavery, no Greek state, no Greek art and science; without slavery, no Roman Empire. Without Hellenism and the Roman Empire as the base, also no modern Europe....

—Friedrich Engels

Them days was hell without fire.

—Former American slave

Slavery is a species of social murder. It reduces human life to a travesty of itself, sacrifices human beings on the altar of violent desire. And slavery teaches us what freedom really is. We have never known freedom without it. The paradigmatic *magnalium Dei* in the Bible is the liberation of slaves. The rupture of the Egyptian slave regime by a rag-tag Hebrew underclass, that ancient huddled mass yearning to be free, was the beginning of freedom. The freedom of that mixed multitude was the beginning of peoplehood. And the interdictions delivered to this delivered people, the revelation of the Law at Sinai, the beginning of an alternative political-economic-religious order, inclusive of human rights. Freedom, peoplehood, human rights: all defined by the previous experience of slavery.

In a critically acclaimed comparative historical study published in 1982, Orlando Patterson defined slavery as the permanent, violent domination of natally alienated and generally dishonored persons (Patterson: 13). Slavery is the exercise of a malevolent alien will against a person in a position of humiliation to the exclusion of all other claims and relations. The slave is a walking social atrocity living in the shadow of another's will without respect and without choice in any respect. Patterson was broadening the standard understanding of slavery. He insisted that the heinous human relation of slavery could not be reduced to "the simple reality" of property, as in M. I. Finley's earlier attempt to place the study of ancient Greek and Roman slavery on a more adequate footing. Patterson argued that slavery must be understood as a relation of persons, not property. It is the unique relation between the master and the slave that distinguishes slavery from other forms of compulsory, degraded labor.

> What . . . are the real differences between slaves and non-slaves who are nonetheless salable even against their will? The first difference is the relative power of the parties concerned and the origins of their relationship. The proprietor's power is limited by the fact that nonslaves always possess some claims and powers themselves vis-à-vis their proprietor. This power has its source not only in central authorities (where they exist) but in a person's claims on other individuals . . . the slavemaster's power over his slave was total. Furthermore with nonslaves, the proprietor's powers, however great, were usually confined to a specific range of activities; with slaves, the master had power over all aspects of the slave's life. (Patterson: 26)

In ancient Greece and Rome, as in the United States, the property relation of slavery was a relation between persons. One person, the master, possessed absolute power over the other, the slave. This power alienated the slave from his own will. This absolute power also alienated the slave from any semblance of dignity. Thus, we must recognize the perennial dishonor of the slave if we are to read rightly the stories of life in bondage under the Roman empire.

Before and after Patterson's study, New Testament studies depended on the very different picture of Greek and Roman slavery constructed by a classics scholarship enamored of classical humanism. Before Patterson's study appeared, New Testament scholars followed classics scholars in arguing that the slavery of antiquity was somehow better, more humane, than the institution in its modern forms. In contrast with how inhuman slavery is depicted in modern terms, slavery in the ancient world was characterized by "a somewhat loftier humaneness" (Stuhlmacher). Yet ancient Greek and Roman slavery, like modern slavery in the United States, applied the sanction of law and custom to kidnapping, rape, torture, and murder. The slaveholding ancient elite agreed with all master classes in all slave regimes that the use of the ruthless physical violence of torture, along with the psychological violence of terror, was more than a prerogative of dominical power. "There is no known slaveholding society where the whip was not considered an indispensable instrument" (Patterson: 4). Masters could and did crucify their slaves, and the excruciating death of crucifixion was recognized as capital punishment especially suited for their dishonored status (see Hengel: 51–63).

Even though Patterson's comparative historical study received awards in fields such as sociology and political science soon after its publication, New Testament studies of slavery either ignored it (Petersen; Bartchy, 1992;

Martin) or attempted to blunt its implications (Harrill; Combes). Scholarly assumptions and practices in the field continue to construct slavery so that its natal alienation and brutality are so obscured as to be invisible. (References and citations in the following discussion are intended as illustrations of the New Testament field, not as criticisms of particular scholars; the latter are working on the basis of standard assumptions in the field, mostly derived from older classics scholarship.)

In an apparent return to modern humanism's justification of the ancient Greeks and Romans we are counseled not to make moral judgments.

> We must avoid a kind of ethnocentrism that does not recognize the diversity of forms, attitudes, and circumstances surrounding human chattel bondage in ancient and modern times. It is both methodologically anachronistic and intellectually inappropriate to hold ancient people to modern standards of morality, although the modern person can and should reject certain features of ancient morality, including slavery. (Harrill)

But terror, mutilation, sadism, unchecked perversity and homicidal rage, the "circumstances surrounding chattel bondage," are no less reprehensible because they took place in antiquity. Men were castrated and humiliated, women raped and prostituted, children molested and exploited. As Patterson has shown, these execrations are perpetrated under slavery in all ages. Ancient Greek and Roman social critics saw these as reprehensible and did not wait for modern liberal sensibilities to denounce the rampant sexual exploitation of slaves: Musonius Rufus (12), Seneca (*Epist.* 47.7), Dio Chrysostom (1.37), Justin Martyr (*First Apology* 27), Clement of Alexandria (*Paed.* 3.3.21.1).

New Testament scholarship that gives short shrift to Patterson's insights, however, does so to its own peril. Failure to recognize the perennial dishonor of the slave leads to misreading of evidence such as Greco-Roman romances. "Even with their upper-class prejudices, however, they [the Greco-Roman romances] provide bits of social history" (Martin: 35). The plot structure of romances supposedly "appropriates and abets the popular theme of the successful slave. In most cases, the hero or heroine is of noble stock and becomes a slave in a tragic twist of fate or divine anger" (Martin: 35). But the "popular theme" in these romances is precisely that the hero or heroine is not a slave at all, but someone noble. The "plot structure" thus underscores the assumption that nobility and slavery are antithetical, that enslavement is a misfortune and an affront to the freeborn, and that slaves, as such, are not successful unless and until they are no longer slaves. Supposedly "Lucian of Samosata offers many insights into how he and other ancients from the propertied classes understood slavery in their society . . . . In his *Fugitivi*, Lucian brings a comical outlook to the plight of slave runaways" (Harrill: 29). But these unhappy protagonists are the characters of comedy. Their misfortunes are in no way tragic nor, dramatically, can they be. Tragedy, as Chaucer succinctly defined it, is the story of the man who "falls from high degree to misery." Tragedy is the preserve of nobility. We may weep with kings, but we may only laugh at slaves because, as Patterson has shown, they are "quintessentially . . . without honor" (96).

The failure to acknowledge the quintessential dishonor of slaves and all those with a servile past also leads to a misreading of the humor of Petronius' *Satyricon* in its mercilessly ridiculous depiction of the *arriviste* freedman Trimalchio.

> Later in the supper, after Trimalchio is quite drunk, he proudly tells his story himself. In his eyes, his low beginnings only emphasize his virtues, sound sense (*corcillum*), and business acumen . . . by which he rose to wealth. He came from Asia as a slave boy. For fourteen years he was his master's sexual pet and entertained his mistress as well. He gained power in the household—by the will of the gods, naturally. He pursued business, overcame hardships, inherited his own master's wealth, and became a powerful and immensely wealthy man in his own right: a first century rags-to-riches success story and all thanks to a well-connected and well-used slavery. Or, as Trimalchio says, "Who was a frog is now a king!" (Martin: 36–37)

The point of Petronius' satire, however, is that Trimalchio, for all his newfound wealth and opulence, is nevertheless still a "frog." Wine is required to loosen the freedman's tongue and allow his lips the history of his "success" that he seeks to repress by his ostentation. And though Trimalchio's wall paintings depict his humble origins at the auction block, it remains for Trimalchio himself to inform his guests of the salacious details of his early life as the toyboy of his former master and mistress. Petronius purchases our laughter at the expense of Trimalchio's honor. Indeed this is Petronius' point and the comfort of all nobility discomforted by the precipitous rise of the parvenu freedmen: they may achieve wealth and influence, but they can never acquire honor.

In New Testament scholarship, on the other hand, Trimalchio is the comic figure of the slave as the Roman imperial version of Horatio Alger. Slavery, properly negotiated, is a way of moving up the rungs of imperial society and escaping the poverty and degradation of those who fail to exploit an exploitative system to their own advantage.

> In Roman society, slaves occupied positions not simply as slaves, but as slaves within particular households, which we might imagine as different ladders. Different households (ladders) themselves had different statuses . . . slaves did not seem to desire manumission simply because it brought individual liberty or because slavery was perceived unambiguously as an evil but because manumission was a step higher on the slave's particular social ladder. It is likely, however, that many slaves of Caesar would rather have remained slaves of Caesar than become freedpersons of some nobody. (Martin: 67).

We have no evidence—anecdotal, epigraphic, literary—that slaves desired to improve their situation by "trading up" to a master of higher status. There was no "social ladder" in Roman imperial society. Between the two classes of the Empire, the wealthy *honestiores* and the impoverished *humiliores* lay not a ladder but a chasm. Non-elites constituted roughly 99% of the imperial population. For this latter class, the overwhelming mass of all pre-industrial societies, scarcity was the rule. There was no mid-range economic group within the Empire of any importance, for the structure of the economy simply did not allow it (Meggitt: 49). The imperial Roman economy had no significant intermediate registers between the wealthy and the wretched. Due to the absence of market mechanisms, there was no autonomous or semi-autonomous mercantile class that could amass wealth by its own initiative. Profit-making was in the hands of the elites and effected by their exclusive use of "political capital." "Upward mobility" is a myth of modern capitalism; wealthy merchants of the Empire cannot be read as ancient Horatio Algers. Indeed the captains of commerce—managers of shops, overseers of absentee estates, business agents, ship captains and merchants marine—were often slaves because this occasionally lucrative but socially and economically marginal activity was appropriate to their socially marginal status.

When slaves of antiquity lamented their lot they did not do so with reference to the social status of their masters. The extant testimonies express aversion to enslavement as such without qualification. We have no indication that slaves had a preference for well-to-do masters. Nor is there any evidence that the lot of the slaves of the wealthy was any better than that of slaves owned by masters of modest means. Artisans, soldiers, peasants, even other slaves owned slaves (Meggitt: 130–31), but there is no suggestion anywhere that these slaves rued their servile lot due to the humble estate of their masters. Our sources suggest that the wealth of Roman elites might be exceeded only by their cruelty toward their slaves. No less than the emperor Augustus prevented the nobleman Vedius Pollio from throwing his slave into a pool of man-eating lampreys (Seneca, *De ira* 3.40.2; *De clementia* 1.18.2; Dio Chrysostom, 54.23.1–4). It is the slave of the wealthy, well-born Roman prefect Pedanius Secundus who in 61 CE rose up and murdered him (Tacitus, *Annales* 14.42.1), and it was Roman elites who were slaughtered by their slaves during the political instability of 70 CE (Tacitus, *Annales* 4.1).

More important and more obvious, however, is the brute fact that elective "upward mobility" was impossible for slaves precisely because slavery meant by definition that the slave had no control whatsoever over the ownership and disposition of his person. The claim that "many slaves of Caesar would rather have remained slaves of Caesar than become freedpersons of some nobody" is inconsequential because what slaves would "rather" do was inconsequential. Slaves have no preferences, no predilections, and to speak of them as exercising prerogatives is to profoundly misunderstand the elementary realities of slavery.

Patterson has explained the function of servile subordinates in the imperial household through the analysis of what he has called "palatine slavery" (Patterson: 14; see 302–306), the servitude of powerful elite registers in imperial and royal administrations. These slaves, though wielding great power and exercising wide-ranging prerogatives on behalf of their masters, were serviceable precisely because they were slaves, mere tools of the sovereign with no will of their own. They could be compelled to go where the emperor needed them; cheap, flexible, indeed disposable. Patterson reminds us that their performance and compliance was also readily forthcoming because "They could literally be whipped into shape" (Patterson: 303). The true precariousness of the power of imperial slaves is clear from their fate attending a change of regime. Those most powerful slaves in the previous administration were always marked for destruction: Vespasian crucified Claudius' favorite Asiaticus, and Icelus, Galba's chief executive, was crucified in turn by Otho. (Patterson: 307). "If this was power," writes Patterson, "then we had better recognize it as a very peculiar and perverse form of power indeed and specify its limitations: that its source was wholly influential; that it was completely noninstitutional in origin, practice, and termination; that it had no authority whatsoever; and that it required natal alienation and dishonor" (307).

Under Roman hegemony, slavery was not salvation. Nor was manumission mercy. Roman law suggested that an adult male slave was to be manumitted at age 30 (Bartchy, 1973). The legal evidence, however, shows not that the slave must be manumitted at age thirty, but rather that he should not be manumitted before his thirtieth birthday—not a prerogative but a prohibition with a view to constraining manumission and not liberalizing it. In other words, this piece of legislation was negative in intent and effect: masters were not being ordered to free their slaves but rather not to free them until their life-expectancy had virtually run out. Augustus, the ultimate sponsor of the law, thought that Romans were already too freewheeling in the manumission of their slaves, and wanted to stem the glut of Roman freedmen. Nor did this prerogative of manumission bode well for the slave. Freedman status was accompanied by its own onerous exactions. As a matter of course masters exchanged grants of freedom for money and obligations to future services or *operae*. A patron could inherit one half of his freedman's estate (Gaius, *Institutes* 3.41, in Jones: 16), and substitute his freedman for himself as a debtor to his creditors (*Digest* 44.5.1.10, Ulpian, citing Cassius, in Jones: 22). All these and other prerogatives of the patron were in effect in perpetuity, an irksome reminder of the freedman's servile past.

But perhaps the greatest liability of manumission was inevitable destitution in advanced years. The life expectancy of a male from birth was about thirty years (Meggitt: 67, n. 157). Thus the manumitted slave, perhaps purchased as a child or even born in servitude, was well past his prime at the age of manumission. He would be forced to struggle not to spend his declining years in penury. Surely the shrewder slave owner was more than happy to dispense with the slave, the ultimate dispensable "tool," after having obtained from him the best years of his life. Those masters who did not exercise this option were faced with the prospect of supporting slaves in their service past their optimal laboring years. An aging philosopher pathetically describes the situation.

> . . . after garnering all that was most profitable in you, after consuming the most fruitful years of your life and the greatest vigour of your body, after reducing you to a thing of rags and tatters, he [the master] is looking about for a rubbish heap on which to cast you aside unceremoniously, and for another man to engage who can stand the work. (Lucian, *De Mercede Conductis*, 39)

The slave could become a slave and remain a slave against his will. The master could even force a slave to be free against his will. Even as slavery defines freedom antithetically, it degrades freedom systemically.

Neither ancient nor medieval authors show the interest that has served as impetus for the deluge of modern treatments that has flowed unabated since the latter half of the nineteenth century concerning the question of Paul's witness on the issue of slavery. For until the modern period, thinkers faced with slave regimes throughout the history of the Western intellectual tradition tacitly agree with Patterson that "there . . . [was] . . . nothing . . . peculiar about the institution of slavery" (vii). Aristotle's insight, if we may call it that, that the slave was property with a soul (*Politics* 1253b32), was analysis enough to last the West two millennia. Virtually no one in antiquity made substantive comment on the legitimacy of the institution itself. As Christian exceptions we may cite Augustine, from whose silence all thralldom would have benefited; he has the dubious distinction of being the first in Christendom to propose that slavery is divinely ordained of God and that perpetual bondage has apostolic sanction (*Quaest. in Heptat.* 11.77).

Yet there is ample evidence that at least some legatees of the heritage of ancient Israel were less than sanguine about slavery. Jubilees 11 attributes the origin of slavery to demons. According to Philo the Therapeutae disavowed slave-holding. Josephus tells us the same of the Essenes. Qumran legislation had no place for slavery. In Rev 18:4 John of Patmos condemns Babylon for the crime of slave-trading as the most egregious of the city's iniquities. References to the purchase of slaves in 1 Cor 7:23, 1 *Clem.* 55.2, and Ignatius' letter to Polycarp (4.3) suggests the practice of Christian corporate manumission (Callahan). Christians used their collective financial resources to buy freedom for their enslaved brethren. Some early Christians had serious reservations about slavery in all its quotidian ignominy, and were willing to put their money where their morals were. By their actions they called into question the norm of violence, dishonor, and alienation that made slavery in their time and for all time what it really was.

The essays in this volume were generated in an attempt to return to Patterson's insights and to broaden the discussion on slavery and the New Testament. The project originated in a conversation between a graduate student and a visiting professor nearly ten years ago. Both were surprised to find that New Testament scholars treating the issue of Paul and slavery were still depending primarily on older classics scholarship that, in its touting of classical humanism, downplayed the severity of ancient Greek and Roman slavery. The work of M. I. Finley appeared in bibliographies, but did not affect the prevailing understanding of ancient slavery as basically benign. Most problematic was that New Testament scholars dealing with the issue of slavery had simply not paid attention to Patterson's ground-breaking comparative analysis of slavery. Our first step was to deliver papers questioning recent treatments of Paul and slavery at the "Pauline Epistles" section at the 1991 SBL Annual Meeting. Robert Jewett, who has done much to bring Paul's epistles to bear on issues of contemporary social concern, suggested that we think about a proposal for an issue of *Semeia* along the lines we were exploring. Thus we set about thinking how the scope and approach and perspective of the New Testament on slavery and particularly on Paul and slavery could be broadened appropriately.

One way to broaden the scope was to change the composition—and announce the changing composition—of those observing and analyzing the evidence. Biblical studies in general is witnessing the emergence of multiple voices and a "radical plurality" of methodological positions and directions (Segovia: 4) because of the growth of non-white, non-male and non-Western individuals in the biblical profession who have pushed biblical criticism to consider the "situated and interested nature of all reading and interpretation" (Segovia: 5). On the issue of Paul and slavery, however, many scholars have not widened their background and perspective to appreciate the contributions of the newer voices. For example, in 1984 Amos Jones, Jr., an African American, presented a discussion of 1 Cor 7:21 (a key text on the issue of Paul and slavery) that was sharply critical of the dominant European-American Protestant assumptions and interpretation, but his study does not even appear in the bibliographies of the recent books on slavery in New Testament studies (Martin, 1990; Harrill, 1995; Combes, 1998). One of our goals then was to promulgate the multiple voices at work on Paul and slavery, and, given the effective history of Paul's witness about slavery in the U.S., to have half or more of the contributors to this volume be African American scholars. In line with this quest for multiple voices, moreover, we have attempted throughout the project to implement a gendered investigation: to find, include, and interpret evidence pertaining to female slaves.

Another effort to broaden our scope and approach was to devise a more adequate critical and comprehensive approach to an issue such as Paul and slavery. We are grateful to the editorial board of this "experimental journal" for allowing us to use its offices and pages to experiment toward a more adequate and comprehensive approach. Our experimentation—our attempt to innovate—will be complex, broadly multidisciplinary and far from neatly defined and packaged. Indeed we find that narrow or uncritical experimentation and innovation on the issue of slavery has become part of the problem. A new approach or even a combination of new approaches can be brought to bear on this and other issues (Petersen, on which see Horsley's second essay below), but unless more basic assumptions are questioned and new approaches are adapted more critically and the basic conceptual apparatus of the field of New Testament studies are questioned, the result can be mere reinforcement of the same old interpretation, in this case, a modern scholarly projection on Paul. One can bring in previously unexamined written source material such as ancient novels and inscriptions (Martin, on which see Wills's essay below), but unless one is aware of the ancient sociology of knowledge and of writing-and-reading, the source material is easily misunderstood and inappropriately construed.

Broadening the scope of New Testament research entails special attention to the social location both of the extant literary evidence and of the various receptions of Paul. Because New Testament studies, and the classical studies on which it is often dependent, have ordinarily not taken class- or social power-relations into consideration, it has often been unclear or imprecise in assessing evidence, particularly literary evidence. By taking the social location of literary evidence into account, it is possible to determine more closely how it can be used—in this case, in the interpretation of ancient attitudes toward slaves and slavery. For example, since ancient "novels" were not "popular" literature in the sense that ordinary people read them, they cannot be taken as evidence for "popular" attitudes toward slavery in the sense of ordinary people's attitudes (see Wills below).

By taking into account the ways ancient slavery and Paul's stance on slavery are treated in a field of study (Paul) heavily determined by the German Lutheran scholars who pioneered the critical scholarship on Paul, one begins to see how important it is to *use* yet *move beyond* historical critical analysis of slavery in the ancient world and of Paul's stance toward slavery. Woven throughout this volume then is an acknowledgment of how the study and interpretation of Paul has been so dominated by Protestant, especially Lutheran, theology, by established academic New Testament studies and by European assumptions and viewpoints. Rather than to take these assumptions and viewpoints as the natural ways of examining Paul and slavery, we determined that it is often necessary to cut through or to by-pass or, better yet, to challenge and confront those assumptions, viewpoints, and conceptual apparatuses.

By taking into account the various receptions of Paul, including the effective history of Paul and slavery, moreover, we seek to explore the power dynamics beyond the text's historical production. Our attention is not exclusively placed on texts, though serious consideration is given to the dynamics about power in the literary evidence about slavery from Israel's scriptures, from Paul and his Jewish contemporaries, and from the larger world of Roman and Greek literature of the first century. Our focus also is directed to receptions of Paul and slavery, for academia—sometimes in its failure to transgress disciplinary boundaries, sometimes in its compliance with received tradition, and often in its quest for authority through putative claims of objectivity—has tacitly supported if not outrightly colluded with forms of oppression. We also think much can be learned from the effective history of Paul and slavery in North America, for that history suggests that persons of African descent were vigorous and astute in their interpretations of Paul and in their discernment of the use of Paul by those who wished to control the identities and the power of blacks and women.

The essays in the volume are grouped into two parts. Those in Part I treat the evidence for slavery in antiquity and attitudes toward it. Those in Part II treat specific receptions of Paul and slavery by persons of African descent in North America. It should be noted that there is a significant discrepancy between the essays in Part I and those in Part II with regard to what "Paul" means. It is standard in the field of New Testament studies to speak of Paul in connection with the "genuine" letters which are by consensus usually attributed to him, with the other letters understood as deutero-Pauline. Ordinary Christian and other readers, however, understood Paul as the author of all the letters, including those in which slaves are instructed in no uncertain terms to be obedient to their masters. Each of the essays below plays a key role in reshaping discussions of ancient slavery and Paul's stance toward slavery in the direction that Patterson has pioneered.

In New Testament studies, inquiries into slavery in the Greco-Roman as the "background" of Paul's stance toward slavery have been dependent on the work of classical historians, especially in Germany. But classical philology and history have been closely linked with European humanism, again especially in Germany. Largely unnoticed by NT studies, classical historians influenced by the work of M. I. Finley and Patterson's more comprehensive theory of slavery have, in the last decade or so, sketched a far more complex and critical view of the Greek and Roman slave systems and of slave experience in these ancient societies. In the first essay of Part I, Horsley sketches a survey of these developments and the difference they make for our understanding of ancient Greek and Roman slavery.

In the Roman empire, however, slavery and the slave system were embedded in a multicultural world empire. Societies such as ancient Judea, that did not have an institutionalized system of slavery similar to that in ancient Greece and Rome, were brought under the political and cultural hegemony of the Roman empire and, in the East, of Hellenistic culture. New Testament literature was produced and shaped in this multi-cultural environment. In particular, Paul and especially the Gospels emanated from ancient Israelite culture recently taken over by the Roman empire. Moreover, we have realized in the last decade or so that even Greek terms for slavery were far from consistent, indeed were complex in having multiple terms and in those terms shifting in their meaning according to context. In his examination of statements pertaining to various forms of servitude in the Hebrew Bible, in ancient Near Eastern context, Callender finds that ancient Israel and other ancient Near Eastern societies had nothing comparable to the institutionalized chattel slavery of ancient Greece and Rome, but only debt-slavery and forced labor. Israel's origin in liberation from the harsh conditions of oppressive forced labor in Egypt, moreover, became the basis for strong objections to the imposition of forced labor by the Davidic monarchy under Solomon and later kings. Indeed because all Israelites are special "servants" of God, it is judged unacceptable that they be subjected to forced labor as "servants" of human rulers such as kings. The term ʿbd, "servant" is used in a variety of ways, including for chattel slavery, but also simply for the high ranking servants of the kings or special envoys of God. Benjamin Wright then examines what happens when the shift is made between the non-slave society of ancient Israel to the slave society of the Hellenistic world and the translation of ʿbd by *doulos* and other terms. The result is a bewildering range of meanings in which *doulos* often has clear connotations of chattel slave status, but can often indicate other relations, including that of an officer commissioned by a king or God.

In discovering the intriguing stories narrated in Hellenistic novels, New Testament scholars were under the impression that this literature that seems far less sophisticated than the standard "classics" of classical Greece and Rome was somehow a "popular literature," giving access to the non-elite of the Hellenistic-Roman world. Informed by recent studies of the very limited literacy of the ancient Mediterranean world, Wills argues that we need to examine the social location of this literature more critically. Pointing to the often unrecognized chasm of wealth and culture that separated the literate elite from the rest of the Hellenistic Roman world, he explains that the Hellenistic novels not only presuppose and address the literate elite, but articulate the social-cultural viewpoint of the elite, including their juxtaposition of their own honor with the degradation of the slaves who make their life of leisure possible.

The paucity of slave revolts in classical antiquity has been used as evidence that slaves were relatively content with their situation. In an examination of slave resistance, however, Callahan and Horsley point out not only that the forms of slave resistance were many and often subtle, but also that a shift to a more critical assessment of historical sources opens up recognition of just how persistent and prevalent those forms of resistance must have been in any slave society. Comparison with slave resistance and revolts in the New World enables historians to read more sensitively the evidence for widespread and sustained slave resistance in the ancient world.

New Testament scholars eager to broaden their horizons to the "social world" of Paul and his contemporaries borrowed what had been almost coextensive with sociology, especially in the United States, in the 1960s. Ironically, the fields of sociology and anthropology had moved past structural-functionalism as being too abstract and concerned with preserving the established order of the large-scale modern industrial societies it was developed to understand. In another essay, Horsley argues that the social science developed to understand the coherence and continuity of a whole modern social system such as the United States may be singularly inappropriate to an upstart movement that was challenging or providing an alternative to the established imperial Roman order. Presupposing the more critical and comprehensive understanding of slavery sketched in his initial essay, Horsley then presents a critical review of recent treatments of Paul's use of slave/slavery imagery and his attitude toward slavery. He attempts to understand the former in the context of Paul's overall arguments in Galatians 3–6 and Romans 6–8 in particular, and the latter in the context of Paul's overall agenda in his mission. He argues that read critically the Pauline textual bases of the standard view that Paul was a "conservative" on slavery and other social issues disappear and that a view of Paul that takes his overall anti-imperial agenda seriously could easily discern that he advocated the transcendence of slavery in the dawning new social order underway in the formation of his *ekklēsiai* as communities of an alternative society to the imperial order. While the better known Pauline disciples who produced the deutero-Pauline literature reverted to the dominant imperial social order based on the slave-holding household, some Pauline communities apparently engaged in the practice of "ecclesial manumission" of members who were slaves, by purchasing their freedom with common funds.

In Part II, Clarice Martin's essay, an examination of the effective history of Pauline texts about slavery, explains how the same texts could be used to create diametrically opposed discourses—a discourse of domination for the proslavers, and a discourse of dignity for enslaved Africans. On the one hand, proslavery apologists approached these texts under the influence of a long tradition of European ethnocentrism and white supremacist thinking and with the presumption that ancient and modern institutions of slavery were relatively benign. On the other hand, enslaved Africans approached these texts under the influence of traditional African moral virtues. These virtues promoted the universal parenthood of God, the dignity of all persons, and the preservation of freedom and justice.

Callahan presents the sheer variety of approaches to Paul by African Americans from the days of United States slavery to now. In this sense, he allows the subaltern voices to speak for themselves rather than essentialize interpretations of Paul into one perspective. The evidence reveals that Paul was sometimes challenged because of his use of scripture or because he was perceived as a generator of a certain type of Christianity, but there is overwhelming evidence to suggest that Paul was viewed as someone whose words critiqued slavery and proffered wise counsel. At times, moreover, Paul's hard sayings were placed in a framework that would maintain Paul's liberative ethos, e.g., the framework of his other more liberative sayings; or in the framework of better, more liberative and less biased interpretations of Paul.

Studies of colonial cultural politics suggest that regimes of representation exert a powerful force in the formation of subjectivity. Certain metanarratives about blackness and whiteness in the 19th century United States discourse were intended to essentialize blackness and thus control the images of African descendants for the benefit of the West in general and the status quo in the United States in particular. Smith's essay examines William Wells Brown's novel *Clotel* for Brown's refusal to allow others to dictate the exclusive terms on which Pauline hermeneutics could be managed. Rather, Brown's novel gives voice to a tradition that was often shunted in the 19th century and that often goes unexamined even today in assessing 19th century black subjectivity in the United States. Smith explores that tradition, the black abolitionist tradition, for its multiple contributions to Brown's re-construction of Paul. Patterson reminds us of the need to evaluate Paul's social morality and political orientation in light of the moral judgments available to him in his own time. Patterson also notes the fundamental contribution of Paul to the concept of freedom carried by post-biblical Christianity into later Western civilization.

The editors are deeply indebted to all the contributors. We are also deeply grateful to the two respondents: Antoinette Clark Wire and Stanley Stowers. Wire reminds us of the importance of attending to evidence for female slaves and reveals in a personal way how importantly the legacy of slavery in North America is still with us. Stowers reminds us of the varying stances which interpreters may take in assessing Paul and of the larger question on the authority of the bible in general and Paul in particular at the dawn of the twenty-first century. Because of the contingencies of academic commitments, not all of the essays were available to both reviewers. We are grateful for the contributions of the respondents as they helped us toward our goal of broadening the scope, approach and perspective of New Testament research on the question of slavery.

WORKS CONSULTED

Bartchy, S. Scott
 1973 ΜΑΛΛΩΝ ΧΡΗΣΑΙ: *First Century Slavery and the Interpretation of 1 Corinthians 7:21*. SBLDS 11. Missoula, MT: Scholars Press.

 1992 "Slavery (Greco-Roman)." *ABD* 6:65–73.

Callahan, Allen Dwight
 1997 *Embassy of Onesimus*. Valley Forge: Trinity Press International.

Combes, I. A. H.
 1998 *The Metaphor of Slavery in the Writings of the Early Church: From the New Testament to Beginning of the Fifth Century*. Sheffield: Sheffield Academic Press.

Finley, Moses I.
 1968 "Slavery." *Encyclopedia of the Social Sciences* 14:307–13.

Garnsey, Peter
 1996 *Ideas of Slavery from Aristotle to Augustine*. Cambridge: Cambridge University Press.

Harrill, J. Albert
 1995 *The Manumissions of Slaves in Early Christianity*. Tübingen: Mohr (Siebeck).

Hengel, Martin
 1977 *Crucifixion*. Trans. John Bowden; Philadelphia: Fortress.

Jones, A. H. M.
 1964 *The Later Roman Empire, 284–602*. 3 vols. Oxford: Oxford University Press.

Jones, Amos, Jr.
 1984 *Paul's Message of Freedom: What Does It Mean to the Black Church?* Valley Forge: Judson.

Martin, Dale
 1990 *Slavery as Salvation: The Metaphor of Slavery Christianity*. New Haven, Conn.: Yale University Press.

Meggitt, Justin J.
 1998 *Paul, Poverty and Survival*. Edinburgh: T&T Clark.

Patterson, Orlando
 1982 *Slavery and Social Death: A Comparative Study*. Cambridge: Harvard University Press.

Petersen, Norman R.
 1985 *Rediscovering Paul: Philemon and the Sociology of Paul's Narrative World*. Philadelphia: Fortress

Robert, J., and L. Robert
 1983 *Fouilles d'Amyzon en Carie*. Paris: de Boccard.

Segovia, Fernando
   1995   "Cultural Studies and Contemporary Biblical Criticism as a Mode of Discourse." Pp. 1–17 in *Reading from this Place*, Vol. 2, *Social Location and Biblical Interpretation in Global Perspective*. Ed. Fernando Segovia and Mary Ann Tolbert. Minneapolis: Fortress.

Stuhlmacher, Peter.
   1981   *Der Brief an Philemon*. Neukirchen-Vluyn: Neukirchener Verlag.

Part I

"All Slavery is Filled with Bitterness": Slavery and Antiquity in the Letters of Paul

THE SLAVE SYSTEMS OF CLASSICAL ANTIQUITY AND THEIR RELUCTANT RECOGNITION BY MODERN SCHOLARS

Richard A. Horsley
University of Massachusetts Boston

ABSTRACT

As the background for their interpretation of Paul and other New Testament literature on slaves and slavery, New Testament scholars have been dependent on portrayals of ancient slavery by classical historians. Since M. I. Finley's trenchant criticism of how Western classics scholars' treatment of ancient Greek and Roman slavery has been determined by the distinctive ideology of classical humanism and anti-communism, and particularly since the appearance of Orlando Patterson's incisive comparative sociological analysis of slavery as "Social Death," more comprehensive and critical investigations into ancient slavery have emerged. Recent studies of slavery as a larger political-economic-domestic system deeply entrenched in ancient society and culture, more sensitive to the lives of the slaves themselves, present a far different picture of the social world addressed by Paul, suggesting serious reconsideration of standard interpretations of Paul and slavery.

In the modern academic division of labor, the history and culture of ancient Greece and Rome have been the jealously guarded turf of "classics" scholars. New Testament scholars of the last several generations have thus depended heavily on classical studies for their knowledge of the Greco-Roman "background" of early Christian and early Jewish literature and history. Nowhere is this more apparent than with regard to slavery.

For the field of classics, however, ancient Greek and Roman slavery was an embarrassment to be downplayed, hedged about with sophisticated apologies, or, if possible, explained away. In the late 1960s, when Scott Bartchy attempted a systematic investigation of ancient Greek and Roman slavery in connection with his dissertation on 1 Cor 7:21, there was no "serious, full-scale history of slavery in the Greco-Roman world" in English or German on which he could draw (1973:30)—and the great surveys by the French scholars Wallon (1847) and Allard (1876) had been largely ignored. The flurry of scholarly investigation into ancient slavery—accompanied by heated debate connected with the Cold War—during the late 1950s and 1960s, moreover, did little to alter the portrayal of slavery available from classics scholars. About the only critical approach available at the time was offered by M. I. Finley in a few then very recent articles, which pointed out the different types of servile labor in antiquity and emphasized the utter powerlessness and social isolation of the vast majority of ancient slaves.

Otherwise Bartchy was dependent on the portrayal of ancient slavery in standard German, British, and American classics scholarship as a relatively benign situation ("much better than modern men are inclined to think"). That there was an "astonishing fluidity of status" between slavery and freedom, including "little difference between a slave and a son" in the Roman household with respect to the legal power of the father, Bartchy (1973:40–44) found in Westermann (1955) and Crook. That the lot of slaves underwent a "definite improvement in the first century (CE) due to a combination of ethical teachings of philosophers and the increasing numbers of slaves born in their owner's house (Bartchy, 1973:67–68) came from Joseph Vogt's Tübingen *Rektoratsrede*, "Wege zur Menschlichkeit in der antiken Sklaverei," and the work of his collaborators such as Lauffer. The "advantages of being a slave" (Bartchy, 1973:71, n250) had been discussed a generation earlier by Barrow (1928, repr. 1968). Since "most slaves were treated well," therefore, it is not surprising that "the vast majority of slaves in the first century accepted their lot and were satisfied with it," partly because of the bright prospect of manumission (Bartchy, 1973:72, 84), as explained by Lauffer and others. The relatively recent West German classicists' ideological attack on the "ideological interests" of recent Marxist scholarship on ancient slavery was the direct source of the sense that the absence of revolutionary impulses among ancient slaves was due to their degree of contentment (Bartchy, 1973:87; Vittinghoff, 1962). It is all the more noteworthy that twenty years later, when Bartchy wrote the *ADB* article on "Slavery" in the New Testament period, the dominant views in classics scholarship on ancient Greek and Roman slavery had not changed all that much, judging from citations in the text (Alfoeldy; MacMullen; Wiedemann, 1981).

The situation is not much different for the few major treatments of Paul and slavery since Bartchy's investigation, which became the standard, widely read treatment of ancient slavery in New Testament studies. Petersen, whose focus is really "the sociology of Paul's narrative world," not concrete historical situations, relies only on Bartchy himself for "the institution of slavery in first-century Greece" (83, n56) and cites only Wiedemann (1981) and Lohse, along with Bartchy, on slave law (73, n11). Martin, emphasizing in passing the complexity of Greek and Roman slavery in general, moves quickly into the opportunities for social mobility that slavery offered. In that connection he depends upon classics scholars such as Barrow, Flory, and Rawson (1966, 1986) for the "unbroken family life" securely counted on by some slaves, and Barrow and Wiedemann for slavery (supposedly) as a method of integrating outsiders into Roman society. Not until the very recent studies of Harrill (1995) and Callahan (1997) did New Testament scholars move beyond the standard portrayals of Western classical scholars and allow the more extensive critical studies of Finley (see esp. 1980; 1982; 1985) and the highly regarded historical sociological study by Patterson (1982) to figure prominently in analysis of ancient slavery as a background for reading Paul and other New Testament texts.

In the same decades that classics scholarship was reprinting old studies of Greek and Roman slavery and generating detailed new ones that reinforced the same picture, two parallel historical dramas were unfolding that one might have thought would have some effect on the study of slavery in the New Testament field, at least in the United States. Outside the academy—and often with some interaction with universities and theological schools—the Civil Rights Movement was growing in scope and intensity, challenging the "second-class citizenship" of African-Americans that remained as a legacy of slavery in the United States. Demonstrations of non-violent "civil disobedience" were rooted in New Testament teachings such as "love your enemies" and "bless those who persecute you." Meanwhile extensive and intensive academic studies of slavery in the United States (and the Caribbean and Brazil) had brought public as well as academic debate over the realities and effects of slavery to a fever pitch. Classical historians, busy defending the "classics" in the curricula of elite colleges and universities in the 1960s, may have seen no immediate significance of ancient slavery, which supposedly was not linked with racial difference. The New Testament, however, particularly the "Pauline" letters, had been quoted for centuries as the divine sanction on slavery, and then cited by slaves themselves and abolitionists in opposition to slavery. It would seem, therefore, that professional students of the New Testament, however belatedly, would be interested in probing somewhat critically the portrayal of Greek and Roman slavery in the classics field, a leading spokesperson of which could still argue in a 1974 publication that "slavery and its attendant loss of humanity were part of the sacrifice which had to be paid" for the remarkable spiritual achievements of Western humanism (Vogt: 25). The following survey is not simply looking for the speck in a neighboring discipline's eye. It is rather an attempt to recognize one of the apologetic logs obscuring our own vision. It may also be of some help in reexamining how New Testament literature legitimated slavery and helped make it work.

Modern Ideology and Ancient Slavery

Vogt, Finley (1980), and Garlan have offered surveys of modern treatments of ancient slavery that may help orient biblical scholars to the classical studies on which we are so dependent. Oversimplifying Finley's more extensive and pointedly critical survey, we will trace the interaction of three strands of interpretation. First we will look at the defense of Christianity as having worked to mitigate the dehumanizing effects of slavery in the Roman world and finally to end it. Then we will consider the strange lack of interaction between (second) the classical humanist apology for ancient slavery and (third) the more fully historical explanation of slavery in ancient Greece and Rome as a product of and fundamental basis for the development of ancient Greek and Roman society. We will afterwards examine the important critical and comparative study by Patterson, and attend briefly to the more critical recent studies by classics scholars that have taken a far more circumspect and holistic approach, under the influence of Patterson and Finley.

In Defense of Christianity

The first great extensive treatment of ancient slavery was also an explanation of how Christianity had worked to end it. Working on the same assumption of the separation of religion and social structures, of personal faith and the established political-economic order, Henri Wallon's massive 1847 treatise, published at the end of a successful campaign for France finally to abolish slavery in the colonies, explained why the ancient Christian opposition to slavery had taken so long to effect any significant change. Accepting the political disposition of society as a condition to which it must submit, Christianity had acquiesced in slavery as a fact of life. Indeed, since the social edifice was already crumbling, it was important to maintain public tranquility and to effect improvement in the lot of the slave progressively through improvement of the master. Tending to its own proper mission, it directed its efforts only to personal morality. But it worked steadily against slavery, which is utterly incompatible with Christian beliefs and values (Finley, 1980:32–33). As further explained by Allard in an 1876 book that won not only the admiring approval of the Holy See but an award from the French Academy, the idea of human equality inherent in Christianity from the start began effectively to influence moral standards only after ancient Roman society became Christianized (Vogt: 175). Such an interpretation of the demise of ancient slavery was not difficult to demolish, as did John Millar in 1771, Franz Overbeck in 1875, and Westermann again in 1935 (Finley, 1980:14–15). Ernst Troeltsch summarized the stance of early Christianity toward ancient slavery: the church accepted it as part of property law and the political order and, indeed, by teaching inward freedom, actually strengthened concrete slave relations in late antiquity (1960:1.132). Vogt (145) nevertheless persists in the belief that Christianity opposed slavery with a fundamentally new view of property and power.

Classical Humanist Apology vs. Historical Explanation

To begin to comprehend the apologetic treatment of ancient slavery in Western classics scholarship, we must remind ourselves of the unique status and authority that classical culture has occupied in "Western civilization." With the Renaissance, of course, came the exciting discovery of ancient Greek and Roman culture. From the Renaissance through the Enlightenment to more recent ceremonial academic occasions, Greek and Roman writers have been cited as paradigms of excellence in style, logic, education, and morals. Athens and Rome were understood as the sources and paradigms of democratic and republican government. The French Revolution draped itself alternatively as the Roman Republic and the Roman Empire. In the United States, public architecture in national and state capitals imitated classical temples, memorializing and celebrating the glories of Athens and Rome.

More directly related to the development of the field of classical studies, the "Great Books" have formed the core curriculum in school and university education for the social elite in Britain and the United States. In Germany the tone for the *Gymnasium* curriculum was set by the New Humanism under the leadership of Wilhelm von Humboldt. The same Spirit (*Geist*) that had inspired the highest development of man's personality and versatility by the ancient Greeks was now to inspire the corresponding development among German youth through a thorough absorption in the classics (Vogt: 171). In the German development of the university with its strict division of labor by academic departments, "classical antiquity became the virtual monopoly of classical philology or *Altertumswissenschaft*, whose goal was to apprehend the high culture, the Geist, the very essence of those incomparable models of spiritual achievement, the Greeks and Romans" (Finley, 1980:38).

The departmentalization of intellectual inquiry, however, inhibited communication across disciplines. Classics scholars certainly proved unreceptive to political economists and historians exploring the role of slaves in the development of Greek and Roman civilization. Certainly classical philologists were put off by treatises on slavery in ancient Greece such as that by Johann Friedrich Reitemeier (1789), arguing that "universal human equality appears to be incompatible with civil society," and discerning in ancient slavery the oldest expression in a civil society of the domination-submission relation. Reitemeier anticipated by generations the concept of the household-economy of Greco-Roman society and Marx's and Weber's later view that slavery played a central role in the historical development of ancient society (Finley, 1980:38). Marx, of course, was instrumental in breaking with "the ethnocentricity of prevailing political economics, which applied modern categories to all the systems of the past, thereby masking the unique features of capitalism itself," and obscuring any differences between antiquity and modernity (Garlan: 4). In his "Notebooks" (*Grundrisse*, 1857–58) written in preparation for writing *Capital*, Marx made an important further distinction between the "ancient" mode of production, dependent on chattel slavery, and the "Asiatic" mode of production (which appeared as slavery or serfdom only from the modern European point of view) in which all producers appeared as servants or slaves of the king or god who embodied the unity of the whole society (Garlan: 5–6). This distinction (made again, in effect, in Finley, 1960) might well have become helpful in historical investigation of biblical and classical societies. This was blocked, however, by a combination of intervening historical factors: the unavailability of the *Grundrisse* until recently, virulent anti-Marxism among key German and British classicists and biblical scholars who dominated those fields, and in the former "Eastern Block," a rigid Stalinist historiographical orthodoxy that boxed all societies into a four-stage scheme of development, omitting the Asiatic mode altogether and heightening the importance of the slavery stage.

Although Marx did exercise some indirect influence on the study of Western antiquity through the sociologists Karl Buecher and Max Weber, he had virtually no influence—or rather a negative influence— upon classical historians. Such influence was most effectively blocked at the end of the nineteenth century by the prestige of Eduard Meyer, who perpetuated precisely the "modernism" that Marx's insights would have undermined in laying the foundation "of our contemporary understanding of slavery in Greek and Roman history" (the opening statement in Westermann, 1935). In *The Decline and Fall of the Roman Empire*, the first modern history of any period of Western antiquity, Gibbon had relegated slavery to a few paragraphs in chapter two. Other historians of antiquity virtually ignored it, except for a few sentences on the helots in Sparta (Finley 1980:22–23). Similarly, the most prestigious German ancient historian, Eduard Meyer, devoted only a three-page section (along with a few other references) to slavery in the fourth and fifth volumes of his monumental *Geschichte des Altertums* (1901–02), on fifth-fourth century Greece.

What became decisive for the understanding of slavery among classical historians, however, were two lectures, on "The Economic Development of Antiquity" (1924b) and "Slavery in Antiquity" (1924a), which "quickly acquired the rank of a binding synthesis" (Christ: 293; cf. 308–11). Meyer insisted that the state, not the economy or culture, is the decisive organism in history and found in antiquity a mirror image of the modern world. Nevertheless, says Meyer, fifth-fourth century BCE Athens stood "under the banner of capitalism" and ancient democracy, like its modern counterpart, derived from the capitalist "spirit." Slavery was a mere interlude and historical irrelevance, a by-product of the peculiar political development of the city-state. It was the corollary, the obverse of liberty, the product of a democracy that was it-self born from the development of commerce and artisan trades (Finley,

1980:44–46; Garlan: 8). Under favorable conditions, moreover, ancient slaves, like modern industrial workers, had opportunities to achieve wealth and upward mobility (Meyer, 1924a). In Finley's judgment, Meyer presents not an argument, but a succession of *ex cathedra* assertions, in highly rhetorical dress, without either evidence or a discussion of the views under attack. In forty pages he makes only eleven references to Greek and Roman sources (1980:47). "In sum, Meyer's lecture on ancient slavery is not only as close to nonsense as anything I can remember written by a historian of such eminence, but violates the basic canons of historical scholarship in general and of German historical scholarship in particular.... What Meyer provided was authoritative support and comfort for already generally accepted views, for the ideology of professional ancient historians" (Finley 1980:48). Meyer's hostility to socialism and intellectual inquiry that might be associated with it "were generally shared in the conservative German academic world." His admirers among classics scholars, moreover, simply "isolated themselves from their colleagues in economics, social science, economic history, and even modern history" (Finley, 1980:49).

Meanwhile, in the estimation of Finley and Garlan, at least, no significant inquiry into ancient slavery was being conducted in Italy, France, England or the United States, including Tenney Frank's *Economic History of Rome* (1919, 1927). Vogt, on the other hand, finds R. H. Barrow's 1928 portrayal of *Slavery in the Roman Empire* "particularly successful, because it avoids... value judgments" (Vogt: 180). Ironically, Barrow was clearly writing from the lofty perspective of British imperialism: "two centuries of experiment and experience in the ruling of subject peoples, of firmness not untempered by tact and sympathy" (xii). In his preface Barrow explains further that slavery played a role in "the spade-work in the task of civilising the world, which is Rome's legacy to later generations," quoting Lord Acton's comment that "it is scarcely an hyperbole to say that slavery itself is a stage on the road to freedom" (xv). Nor does Vogt catch the irony of his positive valuation of A. M. Duff's 1928 book on *Freedmen in the Early Roman Empire*, which in good "orientalist" fashion views "the population mixture brought about by the presence of slaves and freedmen" as "one of the causes of Roman decline" (180). In the *Pauly* encyclopedia article of 1935, expanded somewhat in his 1955 book, Westermann, a student and admirer of Meyer, produced simply another antiquarian exercise the mistakes and limitations of which have received ample attention in critical reviews (Vogt: 181–82; Finley, 1980:53–55; Garlan: 8). Vogt's own history of the Roman Republic (second edition, 1951), finally, "displays more than normal disinterest in slavery" (Finley 1980:58).

In 1951 came an announcement that the Mainz Academy was about to embark on a massive program of research into ancient slavery, under direction of Joseph Vogt. In retrospect, Wiedemann, Vogt's translator, detects an attempt at atonement after the Holocaust, "a kind of 'intellectual reparations' to a dispossessed and exploited class to make up for his failure, as a committed Catholic, to stand up publicly against Nazism" (1987:8).

Finley notes that two broader political-cultural currents exercised the decisive influence on the research program spearheaded by Vogt in the 1950s. The first was the "third humanism," a revival of "classical humanism." For Werner Jaeger, one of its leaders, whose stature as one of the greatest philological scholars of the day strengthened his impact, classical humanism was the work of "the German-Protestant Geist" (Jaeger). The earlier humanism of Humboldt, of course, had accepted slavery as a necessary condition of "that liberal spirit which has not reappeared to a similar extent among any other people, that is to say, the spiritual role of noble and great attitudes truly worthy of a free man." The third humanism simply "turned its head." "Slave/slavery" "does not appear in the detailed indices" of Jaeger's highly regarded three-volume *Paideia* (Finley, 1980:56–57).

In his new research program on ancient slavery, Vogt on the one hand returns to older humanist apology, now for humanism as well as for slavery. At the conclusion of his 1953 essay "Slavery and Humanity" he wrote

> We can appreciate Greek slavery as due both to that vitality which demanded that a man have a complete and active life even at the expense of others, and also to that way of thinking which looks on power not as the aimless discharge of brute force but rather as a rational instrument to bring about order. Slavery was essential to the existence both of this basic will to live and of the devotion to spiritual considerations. . . . Slavery and its attendant loss of humanity were part of the sacrifice which had to be paid for this achievement. (Reprinted in Vogt: 25)

On the other hand, Vogt claims and requires an ominous responsibility for classics scholars, not only to uphold the glorious humanistic standards, but to acknowledge the negative aspects of slavery as well. "Perhaps it has been left to the Classics to uphold the existence of intellectual standards in all areas of knowledge and skill, under conditions of general equality and universal freedom." If "the Humanism of classical studies is to survive in our world," however, we must abandon the old humanist "tolerance of the inhumanity that enabled the Greeks and Romans to secure their development as human beings"; we "must portray human society as it really was without concealing or extenuating its negative aspects." (1974:208–10).

Finley (1980:60) suggests that the sudden new interest in slavery by Vogt (and his students) constituted "a kind of 'saving the phenomena,' rescuing 'classical humanism' by certain concessions." In any case, "human society as it really was" turns out to have been not all that bad, as Vogt found that "humanity" was "constantly cropping up in the practice of slavery itself" (Finley 1980:60; cf. Stuhlmacher). As Garlan (14) points out, Vogt and his collaborators emphasized that slaves were assimilated and integrated into ancient society and that the elite whose progress benefitted from slavery responded by improving the lot of the slaves—somewhat in line with the paternalistic tradition particularly strong during the nineteenth century, in slaveholding America, and in Fustel de Coulanges's *The Ancient City*. Not surprisingly, Wiedemann (Vogt's translator) assembled his collection of texts (1981) in somewhat the same spirit.

The second political-cultural concern driving Vogt and his co-workers' programmatic research clearly arose from the Cold War that had divided Germany in particular. It is significant that Vogt and company began to deploy their research offensive even before research by Soviet and Eastern European scholars had begun to be published. As Finley (1980:60–64) and Garlan (13–14) both explain, however, the West German *Altphilologen* provoked a major confrontation at the 1960 International Historical Congress and in the journal *Saeculum* in preparation for it. In publications connected with that Congress and in the decades following, Vittinghoff (1960, 1962) and others engaged in a blatantly ideological, even defamatory, caricature of Soviet and other Marxist scholarship on ancient slavery, which (then and since) is by no means monolithic. One wonders, however, if Finley's critique quite captures what may have been driving the West German humanistic *Altphilologen* such as Vogt. If slavery was as important in the beginnings of Western civilization as indicated in Marxist analysis, then portraying ancient slavery "as it really was without concealing its negative aspects" might not be sufficient to vindicate the enduring eternal value of the classics. In such an ideologically charged academic atmosphere, Western classics scholars were unlikely to include the broader social, economic, and political issues involved in ancient slavery that were being explored, however schematically, by Marxist scholars. As Wiedemann comments on the sociology of modern knowledge of antiquity, given "the career structure of German universities, in which young scholars are well advised not to write anything controversial," it is not surprising that the intensive new research agenda led by Vogt resulted largely in a series of detailed empirical studies of particular problems. "Disappointingly [they] fail to relate these to a wider picture of ancient slavery" (1987:8). After all, as Vittinghoff (1960:94, n 36) noted, "Everything essential was already said by Eduard Meyer in his foundational lecture of 1898."

By far the most significant development in classics scholarship on ancient slavery was the series of studies by M. I. Finley between 1959 and 1965 (most republished in Finley, 1982), followed by the set of essays on *Ancient Slavery and Modern Ideology* in 1980—partly because he brought historical explanation together with classical philology in the study of ancient Greek and Roman slavery. Trained as an historian, influenced by Marx, Weber, and the medieval historians Marc Bloch and Henri Pirenne and German critical theorists (of the "Frankfurt school") who had fled Nazi Germany in the 1930s, Finley recognized in all of his work that ancient Greek or Roman society must be viewed as an interrelated whole, that the various facets of ancient life, economic, political, intellectual, religious, could not be studied in isolation. Even during the heyday of "objectivity" among historians, he recognized that the historian cannot be a disinterested observer. In his reviews of others' work "Finley sought to strip away the facade of objectivity by pointing out the connection between current 'politics' and the fundamental premises of the works under review" (Shaw and Saller, in Finley, 1982:xvi). He believed the intellectual should be engaged critically in the political issues of his own society.

In his early work on ancient Greek slavery, Finley recognized the diversity of vocabulary in various sources and, particularly importantly, the different types of servitude operative at different times and places in Greek antiquity. Rejecting the Marxist concept of class, he adapted the Weberian sociological categories of order and status, partly because the vagueness of the latter allowed recognition of the psychological dimension involved for the slaves themselves. In what may have become a subsequently misunderstood concept, he delineated a "spectrum" of different servile "statuses" among the particular political-economic patterns prevailing in different societies, times, and locations, including those that were "between slavery and freedom" (articles from 1959, 1960, 1964, and 1965 republished in Finley, 1982). Ironically, some of the historical variations of "servile status" he was painstakingly differentiating had been discerned by Marx in the *Grundrisse* which had been unavailable to him and to the Marxists whose concept of class he had rejected (until the mid 1960s). Finley's second major contribution to the construction and interpretation of slavery in the context of ancient Greek and Roman society has been to expose the conflictual power relations, including use of violence, and to induce ancient historians to think more critically about the interests and agenda of their sources. He does this in an often almost polemical way that makes unavoidable the difference between his own critical view and alternatives. Given the historical roots and continuing agenda of classical studies discussed above, his blunt challenges have been instrumental in clearing some intellectual-academic space for more critical and holistic approaches to ancient Greek society and the Roman imperial order and the important role of slavery in maintaining them.

The Historical Sociological Interpretation of Patterson

In 1982 Orlando Patterson published a monumental comparative historical sociological study, *Slavery and Social Death*, which won prominent awards from both the American Sociological Association and the American Political Science Association. Patterson's research is comprehensive, drawing on virtually everything available at the time in studies of ancient Greek and Roman history, literature, law, social structure, religion, etc. pertinent to ancient Western slavery, as well as parallel studies of slavery in virtually every known historical case around the world. He also draws on significant social scientific theory pertinent to slavery considered in historical societal context, generating important new insights. His study is unusually strong with respect to ancient Roman slavery and makes important suggestions for the understanding of slavery in the context of Roman imperial culture in particular. Until very recently, however, important studies of slavery, particularly of Paul and slavery, by New Testament scholars made no reference to Patterson's knowledgeable, critical, and comprehensive work (Petersen; Martin; Bartchy, 1992). Only in the last few years, in the SBL presentations that led to this issue of *Semeia* (Callahan, 1991; Horsley, 1991) and in the work of Harrill and Callahan (1997) have New Testament specialists recognized that Patterson's study forms the basis for future work on ancient Greek and Roman slavery and on how slavery in New Testament literature and history can be understood in that context. Since Patterson should be read directly, the following paragraphs attempt only a brief summary of his original and stimulating analysis and interpretation.

Slavery was created and maintained by systematic, overt, institutionalized violence (Patterson: 3). In Greek and Roman antiquity this was practiced primarily by the state, often in acts of imperial conquest or re-conquest. Much of the domestic terminology of Roman slavery was derived from Roman military usage and organization (Weaver, 1964). Slaves' powerlessness originated (or was conceived as originating) as a substitute for death. For example, in 4 BCE the Romans simply crucified two thousand Judeans who, they thought, were active in rebellion. Usually, however, the Romans enslaved the young and able-bodied inhabitants in a (re-)conquered area of Judea or Galilee, after slaughtering the rebels, the aged, and the infirm, according to many of Josephus' reports (e.g., *B.J.* 1.180, 222; 2.68, 75; *Ant.* 17.289, 295). The enslaved thereafter lived under a conditional commutation: execution was suspended so long as they acquiesced in their slavery. "The slavemaster's power over his slave was total" (Patterson: 26).

Having been torn violently out of their previous life-situations and removed in chains to a a strange new society, slaves thus lived in a state of natal alienation. They were socially dead persons, without birthright, isolated from the social heritage of their ancestors, "not allowed to inform their understanding of social reality with the inherited meanings of their forebears, or to anchor the living present in any conscious community of memory" (Patterson: 5). As aliens, slaves also lacked a place in the cosmos. Slaves were literally (including linguistically) and forcibly "resocialized." They had no connection with the larger society except through their master. They were of the lineage but not in it—given an often demeaning name ("Little Greek," "Lucky") and regularly addressed as "boy" (Patterson: 63). Older classics scholars, often writing from the perspective of the Greek and Roman slaveowners, had a telling way of describing slavery as "the integration of foreigners" into society. But it was precisely the "alienation of the slave . . . from any attachment to groups or localities other than those chosen for him by the master that gave the relation of slavery its peculiar value to the master (Patterson: 7). This is what made the slave, as Aristotle articulated, an animate tool or an animate piece of property, imprintable and disposable at the will of the master. It would have been extremely difficult for an enslaved Galilean or Judean, bought by a wealthy and powerful head of household in Rome or Corinth, and forcibly integrated into a slave *familia* with a Syrian, a Thracian, a Galatian, and others from various subject peoples, to have maintained an identity and the traditions of his/her ancestors when all communication and interaction was taking place in the ethos of a large elite Roman or Corinthian household.

With M. I. Finley (1968:307–13), Patterson emphasized the "outsider" status of slaves as a key aspect of their condition. This has wide-reaching implications for social relations and "symbolic universes" and their interrelation in Greco-Roman society. In "slave society" the marginal position of slaves is essential to its social and cultural forms as well as to its economic survival. To focus on only a few aspects: (a) "The slave, in not belonging, emphasized the significance of belonging" (Patterson: 47). (b) Slaves, in being enslaved (not being free) or not having rights manifested the significance of being free or having rights. To undergird the binary division between those who possessed true humanity and those who were mere property procedures were required that undermined the slaves' humanity, such as corporal punishment, torture, and availability for the sexual satisfaction of the masters (Finley, 1980:95–96). (c) Those binary distinctions come to appear universal (*ius gentium* in Roman law) or perhaps even natural (Aristotle), and the (threat of) violent coercion by which slavery was maintained appeared natural, legitimated in the nature of things. Says Callicles in Plato's *Gorgias*, "For the suffering of injustice is not the part of a man, but of a slave, who indeed had better die than live; since when he is wronged and trampled upon, he is unable to help himself, or any other about whom he cares" (2.543, trans. Jowett).

Slavery, finally, affirms Patterson, was central and essential in the value of honor that dominated Greek and Roman culture and social relations. In classical Greece, the expanding system of slavery reinforced timocracy's grip on the society. "The preexisting timocratic value system, along with new economic forces, encouraged the development of large-scale slavery. At the same time, the enormous growth of slavery not only reinforced the timocratic character of the ruling class but stimulated its diffusion among all classes (Patterson: 87). To work for a living was utterly despised. To work for another was utterly shameful and degrading. The master's honor was thus manifested and augmented by the ownership of slaves, who had no being except as an expression or reflection of the master's being. Besides doing the work, slaves thus also served the master's psychological need to dominate—indeed to dominate other human beings absolutely, to the point that they were not really humans in the same sense as the master. Even Vogt (8) admits that "slaves were irrevocably degraded in the eyes of the public." The Romans had an even more highly developed sense of honor than the Greeks. Perhaps the most striking manifestation was their need to demean the culturally superior Greeks whom they enslaved by public denigration of Greek character flaws or naming a Greek slave "Little Greek." Other subject peoples, of course, such as Judeans, Syrians, Lydians, Medes, indeed all Asiatics, were viewed as "born to slavery" (Finley, 1980:119). Even for the mass of ordinary Romans and inhabitants of cities around the empire, "the presence of a substantial number of slaves in Roman society defined free-citizens, even if they were poor, as superior" (Hopkins, 1978:112).

Recent Critical Studies of Slavery in Ancient Greece and Rome

Since the early articles of Finley and particularly since the highly suggestive historical sociological interpretation of Patterson, a whole range of studies by classical historians has dramatically widened and deepened the resources available to New Testament scholars on multiple aspects of ancient Greek and Roman slavery and slave systems. The book-length studies mentioned form much of the basis of the summary study of the ancient Greek and Roman slave systems in the next section.

Hopkins (1978) provides a systematic and well-documented analysis of the development of the slave system that provided the economic basis of the Roman imperial elite. He explains and details the integral historical relationship, during the last two centuries of the Republic, between the escalating wars of conquest, the introduction of millions of slaves into Italy, and the impoverishment of the Roman-Italian peasantry, who then joined the urban mobs or became colonists elsewhere in the empire. Not until Ste. Croix did Western classics scholarship finally produce a full-scale "historical materialist" presentation of ancient Greek and Roman societies (including a wealth of documentation). After working through his analysis of the ancient Greek and Roman slave systems, it is difficult again to ignore how important an economic foundation slavery provided for the cultures of the Greek *polis* and the Roman empire. As Garlan points out, however, one must look elsewhere for serious analysis of "the politico-legal dimension which the exercise of extra-economic constraints invariably confers on relations of production and which affects the corresponding theoretical positions adopted" (12). Garlan himself (1988) presented a critical systematic overview of slavery in ancient Greek society.

Critical approaches have been brought to a number of the key aspects of ancient slavery, some of which had not been examined previously. Bradley's books focused directly on Roman slavery (1984; 1989; 1994) present well-balanced analyses of matters such as the intense conflict inherent in a coercive slave system, the manipulation and abuse of slaves, and slave resistance, and are informed by his other research into matters such as wet-nursing and the slave-trade (1986; 1987). The intense recent social-historical focus on the history of the family (Bradley, 1991; Dixon; Rawson, 1986; Saller, 1994) has necessarily included the roles of slaves in the Roman household, since most inscriptional as well as literary evidence concerns the large households of the elite. Saller in particular has demonstrated the relationship between the regular whipping of slaves and the importance in Roman society of sharply enhancing the honor of the wealthy and powerful by dishonoring and dehumanizing slaves. One still finds apologetic attitudes in classics scholarship, e.g., that despite slavery, which can be "rightly deplored," nevertheless "let us admire the Romans and the Greeks for themselves" (Starr: 68). Recent classics scholarship on slavery, however, has developed a far more critical and methodologically sophisticated understanding of the slave systems of ancient Greece and Rome and of what they meant for the lives of the millions of subject people who were enslaved. On the sound theoretical and methodological bases established by Finley and especially by Patterson, these more critical recent studies of ancient Greek and Roman slave systems can provide a more secure foundation for New Testament scholars' attempts to understand the ancient Greek and Roman slavery as the context of early Christian movements and literature.

Slavery and Empire

"In Rome and the Americas, and perhaps in Athens too, mass slavery was a direct consequence of imperial expansion." Since the Roman economy was far less differentiated and developed than that of modern northwestern Europe and north America, however, Roman slavery "was more directly a product of war: booty capitalism, as Weber called it, instead of industrial capitalism" (Hopkins, 1978:113). We do not need to enter the debate over whether ancient Greece and Rome were "slave societies." The key historical point is that both classical Athens and especially late Republican and early imperial Rome created an institutionalized system of large-scale dependence on slave labor for the major portion of basic production by a wealthy aristocracy that presided over an empire. Roman intellectuals themselves understood this, as illustrated by a jurist's etymology which, while surely false, nevertheless reveals the historical awareness that slavery was the direct result of warfare: "Slaves [*servi*] are so called because commanders generally sell the people they capture and thereby save [*servare*] them instead of killing them. The word for property in slaves [*mancipia*] is derived from the fact that they are captured from the enemy by force of arms [*manu capiantur*]" (Florentinus,

Digest 1.5.4.2–3). Other ancient intellectuals confirm the connection between slavery and warfare (e.g., Dio Chrysostom, 15, 25; Varro, *Res Rust*. 2.10.4).

In a complex and contingent development, enslaving millions of subject people was an essential condition and instrument for the emergence of the Roman imperial order during the late Republic. Indeed, the conquest and plunder of a massive empire and the enslavement of millions of conquered people transformed the earlier political-economy of the city of Rome in the course of the last several generations of the Republic. Keith Hopkins (1978) has laid out a systematic analysis and explanation of how this transformation took place—with the exception of his occasional projection of a market economy onto late Republican Rome. Through the plunder taken in their "triumphs" the noble Roman warlords gained massive wealth, the only socially acceptable investment for which was land. Meanwhile, the military campaigns in which the nobles could make their fame and fortune forced prolonged military service on tens of thousands of peasants. More than ten percent of the adult male population in Italy was commonly serving in the army during the last two centuries BCE. Such prolonged military service drove peasant families into debt and impoverishment. Hopkins calculates that in the seventy-two years between 80 and 8 BCE, "roughly half of the peasant families of Roman Italy, over one and a half million people, were forced mostly by state intervention to move from their ancestral farms" (1978:7).

The increasingly rich nobles were only too ready to take advantage of the impoverished peasant families. "The rich ... acquired the plots of the poor, sometimes by purchase with persuasion, sometimes by force so that in the end they cultivated large estates not farms (Appian, *Civil Wars* 1.7). This systematic land-grabbing by the elite also required the legal transformation of traditionally inalienable land through new laws that guaranteed secure private ownership of land by the heads of the great households (as Weber saw, 67–76, 119–24). With hundreds of thousands of slaves generated by their conquests, they then reorganized the land into large estates run by gangs of slaves to raise the produce (including fine wine and olive oil) required for their luxurious palaces in Rome, Pompeii, and elsewhere, and their large staff of domestic slaves. The Roman elite knew exactly what they were doing: "After a time the rich men in each neighborhood, by using the names of fictitious tenants, contrived to transfer many of these holdings to themselves, and finally they openly took possession of the greater part of the land under their own names.... The result was a rapid decline of the class of free small-holders all over Italy, their place being taken by gangs of foreign slaves, whom the rich employed to cultivate the estates from which they had driven off the free citizens" (Plutarch, *Life of Tiberius Gracchus* 8). The Roman peasant-soldiers were thus used to fight the wars of conquest in which they captured the provincials who replaced them farming what were once their own lands but now taken over by their commanders who took advantage of their impoverishment that resulted from their prolonged absence. "The sale of western prisoners took place on a vast scale: the wars in the valley of the Po, Liguria, Corsica, and Sardinia have been described as mere slave hunts" (Gordon: 109). From his glorious conquests of the Gauls the great general Julius Caesar may well have introduced as many as a million slaves into Italy, primarily to be deployed on the expanding estates of wealthy and powerful Roman nobles. Large numbers of slaves also came from Asia Minor and Syria (and Judea) through piracy as well as wars of conquest (Gordon: 94–95).

The result was a massive displacement of Roman and Italian peasants. As the popular tribune and reformer Tiberius Gracchus supposedly told his listeners: "The wild beasts that roam over Italy have their dens and holes to lurk in, but the men who fight and die for our country . . . [must] wander with their wives and children, houseless and homeless, over the face of the earth" (Plutarch, *Life of Tiberius Gracchus* 10). Tens of thousands of the displaced peasants migrated into the cities. Others the Roman state removed to colonies. Over a hundred such colonies were established between 45 and 8 BCE, one of the best known of which was that founded at Corinth by Julius Caesar in 44 BCE and settled largely by freed slaves and other "riff-raff" from the city of Rome. Still others joined the increasingly professionalized army, after service in which they too were settled in colonies at strategic points around the Mediterranean. "Between 80 and 8 BC . . . roughly half the free adult males in Italy left their farms and went to Italian towns or were settled by the state on new farms in Italy or the provinces" (Hopkins, 1978:66). In the complementary flow, albeit over a longer period of time, "many more than two million peasants from the conquered provinces became war captives and then slaves in Italy" (Hopkins: 1978:8–9).

Nor, contrary to earlier classical scholarship on slavery, did the wars of conquest and enslavement end with Augustus' establishment of the imperial "peace." Forty-four thousand Alpine Salassi were reportedly enslaved in 25 BCE, numbers of the Cantabri and Astures in Spain sold into slavery in 22 BCE, the men of military age in Pannonia enslaved in 12 BCE, and some of the Bessi in Thrace enslaved in 11 BCE (Strabo 4.6.7; Dio 53.25.4; 54.5.2; 31.3; 34.7). The intensity and scope of Rome's wars of conquest and expansion gradually lessened under the early Empire, yet wars and re-conquests continued as a principle source of slaves on into the second century (Harris, 1980:121–22; Bradley, 1987:48–49), as those familiar with the history of Roman rule in Palestine will readily recognize. It is likely that the first conquests of Judea and Jerusalem by Roman armies poured thousands of slaves into Roman slave-markets (*Psalms of Solomon* 2:6; 8:21; 17:12; Plutarch, *Vita Pomp.* 45.1–5). Cassius reportedly enslaved thirty thousand at Tarichaeae in Galilee in 52 BCE, then several years later enslaved four district towns in

Judea, including Emmaus (Josephus, *B.J.* 1.180; 2.222; *Ant.* 14.275; Josephus probably exaggerates the numbers). In suppression of the revolt in Galilee following the death of Herod the Romans supposedly enslaved the populace in or around Sepphoris (*B.J.* 2.68; *Ant.* 17.289). Josephus, who was himself involved in the Roman re-conquest of Galilee and Judea in 67–70 CE, mentions explicitly that Vespasian and Titus, after slaughtering the majority of people besieged in villages and towns such as Japha, Jotapata, and Tarichaeae, enslaved thousands of women and children (*B.J.* 3.7.31 #304–305; 3.7.36 #337–38). Of the fugitives who had fled into Tarichaeae and then Tiberias, he sent six thousand of the most robust youths to work on Nero's pet project of cutting a canal through the Isthmus of Corinth, then sold thirty-thousand more into slavery elsewhere (*B.J.* 3.10.10 #540–42). When Jerusalem finally fell to the prolonged Roman siege,

> Caesar issued orders to kill only those who were found in arms and offered resistance, and to make prisoners of the rest. The troops slew the old and feeble; while those in the prime of life and serviceable they drove together into the temple. Caesar's friend Fronto reserved the tallest and most handsome of the youth for the triumph; of the rest, those over seventeen he sent in chains to the works in Egypt, while multitudes were presented by Titus to the various provinces, to be destroyed in the theatres by the sword or by wild beasts; those under seventeen were sold [into slavery]. . . . The total number of prisoners taken . . . amounted to ninety-seven thousand. (*B.J.* 6.9.2 #417–18)

Further tens of thousands of Judeans may well have been enslaved during the prolonged Roman suppression of the Bar Kokhba Revolt in 132–35 C.E. (Fuks: 29). The vast majority of those enslaved by Rome's wars of conquest probably ended up in the huge gangs of slaves working the estates of the Roman warlords, although some undoubtedly wound up as domestic slaves in Rome itself—and some of those later became freedmen/women (Fuks: 30–31; cf. Harris, 1980:122—"in excess of 100,000"). Thus, although the need for slaves was surely not the sole motive force, it is difficult to understand how Rome's relentless wars which brought glory to the generals and imperial control of the Mediterranean to the Senate were not also "slave hunts" (Weber; Hobson: 247–48; Harris, 1979:83–85).

Once the Roman slave-system was well-institutionalized there was a constant demand for slaves. And other sources of slaves were developed, primarily slave-breeding. The latter did not begin only with the establishment of empire and the supposed end of wars of conquest, but was well-developed already under the Republic, then became relatively more important under the empire (Harris, 1980:118–21; Bradley, 1987:42–55). The first references to large-scale breeding of slaves come in Cornelius Nepos, *Att.* 13.3; Horace, *Epod.* 2.65; Varro, *Res Rust.* 1.17.5; 2.10.6; Columella, *Res Rust.* 1.8.5, 19. Another principal source of slaves was the exposure of unwanted infants commonly practiced in ancient Greek and Roman society. It was generally expected that an abandoned baby would be picked up and enslaved. Gender, moreover, was clearly a factor: "Everyone raises a son even if he is poor, but exposes a daughter even if he is rich" (Posidippus, 11E = Stobaeus, *Flor.* 77.7). The frequency of self-sale into slavery and its importance for maintenance of the system has been blown way out of proportion by previous and even current studies. Here is a good illustration of the limitation of uncritical use of Roman law as a historical source, in this case its simple distinction between "those slaves reduced to our ownership by the civil law if a person more than twenty years old allows himself to be sold" and "those slaves who are ours by the law of nations who are captured from the enemy" (*Digest* 1.5.1). That formal distinction indicates nothing about numbers (*contra* Watson, 1985). It is generally agreed, however, that "the self-sale as a mode of enslavement was of negligible importance in the central period of Roman history" (Harris, 1980:124; Bradley, 1988:482).

Enslavement of exposed children and kidnapping and piracy continued as important sources of slaves throughout Western antiquity (Harris, 1980:123), and kept a steady supply of newly enslaved subjects of empire flowing through the slave-markets in Cos, Corinth, and elsewhere. For students of the New Testament, it is noteworthy not only that Syrians and Judeans were thought to be inferior human beings appropriate for enslavement, but that "the great source" of slaves was Asia Minor. "Over and over again we hear of the typical slave as a Cappadocian or a Phrygian" (Harris, 1980:122). Also, "Galatia, like Phrygia of which it originally formed a part, was an important reservoir of slaves throughout antiquity" (Mitchell: 47). That kidnapping continued to be such an important source for slaves, finally, indicates how the slave system generally depended on the imperial order. For it was the need for slaves among the imperial elite in Rome and other metropolitan centers that drove the demand for slaves and it was the imperial administration that maintained the social-political order in which slave-hunters could conduct their kidnapping in the provinces to supply the burgeoning markets in Italy and key imperial metropoles.

Social Control of Slaves by Masters

The Inherent Conflict in the Slave System and in the Master-Slave Relationship

Both the Greek and the Roman slave-holding elite had a disquieting sense of insecurity with respect to their slaves, upon whose involuntary labor they depended for their positions of wealth and power. Xenophon wrote as if there was a perpetual state of aggressive antagonism between masters and slaves: citizens are "unpaid bodyguards of each other against their slaves," since "masters have often died violently at the hands of their slaves" (*Hiero* 4.3; 10.4). Lysias (7.35) and Demosthenes (21.49) speak of a natural enmity between masters and slaves. Plato (*Rep.* 578d–579a) conjures up the horrifying image of an owner of fifty slaves in mortal danger once he had been carried away with his family "to some desert place where there would be no other free man to help him." The wealthy and powerful Roman slave-owning class similarly viewed their slaves as essentially criminal (e.g., Columella, *Res Rust.* 1.1.20; 1.3.5; 1.6.8; 1.7.6; 1.8.1–2, 15, 17, 18; 1.9.1, 4; 7.4.2; 9.5.2; 11.1.12, 14, 16, 19, 21, 23, 25, 27; 12.3.7; Tacitus, *Ann.* 1.17.1; 2.12.4; 2.39.2; 6.10.3; 12.4.1; 13.46.4; 14.40.1; 15.45.5; *Hist.* 1.46,48; 2.59; 3.32; 5.9) . In early Latin literature such as the *De Agricultura* of Cato and the comedies of Plautus, in portrayals for which there are no earlier prototypes, slaves appear as cruel, unruly, pilfering, intransigent, conniving, deceitful (Cato 2.2; 4; 5.1; 67.2; Duckworth: 249–52, 288–92; Bradley 1984:28–30). Columella's treatise on the management of an agricultural estate (*Res Rustica*) has an urgent tone about the dangers of slave ownership and the potential for slave revolt. Slaves must be ruled by fear (1.8.17–18; 1.2.1; cf. Cato, *De Agr.* 5.1–5; Varro, *Res Rust.* 1.13.1–2), balanced by kind considerations. He writes from a kind of a prison-camp mentality, viewing everything in terms of security and control of the slave laborers (Bradley, 1984:23–24). Slaves must be kept in chains and quartered in an *ergastulum* at night.

Similar anxieties haunted slave-owners about their own domestic slaves tending to their every need in their urban mansions. One of the reasons Augustus established a city prefecture was to discipline slaves in Rome itself. And the murder of the senator L. Pedanius Secundus by a slave revived concern among the patricians that urban slaves had to be ruled by fear, particularly considering the large foreign element (Tacitus, *Ann.* 6.11.3; 14.44.5). Slave-masters were anxious not only about the stability of the slave-system as a whole, on which their wealth and positions of power and privilege were dependent, but about their personal vulnerability in households surrounded by their "domestics." As the younger Pliny commented (*Ep.* 3.14), on the death in 108 of the senator Larcius Macedo, who had been assaulted by his slaves while bathing, "No master can feel safe because he is kind and considerate." The Roman proverb, "the number of one's slaves equals the number of one's enemies" (*quot servi, tot hostes*, Seneca, *Ep.* 47.5; Macrobius, *Sat.* 1.11.13), articulates succinctly the elite's fear for their own safety and the antagonism with which masters regarded their slaves.

Slaves, for their part, resisted in whatever ways they could discussed more fully in the article on "Slave Resistance" below. When they saw opportunities, slaves fled, as we know from the lengths their owners went to contain them or, failing that, to recapture them (Bellen). Toward the end of the Peloponesian War 20,000 slaves took the opportunity to flee their servitude in Attica (Thucydides 7.27.5). *Drapetēs* came to mean specifically a runaway slave, and *drapetagōgos* a "slave-catcher," as in a fourth-century comedy by Antiphanes by that title. Among the finds from antiquity are some of the iron collars worn by slaves, containing instructions for their return to their owners if captured. Roman law addresses the problem, and slave-owners could hire professional slavecatchers (*fugitivarii*) to recapture fugitives (Daube; Bradley, 1984:32). Occasionally they murdered their masters and, albeit rarely, even managed collective revolt. That slave resistance was a regular feature of Roman life is indicated by repeated incidents mentioned by historians such as Tacitus or Appian. The latter, for example, having recounted Cinna's massacre of slaves who had earlier plundered and murdered, commented: "Thus did the slaves receive fit punishment for their repeated treachery to their masters" (*Bellum civile* 1.74, Loeb trans.)

The relationship between an involuntary labor force initially forced into slavery by military violence and their masters dependent on their coerced labor was fraught with conflict from the outset. Obviously, maintenance of such an inherently conflictual system required complex means of social control. Ancient Greek and Roman slavery depended upon systematic management and manipulation of the slaves.

Dehumanization, Degradation and the Climate of Fear

Roman literature reveals a consensus among the slave-owning class that it was necessary to create a climate of fear among their slaves. "Severity must be employed by those who keep subjects under control by force—by masters, for example, towards their slaves" (Cicero, *Off.* 2.24). Following a slave's murder of a senator it was argued in the Senate that "you will never coerce such a mixture of [strange] humanity except by terror" (Tacitus, *Ann.* 14.14; cf. 13.2). It was particularly important in the Romans' mind to inculcate fear among slaves (Tacitus, *Ann.* 14.44); it produced greater loyalty (Propertius 3.6.6; Bradley 1984:113–14). Early Christian writers reflect this ethos of master-slave relations: "Slaves, obey your earthly masters with fear and trembling"—with a mild exhortation to slave-masters to "stop threatening" (Eph 6:9). To instill the fear requisite to maintaining the slave-system, therefore, the Romans employed various forms of dehumanization, degradation, and humiliation.

The slave-trade. The dehumanization entailed in ancient slavery began with the Greek and Roman disposition of subject people they captured in warfare. From accounts by Josephus and other historians, Judean and Galilean and other captives would have experienced the slaughter of many of their neighbors and family, very likely their parents, and their own sale to slave dealers who shipped them across the Mediterranean to cities such as Rome or Corinth. As if the traumas of capture and removal far from home were not enough, the slave trade itself entailed further humiliating practices and slave-dealers were notorious for their abuse of the human "stock" in which they traded. A century and a half ago, Wallon (2.51–60) sketched an illuminating picture of the ancient slave-market, with its total humiliation of the human beings involved, which was simply taken for granted by the Greeks and Romans. If it is permissible to indulge in a little comparative history to illustrate the "natal alienation" involved in the slave-trade, we can listen to the eighteenth-century African Olaudah Equiano describe his own experience:

> We were not many days in the merchants' custody before we were sold after the usual manner, which is this:—On a signal given, such as the beat of a drum, the buyers rush at once into the yard where the slaves are confined, and make choice of that parcel they like best. The noise and clamour with which this is attended, and the eagerness visible in the countenances of the buyers, serve not a little to increase the apprehensions of the terrified Africans, who may well be supposed to consider them the ministers of that destruction to which they think themselves devoted. In this manner, without scruple, are relations and friends separated, most of them never to see each other again. (Gates: 37–38)

Enslaved war-captives were likely sold more than once along the route to their final destination in Italy or elsewhere. Their humiliating journey began with sale to one of the *canabae* or parasitic "camp follower" slave-traders who followed the army ready to obtain war-captives "wholesale" and then sell them for handsome profits to "retailers" of "speaking tools." Now utterly isolated socially and culturally (linguistically!), enslaved war-captives were dragged in chains into the unknown, never to return home. On the stele of the Black Sea slave-trader (*sōmatemporos*) Aulus Kapreilius Timotheus a file of twelve slaves walks along in chains. Others were taken into slavery by kidnappers (cf. 1 Tim 1:10; NSRV = "slave-traders"). A papyrus mentions the ten-year-old girl Abaskantis from Galatia, sold in 142 CE in the Pamphilian coastal city of Side to the slave-dealer Pamphilos from Alexandria in Egypt. Another mentions a seven-year- old boy taken from Mesopotamia purchased in Egypt. Once placed on sale in Roman slave-markets, slaves were obliged to stand naked on a raised platform, with chalk marks on their feet indicating foreign origin. Legally required information about their particular qualities was suspended from their necks. In the case of slaves as well as cattle and beasts of burden, statement of defects was legally required (e.g., "a discrepancy between jaws, eyes, or arms is no ground for rescission if it does not affect the slave's ability to perform his duties"—Ulpian, *Digest of Justinian*, Book 21; cf. Plato, *Laws* 11 916a.). Potential purchasers could poke and prod. "When you buy a horse, you order its blanket removed; so too you pull the garments off slaves" (Seneca, *Ep.* 80.9).

Nor was the slave-market located in some out of the way place where the degrading display would be inconspicuous. It was rather in the center of public "civilized" life, the Roman Forum itself, the *agora* of a Greek city, or the shrine of Isis (at Tithorea in Phocis, Pausanius 10.32.15; see further Harris, 1980:126). Major slave-trading centers during the late Republic and Empire, besides the older center Cos, were Byzantium, (Phrygian) Apamea, Tarsus, and especially Ephesus (Harris, 1980:127–28). Although slave-dealers were viewed as disreputable social pariahs in some Latin literature, there is substantial evidence that some were socially well-connected (even with the emperor), respectable authors of public inscriptions (to the Roman magistrate at Ephesus and in honor of the genius of the slave-market; Harris, 1980: 129–30).

For the enslaved, however, their social homicide and/or that of their children may have continued in the humiliations of the slave-trade. Slaves were sold and resold. "Throughout the Mediterranean . . . slaves were bought and sold from one owner to another as a matter of course . . . part of what the Roman jurist Papinian once offhandedly termed 'the regular, daily traffic in slaves'" (Bradley, 1992:126). The Roman *aediles* responsible for supervising markets propounded rulings for the marketing of slaves similar to those for the marketing of cattle. These functioned, in effect, as ancient equivalent of "lemon-laws," requiring slave-traders to inform potential buyers of defects in their merchandise, such as a slave having had his tongue cut out, a woman whose offspring are still-born every time, or slaves who were suicidal or prone to run away (Crook: 181–84).

We can easily deduce from the frequency of slave sale and from the limited surviving papyri that slaves were further dehumanized by the standard disregard of the intimate friendships and family relations they developed while in slavery. A study of the slave trade estimates an annual sale of 250,000 slaves in the early Empire (Harris, 1980:121). There are a handful of cases of mothers with young children, but no examples have yet been found of a sale of slave partners or of slave parents and child. The overwhelming majority of attested slave sales are of individual slaves. Tabulation of Egyptian papyrological evidence indicates sale of individual women slaves ranging in age from four to thirty-five, of individual male slaves from two to forty. That means not only that children were sold away from their parents, but that there was a brisk traffic in slaves, particularly women, during their prime child-bearing age, from thirteen to thirty-five (Bradley, 1984:53–57). In several known cases, slaves had already been sold three or four times, even before the age of fourteen, and had been sold far from their place of origin in Pontus, Phrygia, or Arabia. "It seems that slave-owners were little troubled about breaking servile family ties when economic considerations made sale of their slaves attractive or necessary" (Bradley, 1984:57–60). The treatment of slaves like other property in inheritance, moreover, resulted in similar break-ups of slaves' marital and familial relationships. The dehumanizing effect of "market forces" and treatment of humans as property in the slave-trade is illustrated, finally, by Furia Spes's dedication to her deceased husband: having loved each other since childhood as slaves, she and her beloved had "married," but after a short time had been involuntarily separated "by an evil hand" (*ILS* 8006, cited in Bradley, 1984:69).

Degradation by torture, beating, and branding. The rhetorical flourish of a Demosthenes that the greatest difference between the slave and the free man is that the slave "is answerable with his body for all offenses" (22.55), did not attract much attention in modern classics scholarship on slavery. As Finley (1980:94) notes, Westermann wrote three sentences on the subject and Vogt avoided it in his essays focused on slavery and humanity—while the older antiquarian Pignoria (1613) spent two chapters on it. Some classics scholars simply argued that "torture was seldom used" (Barrow: 31–35). That torture of slaves was a regular practice among Greeks and Romans could no longer be ignored, however, with the discovery in Puteoli of a Latin inscription dated to the late Republic or early Empire listing one of the duties of the city funeral director as the torture of slaves as requested by magistrates or private individuals, replete with details on the techniques and instruments of the trade. "If a slave is a property with a soul, a nonperson and yet indubitably a biological human being, institutional procedures are to be expected that will degrade and undermine his humanity and so distinguish him from human beings who are not property" (Finley, 1980:95). Torture and beating were the two most important "institutional procedures" of degradation among the Greeks and Romans.

Since they could not trust the testimony of free men in court, the Greeks developed a means of gathering testimony that they believed trustworthy, that extracted by *torturing* the bodies of slaves (Aristophanes, *Frogs* ll. 618–25; Pseudo-Aristotle, *Rhet. ad Alexandrum*; Garlan: 42–43; see now duBois, 1991). This practice was continued by the Romans. Torture of slaves, however, was not confined to court cases. Professional torturers (*tortorēs*) were available for hire. Administering a brutal beating was an exhausting undertaking (Cicero, *Cluentio.* 177; Seneca, *Ep.* 66.18, 21, 29). Petronius portrays Trimalchio as keeping two *tortorēs* on staff simply to punish his errant cook (*Satyricon* 49); Juvenal depicts a cruel mistress who kept a *tortor* on retainer (6:480). "Just like other artisans, the *tortor* had his place of business, where the variety of the tools of his trade could be counted on to chill his prospective victim to the bone" (Saller, 1994:148, citing Juvenal 6.0.29). It can no longer be pretended that instruments of torture such as spiked whips, racks, and hot irons were seldom used (Cicero, *Pro Cluentio* 177; Wiseman 1985:5–10; Saller, 1994:134, 147–48).

Roman literature indicates that slaves were regularly subject to *beatings*, the second principal means of degrading slaves. They were treated "not as if they were men, but beasts of burden," by masters who were cruel and insulting; a slave would be beaten even for disturbing the master's dinner by coughing (Seneca, *Ep.* 47.3, 5, 11, 17–19). Cato, a man of traditional Roman values, flogged his domestic slaves for mistakes in the preparation and serving of dinner (Plutarch *Cato maior* 5.1; 21.3). The regularity with which Roman slaves were beaten is indicated in Tacitus' contrast of Roman brutality with the Germans' restraint in beating their slaves only rarely and not in matters of routine discipline (*Germ.* 25). In literature the life of the slave was linked unavoidably with the whip. A slighted wife transfers the target of her anger from her husband to her helpless slaves (Juvenal 6.481). In Plautus' comedies (before 200 BCE), a young man beats his slave, thus literally a "whipping boy," because he is frustrated in love (*Poenulus* 146, 410, 819), and apparently the stringing up and beating of elderly female slaves was meant to be funny (*Truculentus* 775–82 and *Aulularia* 48; Saller, 1994:148).

The regular subjection of slaves to the whip, however, was far more significant in Roman society than as a mere punishment. It was the principal means and symbol of slaves' degradation. In the widely read *A History of Private Life*, influential among those such as biblical scholars dependent on classics scholarship for their understanding of Greco-Roman slavery, Paul Veyne "deliberately minimizes the distinction between *filiusfamilias* and slave" (Saller, 1996b:144). He pictures the life of children as "a kind of slavery" (29), in comparison with which the life of slaves, in which "the master commanded with love," appears benign. In his recent study of *Roman Slave Law*, moreover, Alan Watson (1987:46–47) repeats the standard claim, based on the abstract constructs of Roman Law, that "in many regards the legal position of a slave was very similar to that of a son—of whatever age—in paternal power." He thus reinforces the belief that Roman slaves "did not fare much worse than the master's wife and children" in suffering merciless beatings (Genovese: 73). However such relations may have worked in the southern United States, slaves were not assimilated to the position of children in Roman households, certainly not with regard to beatings. Cicero, following Greek philosophers, wrote that "different kinds of domination and subjection must be distinguished." A father governs his children who follow out of readiness to obey, but a master must "coerce and break his slave" (*Rep.* 3.37). The primary instrument deployed to "break" slaves in (Roman) antiquity, as in the Southern United States, was the whip. Indeed, the use of the whip was precisely what distinguished slaves from the free children of Roman households—besides the fact that the sons inherited, while of course the natally-alienated slaves did not. .

In a critical and probing analysis of Roman social relations Richard Saller (1994; 1996a; 1996b) has recently explained that when Romans regularly *and legitimately* (in their own eyes) inflicted severe beatings on their slaves that maimed and even killed, more was at stake than raw physical pain. To the Romans whipping was primarily an insult to *dignitas*. As the grossest form of invasion, whipping was thus a deep humiliation. "The special potency for

Romans of the symbolic act of beating hinged on its association with slavery. One of the primary distinctions between the condition of a free man and a slave in the Roman mind was the vulnerability of the latter to corporal punishment, in particular the lashings at another man's private whim" (Saller, 1994:137). In Roman comedies, slaves are addressed with variations on the word *verber*, with *verbero* or "whipping post" being common, and the distinguishing marks of slaves are the scars on their backs from past whippings. Conversely the slave's metaphor for staying out of trouble was "to protect his back" from the whip (Saller, 1994:137–38, with many references). It is precisely the whip that distinguishes the master-slave relationship, in distinction from the father-child relationship. In his tract on child-rearing, Plutarch insisted that "children ought to be led to honorable practices by means of encouragement and reasoning, and most certainly not by blows nor by ill treatment; *for it is surely agreed that these are fitting rather for slaves than for the freeborn (De Lib. Educ.* 12). Similarly, Quintilian disapproved of whipping students, "because it is a disgraceful form of punishment and fit only for slaves, and in any case it is an insult" (1.3.13). Formally fathers did indeed hold the power of life and death over their children as well as over their slaves. Other than a famous legend or two, however, no evidence exists that such paternal power over children was ever used. By contrast, masters really did execute slaves, against which legal restraint was finally brought under Hadrian— although Constantine later ruled that a master who beat his slave so severely that the slave died was not to be charged with murder (Saller, 1996a:117–18). The whipping of slaves was a symbolic degradation as well as punishment. "The master's authority had to be coercive (to 'break' the slave), because the master-slave relationship was inherently exploitative. The servile spirit was one motivated by grudging fear, goaded by the lash; the servile back was marked with scars from past whippings" (Saller, 1994:151).

Closely related means of social control were the *branding* and especially *tattooing* of many slaves and the temporary or perpetual *shackling* of slaves (C. P. Jones). Small wonder that one finds in Roman law and literature "a strong suspicion that slavery was detrimental to the slave's character" (Watson, 1987:39). Law codes make frequent references to the likelihood that slaves had been "chained," "branded," even that a slave-master's will provided that a slave "be kept perpetually in chains" (*Digest* 47.10.15.44; Gaius, *Inst.* 1.13; Justinian, *Codex* 3.36.5). Slaves bore on their bodies the marks of the institutionalized practices of their humiliation. As Macrobius commented candidly, "At home we become tyrants and want to exercise power over slaves, constrained not by decency but capacity" (cited in Hopkins, 1978:119 n 43). "The hostility of masters to their slaves ran just below the surface of Roman civilization" (Hopkins, 1978:120). Not surprisingly, the Roman state backed up the "terror" that the master attempted to exercise in his *familia*. By ancient custom, all the slaves in a household of a master killed by one of his own slaves were to be tortured and killed. Sure enough, when one of his household slaves killed the Urban Prefect Pedanius Secundus in 61 CE, all four hundred of the latter's household slaves were executed, over the protest of the urban poor at such inhumanity (Tacitus, *Ann*. 14.42–45).

Sexual exploitation. Slaves were habitually subjected to sexual abuse. That slaves' bodies were available to their masters without restriction is "a commonplace in Graeco-Roman literature from Homer on; only modern writers have managed to ignore it" (Finley, 1980:95–96). Both male and female slaves were sold as prostitutes, available for continuous sexual exploitation at the command of the masters (Henriques, 1962:89ff.; Pomeroy: 201). Martial sought a slave from a patron for sexual purposes, as if it was a common request (*Epig*. 8.73). Anecdotal evidence, rules on the registration and taxing of prostitutes, and the notoriety of the Subura area in Rome suggest that large numbers of slaves worked in brothels, which were a standard feature of Roman society (references in Bradley, 1984:116–17). Because of the special demand for young boys, owners attempted to delay the onset of puberty by various means, including castration (Pliny, *Nat Hist*. 30:41; 21.170; Martial, *Epig*. 9.6; Juvenal 6.373AB).

More common would have been slave-masters'—and probably their families' and friends'—regular gratification of their sexual desires among the slaves of their own *familiae*. The elder Seneca stated bluntly the perpetual sexual vulnerability of the slave: "Unchastity is a crime in the freeborn, a necessity for a slave, a duty for the freedman" (*Controversies* 4, Praef. 10; Veyne, 1978 [from Finley, 1980:170, n 15]). Martial's poems allude frequently to slave-owners' casual encounters with their slaves, both heterosexual and homosexual, including young boys and girls purchased specially for sex (*Epig*. 1.84; 2.33; 3.33; 4.66; 6.39, 71; 11.70; 12.58, 96). The freedman Trimalchio's comments reflect the vulnerable position of the slave: "For fourteen years I pleasured him; it is no disgrace to do what a master commands. I also gave my mistress satisfaction" (Petronius, *Satyricon* 75.11). The first-century CE Stoic philosopher Musonius Rufus was unusual in his complaint about anyone "who has relations with his own slave girl, a thing which some people consider quite without blame, since every master is held to have it in his own power to use his slaves as he wishes" (Fragment 12, "On sexual indulgence"). Plutarch counselled a wife to acquiesce in her husband's sexual exploitation of slave girls because it was "respect for her that led him to practice his debauchery, licentiousness, and wantonness with another woman" (*Moralia* 140B). Such moralists disapproved of the master's lack of self-restraint, but voiced no concern about the dignity of slave women (Saller, 1996a:126–27). For Romans as well as Greeks, active and passive sexual roles corresponded symbolically with domination and subordination. The ancient elite would therefore have been bothered by a matron's liaison with a male slave. Otherwise the standard values appear to have been expressed by

Horace. As Finley (1980:96) says, he "was not being satirical when he recommended his own preference for household slaves, male or female: 'I like my sex easy and ready to hand' (*Satires* 1.2.116–19)." Although Romans refrained from sexual relations with freeborn boys (hence the *bulla* amulet worn by freeborn youth at the festival of Liberalia), there was nothing disreputable about sex with male slaves (Plutarch, *Moralia* 288A). And of course since Romans saw nothing wrong with sexual exploitation of slave women, they were perpetually subject to their masters' advances (Weaver, 1991/96: 178; Buckland 1908:76–77).

The degradation of the powerless slave could not help but have been internalized, although here we must speculate on the basis of non-slave witnesses. It is not difficult to imagine the effect on a person of constantly having the threat of violence overhead, or of always being available sexually to satisfy the master's or his relatives' desires. One of Plautus' characters speaks explicitly of the internalized violence, of "a force (she fears) which forces me to do violence to myself" (*The Rope and Other Plays*, 116–17). This internalization of violence was one of the principal factors that created the "faithful" slave. "Natally alienated" and (as seen in Nazi concentration camps) "brutally deracinated human beings seeking new ties, new psychological attachments, not infrequently turn to those in whose power they find themselves" (Finley, 1980:104).

On the other side of the master-slave relation, however, Finley finds no general evidence for any doubts or guilt-feelings among ancient slaveowners (1980:99). That suggests that Greek and Roman society had developed a powerful legitimating cultural ideology in which they felt quite comfortable sexually invading or brutally humiliating the "bodies" that they owned. While Finley emphasizes that slaves were the property of their masters, Patterson includes this aspect in the broader context of power and domination of the slave by the master, which was absolute. Yet this shift of emphasis in the standard point about the slave (as the only human thing) being the property of the master serves only to make the point all the more central and telling. The modern capitalist concept of property has always been problematic when applied to modern political-economic relation and even more so when applied to traditional societies most of which lacked anything close to "private property." The Romans developed a radically new and unprecedented legal concept, that of absolute ownership of things. Scholars of Roman law suggest that the Roman *dominium* was not just a certain relation between a person and a thing, but absolute power, power not just to use (*usus*) or enjoy the fruits, but to use up (*ab usus*) or alienate or have inner power over a thing (see Patterson's summary, 1982:31). Patterson ventures the compelling hypothesis that behind the Roman drive to develop this legal fiction was slavery, as illustrated in the early original meaning (third century BCE) of the term *dominus* not as "owner" generally but as "slavemaster" in particular. In effect, the slave, as the only human *thing (res)*, was the paradigm of the concept of private property developed by the Romans. This development was correlated with the dramatic transformation in the Roman economy in which slaves, along with land, became the most important basis of wealth (Patterson: 29–32).

Inducements and Manipulations

Sexual relations and families. We may presume the desire for sexual relations among slaves. Epigraphic evidence indicates that slaves also valued long-range marital and familial relations when they had a chance (Bradley, 1984:48–49). Slaves' desires for sexual relations and families were exploited by slave-masters to induce acquiescence and obedience. Because technically, legally, slaves could not marry and produce recognized families, the existence of slave marriages and families presupposes the toleration if not encouragement of the masters. Roman slave-masters state explicitly their manipulation of their slaves in these respects. With regard to herdsmen in mountain valleys Varro commented that "it was advisable to send along women to follow the herds, prepare food for the herdsmen, and make them more diligent" (*Res Rust.* 2.10.6). Tertullian stated that discipline among slaves is better if they marry within the same household (*Ad. Ux.* 2.8.1). The manipulation of sexual and marital desires could be particularly important with regard to slave overseers. "The foremen are to be made more zealous by rewards, and care must be taken that they have . . . mates from among their fellow slaves to bear them children" (Varro, *Res Rust.* 1.17.5 Loeb). "The overseer . . . should be given a woman companion to keep him within bounds and yet in certain matters to be a help to him" (Columella, *Res Rust.* 1.8.5). The satisfaction of having "companions" and children, however, was not the only way in which such "perks" proved manipulative for slaves. Given the frequent sale of slaves away from their loved ones or from their children or parents, anxiety about forced severance from those family members must have plagued slaves, leading to their "good behavior" and "loyalty" to their masters.

Most of the slave marriages and children attested in inscriptions must have been from urban households. Recognition of the living arrangements in large urban households reveals another respect in which masters' allowing their slaves companions and children would have "domesticated" their household slaves. Living arrangements in such households were at virtually the opposite end of the spectrum from those of the modern Western nuclear family isolated in its separate apartment or three to five bedroom house. Slaves, freedmen/women, their children, and the children of the master all occupied the same physical, domestic space (Bradley, 1991:91–92). Privacy was minimal, confined to the few hours spent sleeping in small cells, if such were available. A slave girl might sleep in the same room with her mistress, slave boy at the feet of his master, the master's children with their slave *nutrix*. All lived in close interaction, which left little or no sequestered site for any moments of independent life. Slaves may well have developed close attachments to others in the household, including children of the master. And they were under constant surveillance, either by the master and mistress or by other members of the *familia*.

The peculium *as inducement*. Clear evidence indicates that slaves of the Romans were allowed what was in effect property of their own. In the imperial period the term *peculium* came to refer specifically to resources at the disposal of the slave. Technically it belonged to the slave-owner, and on the death of the slave reverted to the master, who retained almost exclusive proprietary powers over the labor, possessions, progeny, as well as the person of his slaves. Also, in many cases it may not have been in effect a bonus, but the resources from which the slave derived her/his own subsistence living. In practice, however, the slave had use and control of the *peculium*, whether cash, food, livestock, other slaves, or grazing rights. Use of the *peculium* thus gave the slave a sense of responsibility and some taste of independence. The assumption that most slaves had such a *peculium* the easy expansion of which would aid them in buying their manumission, led apologetic interpretations of ancient slavery to argue that it was mild and unoppressive. Far from being primarily a factor mitigating slavery, however, the *peculium* and the other little perks of "humanity" were precisely what made the system work. Another of the "rewards" that slave foremen, according to Varro, should have, is "a bit of property of their own . . . for by this means they are made more steady and more attached to the place" (*Res Rust.* 1.17.5). Xenophon (*Oeconomicus* 5.16; 9.11–17; 12.6–10; 15.1) exhibits that the Greeks had preceded the Romans in understanding how to use "a bit of property" to control and manipulate their slaves. As Patterson observes, the *peculium* "was the best means of motivating the slave to perform efficiently on his master's behalf. It not only allowed the slave the vicarious enjoyment of the capacity he most lacked—that of owning property—but also held out the long-term hope of self-redemption for the most diligent slaves" (1982:185–86).

The use of this device to control slaves, of course, was not universal, perhaps not even extensive. "Very few slaves, relatively speaking, can ever have controlled truly substantial sums of money, and for many the *peculium* was vital to their material welfare and simple survival" (Bradley, 1988:485). Slaves' entrepreneurial and industrial use of their masters' property, however, became very important in the diversification of the Roman imperial economy. Much of the commercial life in Roman society was conducted by slaves exploiting their *peculia* on behalf of their owners. But such economic rewards for the minority of slaves also served to reinforce the slave system. The diversity of wealth among the minority of relatively well-off slaves, comparable to the diversity of their occupations, helped prevent any sense of corporate identity from developing among them.

Manumission and manipulation. Westermann (1955) and others claimed a high frequency of manumission, even that most slaves were freed after age thirty. After all, Syme (446) had declared that "slaves not only could be emancipated with ease but were emancipated in hordes," and Jones (133) still wrote of "the massive influx of freed slaves into the citizen body" as a social problem confronting Augustus. Such classics scholars led New Testament scholars to understand that "all [domestic and urban] slaves in the first century could reasonably expect that they would be manumitted after serving their owners for ten to twenty years beyond physical maturity" (Bartchy 1973:118). That manumission was virtually automatic then became the basis for two further claims: it made for relative contentment among slaves, thus relieving any pressures that might have led to slave revolts (cf. Bartchy, 1973:85), and that slavery was a mechanism for the integration of outsiders into Roman society (Wiedemann, 1981)—one of the standard defenses of ancient Roman slavery. Slavery somehow constituted a "transitional state" which, with manumission, led the vast majority, who were freed, into a recognized if not fully equal status as Roman citizens (Alfoeldy). Arguments for widespread manumission were based on two types of evidence: inscriptions from large households in Rome and Augustus's decrees supposedly placing limits on the large numbers of slaves being freed at the end of the first century BCE.

The inscriptions about slaves and freed slaves, however, 98% of which are from large urban *familiae*, are highly atypical, representing slaves with easy access to and good relations with their masters (Wiedemann, 1985:163). The *familia Caesaris*, represented in many of the inscriptions, was utterly atypical. Hence epitaphs that indicate that slaves in the emperor's household regularly achieved manumission between the ages of 30 and 35 does not support the claim that "manumission was not difficult for an intelligent, energetic and thrifty slave in the early Empire" generally (*contra* Weaver, 1972:97–104). The Lex Aelia Sentia in 4 CE, moreover, does not provide evidence that most slaves were freed soon after the age of thirty. It was concerned rather to enhance the prospect that slaves freed and granted full Roman citizenship were of good, responsible character. "Not content with making it difficult for slaves to acquire freedom, and still more so for them to attain full rights, by making careful provision as to the number, condition, and status of those who were manumitted, he added the proviso that no one who had ever been put in irons or tortured should acquire citizenship by any grade of freedom" (Suetonius, *Augustus* 40.4). What the imperial legislation thus did was to give masters an excuse for not freeing slaves who deserved to be freed (Wiedemann 1985:168). An inscription from central Italy illustrates how masters who fully believed in manumission for faithful slaves and who were even fond of their slaves could avoid manumission because of this law.

> Debita libertas iuveni mihi lege negata
> morte immatura reddita perpetua est. (CIL X, 1.4917)

The frequently cited passage in a Senate speech by Cicero, moreover, is merely a rhetorical analogy; he mentions six years as a sufficiently long time for a captured slave to serve because it had been six years since Caesar's crossing of the Rubicon, during which time the Roman state had been politically enslaved. Cicero himself certainly did not practice manumission after six years. He did not set his "most trusted and versatile" slave Tiro, who had been born into the *familia*, free until he was forty-nine or fifty (Treggiari, 1969:259)—i.e., virtually useless.

Much of the previous scholarly discussion regarding manumission, furthermore, takes on a tone of unreality once we ask about life-expectancy in the ancient Roman empire. Life-expectancy at birth for the population as a whole has been estimated at 20–30 years (Hopkins 1966–67:263–64; Durand, 1959–60:365–73; Frier, 1982:213–51; 1983:328–44). Thus, "it is hard to believe that in the Roman Empire slaves' life-expectation at birth exceeded twenty years" (Harris, 1980:118). Even assuming that one-third of children died in infancy, it would still appear that most slaves would hardly have reached 30 or 35, at which age the privileged slaves of the *familia Caesaris* were being manumitted.

In his reversal of his overly apologetic previous position, Wiedemann argues that regular manumission was an ideal, something the Romans wanted to believe, i.e., that if a slave served faithfully, s/he would be rewarded. As it affected practice, however, it had virtually the opposite effect. The slave-master had no obligation to free a slave whom he did not deem faithful. Law codes contain much evidence that masters displeased with their slaves would include in their wills clauses prohibiting them from ever being freed. The literary evidence adduced to show that Romans practiced regular manumission indicates only that they believed they should do so. The evidence of the jurists suggest that when a Roman slave-owner provided for ultimate manumission in his will or in a contract of sale, he paid scant attention to the ideal that a faithful slave should be manumitted" (Wiedemann, 1985:175). It is impossible to reach anything close to a statistical probability, but it is now believed "that emancipation was a comparatively rare reward," with perhaps only one out of five slaves having been freed. Such acts of generosity by Roman slave-masters were the exception, not the rule (Bradley, 1984:83–91; 1988:483; *contra* Watson, 1985:23). "Roman society was not marked by altruism" (Hopkins, 1978:117).

For the slave, manumission brought an improvement in moral, legal and, for slaves of Roman citizens, political position. S/he was no longer completely subject to the master's whim and could gain a degree of self-respect, being less subject to the most extreme forms of regular humiliation that slavery entailed. Many slaves of Roman masters became Roman citizens upon manumission, a practice unusual among slave-holding societies which drew comments from the Greeks, who did not grant citizenship with manumission. Economically and socially, however, not much changed for the freed slaves. The status of a freedman/woman has frequently been compared with that of a client of a Roman patron and the manumission phase of ancient slavery in particular assimilated to the vertical patron-client power relations into which a large proportion of the freeborn were forced during the late Republic and early Empire.

Freedmen/women, however, had far greater obligations to their patrons/former masters and were of distinctively lower status than freeborn clients. The relationship between ex-slave and ex-master was always stronger than that of the usual client and patron and had a distinctively involuntary quality. It cannot be viewed in isolation from the slave relationship it replaced (Patterson: 241). The ex-master could and usually did exercise three kinds of claims on his freedmen/women: *obsequium*, or the regular demonstration of proper reverence and gratitude to their patron and his kin (e.g., joining in the humiliating daily ritual of the morning *salutatio* in which clients would line up at the patron's house hoping for hand-outs); *operae*, obligatory work for the patron a specified number of days a week/year; and a claim to half or all of the freedpersons' estates on their death, which might also be inheritable by the patron's heirs (Treggiari,1969:69–81; Wiedemann 1981:50–60). Many a freedperson must have faced economic hardship (e.g., the wry comments of the former slave Epictetus, *Diss.* 4.1.35–37). Special conditions were often stated in testamentary manumission. The will of Acusilaus, resident of Oxyrhynchus, specified that five female slaves set free were still subject to the condition that their services and earnings were to remain at the disposal of his wife as long as she survived, while his son was given claim to any children borne by the women in the future. (*P. Oxy.* 494). The slave woman Arescusa "by last will was ordered to be free if she gave birth to three children" (*Digest* 1.5.15).

For most freedpersons, their post-manumission destitution came after years of struggle and sacrifice to raise the "purchase price" of their freedom. Since the slave's *peculium* was really (legally) the property of the master anyhow, what was involved was more like a "gift-exchange," the slave's surrender of the *peculium* for the master's gift of freedom—except that in receiving the gift of freedom, the ex-slave then came under new obligation to the former master, for *operae*, etc. In any case, the "exchange" which cost the master nothing (providing the replacement cost for the freed slave) cost the slave dearly in terms of long-term sacrifice and struggle. "The money which slaves have saved up by robbing their own stomachs, they hand over as the price of liberty" (Seneca, *Mor.* 80.4). Cost of manumission was probably close to or somewhat higher than the market price of slaves. Petronius gives HS4,000 as one figure, but a slave doctor paid HS50,000 (Duncan-Jones: 349–50; HS1,000 could provide basic rations for one person for four to eight years). Purchase prices varied according to the skills and ages of the slaves. It seems unlikely that the vast majority of slaves would ever have had opportunities to acquire such substantial sums (Bradley 1984:107). How long it might take for those who did is illustrated by two cases from Egypt. In the late first century a homeborn slave named Euphrosyne was set free by her owner Aline on payment of a ransom sum (plus tax) at the age of thirty-five; in the late second century a woman named Zosime was manumitted by her owner Tasucharion after payment of ransom at the age of forty-four (*P. Oxy.* 2843). Many scholars of ancient slavery suggest that prostitution was one of the principal means by which slaves worked at raising the price of their freedom.

Manumission of slaves in Greece during the last two centuries BCE is particularly well-documented by a thousand recorded cases involving 1200 slaves in Delphi (paralleled by others from the island of Calymna, near Cos). Especially interesting among these are the cases of so-called *paramonē* or suspended release, in which "bodies" (*sōmata*) formally bought freedom, but bound themselves contractually to remain, just as though they were still slaves, until their masters' and/or mistresses' deaths, and perhaps to meet some additional condition (see esp. Hopkins, 1978:chap. III). Of the 83% who were adults, 63% were female. The high average cost of 400 drachmae, enough to feed a poor peasant family for over three years, suggests that these slaves had unusual access to earnings, hence were not typical (Hopkins, 1978:168). That even relatively advantaged slaves would struggle to obtain such an amount of funds for only a conditional release suggests just how onerous and degrading slavery must have been, how intensely slaves desired their own even nominal freedom or that of their children. Such conditionally released slaves basically remained in all the basic conditions of slavery. The contracts emphasize the masters' right to punish: "If Eisias does not serve or do as she is ordered let Kleomantis have power to punish her in any way he wishes; he may beat her, chain her or sell her" (*FD* 3.3.329). The savings of conditionally freed slaves, just like those of a slave, were claimed by the master. Most interestingly, many of these conditionally released slaves (men and women) were required to produce one, two, or even three (already weaned) children for their masters or their heirs: "Let Epaphro give to my grandson Glaukias three babies, each two years old. And let Epiphanea give to my son Sostratos one three-year-old child after five years, and another three-year-old child to my grandson Glaukias after three years" (*FD* 3.6.38). In some cases parents were thus placed in situations where they "left children behind in slavery to win freedom for themselves as adults"—perhaps hoping to be able eventually to free their children as well (Hopkins, 1978:166).

In social status the freedman/woman had made the important transition from a non-person, subject to the power of a master, to a human being with (limited) rights, yet remained stigmatized by the shameful previous status as a slave. "The stigma of former slavery meant that the freedman was rarely perceived as an equal. Only time could blot out the memory of the debased condition [of slavery]. Hence, full freedom came only to his descendants" (Patterson, 1982:247). As a marginal person, moreover, the freedman continued to be viewed as something of an anomaly and, like all persons in transitional states, was regarded as potentially dangerous" (249). Custom, law, and prejudice conspired to keep even those who became Roman citizens in a position of second-class citizenship (Treggiari, 1969:36–68). The stigma of slavery, still suffered by the sons of freedmen, disappeared only after two or three generations. Nevertheless, to finally be free of having to constantly yield to the commands and whims of the master brought a sense of self-respect and pride. Slaves coveted freedom, were eager to move to the other side of the institutionalized Greek and Roman division between slave and free that meant having minimal human rights, being treated like a human being (even if of the low status) instead of like a beast, and having familial relationships recognized by the society.

Manumission served the interests of slave-master in several ways. It entailed little if any economic loss. The *peculium* was his anyhow, and his freedmen/women paid for their freedom. Freeing slaves before his own death added to his train of clients, increasing his prestige in comparison with his patrician peers. Testamentary manumission at his death brought admiration for his generosity and magnanimity. In both cases the actions thus added to his *dignitas* (Harrill: 171).

Whatever the benefit to a minority of domestic slaves who finally attained their freedom, the basic function of manumission was as an incentive to acquiescence, obedience and productivity among urban domestic slaves. (Agricultural slaves, of course, were apparently hardly affected by the promise, much less the reality, of manumission.) As Tacitus indicates, conferring freedom on a slave was a *beneficium*, an act of generosity by the master, which followed evidence of servile *obsequium*. Greek writers (e.g., Pseudo-Aristotle, *Oikonomikos* 1.5.6) stressed the efficacy of promising slaves their freedom, as an encouragement to co-operation and a disincentive to resistance" (Wiedemann, 1985:175). Columella indicates precisely how Roman slave-masters were thinking about manumission and how they manipulated their slaves with the prospect of freedom: "To women, too, who are unusually prolific, *and who ought to be rewarded* for the bearing of a certain number of offspring, I have granted exemption from work and sometimes even freedom after they had reared many children. For to a mother of three sons exemption from work was granted; to a mother of more her freedom as well (*Res Rust.* 1.8.19).

Testamentary manumission was the most popular mode among the Romans because it retained the services of slaves to the very last moment in which their owner could use them; it kept the slaves in a suspense of good conduct to the end (Patterson: 223). The effect of the *lex Fufia Caninia* of 2 BCE and the *lex Aelia Sentia* of 4 CE was to give testamentary manumission "something of the character of a competition, the rules for which had to be compliant behavior, loyalty, and obedience . . . . [they] made full manumission a reward to the slave who reached a deserving age, or . . . a slave who displayed conformity to the established values of free society" (Bradley, 1984:91–93). Correspondingly, refusal of manumission could be used as a punishment which, when known to other slaves, would have the same effect of an incentive toward good behavior: The will of Dasumius, of the Roman elite of second century, expressly bans the manumission of certain slaves at any future point in their lives, which was sanctioned by law. "I ask that Menecrates and Paedaros not be manumitted but kept in the same occupation as long as they live . . . because they have given me great offence by their lack of merit" (FIRA 2ed, III no. 148, ll 80ff). Slaves thus knew that submission to the interests and commands of the master—whatever their true sentiments—was required in order to earn his favor and cultivate the possibility of manumission. Masters could further manipulate their slaves by making known in advance the contents of their wills, thus eliciting continued compliance to their will through a prolonged period of time, since changes could be made. "It was the element of uncertainty which surrounded manumission which made freedom an effective form of social manipulation" (Bradley, 1984:99, 112).

Manumission thus served as an incentive for obedient servitude mainly for domestic slaves, most of whom never attained their freedom. Because slaves were systematically dehumanized on the one hand and thus intensely desired freedom on the other, Greek and Roman slave-masters could use the possibility of manumission to manage and manipulate their household staff. "For the masters, manumission was economically rational, partly because it tempted slaves to increase their productivity and lowered the cost to the master of supervising his slaves at work, and partly because the slave's purchase of freedom recapitalised his value . . . . Manumission, for all the benefit it gave to ex-slaves, thus served to strengthen slavery as a system" (Hopkins, 1978:131). "By holding out the promise of redemption, the master provides himself with a motivating force more powerful than any whip" (Patterson: 101).

Some Special Aspects of Roman Slavery

Wet-Nursing

Women, like slaves, have usually been "hidden from history," and perhaps women slaves most of all. A further important aspect of the experience of many enslaved women in ancient Roman society has been brought to light by recent research. Both classical literature and Roman inscriptions indicate that elite families used wet-nurses and other care-givers to nurture their children (Bradley, 1986; 1991). To a degree they employed poor free-born women (Dio Chrysostom 7.114), but mostly they used slaves (or freedwomen) in their own households. Slave-owners thus exploited their slaves' own recent delivery to their own benefit. The *nutrix* inscriptions from Rome, however, also indicate that slave infants were also nursed by women other than their mothers (Bradley, 1986:210). We can imagine various contingencies behind this practice: the death of the mother, separation of child from mother through sale (or inheritance) of mother or infant, or a master's scheme for efficiency in a certain division of labor within the slave staff, with a mother going back to her assigned work while another slave nursed an additional child. Thus some of the wet-nursing practiced was apparently due to slave-breeding, which became more important in the early Empire (Bradley 1986:211-12)

Roman writers, however, viewed the common practice of having slaves nurse upper class children as threatening the proper socialization as well as physical nurture of the child. Favorinus feared the corrupting moral as well as physical influence on a child from a slave, particularly one of a foreign and barbarous nation, . . . dishonest, ugly, unchaste and a wine-bibber—partly because the nurse's milk transmitted her moral characteristics to the child (Aulus Gellius 12.1.8, 11–2; cf. Plutarch, *De Liberis Educandis* 5). Quintilian (1.1.4–5) and Tacitus (*Dialogus* 28.4—29.2) were concerned that children would be morally corrupted by the speech, stories, and beliefs of nurses and other disreputable slaves—concerns that may not have been unfounded, as we shall explore below. The slave nurse, who was the living embodiment of imperial power of conquest and control, thus became the symbol of decadence once she was placed in the intimate position of nurturing the heirs-designate of the imperial elite.

The threat of the "bad" nurse was mitigated somewhat by the stereotype of the "good" nurse, lovingly loyal to her master-nursling and utterly untainted by the resentment or resistance assumed for other slaves. Indeed, the good nurse became a symbolic comforter figure in literature. On the basis of such literature some historians have constructed a romantic view of the parent-child-nurse triangle and have imagined the Roman urban *familia* as a comfortable world free from the tensions and conflicts inherent in the master-slave relationship (Treggiari, 1975:56; 1976:76–104, esp. 89; Vogt: 105–109; Barrow: 37–38). The relationship between slave nurse and elite child was no doubt often close and affectionate, although in practice the senatorial and equestrian slave-holders knew that it was necessary to exercise the proper control of those charged with care of the children. However, this situation also set up the possibility of conflict, insofar as the nurse entered the child's familial world through compulsion rather than choice. A decree by Constantine in 326 suggests that there was always another possible scenario, that of subtle subversion by slave nurses: "Since the watchfulness of parents is often frustrated by the stories and wicked persuasions of nurses, punishment shall threaten first such nurses whose care is proved to have been detestable and their discourses bribed, and the penalty shall be that the mouth and throat of those who offered incitement to evil shall be closed by pouring in molten lead" (*Theodosian Code* 9.24.1.1). Joshel draws on testimony of masters and slaves from the American south to indicate how the nursling's view of the relationship, which is what is usually represented on Roman *nutrix* inscriptions, may not correspond to the experience of the slave nurse. "The nurses affection and loyalty were there, but not in the way understood by masters who had difficulty seeing beyond their own feelings and their need for the nurse's love and trust" (Joshel: 12). For example, after she was liberated from a Georgia plantation, Louisa continued to tend the children left under her care. But when asked why she did not object to the Union soldiers setting fire to her master's house, she explained: "Cause there has been so much devilment here, whipping niggers most to death to make 'em work to pay for it" (Litwack: 163).

The Familia Caesaris and Other "Managerial Slaves"

That tiny faction of ancient Roman slaves who came into positions of considerable influence and responsibility has recently exercised a particular fascination on classics scholars and others. It has been claimed, for example, that with regard to the ordinary activities of managerial slaves, "it would have been difficult to distinguish them from free or freed people," except for the fact that they were "representatives of powerful people" and thus *appeared* "powerful, not weak" (Martin: 22). The first part of that statement is questionable because of the dominant values of Roman society. Not only was it beneath the dignity of honorable Greeks and Romans to work with their hands, but it was shameful to work for another person.[1] That presented a serious problem for a wealthy magnate who needed agents to manage their *latifundia* and other enterprises and a particularly serious problem for Augustus who, as *princeps*, suddenly faced the problem of a burgeoning imperial administration.

Because slaves were not only "the ultimate human tool" but also dishonored and "natally alienated" they were available to do any work for another person, available for any assignment, susceptible of being trained for whatever task their master required, moved physically and occupationally at beck and command. Thus the availability of slaves provided a ready-made

---

[1] As suggested by Patterson's discussion (34), another reason why classics scholars, who have deep roots in aristocratic and bourgeois values, gloss over the realities of ancient slavery is that slavery exposes the demeaning nature of all labor for others, which took a distinctive new form in modern capitalism.

solution to the social and legal problem of having individuals act as agents for another person. For example, "the slave's lack of separate legal personality enabled him to handle funds directly on behalf of his master" (Weaver, 1972:205). Similarly, for the problem of administering both the empire and the extensive personal property of the emperor, the slaves of the emperor, the *familia Caesaris*, were the ideal solution. "As natally alienated persons with no other anchor in Roman society or as freedmen owing their status solely to the emperor, their interests were completely identified with his own and he could use and abuse them as he wished" (Patterson: 304). Such slaves' influence and standing, however, was always dependent. Even freedmen in such positions were considered people without honor (Garnsey: 122). Such slaves' position was thus also always insecure at best. Their masters retained the power to torture and kill even the most powerful managerial slave. "Of necessity, the power of freedmen and slaves was utterly precarious; it existed solely at the whim, feeblemindedness, or design of the master. Often carnage ensued as the new emperor cleared the deck and settled scores.... Vespasian crucified Asiaticus, his predecessor's favorite; Otho executed Galba's favorite, Icelus, to public rejoicing; and so on" (Patterson: 307).

The wealth they acquired and influence they wielded did not give the "managerial" slave or freedperson any dignity or standing in the society. As literary sources, particularly satire, indicate quite clearly, the more wealthy and powerful the slave or freedperson, the more contemptuous he would be in the eyes of honorable people. "Indeed, to the degree that elite slaves used their master's power in relation to others, to that degree were they despised. It was precisely because they were without honor that they had risen to their positions in the first place" (Patterson: 331–32).

The Question of Social Mobility

Studies by classical scholars on manumission have been of singular importance recently in New Testament studies well beyond the particular issue of slavery in the sociological analysis of the "first urban Christians" by Wayne Meeks, focused on the "status inconsistency" of upwardly mobile individuals. He makes the sound observation that "the most fundamental change of status for a person of the lower classes was that from slavery to freedom—or vice versa" (20). Focusing on freedmen "because they provide an especially vivid instance of social transitions and the resulting dissonance of status indicators" (21), he draws evidence only from "recent intensive studies of the inscriptional evidence [documenting] the restless upward movement of the imperial slaves" (22), particularly by Weaver (1974; 1972).

Weaver (1974) indeed suggests that inscriptions from members of the *familia Caesaris* "can be of general significance in Roman society ... [to] throw light on the process of social mobility in general" (123), yet offers no other evidence for social mobility of freed slaves. Two thirds of the males of the *familia Caesaris* did indeed marry freeborn wives. By the end of the study of "social mobility," however, Weaver must actually conclude that, for all the high status of the imperial freedmen, the upward mobility of imperial freedmen into the equestrian order "was the merest trickle"(1974:136). In a more recent study (1991/1996) Weaver sharply questions the whole thesis of the upward mobility of freed slaves. He declares that the burial inscriptions from Rome are not typical of Italian towns and are even less relevant to provincial communities. Evidence from Rome itself over-represents the numbers of freedmen and freedwomen and their offspring (1991/96:189). Moreover, "the marriage pattern of the *familia Caesaris*, as of public slaves, is demonstrably abnormal for slaveborn society in general" (177). Weaver refers rather to "perceptive studies of the lower classes in Roman society [which indicate that] the effects of slavery on family life at those levels cannot be overemphasized—slave breeding, sale of children, forced separation of families, the general imputation of moral inferiority to slaves of all ages. These effects persisted to a considerable degree past the barrier of manumission and left their stigma on the next generation as well, even those fortunate enough to be freeborn." (1991/96:177; citing Rawson 1966:71ff., 1986a:170ff.) The most we can imagine is that freedmen's marriage "with freeborn women of citizen status would create the possibility of whole families of freeborn citizen children. This would enable the taint of servile blood to be minimized and enhance the social mobility of their descendants. But, in the absence of conspicuous wealth, this would not necessarily be achieved in the first generation, and not easily in sufficient numbers to produce a social invasion from below" (190). Not only was social mobility of freedmen nowhere near what was previously imagined, but the orientalist anxieties about Roman blood, and the civilization to which it gave rise, having run the risk of contamination from the East was historically unfounded.

Roman imperial society generally consisted of a static pyramid of legally mandated orders and a relatively rigid hierarchy of statuses. For what minimal social mobility there was, slavery, even most "managerial" roles, would not have provided a very promising launching pad, considering the social stigma that still attached to the minority of slaves who became freedmen/women—unless we are thinking of a social mobility that happened over three or four generations. The experience of the vast majority of slaves cannot be mitigated by focusing on the unusual influence or atypical mobility of a "select few." Nor would it be methodologically sound to juxtapose evidence for the perks available to that "select few" with the generally depressed circumstances of the vast majority of free people in the Roman empire. That some sold themselves into slavery says more about the condition of the masses of free people than it does about "the positive meaning of slavery." As noted above, for example, the dramatic social changes wrought precisely by the expansion of the slave system in the late Republic brought impoverishment to the majority of Italian peasants in a wide radius around Rome. Not only did slavery not mean "upward mobility" for the vast mass of slaves, but the masses of freeborn people were experiencing a downward slide in both economic circumstances and social-legal status. Finley calls attention to "an important symbol of the changing social structure and accompanying social psychology which [had] set in by the second century CE that so-called *humiliores* [humble freeborn people] were transferred by law to the 'slave category'" in respect to corporal punishment and torture. The extension of humiliating indignities to "the lower classes among the citizen population . . . was a qualitative transformation in social values and behavior" (1980:95).

Implications for New Testament Studies

Slavery, as an integral aspect of Roman imperial society, impinges on the New Testament in numerous ways and with profound impact: in the historical condition out of which the Jesus movement and the early mission of Paul and others arose; in the focal symbols of the gospel message; and in the households and individual people who joined the movement(s).

According to Josephus and other sources, as noted above, Roman warlords enslaved tens of thousands of Judeans and Galileans who then ended up in slave markets in Rome and elsewhere in the generations before, during, and after the life of Jesus, Paul, and their associates. Cassius reportedly enslaved 30,000 people at Magdala two generations prior to Mary Magdalen. In retaliation against the popular messianic movement led by Judas son of Hezekiah in 4 BCE, right about the time Jesus was born, the Romans enslaved the people in Sepphoris or its environs near the village of Nazareth. After reconquering Galilee during the Jewish revolt in 67, Vespasian sent six thousand slaves to work on the canal at the Isthmus of Corinth. This meant not only collective trauma within Judean and Galilean society in the aftermath of mass enslavement. It also meant that tens of thousands of Judean and Galilean peasants ended up as slaves in Rome itself or other cities of the empire in which missionaries such as Paul catalyzed communities of a movement rooted in Israelite tradition. A substantial portion of the Jews living in Rome were apparently slaves or freedmen/women (Fuks; Lampe). Other subject peoples to whom Paul and others took their mission had also suffered the trauma of mass-enslavement—e.g., the Galatians, to whom Paul addressed an impassioned message about "freedom" and not falling back into "slavery" (Galatians 3–5).

In the areas of mission to the Gentiles the fundamental gospel message resonated with the experience of slavery. In the context of a recently subjected country such as Judea and Galilee, crucifixion would have been experienced and understood as the form of torturous execution practiced against insurrectionaries fighting to preserve their indigenous culture and way of life. In the context of Greek cities long since "pacified" and assimilated into the Roman imperial order, crucifixion would have been experienced and understood as the form of execution practiced against trouble-making slaves. It may not be surprising therefore to find in an early (pre-Pauline) hymn that "taking the form of a slave" is the key image for the "incarnation," the lowest of the low in a dehumanized and degraded condition (see further Briggs). As Patterson points out, even a message of freedom, such as Paul's exhortation to the Galatians (Galatians 3–6), depended on experience in a slave-holding society, for freedom had meaning only in contrast with slavery.

In the synoptic Gospel traditions, particularly the parables, derived from and rooted in Galilean Israelite culture not permeated by typical Greek and Roman slavery, perhaps most of the *douloi* would have originally been understood as "servants." Some *douloi*, however, such as those in the parable of the tenants (Mark 12:1–9 & par.), are clearly the "slaves" who comprised the staff of the large "households" of the ruling elite. Those who heard/read the Gospels with the assumptions shaped by their socialization into the dominant Roman imperial society, however, may well have taken any *douloi* as slaves.

Slavery, finally, figured prominently in the membership and structure of the "assemblies" that were the local forms of the overall "assembly" (*ekklēsia*) of the movement. Whenever a "household" is mentioned, as in those of Stephanus, Gaius, and Crispus in Corinth (1 Cor 1:14–16; 16:15–16; cf. Rom 16: 10–11, 23), it is possible that a whole household including its slaves (or freed-slaves?) was involved in a local "assembly." Paul even mentions the "saints in the emperor's household" (i.e., the *familia Caesaris*, through which the empire was administered), although we have no idea whether such "saints" were menial or "managerial" slaves. Actual or hypothetical slaves also crop up that we may miss, unless we are familiar with the patterns of slavery in antiquity. For example, it is at least likely that the "prostitute" mentioned hypothetically in 1 Cor 6:15–16 would have been a slave. By the third if not the second generation at least some assemblies of the young movement had assimilated to the dominant pattern of Roman imperial society, based in slave-holding households. Thus the deutero-Pauline letters and other early Christian documents include in their standard exhortations to the faithful that "slaves . . . " (e.g., Eph 6:5–8; Col 3:22–24; 1 Tim 6:1–2; Tit 2:9–10; 1 Pet 2:18–25 [here not *douloi* but *oiketai*]).

Finally, over against apologists for Christianity working from liberal individualistic perspectives and assumptions, it must be recognized that taking a stand in favor of abolishing slavery in Greek and Roman antiquity would not have occurred to anyone. Slavery was part and parcel of the whole political-economic-religious structure. The only way even of imagining a society without slavery would have been to imagine a different society.

WORKS CONSULTED

Alfoeldy, Geza
    1972   "Die Freilassung von Sklaven und die Struktur der Sklaverei in der römischen Kaiserzeit." *Rivista Storica dell' Antichita* 2:97–129.

Allard, Paul
    1876   *Les esclaves chrétiens.* Paris: Lecoffre.

Barrow, R. H.
    1928   *Slavery in the Roman Empire.* London: Methuen.

Bartchy, S. Scott
    1973   ΜΑΛΛΩΝ ΧΡΗΣΑΙ: *First Century Slavery and the Interpretation of 1 Corinthians 7:21.* SBLDS 11. Missoula, MT: Scholars Press.

    1992   "Slavery (Greco-Roman)." *ABD* 6:65–73.

Bellen, Heinz
    1971   *Studien zur Sklavenflucht im römischen Kaiserraich.* Wiesbaden: Steiner.

Bradley, Keith R.
    1984   *Slaves and Masters in the Roman Empire: A Study in Social Control.* Brussels: Latomus.

    1986   "Wet-Nursing at Rome: A Study in Social Relations." Pp. 201–29 in *The Family in Ancient Rome: New Perspectives.* Ed. B. Rawson. Ithaca: Cornell University Press.

    1987   "On the Roman Slave Supply and Slave Breeding." Pp. 42–64 in *Classical Slavery: Slavery and Abolition Special Issue 8.* Ed. M. I. Finley. London: Frank Cass.

    1988   "Roman Slavery and Roman Law." *Historical Reflections* 15:477–95.

    1989   *Slavery and Rebellion in the Roman World: 140 B.C.–70 B.C.* Bloomington, IN: Indiana University Press.

    1991   *Discovering the Roman Family.* Oxford: Oxford University Press.

    1992   "'The Regular, Daily Traffic in Slaves': Roman History and Contemporary History." *Classical Journal* 87:125–38.

    1994   *Slavery and Society at Rome.* Cambridge: Cambridge University Press.

Briggs, Sheila
    1989   "Can an Enslaved God Liberate?: Hermeneutical Reflections on Philippians 2:6–11. *Semeia* 47:137–53.

Buckland, W. W.
    1989   *The Roman Law of Slavery.* Cambridge: Cambridge University Press.

Callahan, Allen Dwight
    1989–90   "A Note on 1 Corinthians 7:21." *JITC* 17:110–14.

1991 "Paul's Epistle to Philemon: Toward an Alternative Interpretation." Paper delivered to the "Pauline Epistles Section" at the Annual Meeting of the Society of Biblical Literature.

1997 *Embassy of Onesimus: The Letter of Paul to Philemon.* Valley Forge, PA: Trinity Press International.

Christ, Karl
1972 *Von Gibbon zu Rostovtseff.* Darmstadt: Wissenschaftliche Buchgesellschaft.

Crook, J. A.
1967 *Law and Life of Rome.* Ithaca: Cornell University Press.

Daube, David
1952 "Slave-Catching." *Juridical Review* 64:12–28.

Dixon, Suzanne
1992 *The Roman Family.* Baltimore: Johns Hopkins University Press.

DuBois, Page
1991 *Torture and Truth.* London: Routledge.

Duckworth, George, E.
1952 *The Nature of Roman Comedy.* Princeton: Princeton University Press.

Duff, A. M.
1928 *Freedmen in the Early Roman Empire.* Cambridge: Heffer.

Duncan-Jones, Richard
1974 *The Economy of the Roman Empire: Quantitative Studies.* Cambridge: Cambridge University Press.

Durand, John D.
1959–60 "Mortality Estimates from Roman Tombstone Inscriptions." *American Journal of Sociology* 65:365–73.

Finley, Moses I.
1968 "Slavery." In *Encyclopedia of the Social Sciences* 14:307–13.

1980 *Ancient Slavery and Modern Ideology.* New York: Viking.

1982 *Economy and Society in Ancient Greece.* Ed. B. D. Shaw and R. P. Saller. New York: Viking.

1985 *The Ancient Economy.* Berkeley: University of California Press.

Finley, Moses I., ed.
1960 *Slavery in Classical Antiquity: Views and Controversies.* Cambridge: Heffer.

1987 *Classical Slavery: Slavery and Abolition Special Issue 8.* London: Frank Cass.

Flory, Marlene Boudreau
    1978   "Family in *Familia:* Kinship and Community in Slavery." *American Journal of Ancient History* 3:78–95.

Frier, Bruce
    1982   "Roman Life Expectancy: Ulpian's Evidence." *Harvard Studies in Classical Philology* 86:213–51.

    1983   "Roman Life Expectancy: the Pannonian Evidence." *Phoenix* 37:328–44.

Fuks, Gideon
    1985   "Where Have All the Freedmen Gone? On an Anomaly in the Jewish Grave-Inscriptions from Rome." *Journal of Jewish Studies* 36:25–32.

Garlan, Yvon
    1988   *Slavery in Ancient Greece.* Ithaca: Cornell.

Garnsey, Peter
    1970   *Social Status and Legal Privilege in the Roman Empire.* Oxford: Oxford University Press.

Gates, Henry Louis
    1987   *The Classic Slave Narratives.* New York: Penguin.

Genovese, Eugene
    1972   *In Red and Black: Marxian Explorations in Southern and African American History.* New York: Vintage.

Gordon, Mary L.
    1924   "The Nationality of Slaves under the Early Roman Empire." *JRS* 14:93–111. Reprinted in Finley, 1960:171–89.

Hands, A. R.
    1968   *Charities and Social Aid in Greece and Rome.* Ithaca: Cornell University Press.

Harrill, J. Albert
    1995   *The Manumission of Slaves in Early Christianity.* Tübingen: Mohr (Siebeck).

Harris, William V.
    1979   *War and Imperialism in Republican Rome, 327–70 B.C.* Oxford: Clarendon.

    1980   "Towards a Study of the Roman Slave Trade." Pp. 117–40 in *The Seaborne Commerce of Ancient Rome: Studies in Archaeology and History.* Ed. J. H. D'Arms and E. C. Kopff. Rome: American Academy.

Hobson, J. A.
    1965   *Imperialism: A Study.* Revised with new introduction by Philip Siegelman. Ann Arbor: Michigan University Press.

Hopkins, Keith
    1966–67   "On the Probable Age Structure of the Roman Population." *Population Studies* 20:263–64.

1978 *Conquerors and Slaves.* New York: Cambridge.

Horsley, Richard A.
1991 "Paul and Slavery: A Critical Alternative to Recent Readings." Paper delivered to the "Pauline Epistles Section" at the Annual Meeting of the Society of Biblical Literature.

Jaeger, Werner
1939–44 *Paideia: The Ideals of Greek Culture.* 3 Vols. New York: Oxford University Press.

Jones, A. H. M.
1970 *Augustus.* London: Chatto and Windus.

Jones, C. P.
1987 "*Stigma:* Tattooing and Branding in Greco-Roman Antiquity," *JRS* 77:139–55.

Joshel, Sandra R.
1986 "Nurturing the Master's Child: Slavery and the Roman Child-Nurse." *Signs* 12:3–22.

Lauffer, Siegfried
1961 "Die Sklaverei in der griechische-roemische Welt." *Gymnasium* 68: 370–95.

Lampe, Peter
1999 *The Christians of Rome in the First Two Centuries.* Tunbridge Wells: Burns and Oates.

Litwack, Leon
1979 *Been in the Storm So Long: The Aftermath of Slavery.* New York: Random House

Lohse, Eduard
1971 *A Commentary on the Epistle to the Colossians and Philemon.* Ed. Helmut Koester. Philadelphia: Fortress.

MacMullen, Ramsay
1974 *Roman Social Relations 50 B.C to A.D. 284.* New Haven: Yale University Press.

Martin, Dale B.
1990 *Slavery as Salvation: The Metaphor of Slavery in Pauline Christianity.* New Haven: Yale University Press.

Meeks, Wayne
1983 *The First Urban Christians.* New Haven: Yale University Press.

Meyer, Eduard
1924a "Die Sklaverei im Altertum." Pp. 169–212 in *Kleine Schriften.* 2nd ed. Halle: Niemeyer. (Orig. 1898)

1924b   "Die Wirtschaftliche Entwicklung des Altertums." Pp. 79–168 in *Kleine Schriften*. 2nd ed. Halle: Niemeyer. (Orig. 1895)

Mitchell, Margaret M.
- 1995   "John Chrysostom on Philemon: A Second Look." *HTR* 88:135–48.

Patterson, Orlando
- 1982   *Slavery and Social Death: A Comparative Study*. Cambridge, MA: Harvard University Press.

Petersen, Norman
- 1985   *Rediscovering Paul: Philemon and the Sociology of Paul's Narrative World*. Philadelphia: Fortress.

Pomeroy, Sarah B.
- 1975   *Goddesses, Whores, Wives, and Slaves: Women in Classical Antiquity*. New York: Schocken.

Rawson, Beryl
- 1966   "Family Life among the Lower Classes at Rome in the First Two Centuries of the Empire." *Classical Philology* 61:70–83.
- 1986   *The Family in Ancient Rome: New Perspectives*. Ithaca: Cornell University Press.
- 1991/96   *Marriage, Divorce, and Children in Ancient Rome*. Oxford: Oxford University Press.

Ste. Croix, G. E. M. de
- 1981   *The Class Struggle in the Ancient Greek World: From the Archaic Age to the Arab Conquest*. London: Duckworth.

Saller, Richard P.
- 1987   "Slavery and the Roman Family." Pp. 65–87 in *Classical Slavery: Slavery and Abolition Special Issue 8*. Ed. M. I. Finley. London: Frank Cass.
- 1994   *Patriarchy, Property, and Death in the Roman Family*. Cambridge: Cambridge University Press.
- 1996a   "The Hierarchical Household in Roman Society: a Study of Domestic Slavery." Pp.112–29 in *Serfdom and Slavery: Studies in Legal Bondage*. Ed. M. L. Bush. London: Longman.
- 1996b   "Corporal Punishment, Authority, and Obedience in the Roman Household." Pp.144–65 in *Marriage, Divorce, and Children in Ancient Rome*. Ed. B. Rawson. Oxford: Oxford University Press.

Starr, Chester G.
- 1987   *Past and Future in Ancient History*. Lanham, MD: University Press of America.

Stuhlmacher, Peter
- 1981   *Der Brief an Philemon*. Neukirchen-Vluyn: Neukirchner Verlag.

Syme, Ronald
    1939   *The Roman Revolution.* London: Oxford University Press.

Treggiari, Susan
    1969   *Roman Freedmen During the Late Republic.* Oxford: Oxford University Press.

    1975   "Family Life among the Staff of the Volusii." *Transactions of the American Philological Association* 105:393–401.

    1976   "Jobs for Women." *American Journal of Ancient History* 1:76–104.

Troeltsch, Ernst
    1960   *The Social Teachings of the Christian Churches.* 2 vols. New York: Harper. (Orig. 1911)

Veyne, Paul
    1987   *A History of Private Life.* Vol. 1, *From Pagan Rome to Byzantium.* Cambridge, MA: Harvard University Press.

Vittinghoff, Friedrich
    1960   "Die Theorie des historischen Materialismus über dem antiken 'Sklavenhalterstaat': Probleme der alten Geschichte bei den 'Klassikern' des Marxismus und in der modernen sowjetischen Forschung." *Saeculum* 11: 89–131.

    1962   "Die Sklavenfrage in der Forschung der Sowjetunion." *Gymnasium* 69:279–86.

Vogt, Joseph
    1974   *Ancient Slavery and the Ideal of Man.* Translated by Thomas Wiedemann. Oxford: Oxford University Press.

Wallon, Henri
    1847   *Histoire de l'esclavage dans l'antiquité.* 3 volumes. Paris: Hachette.

Watson, Alan
    1985   *The Evolution of the Law.* Baltimore: Johns Hopkins University Press.

    1987   *Roman Slave Law.* Baltimore: Johns Hopkins University Press.

Weaver, P. R. C.
    1964   "Vicarius and Vicarianus in the Familia Caesaris." *Journal of Roman Studies* 54:118.

    1972   *Familia Caesaris: A Social Study of the Emperor's Freedmen and Slaves.* Cambridge: Cambridge University Press.

    1974   "Social Mobility in the Early Roman Empire: The Evidence of the Imperial Freedmen and Slaves." Pp. 121–40 in *Studies in Ancient Society.* London: Routledge.

1991/96 "Children of Freedmen (and Freedwomen)." Pp. 166–90 in *Marriage, Divorce, and Children in Ancient Rome*. Ed. B. Rawson. Oxford: Oxford University Press.

Weber, Max
1891 *Die Röemische Agrargeschichte*. Stuttgart: F. Enke

Westermann, William L.
1935 "Sklaverei." Pp. 894–1068 in *Pauly, Realencyclopedie* Suppl. vol. 6.

1955 *The Slave Systems of Greek and Roman Antiquity*. Philadelphia: American Philosophical Society.

Wiedemann, Thomas. E. J.
1981 *Greek and Roman Slavery*. Baltimore: John Hopkins University Press.

1985 "The Regularity of Manumission at Rome." *Classical Quarterly* 35:162–75.

1987 *Slavery*. Oxford: Oxford University Press.

Servants of God(s) and Servants of Kings in Israel and the Ancient Near East

Dexter E. Callender, Jr.
University of Miami

ABSTRACT

In contrast with ancient Greece and Rome, chattel slavery played a minor role in societies of the ancient Near East, including Israel. Yet the people in general and officers in particular were understood as "servants" of the king and, by analogy, "servants" of the gods. The Hebrew Bible, however, is sharply critical of various forms of human servitude. Its critique is rooted in Israel's formative memory of having been "redeemed from slavery" in Egypt, on the basis of which Israelites are expected not to enslave fellow Israelites and to care for the destitute.

Pauline letters supplied the principal biblical warrant for slavery in the southern United States. The exodus story in the Hebrew Bible, however, provided the biblical paradigm for emancipation from slavery. Clearly the literature of the Christian Old and New Testaments have different views of slavery. And those are rooted respectively in very different historical experience and societal patterns of power-relations. Paul's letters were addressed to communities in Roman imperial society in which chattel slavery was integral to patriarchal households in particular and to the economy generally. By contrast the Hebrew Bible refers regularly to the people generally as "servants" (ʿbdym) of God, on the one hand, yet attempts to restrict the possibility of chattel slavery, on the other. With regard both to the understanding of people generally as "slaves/servants" of the god(s) and to the limited role of chattel slavery, ancient Israel appears to have been similar to other ancient Near Eastern societies, and very different from classical Greek and imperial Roman societies. Yet the Hebrew Bible also articulates an opposition unusual in antiquity, to various forms of servitude, one that appears rooted in Israel's formative deliverance from bondage in Egypt, the basis of its own distinctive social identity.

People as Servants of the Gods and Kings in the Ancient Near East

Forging an understanding of the concept "slavery" in the ancient Near East poses an almost intractable problem of definition. At present there is a notable lack of consensus with regard to terminology. The problems attending the use of the term slavery are basic to the very nature of language. The meaning of the term "slavery" is determined not only by the spoken or literary setting, but also by the effective history of a given people. The term "slavery" in the modern western anglophone world has been influenced by the course of the African slave trade and its ultimate manifestation in the American South. For Americans in particular, then, caution must be exercised in discussing slavery in the context of antiquity. What exactly is a slave? A common understanding suggests a person deprived of freedom, who may be purchased or sold and, as such, is the property of another, used in accordance with the will of that owner.

A seminal understanding of the term has been offered by Orlando Patterson, who saw property as merely a small and potentially misleading aspect of a definition of slavery. Slavery is not simply an issue of one having proprietary rights over another. Strictly speaking, property in this sense refers simply to a set of relationships between people. Patterson, instead, is informed by the historical development evident in what he refers to as the Roman "legal fiction" of *dominum*, i.e., "absolute ownership," which changed the relation to one between a person and things and the subsequent absolute power of person over thing (31). The legal fiction was created, he argues, to buttress and virtually redefine the burgeoning economic role of slavery, previously devoid of such far-reaching philosophical underpinnings.

The place of slavery in the ancient Near East has been the subject of considerable discussion over the course of the present century particularly in view of its relation to the later and more clearly defined systems of Greece and Rome. Something of a consensus has emerged, but a lack of unambiguous sources has provided the conditions for continued debate. The reigning consensus has been that slavery in the ancient Near East differed markedly from that found in classical Greek and Roman societies (Dandamaev: 67–80). Among the most widely recognized differences is that which pertains to the property aspect of slavery. "In Israel and the neighboring countries, there never existed those enormous gangs of chattel slaves which in Greece and Rome continually threatened the balance of social order. . . . Nor was the position of the slave ever so low in Israel and the ancient East as in republican Rome, where Varro could define a slave as 'a sort of talking tool'" (de Vaux: 80).[1] Degradation and dishonor of slaves were fundamental features of Greco-Roman society. In his classic treatment of the subject, Isaac Mendelsohn attempted to define the nature of slavery in the ancient Near East. He argued that Near Eastern slave institutions were essentially the same in origin, func-

---

[1] Wiedemann and many other classics scholars sought to cast Greek and Roman slavery in a more palatable light. See further the survey by Horsley in this volume (19–66).

tion, and character. In Babylonia, Assyria, and Syria-Palestine, factors such as private ownership of land and intensive agriculture led to a system in which chattel slavery played a relatively minor role. Rather, the basis of Near Eastern society was the free tenant-farmer and share cropper in agriculture and the free artisan and day laborer in industry. True chattel slavery indeed existed, but such slaves were nonetheless regarded as human beings possessing basic inalienable rights, as evidenced in the law codes (1949:121–22).

I. M. Diakonoff approached slavery from the sphere of economics rather than law. He perceptively pointed out that in ancient Near Eastern societies "'slave' is not an absolute, but a relative, concept. Here one does not contrast 'slave' with 'free', as in the Greek opposition *doulos—eleutheros*" (1987:1–2).[2] He observes that among inhabitants of the ancient Near East "everyone who has a 'lord' is automatically a 'slave' of that lord. No person is without his or her lord (human or divine), and, thus, as was already noted in antiquity by Herodotus and again by Marx, everybody is someone's slave. This makes it absolutely clear that a social or legal frame of reference is useless for the economist." Diakonoff finds that there are three types of relations to production and to property in the means of production in ancient Near Eastern societies. First, those sharing property rights in the means of production but not partaking in any process of production. Second, those sharing property rights in the means of production and who partake in the process of production in their own interests. Third, those who are devoid of property in means of production and who take part in the process of production in the interest of others. These would include chattel slaves, patriarchal slaves (who worked alongside their masters), debt slaves, and other "quasi slaves," as well as "helots" or "serfs" (the term preferred by Gelb). Diakonoff finds the third category appropriate for the "slave" (1987:3).

It is generally recognized that the numbers of chattel slaves in ancient Mesopotamia was generally small and that for the most part they were privately held (Oppenheim: 74–76). In the Ur III period, chattel slaves were virtually insignificant in number and economic impact. The bulk of the labor force consisted of people referred to by the terms *guruš* and *geme2*. The socioeconomic status of these has been variously interpreted. According to Gelb, such were native-born "semi-free serfs," possessing means of production and perhaps family life, who worked part- or full-time mainly in productive type of labor in the public sector. Slaves, on the other hand would have been foreign-born workers who possessed neither family life nor means of production, and who labored on a full-time basis in large households. Diakonoff, as we have seen, would have considered both of these groups "slaves," but in economic terms alone, not in a legal sense. In addressing these issues,

---

[2] Note, however, regarding the opposition *doulos:eleutheros* the term in the Hebrew Bible, *ḥpsy*, which signifies the "emancipated" slave. For discussion and bibliography see Lohfink.

P. Steinkeller has declared that the question as to whether the position of the serf differed sufficiently from the slave to warrant a socio-economic class distinction has reached an impasse (74). His study on foresters in Umma revealed the difficulty in detecting clear social distinctions between workers.

According to the code of Hammurabi, Babylon at the time of the First Dynasty distinguished three principal groups within society. The *awilūm*, the *muškenūm* and the *wardūm*. The term *(w)ardū(m)* was the most common designation for what is generally agreed upon as "slave" in Babylonia in the second millennium, and in all periods in Assyria. The neo-Babylonian period witnessed the appearance of a number of terms unattested in earlier texts (as discussed by Dandamaev: 82). In writing about the situation in Babylonia, Driver and Miles noted that a slave in Babylonia preserved his identity and had a family, and his master did not have the power of life or death over him (Dandamaev: 68).

Market conditions played no mean role in the extent of chattel slavery. The average price for a slave in the Old Babylonian period was approximately 20 shekels of silver, sometimes rising to as high as 90. The average wage paid to hired labor was some 10 shekels a year. Because it was far cheaper for a landowner to employ seasonal labor than to own a slave specifically for agricultural work, private slaves were relatively uncommon, and were employed mainly in domestic service (Oates: 70). Oppenheim also attributed the apparent small holdings of slaves in private households "partly to the specific nature of their relationship to their masters and partly to the absence of any interest in industrial production on the home level, a characteristic of the Greek city-dwellers." Such production, he continues, "was restricted in the ancient Near East to the great organizations, that is, ultimately to the manor-level, the house of the ruler or the god" (76). Otherwise, in addition to the corvée, the most common system of working the land was that of tenant farming, whereby the tenant received seed, animals, and implements, for the most part in the form of non-interest bearing loans, for which the tenant returned a set percentage of the harvest.

Servitude in Ancient Egypt appears to have existed in different forms and degrees. Bakir detects a fundamental classification of free or unfree people, yet those who were "unfree" had various degrees of liberty (8). Attempting to locate an Egyptian concept of "slavery" involves negotiating a variety of terms. The term *isww*, from *isw* "price, equivalent" designates people acquired for an equivalent, that is, people who have been purchased. The term *b3k* derives from a verb, which may describe voluntary or forced labor. The term *mr(y)t* appears beginning in the Old and Middle Kingdoms to describe people belonging either to individuals or to religious institutions. They are often closely associated with land and cattle, and along with the term *mr(t)* denote people who are put to work especially on land (Bakir: 27). In the Middle Kingdom, the term *ḏt* was frequently used to denote people who were owned and could be bequeathed. The work they perform usually pertains to funerary service (37). The term ḥm occurs regularly beginning in the Middle Kingdom, but by Dynasty 18 all evidence suggests it becomes the most popular term for denoting true chattel slaves (Bakir: 34). But it is interesting to note that a ḥm could be a land owner (32). In fact, evidence suggests that from Dynasty 18 onwards, the socio-economic position of the slave was not that of the most wretched poverty and abject misery. One cannot deny the existence of chattel servitude, whereby a person could come under the ownership of another, who would obtain exclusive rights to make use of that person as any other form of movable property. Nonetheless, although the worker was regarded as chattel, the worker was allowed to marry, testify in law courts, and refuse instructions not issued by the owner. Texts also reveal that owners could be beneficent, rewarding good behavior with emancipation (Bakir: 90).

The realities of living in Egypt, the place called by Herodotus "The Gift of the Nile," with its unusually arid climate and low levels of rainfall, made the maintenance of irrigation systems of paramount importance. This placed a premium on cooperation and authority, which led ultimately to an emphasis on praedial servitude connected to the land. Thus, it was praedial servitude that ensured continued existence in the region. From the period of the Old Kingdom on, and intimately related to the need to work the land, Egypt developed a system of forced labor, which included not only peasants but also people who were not normally involved in agricultural occupations. Even those in positions of stature were not exempted by virtue of their position alone (Bakir: 2). The need for an agricultural workforce led to what Bakir describes as a *de facto* status of bondage to the land, which ultimately, became manifest in compulsory service. In areas other than agriculture, the available evidence precludes assessing what proportion of men were permanently employed in areas such as quarrying and building. Urk. I, 44, 3–4 tells of a mission that was carried out by "all crews from the residence," and an expedition of a group of 'state-people' pr-ʿ3, a group of people which may have been regularly connected with the state for service, although their status and functions are unknown" (Eyre: 13). The mass of people needed for basic labor on any project can only have been provided by corvée, but information is sparse and mostly indirect.

Chattel slavery thus played a limited role in the political-economic systems of major ancient Near Eastern societies. The extent to which it and other forms of servitude played a role in the ideological life or symbol systems of these people is a separable question. In the mythological traditions of Mesopotamia, the notion of unpaid servitude on behalf of another plays a prominent role in texts that discuss creation motifs. The notion of humans being created as servants of the gods is one that belongs to the official fabric of Mesopotamian thought. This idea is found in the opening sections of the Atrahasis myth (Old Babylonian version). Before the creation of mankind, the lesser gods carried out the "heavy forced labor" imposed on them by the great gods. Mankind is then created to "bear the yoke . . . the drudgery" (of canal construction, etc.), the ultimate purpose being the production of provisions for the gods. The same idea of creating humankind to "bear the gods' burden that they may rest" appears again later in the Babylonian epic of origins, "Enuma Elish." Once again, the work concerns provisions for the gods (Enuma Elish V.139, where the gods remark, "let them bring us our daily portions"). The notion of mankind being created to bear the burden of the gods is also expressed in a bilingual Sumerian and Akkadian text (Pettinato: 74–77), which presents the work in similar terms, and centers it around the temple.

> The work of the gods shall be their work
> that they might lay down the border trenches forever,
> place the pickaxe and the basket,
> for the temple of the great gods, . . .
> That they make flourish the grainfield of Anunna,
> to increase the abundance in the land,
> to appropriately celebrate the feast of the gods.

Particularly interesting here is that the hard work signified by the pickaxe and pannier and by the digging of borders and dykes has an agricultural orientation and goal, expressed in the growth of "all sorts of plants", "increase" in grain, and "abundance" in the land. From these texts we may conclude that according to this conception, man was created to work not simply in place of the gods, but on their behalf—to do work of direct benefit to them. This work involves the divine dwelling, the temple, and is agricultural in nature (Lambert: 298). Not only were ordinary humans considered the servants of the gods, but the king as well considered himself an agricultural worker. The conception of the king as gardener is seen most clearly in the epithets of Akkadian and Sumerian rulers: "farmer, landworker," and "gardener." In the so-called "Legend of Sargon" Sargon was rescued by a gardener and trained as a gardener. These varied images suggest the extent to which the notion of the servant-lord relationship played a significant role in defining and articulating the relationship between humanity and the divine.

In sum, by contrast with the developed slave-systems of classical Greece and the Roman empire, chattel slavery was not very important in the ancient Near East. The people understood themselves as generally in servitude to gods, entailing agricultural production in order to provide for the gods in the style to which they had become accustomed and forced labor on irrigation works, temple-building, and other "public works."

Servants of YHWH vs Forms of Slavery in Ancient Israel

Variety and Ambiguity in the term ʿbd

Relations of servitude in ancient Israel were in many respects analogous to what is found in its ancient Near Eastern environment. The situation met with in the traditions of the Hebrew Bible is by no means easy to apprehend. Here, the chief problem is the broad semantic range of the term ʿbd. In a broad sense ʿbd refers to a person who is subject to the will of and serves another. It is used for a wide range of relations, from that of a social inferior to a social superior to chattel slavery.

The word ʿbd is used for the all subjects of the king in general and for his mercenaries, officers and ministers in particular. Subjects routinely refer to the king as "lord" and to themselves as "servants." This extended even to family members, including the monarch's wives, sons, and brothers (2 Sam 13:24; 1 Kgs 1:17). The word was also simply a term of courteous address, as some have compared with "the development of its equivalents 'servant' in English or 'serviteur' in French, both derived from *servus*, 'slave'" (de Vaux: 80).

By analogy, ʿbdym is also frequently used for the people of Israel in relation to YHWH their God, as can be seen in poetic parallelism such as the very early Song of Moses, Deut 32:43, and later Ps 105:25:

> He turned their hearts to hate his people,
> to deal craftily with his servants (ʿbdym).

This relationship can also be seen clearly in the fact that the God of Israel is regularly addressed as "Lord" (ʾdwny). Such language reflects a conscious servant-lord relationship that extends beyond the expression of simple politeness or respect. Indeed, the roots of this type of expression must certainly lie in the socio-economic servant-lord relationship. Cultic service is simply another aspect of this relationship, since there was no separation of the religious dimension from political-economic relations in ancient Israel.

"Servant of the Lord" can thus also be a title used in a special sense to denote significant individuals, such as the patriarchal figures Abraham, Isaac, and Jacob. Likewise, David, Solomon, and other kings are referred to as "servant of YHWH." David expresses his relationship with YHWH in 2 Samuel 7: "What more can David say to you, for you know your servant (ʿbd), O Lord (ʾdwny) God." This special sense is applied to prophets as well, who obediently pronounce the will or carry out the orders of YHWH their lord. Because the will of the deity is communicated in the words and actions of the prophet they are to be heeded.

Chattel Slavery

Besides all Israelites being "servants of YHWH" and, under the monarchy, "servants of the king," some Israelites were involved in other forms of servitude. Three principal types of servitude can be distinguished, two of which were referred to with the term ʿbd. As in the rest of the ancient Near East, chattel slavery was nowhere near as prevalent and important to the political economy as it was later in classical Greece and late Republican and

Imperial Roman society. People were indeed bought and sold, owned and utilized as slaves, usually in domestic capacities. As indicated explicitly in the Holiness Code of Leviticus, "it is from the nations around you that you may acquire male and female slaves" (ʿbd wʾmh; Lev 25:44). Covenantal laws and teaching, however, placed severe restrictions on chattel slavery. Israelites were forbidden to force other Israelites to serve them or to sell fellow Israelites abroad as slaves. "If any . . . become so impoverished that they sell themselves to you, you shall not make them serve as slaves (ʿbdt ʿbd). They shall remain with you as hired or bound laborers" (Lev 25:39–40). Similarly, Israelites were not to become or be sold as slaves to non-Israelites, either resident aliens or to foreigners outside Israel. An Israelite sold to a resident alien could be "redeemed" (Lev 25:47–53). Furthermore, not as a chattel slave but rather "as a wage laborer (śkyr) year by year shall he be with him; he shall not rule with harshness over him in your sight" (25:53). The very existence of such laws, of course, indicates that Israelites were enslaved and/or sold abroad. Prophets such as Amos deliver sharp indictments against wealthy creditors "because they sell the righteous for silver, and the needy for a pair of sandals" (2:6).

Debt Slavery

The laws of slavery themselves reveal another type of slavery different from chattel slavery. Although the precise relation in a practical sense is unclear, this would appear to be what is often known as debt slavery. Israelites who became heavily indebted could be forced to surrender or sell children or themselves as "men-servants" (ʿbd) or "women-servants" (ʾmh) to the creditor. In a passage that also exemplifies the different relations that could be indicated by the term ʿbd,

> Now the wife of a member of the company of prophets cried to Elisha, "Your servant (ʿbdk) my husband is dead; and you know that your servant feared the LORD, but a creditor has come to take my two children as slaves (lʿbdym). (2 Kgs 4:1)

The various legal codes place strict time limits on this type of servitude. The so-called Covenant Code stipulated release after a maximum of six years of service and provided further provisions supposedly protecting the rights of "women-servants" (Exod 21:2–3, 7–11). This is echoed and expanded upon later in the Deuteronomic Code (Deut 15:12–14). The later Holiness Code virtually eliminated such limits on debt-slavery, allowing such a relationship to continue beyond normal life-expectancy to a maximum of 49 years (Lev 25:39–43). If the debt-slave consented, of course, the servitude could become permanent, a relationship that must have been close to chattel slavery (Exod 21:5; Deut 15:17). Clearly debt-slaves were extremely vulnerable to being forced into chattel slavery. The prophets railed against the powerful for selling debt-slaves into chattel slavery (again see Amos 2:6). And after the exiled Judean ruling class had returned from exile, exploited Judean peasants complained bitterly to the Persian appointed governor Nehemiah that for their debts (apparently) the "nobles and officials" were "forcing our sons and daughters to be slaves (ʿbdym), and some of our daughters have been ravished" (Neh 5:1–13, esp vv. 5–6).

Forced Labor

In contrast with other ancient Near Eastern societies, Israel distinguishes another type of servitude, "forced labor," from the general service owed to lords such as gods, kings, high priests, and other "lords." The Davidic monarchy utilized forced labor for state projects such as the building of Solomon's temple. The Hebrew term *ms*, used for forced labor on behalf of the monarchy, is a word of uncertain etymology (North: 427). Conscripted labor was instituted already under the reign of David himself, then dramatically expanded under Solomon, and apparently continued throughout the Judean monarchy until Jehoiakim, just before the conquest by Babylon. That both David's and Solomon's regimes included as one of their principle officers an overseer of "forced labor" (2 Sam 20:24; 1 Kgs 4:6) reveals the extent and relative importance of conscripted labor for the early Israelite monarchy. The institution of forced labor in the Davidic-Solomonic empire may have been based on an Egyptian model (Redford: 369–74).

The Deuteronomic history makes a distinction between forced labor imposed on conquered peoples and forced labor imposed on Israelites themselves. David appears to have required forced labor from the Ammonites after defeating them (2 Sam 12:31, although the text does not explicitly use the term *ms*). That servitude to a foreign regime was at least one of the fates that a conquered people might expect appears in the later 8th century oracle of Isaiah (31:8), a notion echoed perhaps even in the exilic period literature (Lam 1:1; see also Gelb). Under Solomon, the Davidic monarchy must have developed an elaborate system of forced labor by conquered peoples. The royal palace, the fortification of Jerusalem, Hazor, Megiddo, Gezer and other towns, the establishment of storage cities, chariot cities, and cavalry, all testify to the existence of a system designed to organize and enforce a labor force requisite for the completion of such projects. According to the notice in 1 Kgs 9:15–22 (echoed later in 2 Chron 2:16–17; 8:7–9), the great building projects of Solomon were accomplished by means of a non-Israelite "conscripted ... forced labor" (ʿbd ms, a term often understood to be a synonym of *ms* (North: 428). The phrase "and so they are to this day" (9:21) suggests a permanent state of enslavement of the Canaanites conquered by David's armies.

Although 1 Kgs 9:22 claims otherwise, 1 Kgs 5:13–16 (Heb 5:27–20) makes clear that Israelites also were subjected to forced labor. "King Solomon conscripted forced labor out of all Israel." The Deuteronomic history connects this with Solomon's building of the temple, but he also required a vast and consistent labor force for his many building projects, including his own palace and those for the princess of Egypt, etc. It is clear, moreover, that forced labor did not end with Solomon, at least in the kingdom of Judah. The last king noted explicitly by the Deuteronomist to have continued the practice of conscripted labor (from which "none was exempt") is Asa of Judah, specifically for the fortification of the cities of Mizpah and Geba (1 Kgs 15:22). Finally, the seventh century prophet Jeremiah, who witnessed the demise of the Israelite monarchy, alludes negatively to the practice of forced labor continuing under Jehoiakim, to construct his royal palace (Jer 22:13). By contrast to the forced labor for "public works" under the monarchy, the later book of Nehemiah, in the absence of a strong centralized government, portrays the rebuilding of the walls of Jerusalem with what amounts to voluntary labor, with some refusing to participate and others scoffing (2:17).

Like chattel slavery and the prolongation of debt-slavery, however, forced labor is unacceptable for Israelites, according to both the Deuteronomic history and prophets such as Jeremiah. In 1 Kgs 12:3–4, a passage reminiscent of the Hebrew foremen's confrontation with Pharaoh (Exod 5:15), Jeroboam and all the assembly of Israel confront Solomon's son and presumed successor, Rehoboam: "Your father made our yoke heavy. Now therefore lighten the hard service of your father and his heavy yoke upon us, and we will serve you" (1 Kgs 12:4).[3] Rehoboam's response, likewise, is reminiscent of Pharaoh's in the exodus narrative (Exod 5:17–18). Following the advice of his younger colleagues his response is harsh and without mercy, "My father made your yoke heavy, but I will add to your yoke; my father chastised you with whips, but I will chastise you with scorpions" (1 Kgs 12:13–14). Particularly instructive for the close relationship between what Israel viewed as intolerable "forced labor" and the general "servile" (ʿbd) relationship between people as "servants" king as "lord" is the diplomatically sage advice of his older advisors (which he immediately disregarded, according to the narrator): "If you will be a servant (ʿbd) to this people today and serve them (ʿbd), and speak good words to them when you answer them, then they will be your servants (ʿbdym) for ever" (12:7). The sage older generation of advisers articulate a view of what would be an acceptable relationship between parties arranged hierarchically in the positions of servant and lord. From the Deuteronomistic viewpoint, the Israelites are willing to compromise on a lightened burden of labor, although forced labor is basically unacceptable. The latter position is more explicitly stated in the so-called anti-monarchic speech of Samuel in 1 Sam 8:11–17, which warns of the dangers of kingship, one of them being the conscription of the people to service. The text is loaded with

---

[3] It is noteworthy that the leader of the group was none other than the chief overseer of the corvée, Jeroboam son of Nebat (1 Kgs 11:26–28; 12:2).

statements that demonstrate the nature of the problem anticipated, as well as use of the term ʿbdym, for the officers of the king, the addressees "menservants" and "his [the king's] slaves."

> These will be the ways of the king who will reign over you: he will take your sons and appoint them to his chariots and to be his horsemen, and to run before his chariots; and he will appoint for himself commanders of thousands and commanders of fifties, and some to plow his ground and to reap his harvest, and to make his implements of war and the equipment of his chariots. He will take your daughters to be perfumers and cooks and bakers. He will take the best of your fields and vineyards and olive orchards and give them to his servants. He will take the tenth of your grain and of your vineyards and give it to his officers and to his servants. He will take your menservants and maidservants, and the best of your cattle and your asses, and put them to his work. He will take the tenth of your flocks, and you shall be his slaves. (1 Sam 8:11–17)

There is no acceptance of a royal ideology of the king controlling the people's labor and resources for the common good. The tone is clearly one of objection: "He will take. . . ." It represents monarchy as an unacceptable slavery: "you shall be his slaves."

Exodus and Covenant

The event celebrated in the exodus narrative formed the basis of Israel's socio-cultural identity, which it forged from the memory of harsh servitude, "slavery" in Egypt. Deuteronomy calls Israel's hard labor in Egypt "slavery," using ʿbd, the general term for servitude. The concept of forced labor, *ms*, or corvée is more instructive in addressing this question than that of chattel slavery for at least two reasons. First, it has the potential to be as severe as any form of servitude and therefore as troubling from a human standpoint. Second, it is corvée that forms the real background of the exodus in the Exodus narrative.

In Exod 1:11–14 the Hebrews are set to building Pharaoh's "store-cities, Pithom and Ra-am'ses . . . with task-masters set over them to afflict them with heavy burdens; [they] made their lives bitter with hard service, in mortar and brick, and in all kinds of work in the field." The labor involved both agricultural work and large-scale building projects. These two kinds of "service," of course, were precisely what was required of people in the ancient Near Eastern societies in their existence as the "slaves of the gods," as noted above—although the text does not employ the term ʿbdym, the term used elsewhere to indicate the people's general servitude to the human as well as divine rulers. Nor is there any suggestion that the Hebrews were chattel slaves (for which ʿbdym again would have been the usual term). There is no hint of a legal change of status, from free to slave. Rather, the language is strongly suggestive of the corvée system: massive building projects, for which "they set up taskmasters over them." The term "taskmasters," "chiefs of *missîm*" (cf. the "forced labor" under Solomon in 1 Kgs 5:13–15), makes the case explicit.

Yet the issue was even more than that of "forced labor." Exod 1:8–10 suggests that xenophobia and imperial oppression of a subject people, lest they generate an insurrection,[4] were also involved. In Exod 1:11 the taskmasters' assignment was not simply to organize human resources and expedite the completion of state projects, but to afflict (ʿ*nh*) the people of Israel through the socially sanctioned means of labor conscription. The term ʿ*nh* connotes the ideas "to bow down," "to lower," or "to humble." Thus, in the Exodus narrative, at least, the Hebrews' "slavery" in Egypt was a systematic program of imperial oppression. And indeed, as the Moses-led movement of the Hebrews' resistance to their oppression emerges, Pharaoh and the taskmasters further escalate the severity of the hard labor, with abusive treatment as well as repressive measures, as narrated in Exod 5:4–19. The NRSV translation that the Israelite foremen "saw that they were in trouble" is simply an understatement. The phrase *br*ʿ may be literally rendered "in evil, calamity." The Israelites/Hebrews here were in a desperate situation. The sense is that the situation was humanly intolerable, outside the bounds of acceptable human relations.

God's deliverance of the Israelites from bondage in Egypt is often called a "redemption" or "ransom" (*pdh*) from slavery, particularly in Deuteronomic literature. One is tempted to think of debt slavery redemption expressed in Leviticus 25, but the term *pdh* is never used in that immediate connection. It is, however, used elsewhere for redemption of slaves, as in the Covenant Code (Exod 21:8) and elsewhere in the Holiness Code (Lev 19:20). There are various aspects of the notion of redemption, and there are different terms used to describe such aspects. One clear observation we may make is that the Deuteronomic literature consistently uses the term (*pdh*) to describe YHWH's action on behalf of Israel. Exod 13:11–16 draws the analogy with the redemption of the first-born animals, the meaning of which is precisely that "the LORD brought us out of Egypt, from the house of slavery." Deut 7:8 and other passages in Deuteronomic literature use the term "redemption" directly for God deliverance from Egypt: "the LORD has redeemed you from the house of slavery" (see also Deut 9:26; 13:5; 15:15; 21:8; 24:18; 2 Sam 7:23; cf. Isa 35:10; 51:11; Jer 31:11). Many of these passages are explicitly linked with Israel's (Mosaic) covenant with the LORD. The combination of the exodus re-

---

[4] Literally "go up" from the land. This may be a reference to an overthrow of the government (rising up from the land) rather than an escape from Egypt. At this point in the narrative, there is no reason for them to "escape."

demption from slavery in Egypt and the Mosaic covenant with YHWH as their literal king, to the exclusion of other kings, human as well as divine (e.g., Judg 8:22–23; 1 Sam 8:4–8), brings to clear articulation the sense that Israelites cannot properly serve any other lord. Israelites are "servants" (ʿbdym) exclusively to YHWH, and therefore cannot rightfully be "servants" of others, whether another god, a domestic or foreign king, or another Israelite.

Israelite exclusive servitude to God is then precisely the basis for its sharp rejection of all forms of human servitude, whether chattel slavery, the prolongation of debt-slavery, or "forced labor," as discussed above. If we read the full passages of legal rulings already cited above, the connection is abundantly clear. The debt-slave must be set free in the seventh year and generously supplied by the creditor with resources for a fresh start. Why? "Remember that you were a slave in Egypt, and the LORD your God redeemed you; for this reason I lay this command upon you today" (Deut 15:12–15). An Israelite who becomes a slave to a resident alien must be redeemed by a brother, or at least go free in the jubilee year. Why? "For to me the people of Israel are servants; they are my servants whom I brought out of the land of Egypt; I am the LORD your God" (Lev 25:55, which probably applies to all of the mechanisms in Leviticus 25 to keep Israelites free on their land).

Redemption from Slavery and Social Justice

Israel's sense of having been "redeemed from slavery" in Egypt and their being "servants" exclusively to YHWH their sole lord, finally, resulted not only in opposition to or limitation of various forms of human servitude. It also carried over into demands for humane treatment of the poor and destitute generally, those who were vulnerable to becoming slaves or otherwise suffering further abuse and exploitation. Again these concerns are articulated particularly in Deuteronomy.

> You shall not deprive a resident alien or an orphan of justice; you shall not take a widow's garment in pledge. Remember that you were a slave in Egypt and the LORD your God redeemed you from there; therefore I command you to do this. (Deut 24:17–18)

The Deuteronomic code continues into other examples of how the redemption from slavery leads to social welfare measures for those who are without the usual protection of a complete household for their economic subsistence: leaving some grain, olives, and grapes for the gleaners (Deut 24:19–22; cf. further, 10:18–19). These statements support humane treatment of those who are destitute, the traditionally vulnerable members of society, the sojourner, the orphan, and the widow. Theirs is a situation broadly analogous to that of the Israelites' oppression in Egypt. Similarly the "credo" preserved in Deut 26:5–9, which reminds Israelites of their "hard servitude" under the

Egyptians and the Lord's deliverance therefrom, serves as a sanction on the bringing of "first fruits" to the Lord, which is in effect yet another form of social welfare to sustain the destitute. Based on its own bitter experience of "affliction" (ʿny), "toil" (ʿml, violent trouble, devastating anguish), and "oppression" (lḥṣ), therefore, Israel was concerned not only to mitigate actual forms of slavery, but more generally to maintain mechanisms whereby they might mitigate other forms of affliction of the destitute. Israel's concern is not simply with the formal institutions of servitude, but beyond that with the disadvantaged generally, those who were the most likely to end up in various forms of servitude and be subjected to maltreatment.

The liberation of Israel in its "founding" moment was thus from an utterly abusive institutionalized system of servitude, particularly in the hard forced labor imposed upon them as resident aliens. The exodus was a liberation from oppression as well as a "redemption from slavery." Egyptian corvée became a symbol of such oppression, including when the Davidic kings instituted oppressive policies such as "forced labor" to carry out the "development" of an imperial monarchy. Further, it reverberated in the legislation regarding other forms of servitude, chattel slavery and debt-slavery. Here we might return to the thinking of Patterson in highlighting human degradation in our definition and use of the term "slavery." The problem was not simply one of servitude but of slavery. The people of Israel were ʿbdym of their God alone, who had redeemed them and now demanded justice from them in their own social relations.

Works Consulted

Bakir, A.
    1952   *Slavery in Pharaonic Egypt.* Cairo: L'Institut Français d'Archéologie Orientale.

Dandamaev, M.
    1984   *Slavery in Babylonia: From Nabopolassar to Alexander the Great (626–331 BC).* DeKalb: Northern Illinois University Press.

Diakonoff, I. M.
    1969   "Slave-Labor vs. Non-Slave Labor: The Problem of Definition." Pp. 1–3 in *Labor in the Ancient Near East.* Ed. M. Powell. New Haven: American Oriental Society.

Diakonoff, I. M., ed.
    1987   *Ancient Mesopotamia, Socio-Economic History: A Collection of Studies by Soviet Scholars.* Moscow: Nauka.

Driver, G. R. and J. C. Miles
    1968   *The Babylonian Laws.* Oxford: Oxford University Press.

Evans, D. G.
1963 "The Incidence of Labour-Service in the Old-Babylonian Period." *JAOS* 83:20–26.

Eyre, C.
1987 "Work and Organization of Work in the Old Kingdom." Pp. 5–47 in *Labor in the Ancient Near East*. Ed. M. Powell. New Haven: American Oriental Society.

Finley, Moses. I.
1980 *Ancient Slavery and Modern Ideology*. New York: Viking Press.

Gelb, I. J.
1973 "Prisoners of War in Early Mesopotamia." *JNES* 32:70–98.

Heltzer, Michael
1987 "Labour in Ugarit." Pp. 237–50 in *Labor in the Ancient Near East*. Ed. M. Powell. New Haven: American Oriental Society.

Lambert, W. G.
1965 "A New Look at the Babylonian Background of Genesis." *JTS* 16: 287–300.

Lohfink, N.
"ḥpšy." *TDOT* 5:114–18.

Maekawa, K.
1987 "Collective Labor Service in Girsu-Lagash: The Pre-Sargonic and Ur III Periods." Pp. 49–71 in *Labor in the Ancient Near East*. Ed. M. Powell. New Haven: American Oriental Society.

Mendelsohn, Isaac
1949 *Slavery in the Ancient Near East: A Comparative Study of Slavery in Babylonia, Assyria, Syria, and Palestine from the Middle of the Third Millennium to the End of the First Millennium*. New York: Oxford University Press.

1962 "On Corvée Labor in Ancient Canaan and Israel." *BASOR*, 167:31–35.

Mieroop, M. V. D.
1997 *The Ancient Mesopotamian City*. Oxford: Oxford University Press.

North, Robert
1997 "*mas*." *TDOT* 8:427–30.

Oates, J.
1986 *Babylon*. London: Thames and Hudson.

Oppenheim, Leo
1977 *Ancient Mesopotamia: Portrait of a Dead Civilization*. Chicago: University of Chicago Press.

Patterson, Orlando
1982 *Slavery and Social Death: A Comparative Study*. Cambridge: Harvard University Press.

Pettinato, G.
1971 *Das altorientalische Menschenbild und die sumerischen und akkadischen Schöepfungsmythen*. Heidelberg: Carl Winter.

Rainey, Anson
1970 "Compulsory Labour Gangs in Ancient Israel." *IEJ* 20:191–202.

Redford, D. B.
1992 *Egypt, Canaan, and Israel, in Ancient Times*. Princeton: Princeton University Press.

Robertson, J. F.
1995 "The Social and Economic Organization of Ancient Mesopotamian Temples." Pp. 443–54 in *Civilizations of the Ancient Near East*. Ed. J. M. Sasson. New York: Charles Scribner's Sons.

Steinkeller, P.
1987 "The Foresters of Umma: Toward a Definition of Ur III Labor." Pp. 73–99 in *Labor in the Ancient Near East*. Ed. M. Powell. New Haven: American Oriental Society.

1991 "The Administrative and Economic Organization of the Ur III State: The Core and the Periphery." Pp. 15–33 in *The Organization of Power: Aspects of Bureaucracy in the Ancient Near East*. Eds. McGuire Gibson and R. Biggs. Chicago: The Oriental Institute.

Trigger, B. G., et al.
1983 *Ancient Egypt: A Social History*. Cambridge: Cambridge University Press.

Vaux, Roland de
1961 *Ancient Israel: Social Institutions*. New York and Toronto: McGraw-Hill.

Wainwright, J. A.
1979/1980 "Zoser's Pyramid and Solomon's Temple." *ExpT* 91:137–40.

Westbrook, R.
1985 "Biblical and Cuneiform Law Codes." *Revue Biblique* 92:247–64.

Wiedemann, Thomas
1981 *Greek and Roman Slavery*. Baltimore and London: Johns Hopkins University Press.

1987 *Slavery*. Oxford: Oxford University Press.

Wittfogel, Karl A.
1957 *Oriental Despotism: A Comparative Study of Total Power*. New Haven: Yale University Press.

Yoffee, N.
1995 "The Economy of Ancient Western Asia." Pp. 1387–99 in *Civilizations of the Ancient Near East*. Ed. J. M. Sasson. New York: Charles Scribner's Sons.

'EBED/DOULOS: TERMS AND SOCIAL STATUS IN THE MEETING OF HEBREW BIBLICAL AND HELLENISTIC ROMAN CULTURE*

Benjamin G. Wright, III
Lehigh University

ABSTRACT

This article explores the impact of the social experience of slavery in the Greco-Roman world on Jews of the Second Temple period. Initially, the article examines biblical slavery—the use of ʿebed to connote any form of subservient relationship, the different rights of the Hebrew ʿebed and the gentile ʿebed, and the limited use of slaves in Israelite society. Next, the author makes a case for Second Temple Jews' familiarity with slavery in the Hellenistic-Roman period, which was essentially a system of chattel slavery exploiting huge numbers of persons for work in mines, manufacturing and agriculture. The argument is based not only on a general assessment of the ubiquity of slaves in the period but more specifically on examination of the uses of Greek terms for slaves in the LXX, Josephus, Philo, Apocrypha, and Pseudepigrapha.

INTRODUCTION

Although the Jews of the Second Temple period possessed divinely sanctioned laws that included regulations about servitude and enslavement, of both Hebrews and foreigners, they lived in a world where slavery played a role different from and greater than that of their biblical predecessors. Jews, in Palestine and in the Diaspora, were in contact with and subject to systems of slavery that differed in basic respects from the slave system practiced in "biblical times." Whereas the world in which the biblical slavery laws developed was apparently not highly dependent on slaves for its economic well being, the Mediterranean world of the Hellenistic-Roman period clearly was.[1] Further, the legal status of the enslaved individual in biblical law was different

---

* This article is dedicated to the memory of my wife, Ann, who died August 17, 1995 of breast cancer. Although some might find it strange that I would dedicate an article on slavery to her, she was always my greatest encouragement, both as a scholar and as a person. She either heard or read everything that I ever wrote. This is the last piece that will have the benefit of her wisdom and insight.
[1] For detailed treatments of slavery in ancient Israel and the Hebrew Bible see Mendelsohn, de Vaux, Flesher, and Dandamayev.

from that of Greek and Roman slaves who were considered little more than their owners' chattel. The purpose of this essay is to investigate the extent to which Second Temple Jewish literature uses the language of Hellenistic-Roman slave systems and thus reflects the socio-cultural realities of slavery in the Hellenistic and Roman Mediterranean rather than those of ancient Israel.

The effects of these systems were probably felt by Jews in a number of ways. First, Jews were part of a social world in which slavery was the norm, and they, for various reasons, were undoubtedly part of the system, both as its beneficiaries and its victims. Many were bought and sold as chattel slaves, or perhaps themselves bought and sold slaves (though probably not Jewish ones).[2] They were certainly the beneficiaries of slave labor, whether they lived in Palestine and utilized, for example, the numerous building projects undertaken by Herod, or in diaspora communities where, for instance, public slaves performed important civic duties. In all areas of the Mediterranean Jews had contact with the products of Greek and Roman slave economies.

Jewish involvement in the social world of Hellenistic-Roman slave systems must have had consequences for the ways Jews used words for slaves, and the use of the two major languages of the Mediterranean in this period, Greek and Latin, must have influenced Jewish thought worlds. In appropriating these languages, Jews took over the Greek and Latin vocabulary for slaves and slavery. It is hard to imagine that the lexical content of the Hebrew ʿebed was simply dumped into the Greek and Latin vocabulary; the idea was socially conditioned as well.

To a great degree, living in the Hellenistic-Roman Mediterranean and speaking (or, at least understanding) Greek or Latin meant transforming the notion of slavery or servanthood from that of the Hebrew Bible to that of the slave systems characteristic of the Mediterranean social world in the Hellenistic-Roman period. Of course, the most critical place in which such a transformation can be found is in the Jewish-Greek biblical translations, and the lexical choices made by the translators to render ʿebed have the potential to have a dramatic impact on the "biblical" concept of servanthood. The term *doulos*, one of the two major translations of ʿebed in the Jewish-Greek Bible, quite simply communicated to the Greek reader in this period something different from what the word ʿebed did earlier. This consideration most probably applies not only to those instances in which an actual servant or slave is meant, but also to metaphorical uses of the terminology.

A corollary to this issue is whether and to what extent the different words for slaves in this period retained their older connotations and distinctions or

---

[2] There is much evidence in literature, inscriptions and papyri that this was indeed the case. Several examples will be noted below. Biblical law does not recognize a Hebrew having another Hebrew as chattel (see Flesher), and Hebrews were required to try to redeem Hebrews who had been enslaved. Non-Hebrews, however, could be bought as slaves, but even their status seems to have been better than the chattel slaves of Greek and Roman slave systems.

were used generally as synonyms for slaves. The degree to which Jewish literature uses slave terms like they are used in the language in general will tell a great deal about whether Hellenistic Jews adopted not only the vocabulary of slavery but the attendant cultural realities/concepts as well.

In what follows, I will look at both of the foregoing problems, because they are connected in important ways. The recognition that Jews in the Second Temple period were not isolated or insulated from Greek and Roman slave practices and that they used the vocabulary of slavery consistently with their larger socio-cultural surroundings helps to build a picture of what slave language meant to Jews when they encountered it or used it in their literature. Or, taken from the other direction, although the Hebrew Bible's uses of the language of servitude, especially the metaphorical uses of such language, may provide a background for understanding the meaning of slave terms in Jewish-Greek sources, such use is only a partial and incomplete background.

I do not intend a review of slavery as it was practiced in the Hellenistic-Roman world (see Finley, 1960, 1987; Garlan; and Horsley's survey in this volume). My task is much more circumscribed than that. Two questions will remain the primary focus of this essay. 1) What was the social experience of Jews with slavery in the Greco-Roman world? and 2) How might that experience impact our understanding of the use of language for slavery in Jewish sources? The major effort here will be descriptive. That is, I want to gather as much of the data together as possible in an attempt to provide a basis for answers to the questions just posed. Although it will be primarily descriptive, this essay, given space limitations, cannot be exhaustive. Consequently, in addressing question 2, I will treat mostly Jewish literature in Greek, and I will concentrate on the two major terms used in the Jewish-Greek scriptures to render the Hebrew ʿebed—*doulos* and *pais*. That the translators of the Septuagint, people working at different times and places, preferred these two Greek terms by a large margin over any other Greek words (and there were many for slavery) indicates their potential importance for getting a handle on the conceptual content of the transformation of Hebrew slave language into Greek.

Slavery in the Hebrew Bible—Summary Statement

Although the Hebrew Bible contains many references to ʿăbādîm there is actually a limited corpus of laws concerning them. In its basic biblical meaning someone is called ʿebed who is in a subservient relationship to another.[3] This relationship does not have to be one of ownership, but can apply to a

---

[3] For more detailed treatments of slavery in the Hebrew Bible, see Callender's essay in this volume and the bibliography cited there. The Hebrew ʿebed is used for a male slave. Hebrew had no word for female slaves from the same root. The standard words for a female slave is ʾmh.

king and his subjects, a god and those who serve him/her, a social superior and inferior. Uses such as that found in 1 Sam 19:4 where Jonathan says, "The king should not sin against his ʿebed David," or in Deut 34:5 where Moses is called the "ʿebed of the Lord," occur frequently in the Hebrew scriptures. But an ʿebed can clearly be in a servile relation to another, and these ʿăbādîm are treated primarily in Exodus 21, Leviticus 25 and Deuteronomy 15.

In ancient Israel the Hebrew ʿebed was distinguished from the gentile ʿebed. In many respects, the Hebrew ʿebed was not really a slave as much as a debt-slave or an indentured servant. A Hebrew could be enslaved/indentured as a result of inability to repay theft (Exod 22:3) or for debt (Lev 25:39?; 2 Kgs 4:1), but the slave/servant worked for six years or until the next jubilee year and then was released (Exod 21:2; Lev 25:40; Deut 15:12). A Hebrew could not be enslaved in perpetuity, unless he voluntarily submitted to permanent slave status.[4] This situation, however, seems to apply to males only, since Exod 21:7–11 says that a daughter who is sold as a slave does not "go out" like a male (probably since she is used as a concubine), but either is redeemed or released a) if her master is not pleased with her, b) if he gives her to his son or c) if he marries another (or takes another concubine) and does not continue to provide for her. Deut 15:12–17, in an apparent updating of the Exodus law, explicitly says that the law applies to the female slave.

The situation of foreign slaves was altogether different. In the case of holding foreigners as slaves, Israelites could, in fact, keep them as they would other chattel. Lev 25:46, for instance, allows the Israelite to will them to his heirs. But, the foreign slave is not treated as chattel exclusively. Gen 17:12–13 requires foreign slaves to be circumcised, and circumcised slaves are permitted to participate in the Passover meal. Circumcised slaves of priests are permitted to eat the priestly rations (Lev 22:11). Thus, the foreign slave is at the same time property and a dependent of the householder (Flesher, chap. 1).

In ancient Israel (and the ancient Near East generally) (debt-)slaves and (indentured) servants were utilized primarily in small numbers in households, not in mass numbers as laborers who worked large agricultural estates or mines. Occasionally large numbers of foreigners might become available as slaves due to military successes, but this was certainly not a frequent or normal occurrence.[5] Those people who were enslaved in ancient Israel had a social and legal status different from that of the chattel slaves who made up the system practiced later in Hellenistic-Roman times.

---

[4] In this case, Exod 21:5–6 describes a ritual where the person voluntarily submitting to slavery has his ear pierced as a sign that he will serve that master for life. This ritual describes men who have been married and had children while in service to their master. Lev 25:41 says that the Israelite should be released on the jubilee year, "he and his sons with him." The text does not state whether the sons are born before or after the Israelite sells himself into servitude.

[5] On the uses, sale and sources of slaves generally, see de Vaux: 80–90.

Jews and Slavery in the Hellenistic-Roman World: General Considerations

Slavery in ancient Greece and Rome was a complex phenomenon, but in general slaves in the Hellenistic-Roman period were their owners' chattel. The slave owned nothing, generally had no independent legal rights and was obligated to do as his/her master commanded. Failure to obey meant discipline or punishment as the master saw fit. In a papyrus from 225 CE concerning the sale of a slave-girl named Soteris, "(Kephalon agrees) that [Apion therefore is master] and has possession and [controls her] and can deal with her in whatever [manner he chooses]" (SB XIV 11277, Llewellyn: 50–51). The slave had no legal family. Anyone to whom the slave was married by the master belonged to the master and any children born to a slave were the property of the master to keep or dispose of as he/she saw fit.

Some incentives were offered to slaves, however, to make the slave system work. Masters occasionally allowed families to stay together. They sometimes set up educated or talented slaves in businesses in which the slave was permitted to keep some of the proceeds. Such is apparently the case in an Oxyrhynchus papyrus where a brother and sister who have inherited a slave from their parents are petitioning two local officials. The slave evidently works independently of his masters, but is refusing to pay them the required monies they think he owes (Horsley: 4.104–106). Slaves were often allowed to keep a *peculium*, a fund that might eventually be used to purchase the slave's freedom. And not all slaves lived difficult lives of backbreaking labor. Some slaves, especially in the Roman imperial households, could be entrusted with significant responsibilities that resulted in that slave accumulating wealth, social prestige and even slaves of his/her own. These slaves also experienced a greater independence from their masters than other slaves.[6]

Enslaved persons were used for a wide variety of tasks at all levels of society. Large number of laborers were used in mines, in manufacturing facilities or on large agricultural estates. They were also used in the household as personal attendants, cooks, bath attendants, etc. As a result, slaves were quite simply ubiquitous in the Hellenistic-Roman Mediterranean.

Because of the general ubiquity of slaves, Jews, no doubt, were familiar with Greek and, subsequently, Roman slave systems from early on. Jewish contacts with the Hellenistic and Roman west were quite extensive already by the turn of the era.[7] These contacts were affected not only by Greek

---

[6] For a good summary of these issues, see Martin, chap 1. But cf. Patterson: 182–86, 300–10.

[7] Abundant evidence exists for Jewish communities throughout the Mediterranean world. N.B. Josephus's celebrated citation of Strabo (*Ant.* 14.114–15) who remarks that Jews can be found in every city and also the report of the speech of Agrippa in *War* 2.398 who says "There is not a people in the world which does not contain a portion of our race." On the contacts between Jews, Greeks and Romans, see Hengel, Stern (1992). On familiarity of gentiles with Jews, see Stern (1976–84). On the various Jewish communities in Asia Minor, see Trebilco.

and Roman military and mercantile traffic in the Near East, but by the general spread of Jewish communities into Egypt, Asia Minor, Greece and Rome. Those living as significant minorities in these diaspora communities would likely have had extensive experience with slavery, both with individual slaves and with its larger institutional forms. In many cases, Jews were among those known to have been slaves. For instance, two inscriptions from Delphi, which date to 163/162 and 158/157 BCE, note the manumission of an unknown Jewish slave and a Jewish slave woman and her two daughters.[8]

Although it is not certain when Jews began to settle in Rome, the greatest population expansion of that diaspora community most likely came about beginning in the first century BCE through the importation of Jews as slaves. Pompey undoubtedly brought back captives, who would be sold as slaves, as part of his triumph. Philo, in the first century CE, remarks that most of the inhabitants of the Jewish community in Rome were brought to Rome as slaves and later were manumitted (*Legatio ad Gaium* 155), and certainly many more slaves were brought to Rome to celebrate Titus's triumph over the Jews in the First Revolt (Fuks).

Several pieces of evidence demonstrate that Palestine also became acquainted with Hellenistic-Roman slave systems at a fairly early period. The Zenon papyri, which give a detailed view of the relationship between Ptolemaic Egypt and Palestine in the third century BCE, provide perhaps the best evidence about early Jewish involvement with Hellenistic slave systems in Palestine. Slaves were but one commodity in an extensive trading network between Egypt and Palestine in this period. One text, *CPJ* 1, will suffice as an example. This papyrus records the sale of a seven year old slave girl, named Sphragis. She was sold to Zenon by a man named Nikanor "in the service of Tobias" (Tcherikover: 1.118–120). Several other papyri testify to Zenon's slave acquisitions in the area (Hengel: 41; Urbach: 13). In the period of the Maccabean revolt, 2 Macc 8:11 notes that the Syrian general Nicanor sold captured Jews as slaves, apparently to Phoenicians on the seacoast, in order to make two thousand talents, the amount due to the Seleucid king as tribute.

These several examples do not exhaust the available evidence. What they demonstrate is that Jews, in Palestine and in the diaspora, were well acquainted with Hellenistic-Roman slavery. If they knew the social reality, they were undoubtedly conversant with the vocabulary of slavery in these periods. Several Jewish writers, Philo and Josephus for example, are very familiar with the variegated terminology for slaves. What all this implies, is that when these writers use terms for slaves, whether general or specific, modern interpreters ought to see the thought world of this language reflecting that of Hellenistic-

---

[8] J.-B. Frey, *Corpus Inscriptionum Iudaicarum*, as cited in Hengel: 42 and Urbach: 13. On the identification of Jews in epigraphic materials, see Kraemer (1989, 1991).

Roman chattel slavery, not what might be termed the indentured servitude more characteristic of the biblical laws. That is, when Philo and Josephus speak of slaves, they speak, on the whole, the language of Hellenistic-Roman slavery. The situation is complicated by the fact that both Philo and Josephus comment specifically on the biblical laws, and a major question is the extent to which the terms that they use for biblical slaves reveal their own attitudes towards slavery. I will try to set out some of those complications below.

The Uses of Slave Terms in Hellenistic Greek

In contrast to Hebrew, which had one principal word for male servants/slaves and two for female servants/slaves, Greek had quite a number. Each of these had important distinctions in the classical period, but evidently during the Hellenistic period, the several different terms for slaves began to be used more often as synonyms, the older distinctions being generally abandoned. The place where this synonymity is most noticeable is in the papyri, most of which come from Egypt. In the Hellenistic through the Roman periods the papyri show these Greek words used in identical or similar ways to indicate slaves.[9]

Of all the terms used to designate male slaves, *doulos* (a general word for slave), *pais* (a less general and more familiar word) and its diminutives, *oiketēs* (a domestic or household slave) and *therapōn* (personal attendant) are found in second-temple Jewish literature. In addition *koine* Greek often uses the nouns *andrapodon* (literally "human footed") and *sōma* ("body") and the adjective *oikogenēs* ("houseborn"). Female slaves are most often designated by *paidiskē, doulē, therapaina* and *korasion* (although in the Jewish-Greek biblical translations *korasion* seems to mean "young girl" rather than "slave").

In the Hellenistic and Roman periods, these words can be found maintaining their usual distinctions with relative frequency, but all can be used of slaves in general and do not have to retain the earlier classical differentiation (Spicq). In several cases *doulos* and *oiketēs* or *doulos* and *pais* are used synonymously (Straus 1976:337, 338) a certain Epagathos is called both a *doulos* and a *paidarion* (Straus 1976:349). Often these different terms may be modified by *oikogenēs* or even by each other. A number of papyri, for example, use *paidiskē doulē* (Straus: 338, 344, n. 40).

Important for the use of these terms in the Greek biblical translations and other Second Temple Jewish literature is J. Modrzejewski's point that there appears to be two vocabularies for slaves (in Straus 1976:347). One is a juridical/official vocabulary which appears "in public acts, in particular requests

---

[9] Gibbs and Feldman (288) and Garlan (21) make this claim without documentation. Straus (1976, 1981) and Spicq set out much of the evidence.

that are submitted to authorities . . ." (Straus 1976:347). The other is a private/daily vocabulary. It is this private/daily vocabulary where the terms for slaves find their most frequent uses as synonyms. Synonymity is possible largely because in such private daily use those involved would know the status of the slave in question. In requests made to authorities, a greater specificity might be expected.[10] What we will see below is that both the Greek biblical translations and other Second Temple Jewish works use those terms that appear most frequently in the papyri as synonyms. Those terms that are used most in Modrzejewski's public vocabulary, like *andrapodon*, or those that are most ambiguous, like *sōma*, occur infrequently.

The LXX and the Translation of Terms for Slaves[11]

Of the close to 800 uses of the Hebrew term *'ebed* in the Jewish scriptures, almost 770 are rendered either by *doulos* or *pais*.[12] Of the remaining equivalents for this Hebrew word only *therapōn* and *oiketēs* amount to any significant portion. The number of occurrences of these words are relatively meaningless in themselves, however. Only some summary of how and where they are used gives them any meaning for understanding the conceptual transformation, if there is any, between the Hebrew and Greek languages.

The Pentateuch. The most immediately noticeable feature of the renderings of *'ebed* in the earliest of the biblical translations is that *doulos* almost never occurs. Genesis, Exodus and Numbers do not use *doulos* at all. Leviticus uses it only twice and Deuteronomy only once. W. Zimmerli (674) understands the translators as reserving *doulos* for "especially severe bondage." But this solution is not entirely satisfactory. The difficulties of determining whether any distinction in meaning is to be made between *doulos* and *pais* can be seen in the several uses of *doulos* in the Pentateuch.

Lev 25:39–44 concerns two issues: the treatment of the Israelite who, due to impoverishment, sells himself to another Israelite and the buying of foreign slaves. In these verses neither the Hebrew nor the way the Greek translator understood it is altogether clear. 25:39 says that the Israelite who must sell himself is not to be worked as a slave (*l' t'ebed bw 'bdt 'ebed*), but as a

---

[10] F. Dunant (in Straus 1976:347-48) argues that this dual vocabulary might be referring to individuals whose status might be termed half-slaves. Modrzejewski's position, that these people are slaves and that the language has to do with the social context, makes better sense.

[11] Because of the number of occurrences of all words in the slave/servant word group and the scope of this article, I will restrict the material below to the nouns used for slaves in Hellenistic Jewish literature. These are primarily, but certainly not exclusively, *doulos* and *pais*.

[12] The statistics will vary depending on which edition of the Jewish-Greek Bible one consults. For detailed treatments of *doulos* and *pais* in the Bible, see Rengstorf, Zimmerli and Jeremias. For a basic overview of some words for servant/slave in the Jewish-Greek scriptures, see Kraft. The words for female slaves are somewhat less problematic, because the Hebrew has no word for female slaves derived from the verb *'bd*. Thus the Greek *doulē* occurs very infrequently. The translators of the Jewish scriptures prefer *paidiskē* when a slave/servant is specifically female.

hired or bound laborer.[13] That Israelite shall be released at the next jubilee year, and he can then return to his family. The reason given in v. 42 is that since the Israelites are God's servants and since he brought them out of Egypt, they should not be sold as slaves are sold (*lʾ ymkrw mmkrt ʿebed*). Verse 44 begins the second issue mentioned above. "As for your male and female slaves (*wʿbdk wʾmtk*) whom you may have, it is from the nations around you that you may acquire male and female slaves (*wʿebed wʾmh*)." The servants of the beginning of this verse must be understood as the same as those at the end—non-Israelite slaves who can be bought from the surrounding nations.

How the Greek translator understood this passage is very unclear and for the most part depends on how one thinks he understood who the slaves/ servants were in each instance. He translates the end of v. 39 *ou doulousei soi douleian oiketou* (lit. "you shall not enslave them with the slavery of a household servant"). In v. 42 the Israelites are called the *oiketai* of God, so they shall not be sold like an *oiketēs*. In these cases, the translator keeps a consistent rendering of the Hebrew, whether one sees the connotation of the passage as good, bad or neutral. In v. 44, however, the translator begins with the *pais* and *paidiskē* who belong to the Israelites, and he finishes the verse with *doulon* and *doulēn*. If the translator construed the beginning of the Hebrew of v. 44 as referring to Israelite slaves, connecting it to what came before, and then understood the end of the verse as referring to non-Israelite slaves, Zimmerli's claim would make sense. If, on the other hand, the translator understood the Hebrew correctly, then *pais* and *paidiskē* are synonyms for *doulos* and *doulē*, and Zimmerli's contention would not appear to hold true. Which is the case is very difficult to tell. Further complicating matters is Deut 32:36 where God's people are not called his *oiketai* but his *douloi*.

The other use of *doulos* in the Pentateuch is Lev 26:13 where God again appeals to his role as deliverer from Egypt, but there is added, "when you were slaves (*douloi*)." In this case the context makes it clear that the idea of chattel bondage is meant. The latter part of the verse proclaims that God "broke the bonds of your yoke and made you walk upright." In other places, however, the Israelite bondage in Egypt is looked back on and expressed through the use of *oiketēs* (Deut 5:15; 15:15). In the passages that narrate that bondage, especially Exod 5:15–16, the Israelites, who do not understand why Pharaoh is being so hard on them, call themselves his *oiketai* and *paides*.[14]

---

[13] The term translated "bound laborer" is *twšb*, which usually indicates a resident alien. The term is used in parallel with hired laborer here and earlier in 25:6. Thus, the terms seem to mean an Israelite who is a hired laborer and a resident alien who hires himself out. See Levine: 170–71.

[14] The end of the verse is difficult. The MT of Exod 15:16 reads, "Look how your servants are beaten, and the sin of your people." The LXX has this last clause as a full independent clause that suggests that the Israelites saw themselves as Pharaoh's people. It reads "And look, your servants are whipped/beaten. Therefore you are being unjust to your people."

Whatever significance one assigns to it, the translators of the Septuagint show a clear predilection for *pais* as a translation of ʿ*ebed* in all its various uses.[15] Several examples will demonstrate the wide variety of uses to which the Septuagint translators put *pais*. Although *pais* can mean "child" with reference to chronological age and so sometimes can refer to a young slave/ servant, it does not often have that meaning in the Septuagint. The slave laws in Exodus 21 use the word to refer to the Hebrew slave who is bought and who serves for six years or until the next jubilee. Even the Hebrew slave who renounces his freedom in order to stay with his wife and children (he clearly is no child himself) and voluntarily consents to stay the slave of his master in perpetuity is called *pais* (21:6). In the Joseph story in Genesis, Joseph is sold as a slave in Egypt to one of Pharaoh's officers. Potiphar's wife calls Joseph a Hebrew *pais* at the same time she is finding him sexually attractive and accusing him of attacking her (Gen 39:17–19). It is this same *pais* who is subsequently put in charge of administering food supplies in all of Egypt.

As has often been noted about ʿ*ebed*, it is a word that does not have to indicate slave status in the absolute, but subservient status vis-à-vis someone or something else. Frequently, one addressing a king or social superior calls him/herself one's servant. Several places in the Pentateuch exemplify this use. In Gen 19:19, Lot responds to the messengers of God who have told him to flee, "Your servant (*pais*) has found favor before you. . . ." Later in Gen 33:5 when Esau and Jacob reconcile, Jacob calls himself Esau's servant (*pais*) as a gesture of humility and reconciliation.

A similar idea is also found in relation to God. In several places in the Pentateuch, people are called servants (ʿ*ebed*) of Yahweh. Although different Greek servant/slave terms are used to express this relationship, *doulos* is not one of them.[16] The most frequently occurring term in this context is *therapōn*. Moses, for example, is called a *therapōn* of God in several places (see Exod 14:31; Num 11:11, 12:7–8). Deuteronomy, however, generally prefers *oiketēs* to *therapōn*; at Moses' death, the Deuteronomist calls Moses a servant of God, rendered *oiketēs kyriou* by the Greek translator. Yet, in Deut 3:24 Moses calls himself a *therapōn* of God. *pais* is not left out of this type of usage, either. In Num 14:24, where God singles out Caleb for believing him, he calls him "my servant (*ho pais mou*)."

Not only individuals, but families and the nation of Israel as corporate entities, are called God's servants. Here too, no one Greek term characterizes this relationship. In Gen 50:17, for example, Joseph's brothers ask him

---

[15] It is the clear favorite rendering in Genesis. The predominance of *therapōn* in Exodus can be attributed to that translator's use of the term to represent the servants/attendants of Pharaoh, a phrase that occurs frequently in the book.

[16] There is considerable discussion of the servant of Yahweh in Zimmerli and Jeremias.

to forgive the "crime of the servants (*therapontōn*) of your father." Lev 25:42, 55 both refer to the Israelites as the *oiketai* of God.

Several instances in particular indicate that the translators may have used these words for slaves/servants as relative synonyms, with only minor distinctions. In the curse of Canaan (Gen 9:25–26), he is to be *ʿebed ʿăbādîm*, translated "the lowest of slaves" by the NRSV, to his brothers, and in v. 26 God blesses Shem and makes Canaan his slave. The Greek translator renders the first phrase *pais oiketēs* and the second *pais*, thus making the two terms synonymous for "slave." Later, in Gen 44:33, Judah pleads with Joseph to allow Benjamin to return to Canaan with his brothers. In his place Judah offers himself as surety that the brothers will return. "I will remain as a slave (*pais*) instead of the boy, a slave (*oiketēs*) of [my] lord/master," begs Judah.[17] For the translator of Genesis, the two uses of *ʿebed* are synonymous, but he uses two different Greek words. *pais* perhaps connotes a slave in a more general fashion while the following use of *oiketēs* has more specificity regarding the duties of the slave. The words should nonetheless be regarded as virtually synonymous. Finally, in Deuteronomy, where the Greek translator uses *oiketēs* to refer to the status of the Israelites as slaves, Moses is called both an *oiketēs* (34:5) and a *therapōn* (3:24) of God.

These data, then, indicate that for the translators of the Pentateuch, the several words for slaves used here *doulos, pais, oiketēs* and perhaps *therapōn* are roughly synonymous, or at least in some cases interchangeable. Zimmerli's distinction between *doulos* and the other terms does not hold in my estimation. Yet, the reason that the translators of the Pentateuch generally avoided *doulos* is not clear to me. Perhaps these translators considered the term derogatory or insulting in a way that the others were not (even though some contexts might lend themselves to insult).

The social realities behind these uses is also difficult to ascertain. In Hellenistic-Roman Egypt were Jewish slaves/indentured servants and non-Jewish slaves both called *pais* and/or *oiketēs* as they are in the Septuagint? On the one hand, those Jews who were enslaved for debt were designated by the same words as foreign slaves, but, on the other hand, the laws in Leviticus, while recognizing the "slave" status of these Jewish servants, also demanded that they be treated as hired workers.[18] At the very least, the Jewish translators are adapting the language of Hellenistic-Roman slavery to a category of Jewish enslavement which has no ready Hellenistic parallel.

---

[17] These same two words appear in Judah's speech to Joseph in 44:16. In this case *pais* is used as a term of social deference.

[18] Westermann (125) notes that the Jewish community near the Black Sea (ancient Panticapaeum) seemed to have expressed "the traditional Hebrew attitude as it expressed itself in slavery," but that "in the formal and external features both of procedure and of publicity of the event, Greek practices and models were copied almost completely." He argues this latter point on the evidence of four manumission inscriptions.

Excursus on the Use of a Jewish Form of Greek

This last point raises the issue of whether the Greek of the Septuagint translators reflects a special Jewish Greek spoken by Jews in this period or whether the Septuagint formed the basis for the development of a special Jewish dialect of *koiné*. That is, did Hellenistic Jews speak a language like that found in the biblical translations? G. H. R. Horsley has, conclusively argued against such a notion.[19]

> The issue of Jewish Greek has been brought clearly into focus by the studies which have appeared in the New Documents Illustrating Early Christianity series. The sample of inscriptions and papyri collected in the four previous volumes provides a tangible weight of evidence which has steadily reinforced the impression that to claim any such cleavage between the koine and "Jewish" or "Christian" Greek is quite inapposite. The erroneous belief in Jewish Greek is dependent on
>
> (a) the acceptance of over-vague terminology and
> (b) lack of contact with linguistic research, particularly in the area of bilingualism. (Horsley 5:6)

Recent linguistic theory has shown that the phenomenon of bilingualism is much more complex than those claiming the existence of a Jewish Greek have recognized. The result is that distinctions must be made regarding bilingualism and the question of fluency in the secondary language, the relative status of the primary and secondary languages, which language is the preferred language (not always the primary language), how a secondary language is learned and whether the secondary language is read and perhaps understood, but not spoken (Horsley 5:24–25). The presence of Semiticisms in Greek, moreover, cannot bear the weight of an argument for Jewish Greek (Horsley 5:26–37).

Although certain "Semitic features" do find their way into the Greek used by Jews and Christians it should be regarded as "the expected phenomenon of interference which manifests itself in varying degrees in the speech and writing of bilinguals" (Horsley 5:40). Jews may well have spoken with an accent, but accents do not make dialects. What distinguished the Greek spoken by Jews in antiquity from other peoples' Greek was the use of technical terms reflecting the particularities of Jewish culture and religion. It was Jewish customs that marked them, not their Greek (Horsley 5:40).

---

[19] Horsley: 5:5–40. This section contains a good history of the scholarly claims made for such a Jewish Greek.

Joshua, Judges, 1–4 Kingdoms. These translations, with the exception of Joshua, restrict the number of terms rendering *ʿebed* to *pais* and *doulos*.

In Joshua, Moses is at the same time called the *pais* of God (1:7, 13; 9:24; 11:12, 15; 14:7[20] and others) and the *therapōn* of God (1:2). Joshua, at his death, is called *doulos kyriou* (24:30 [29]).[21] The deceit of the Gibeonites reported in Joshua 9 contains the other major uses of slave language in Joshua. The Gibeonites come pretending to be people from a far away land who want to make a treaty with Joshua. In trying to make the ruse convincing they twice use language of humility claiming to be Israel's "servants/slaves." In the first instance, 9:8, they call themselves *oiketai*, and in the second, 9:9, they use *paides*. It is unclear whether the translator intends these terms as synonyms, or whether he wants to convey a more subservient status, foreshadowing what is to come a few verses later, because in 9:23, Joshua curses the Gibeonites for deceiving him and says that they shall always be slaves (*doulos*), wood cutters and water bearers for the "house of my God." The passage clearly understands being a *doulos* as an undesirable position in which to be, but it sheds little light on the meanings of the two terms used previously.[22]

Both *doulos* and *pais* appear frequently in 1–2 Samuel and 1–2 Kings. About their uses in these books, Zimmerli argues that "[o]ne may discern a careful distinction between them. *pais* is used only for the freer servants of the king (soldiers, minister, officials) who by their own choice enter his service ... *doulos*, on the other hand is used for slavery proper" (Zimmerli: 674). I confess to being a bit puzzled about this claim, however. A careful look at the use of the two terms in 1 Sam 16:14–17:38 illustrates the difficulty of making such a sharp distinction.

In 1 Sam 16:14 an evil spirit enters Saul and torments him. In 16:15 he calls his *paides* who diagnose the spirit. They reply, "Let your servants (*douloi*) speak and let them seek for our master a man. . . ." Saul then requests that his *paides* find such a man. In chapter 17, Goliath issues his challenge, that if he defeats an Israelite they will be the slaves of the Philistines and if the Israelite triumphs, the Philistines will be slaves of the Israelites, with the term *doulos*, clearly indicating enslavement for the vanquished. David then appears on the scene and volunteers to fight the Philistine. He convinces Saul and in his argument uses the term *doulos* three times (17:32, 34, 38) to describe his relationship to Saul.

In the first passage, the Greek translator actually turns the Hebrew text around a bit. The MT has Saul's servants reply, "Let our lord say to your ser-

---

[20] Rahlfs prints *pais* in his text; Ms A reads *doulos kyriou*.

[21] In 7:7 the Greek has Joshua call himself *pais*, but there is no extant Hebrew for this phrase in the MT.

[22] Another passage may help a bit here. In 5:14, the commander of the army of the Lord meets Joshua, who falls on his face and calls himself the *oiketēs* of the divine warrior. Here, although the term indicates humility and inferiority, it does not seem to have a negative connotation.

vants who are before you . . ." The Greek makes the servants, here called *douloi*, the subject of the verb, and thus more obviously the same group of servants just called *paides*. By rearranging the text in this way, the two Greek terms must be synonymous, and thus Zimmerli's distinction breaks down. In chapter 17, the same Greek term is used to indicate the status of the vanquished people, reflecting Zimmerli's idea that *doulos* is reserved for slavery, but David immediately thereafter calls himself *doulos* in a passage where he is clearly volunteering to enter the service of the king. So, while it is possible that the distinction that Zimmerli claims for these translations might generally apply, it cannot be maintained throughout. I would see these two terms as having an overlap in meaning with the tendency of *doulos* to indicate slavery and that of *pais* to refer to voluntary service to the king.

The Later Books. Most of the other books use both *doulos* and *pais* to render ʿ*ebed*. Some, like the Minor Prophets and Ecclesiastes, use *doulos* as the stereotyped rendering of the Hebrew. Most, however, use both to some degree. Psalms is a good example here. While Psalms clearly favors *doulos* (*pais* only appears four times in Psalms), both terms designate a servant/slave of God, *doulos* many times and *pais* in Pss 85(86):16 and 68(69):18. The same situation can be found in the Greek of Isaiah. The general conclusion one can reach for these translations is that *doulos* and *pais* have become fairly interchangeable as translations of ʿ*ebed*, and the alternatives found most frequently in the earlier books have now fallen out of use.[23]

The one major exception, of those books for which Hebrew is extant, is the Wisdom of ben Sira. Ben Sira uses neither of the two major Greek terms, but he renders ʿ*ebed* by *oiketēs* in every instance. In this case, the use of *oiketēs* seems to indicate a foreign slave, who is considered chattel. 7:20–21 encourages a master not to abuse a faithful slave and not to withhold freedom from an intelligent slave.[24] Later in 33:25–33 on the treatment of slaves, ben Sira advises a master to work a slave hard because idleness will cause a slave to "seek liberty." Thus, a slave is to have "bread and discipline"; for a wicked slave ben Sira recommends "racks and tortures." If a slave does not obey, he says, "make his fetters heavy." These do not sound like the recommendations for an Israelite slave who is not to be treated like an *oiketēs* (see above on Pentateuch), laws ben Sira certainly knows. The only exception to this trend is in the prayer contained in chapter 36. Verse 22 refers to the Israelites as the *oiketai* of God, a use of the term also found in the Greek translation of the Pentateuch.

---

[23] Except for the translator for Job who prefers *therapōn* and the translator of Proverbs who also has a predilection for *oiketēs*.

[24] Skehan and di Lella: 205, refer to the law of release of the Hebrew slave after six years. It does not appear from the biblical laws, however, that an Israelite master could withhold that freedom, so my inclination is to understand ben Sira as speaking of foreign slaves which could be considered chattel and either be freed or kept.

Conclusions. The lack of use of *doulos* in the Pentateuch would appear to be intentional on the part of the translators. The reasons for that avoidance are not so obvious, however. Perhaps the use of this particular term was not thought to be appropriate for slaves who would have been used primarily in the household while other terms would. Yet, as we saw, the few cases of *doulos* that do occur in the Septuagint proper serve to blur this distinction. The Pentateuch does contain a broader vocabulary for slavery than do the rest of the Greek translations, which tend to restrict their uses to *doulos* and *pais*, both for actual slaves and in figurative uses.[25] This situation may perhaps be attributed to one specific problem facing the Greek translators of the Pentateuch, namely, that the category of Israelite slave represents an in-between category which does not exist in Hellenistic slave systems. Yet even in these instances the translators did not restrict the use of some terms to Israelite slaves and other terms to foreign slaves, further complicating the problem. Later translations narrow the range of possible terms, but they also eliminate distinctions in the meaning of the terms that they use.

What appears to me to be the case is that the translators were struggling to find ways to represent what was a completely different lexical and social world from theirs. Ancient Israelites had a single term for various forms of servitude. An Israelite enslaved to another Israelite, a foreigner enslaved to an Israelite, a free person voluntarily serving a king, a person expressing social deference to another, a person addressing God, all are designated by the same term, *ʿebed*. Socially, ancient Israel does not seem to have had a slave-dependent economy. Few persons would have held large number of slaves, and most slaves were attendents in a household, in close contact with the master and his family.

This was not the lexical and social world of Jews in the Hellenistic period. Greek was replete with words for slaves. A household slave, a field slave, a house-born slave, a personal attendant, all had different designations in Greek. And, although conditions varied throughout the Mediterranean, it can probably be said that the economy of the Hellenistic-Roman world was much more dependent on slave labor than anything ancient Israel knew.

The translators of the Hebrew Bible lived in the latter world, and their use of terms for slaves in the Jewish-Greek translations reflects their attempts to transform the monolithic slave/servant language of Hebrew to their own. In doing so, these scholars not only lexically translated, but culturally transformed the biblical language of slavery for those who used the texts after them.

---

[25] It should at least be noted that the Greek translations of the Jewish Bible are not the only places where someone can be a slave to a god. To be a slave of a god is used often in the magical papyri. The extant collections of magical texts, for the most part, post-date these transltions, and are of minimal use in evaluating the novelty of this translation choice.

SLAVE TERMS IN JOSEPHUS

In contrast to the Septuagint, Josephus's usual term for slave is *doulos* which almost certainly connotes for him a chattel slave. This is most forcefully demonstrated in speeches attributed to Jewish leaders in the *Jewish War*. To be a *doulos* is, for Josephus, to lose all of one's freedoms. This is not the limited servitude of the biblical laws. More than once are slaves contrasted with free persons. In Agrippa's speech in *War* 2.356 the *doulos* stands opposite the *phileleutheros*, the lover of freedom. In *Ant*. 3.357 to surrender to the Romans is to become a *doulos*. Here Josephus is certainly referring to the Roman practice of selling captives of war as slaves. *douloi* in Josephus's social world seem to occupy a very low place. In *War* 4.508 when Simon bar Giora frees slaves, Josephus links them with evildoers (*ponēroi*). He also remarks that Simon's army is made up of slaves and brigands (*doulōn. . . lēstōn*). In War 5.443 he calls Simon son of John and his supporters "slaves and rabble and the bastard outcasts of the nation" (*douloi kai sygklydes kai notha tou ethnous phtharmata*).

Josephus also utilizes a broader vocabulary of slavery than do the Greek biblical translations. Of the nouns used to designate a slave several appear in common with the Greek Bible, *doulos*, *oiketēs*, *therapōn* and *pais*. In addition, several other Greek words refer to, or may refer to, slaves. The most frequently used are *aichmalōtos* (referring to war captives) and *andrapodon* (which does not occur in the Greek biblical translations).[26] What John Gibbs and Louis Feldman conclude from the use of these terms is that Josephus did not distinguish very carefully among his words for slaves, generally using them as rough synonyms.[27] They cite several pieces of evidence, all of which justify this conclusion. Two seem most convincing to me.

First, in a number of cases where parallel passages exist between the *Antiquities* and the *Jewish War*, Josephus changes the term used to designate a slave. For instance, in *War* 1.233, Herod, as part of a ruse, sends a servant (*oiketēs*) ahead on the pretext of preparing a meal. When that same incident is narrated in *Ant*. 14.291, the *oiketēs* is now a *therapōn*. In *War* 1.620 when certain informers are produced for Herod, some come from the *oiketai* of Antipater's mother. The same event in *Ant*. 17.93 finds them called *douloi*.[28]

The second point made by Gibbs and Feldman is one on which I want to expand. A good way to ascertain how Josephus uses these terms would be to compare them to places where he is treating biblical texts. Gibbs and Feldman

---

[26] For locations and discussion of other nouns and word groups in Josephus having to do with slavery, see Gibbs and Feldman.

[27] Gibbs and Feldman: 290. I came upon this article after I had examined the uses of these words in Josephus and had come to the same conclusion.

[28] These two examples were taken from Gibbs and Feldman. For a more detailed list see Gibbs and Feldman: 288.

look closely at 1–2 Samuel and 1–2 Kings.[29] They note at several places that Josephus has apparently substituted *doulos*, or some form of it, for another word. They further point out that since Josephus probably had some "proto-Lucianic" form of these books definite conclusions are difficult to make.[30]

One finds a similar trend elsewhere in Josephus where he cites or paraphrases biblical passages. I will examine Josephus's use of pentateuchal traditions here. At the beginning of *Antiquities* 2, Josephus tells the story of Joseph. Both in places where he adds to the wording of the biblical narrative and in those passages where slave terms occur already, he primarily uses *doulos*. In the interpretation of the brothers' initial dream, Josephus sees the sheaves of his brothers bowing down to his "like *douloi* before their masters." This is a clear expansion of the biblical text, but it represents the language Josephus has chosen for this story. When Joseph is sold in Egypt as a slave and he has his encounter with the libidinous wife of Potiphar, she calls him a wicked *doulos* although the Septuagint uses *pais* (also in *Ant.* 2.78). Later, after Joseph sets up Benjamin as a thief, Judah pleads with him to let Benjamin go and to keep him as a slave. Josephus uses *doulos* here whereas the Greek of Gen 44:33 has *oiketēs*.

In other expansions of the biblical law, Josephus adds slaves (*douloi*) to the list of those who are to hear the reading of the Law (see *Ant.* 4.209 and Deut 31:10). Although Deuteronomy 17 and 19 do not specify them, Josephus (*Ant.* 4.219) also says that *douloi* cannot be counted as possible witnesses in criminal cases due to the "baseness of their soul" (*tēn tēs psychēs ageneian*). In the law concerning debt slavery, Exodus 22 does not designate by a noun the Israelite who is sold as a slave. Josephus (*Ant.* 4.272) calls him a *doulos*. Finally, regarding the law concerning the ox which kills a male or female slave, Exod 22:32 calls the slaves *paida . . . ē paidiskēn*; Josephus (*Ant.* 4.282) designates them *doulon hē therapainan*.

While Josephus uses *doulos* and *oiketēs* by far and away more times than any other term to designate a slave,[31] the one term that really drops out of use as a primary designator for a slave is *pais*. The lack of this word's use to mean slave is especially striking when one remembers how it often far outnumbered uses of *doulos* in the Greek biblical translations. Of the over 700 occur-

---

[29] A crucial issue for the study of Josephus is whether he used a Greek or Hebrew text of the Bible. Gibbs and Feldman (297) claim that one finds in 1–2 Samuel and 1–2 Kings the "strongest evidence that Josephus used a Greek text. . . ." See Attridge (211), who concludes for Josephus that his "text of scripture used throughout is a Greek version. Josephus may, in some instances, have consulted a Hebrew or Aramaic targum, but the evidence for such Semitic sources, and particularly for the use of targum, is slender at best."

[30] For a complete listing of the comparable Greek biblical passages with Josephus and the conclusion cited here, see Gibbs and Feldman: 298–99.

[31] *Aichmalōtos* occurs more frequently than either of these, but it does not always refer to a slave, so it is not includeed in this section.

rences of *pais* in the works of Josephus only a very few could or do mean slave; the rest refer to children.[32]

In several other cases, *pais* clearly means child in a context where slavery is discussed, and thus the meaning of the term stands in contrast to slave. In *War* 7.334 Eleazar exhorts the people on Masada to commit mass suicide by arguing that such an end is more tolerable than surrender to the Romans. He says, "Let our wives thus die undishonored, our children (*paides*) unacquainted with slavery (*douleia*)." In *Ant.* 19.129, Josephus gives a list of people who cannot believe that the emperor Gaius could be killed. He includes women, children (*paides*) and slaves (*douloi*). *Ant.* 12.109 and 217 is probably the most interesting passage of this kind. Hyrcanus, who is several times in this entire section called a boy (*pais*), is sent by his father to Alexandria to honor Ptolemy's newborn child. He buys from a slave dealer 100 *paidas* and 100 virgins (*parthenous*) as a gift for Ptolemy. He then presents them to Ptolemy and Cleopatra each carrying a single talent. Even though Hyrcanus buys them from a slave dealer, and they are to be considered slaves, the use of *pais* together with "virgins" indicates that Josephus is interested not in their servile status, but in their ages. These are young boys and girls.[33]

Conclusion: This brief discussion confirms the general conclusion reached by Gibbs and Feldman. Josephus has a varied vocabulary for slaves and generally uses the terms without making hard distinctions between them. Although a few uses of *pais* mean "slave," the term means "child" in the vast majority of its occurrences in Josephus's writings. In this, Josephus is certainly different from the Greek biblical translations which use *pais* often to designate a slave.

Slave Terms in Philo of Alexandria

Given the large corpus of Philo's writings, one might expect terms for slaves to occur fairly often; they do. His vocabulary for slaves is even more widely varied than the Greek Bible's or Josephus's. The main words that Philo utilizes, however, are the same ones on which Josephus relies: *doulos, oiketēs, therapōn* and sometimes *pais*. Philo speaks about actual slaves and slavery, but since his agenda is frequently philosophical, slave language is also employed by him in philosophical arguments and thus serve metaphorically.

---

[32] Gibbs and Feldman (296) list 3 cases in *War*, 1.82 (twice) and 1.340. These are paralleled by passages in *Ant.* 13.314 and 315 where the same term is used. Of the ten places cited in *Antiquities*, three are parallel to the passages just noted. The two occurrences of the term in *Ant.* 12.209 and 12.217 listed by them as denoting slaves, probably mean simply "boys."

[33] *Contra* Gibbs and Feldman (296).

His most common philosophical use of slave language is in the relationship of a person to his/her desires or emotions. For Philo, as for many Hellenistic philosophers, one can be enslaved to one's desires, passions, emotions or appetites. To be a slave (for Philo, primarily *doulos*) of these desires is to lose one's freedom completely and to be "owned" and controlled by those desires. The result is that such people cannot exercise reason.[34] Philo contrasts slavery, in good Greek fashion, with freedom. Sometimes he does this for actual situations, but other times the slave/free contrast is metaphorical, especially when he speaks about the nature of human beings. Thus, one can be a slave in the body; that is, someone may own/control a person's physical self, but that person may still be truly free. Philo's clearest explication of this idea comes in the tractate *Every Good Man is Free*.[35] Physical slavery, Philo argues, is often simply dependent on bad luck, and "anyone who thinks that people put up for sale by kidnappers thereby become slaves goes utterly astray from the truth" (37). And, Philo continues, just as a lion may be captured, but not tamed, still less can a wise man be a slave (40). He concludes a long argument by saying, "Consequently none of the good is a slave (*doulos*), but all are free. By the same line of argument it will appear that the fool is a slave (*doulos*)" (50–51).

In other clearly metaphorical contexts Philo speaks of the statesman as the slave (*doulos*) of the people, an image evidently drawn on deliberately by orators (*Ios*. 35, 67, 76). In *Abr*. 45 Philo reveals his own understanding of social order when he argues, in a discussion about the Flood, that if human beings were destroyed "none of the inferior kinds would be left, since they were made for humanity's needs, as slaves in a sense, meant to obey their masters' orders."

In the course of these discussions, as well as others, Philo reveals his own social understanding of the place and function of slaves, and though he certainly is aware of the biblical laws (as we will see below), his own social attitude towards slaves seems much more conditioned by the practices he sees around him. Slaves occupy the lower rungs of the social order. He makes this clear in *De Decal*. 165. "Parents belong to the superior class (*tē kreittoni ... taxei*) in which belong elders, rulers, benefactors and masters while children (*paides*)[36] belong in the lower (*tē katadeestera*) in which belong juniors, subjects, receivers of benefits and slaves (*douloi*)." In his discussion of how virtuous

---

[34] This theme is frequent in Philo. See, for example, *Opif*. 167; *Leg*. 3.156, 3.194; *Spec*. 4.91, 113; *Prob*. 11, 159. Several of these kinds of passages are Philo's allegories of biblical stories to achieve philosophical purposes.

[35] Philo does, however, treat this issue in other places as well. See, for example, *Spec*. 2.69, where Philo argues that no person is by nature a slave or *Abr*. 251 in which Sarah's slave Hagar is described as outwardly a slave, but inwardly free.

[36] See below on the use of *pais* in Philo.

people are not usually honored, Philo says that they do not enjoy the privileges of subjects peoples "or even slaves (*doulōn*)" (*Det.* 34). Although Philo says, and probably believes, that no good person is a slave, in *Spec.* 2.123 his aristocratic sensibilities surface in a discussion of the fact that the biblical law allows the buying of foreign slaves. He says that there are two reasons for this allowance. "[F]irst, that a distinction should be made between fellow-countrymen and aliens; secondly that the most indispensible possession, domestic service (*therapontas*), should not be excluded from his [God's] commonwealth. For the course of life contains a vast number of circumstances which demand the ministration of slaves (*tas ek doulōn hypēresias*)." He recognizes that slaves can be and were beaten (*Opif.* 85; *Leg.* 3.200), that people can be forcibly enslaved (*Somn.* 2.136), that "bad" slaves take advantage of the kindness of a master and act as if they had not been slaves (*Somn.* 2.294), and that even though enslaved, sometimes slaves can be entrusted with great responsibility and can purchase, lend or pursue other relatively free activities (*Prob.* 35). In general then, the way that Philo describes the position and use of slaves in his writings seems consonant with their place and use in Hellenistic-Roman slave systems.

The terms that Philo uses when speaking of slaves also represent the usual Greek spectrum of terms for enslaved persons. While *doulos* occurs most often, several other terms appear to be used synonymously with it. One of the best texts in which to see these terms being used without distinction is in *Spec.* 2.65f. where Philo is discussing the Sabbath law. He is quick to note that the law not only requires free persons to rest, but also servants and animals. In the course of his explanation of the reasons for this requirement, he says that masters must get used to working for themseves without the attendance of their *oiketai*, and that these *oiketai* should interpret this Sabbath rest as a taste of freedom. He then recapulates this notion using both *oiketēs* and *doulos* in the same sentence as synonyms. He moves on to animals, who are also given a Sabbath rest, because "[f]or servants (*therapontes*) are free by nature, no man being naturally a slave (*doulos*), but the unreasoning animals are intended to be ready for the use and service of men and therefore rank as slaves (*doulōn*)." Not only does this passage reveal Philo's attitude toward slaves, it also shows the relative ease with which he can substitute one slave word for another. In another place in *Special Laws* (1.126), Philo comments on the right of priestly slaves to partake of priestly food. In this case Philo refers to the house-born slave (*oikogenēs*) and the bought slave (*argyrōnētos*). The subsequent discussion contains *doulos*, *oiketēs* and *therapōn*, all meaning slaves, although *oiketēs* probably has here the narrower meaning of domestic slave.

While the previous examples show that Philo could use certain slave words interchangeably, his writings also reveal that *pais* is a special case as it was in Josephus. As in Josephus, *pais* for Philo seems to have the primary meaning of "child." Only a few times does it unequivocally mean "slave." Several passages have *pais* and slave words together where *pais* clearly indicates a child. In *Det.* 13–14 Philo addresses the plausibility of the Joseph narrative. Why, he says, would a father who has slaves and attendants (*oiketēn hē hyperetōn*) send out his son to find out about his other children (*tōn allēn paidōn*)? In *Fug.* 3, he gives reasons that people might flee others, including "children (*paides*) their parents and slaves (*oiketai*) their masters." Finally, the passage mentioned above from *Det.* 165, where slaves and children occupy the lower classes of society, has the two words in the same context.

The most interesting aspect of Philo's use of *pais* is that when it means "slave" he is almost always using the term in dependence on the Greek biblical translations. On the one hand, in sections on the slavery laws from the Bible, he often has *doulos* where the biblical translations have some other term, frequently *pais*. In several different places Philo treats the slave laws from Exodus 21, Leviticus 25 and Deuteronomy 15. His treatment of the laws that distinguish between an Israelite and foreign slave is potentially very revealing. In *Spec.* 2.79ff. Philo cites Deut 15:12 and speaks about the importance of the text using the word "brother" of the debt servant. He further recognizes the biblical injunction to treat that "brother" as a hired laborer rather than as a slave. He then says, "For people in this position, though we find them called slaves (*doulous*), are in reality laborers who undertake the service just to procure themselves the necessities of life." The biblical text does not call these people *douloi*; Deuteronomy does not use the word slave, and Exodus says, "If you buy a Hebrew *paida*." Does Philo's remark indicate that in his social context the biblical word is not used for these debt slaves, but that the usual Greek word *doulos* is? That would appear to be the implication here. The apparent change from *pais* to *doulos* may indicate that the use of these words by Jews may be following contemporary Hellenistic Greek usage in which *pais* is found less and less with the meaning "slave."[37] Several other passages have *doulos* instead of *pais*: *Leg.* 3.198 (Exod 21:5) on the debt slave who chooses to remain a slave (LXX = *pais*, Philo = *doulos*), *Sobr.* 51, a citation of Gen 9:26–27, the curse of Canaan (LXX = *pais, oiketēs, pais,* Philo = *pais, oiketēs, doulos*),[38] *Ios.* 228 (Gen 44:33) in which Judah asks to be a slave in return for Benjamin's freedom (LXX = *pais*, Philo = *doulos*), *Spec.* 3.145 (Exod 21:32) concerning the killing of a slave by an ox (LXX = *pais*, Philo = *doulos*), *Virt.* 124 (Deut 23:16) on the runaway slave (LXX = *pais*, Philo = *doulos*).

In other instances where the Greek Bible uses *pais* to mean "slave," Philo retains it and its meaning. In some cases Philo cites the text directly, and in

---

[37] Although the diminutives of *pais* are used frequently. A similar discussion occurs a bit later in 2.122–23. In this case the person who is bought (*argyrōnētos*) is not a *doulos* by nature.

[38] In this case the citation is very close and the question arises as to whether Philo may have a variant Greek text of Genesis which used *doulos*.

others he paraphrases, but retains *pais* rather than change it. In *Det*. 30–31 (see also *Congr*. 111) Philo allegorizes the story of Isaac and Rebecca in Genesis 24. Abraham has sent a servant (*pais* in both Genesis and Philo) to find a wife for Isaac. The servant finds Rebecca and as Isaac approaches, she asks the servant who it is that is coming. The servant replies, "It is my master," a clear indication of the servile status of the *pais*. In a citation of Gen 26:32 (see *Plant*. 78 and *Somn*. 1.38), Isaac's *paides* report to him about wells they have dug. Philo simply reproduces the word used in the Septuagint, here clearly referring to slaves. In one of the two uses of *pais* in the curse of Canaan, Philo retains the *pais* found in the Septuagint (see above). He cites Num 31:49–50 in *Ebr*. 114 in which Moses' officers (called *paides* in the Greek Bible and in Philo) report to him.

There are other instances where it seems as if Philo is deliberately playing on the lexical ambiguity of *pais*. In a passage on the value of wisdom (*Cher*. 71–73), he quotes Exod 21:5–6 on the indentured servant who chooses to remain a slave, this time retaining the *pais* of the Septuagint. He draws the conclusion that the mind that has heard lofty and wise words and rejects them is "a *pais* in very truth and wholly childish (*nēpiou*)." Here *pais* might as well mean "boy" as "slave." Philo apparently wants the lexical ambiguity at work. Another very interesting passage is *Congr*. 154 in which Philo is treating Gen 16:6 where Sarah sends Hagar away. The Greek Genesis calls Hagar *paidiskē*, and about this title Philo comments, "Indeed in calling her *paidiskē* he [Abraham] makes a double admission, that she is a slave and that she is childish, for the name suits both of these. At the same time the words involve necessarily and absolutely the acknowledgment of the opposites of these two, of the full grown as opposed to the child, of the mistress as opposed to the slave." In this passage Philo not only understands, but intentionally plays upon the duality and ambiguity of *pais* words used for slaves.

Some of this ambiguity may be present in one specialized use of slave language in Philo, the servant/slave of God. To be a slave of God (the Jewish God, that is) is not a bad thing, but is valued positively by Philo. His language of slavery to God is varied, like his other uses of slave terms. Sometimes this service can be described using *doulos* language. In *Det*. 56, Philo speaks of loving God by which "we mean some such service as slaves (*douloi*) render to their masters. . . ." Philo also deals with God's concern for the world in *Mut*. 46. He concludes, "Shall we then his slaves (*douloi*) follow our Master with profoundest awe and reverence for Him Who is the Cause, yet not forgetting the calls of our common humanity." The slave of God designated by *therapōn* is also frequent in Philo and the word is used synonymously with *doulos* in *Her*. 6 where Philo is interested in speaking with God.[39] A slave, Philo argues,

---

[39] For instances of *therapōn theou*, see *Det*. 62; *Fug*. 67; *Spec*. 1.242 (of priests). That *therapōn* is also a normal word for slave in Philo's vocabulary is evident from many places.

properly speaks to his master when his words and actions are all for the master's benefit. Thus, "when else should the slave (*doulos*) of God open his mouth freely to Him who is the ruler and master both of himself and of the All . . . , when he feels more joy at being the servant (*therapōn*) of God than if he had been king of the human race. . . ."

As with the more usual uses of *pais*, its lexical ambiguity extends to figurative uses as child/slave of God. It is apparent from the examples given above that Philo does play on that ambiguity. One passage, *Conf.* 147, shows how that problem extends to figurative uses of *pais*. Philo cites Gen 42:11 according to the Septuagint, "We are all sons (*huioi*) of one man." He then continues, "For if we have not yet become fit to be thought children (*paides*) of God yet we may be [children] of his invisible image, the most holy word." Here *pais* almost certainly means "children," but what impact does such use have on other places, like *Abr.* 132 where Philo discusses the singularity of God. He cites Gen 18:3. "Sir, if indeed I have found favor with you, do not pass your *pais* by." Is it child or slave/servant, especially since these ambiguities seem to be present when Philo quotes or uses a biblical passage that has *pais* as the central term?

Conclusion: The uses to which Philo puts nouns for slaves, then, are similar to those found in Josephus and, to a degree, in the Greek biblical translations. *doulos, oiketēs* and *therapōn* are used mostly as synonyms. Occasionally, *oiketēs* may be used to indicate a household servant particularly, but certainly not in every case. *pais* in Philo's writings has a clear lexical ambiguity on which Philo plays. Yet, most of Philo's uses of *pais* to mean "slave" come in contexts where he is dealing with biblical passages in which the word has that meaning already. In other places, Philo would seem to prefer some other word. This general synonymity would put Philo, like Josephus and the Greek Bible, in agreement with the uses of the terms in other contemporary Hellenistic literature.

Slave Terms in the Apocrypha and Pseudepigrapha

The situation in the Apocrypha (except ben Sira which I discussed above) and the Pseudepigrapha that are extant in Greek is not too much different from what was the case for the biblical translations, Josephus and Philo. The usual slave terms seem to refer to chattel slaves when actual slaves are the referent. What is somewhat surprising is the frequency with which *pais* means "servant/slave" in addition to its meaning of "child." One might not expect this given Josephus's and Philo's apparent lack of interest in this meaning of the word. The use in the Apocrypha and Pseudepigrapha may perhaps be attributed to the frequent occurrence of the word in the Jewish-Greek scriptures with the meaning of slave/servant. The best example of this kind of usage is in the *Testament of Abraham* where in 7:8 *pais* refers to Isaac and means "child/son," but later in 15:5 at the end of Abraham's life his servants (*douloi*) gather around him. In 15:6 these servants are called *paides*. In 20:7 where the scene is reprised, *doulos* is the term used. In 17:18 and 18:3, 9 Death kills a large number of Abraham's slaves, called *paides*.[40] *pais* also is used to mean "slave" in passages in *Testaments of the Twelve Patriarchs, Joseph and Asenath*,[41] the letter of *Aristeas*, Judith, 1 Maccabees.[42]

The title "servant of God" appears a number of times in these works with both *pais* and *doulos*, sometimes in the same work. In the *Testament of Levi*, for example, the Aramaic Prayer of Levi, extant in Greek in Mount Athos ms e and in Aramaic in 4QAramaic Levi, has ʿ*ebed* in relation to God twice in the text and once as a fairly certain reconstruction. The Greek uses *doulos* once and *pais* two times, apparently as synonyms.[43] In *Paraleipomena Ieremiou* 6:19 Baruch is called the *doulos* of God and in 6:24 Jeremiah is God's *pais*—both apparently meaning "servant/slave."[44] *Psalms of Solomon* may witness a distinction between the two Greek words. *pais* is used twice, in 12:6 and 17:21. In each case Israel is being singled out as the servant of God. The three cases of *doulos*, 2:37, 10:4 and 18:2, all are used in an indefinite plural to refer to God's slaves. Israel is the *pais* of God; individuals are his *douloi*.[45] All the uses of servant of God in 1–2 Maccabees use *doulos*.

The one work in which the use of *pais* of God shows some ambiguity is Wisdom of Solomon. The book does use *doulos*, and the speaker in 9:5 calls himself God's *doulos* "the son (*huios*) of your serving girl, a man who is weak and short-lived with little understanding of judgment and laws." 18:11 speaks about the killing of the Egyptian firstborn and remarks that the slave (*doulos*) was killed along with the master. Both uses of *doulos* designate a chattel slave, one in relation to God.

The occurrences of *pais* where the meaning is clear serve to illuminate those places where the meaning is not. In 8:19. the speaker remarks that as a child (*pais*) he was "naturally gifted" that he had "entered into an undefiled body." The three occurrences of *pais* in chap 12 all seem to mean "child/children." 12:3–11 deals with the sins of the Canaanites and the giving of the land to the Israelites. The author singles out the original people of the land as those who sacrificed their children (*teknōn*). He returns to this theme in v. 6, refer-

---

[40] These passages are in the A recension.

[41] Primarily as the servants of Pharaoh. The same Greek is used of Pharaoh's servants in the biblical translations.

[42] 3:41 is the only place I have encountered where *pais* seems to refer to war captives being sold as slaves.

[43] For the text of the prayer in 4QAramaic Levi and the Mount Athos manuscript, see Stone and Greenfield.

[44] For the text, see Kraft and Purinton.

[45] Text is taken from Rahlfs.

ring to "parents who murder helpless lives." As a result, God gave the "land most precious" to him to the Israelites, a "worthy colony of the *paidōn* of God." In the context, "children" of God seems to me to make the best sense.[46] 12:20–21 continues the theme with "For if you punished . . . the enemies of your *paidōn* . . . with what strictness have you judged your *huious*." The use of *huios* and *pais* in parallel suggest that *paidōn* means "children" here. Finally in vv. 24–25 the Egyptians, who worshipped animals and were deceived like "foolish infants (*nēpiōn*)," are judged by God as "children (*paisin*) with no reason." The parallelism makes the meaning clear. The context of 18:9–10, the killing of the Egyptian children, makes the use of *pais* in the phrase "holy *paides*" clearly mean children.

That leaves 2:13, 9:4 and 19:6. 2:13 refers to an individual against whom the ungodly conspire. This righteous man calls himself "*paida kyriou*." Both 9:4 and 19:6 refer to the people of God with the plural *paides*. Since the other plural uses of *pais* mean children, these probably do as well. 2:13, as the only use of the phrase *pais* of God in the singular in this book, is more uncertain, but should also probably be rendered "child."

Conclusion: Generally in the Apocrypha and Pseudepigrapha slave terms do not seem to have any clear cut distinctions in use, even in their religious contexts. This situation is not very different from the other Jewish literature of the Second Temple period discussed above. The terms seem largely interchangeable. With the exception of Wisdom of Solomon, where *pais* of God should be translated "child/children of God," the uses of *pais* with reference to God probably mean "servant/slave," especially in these places where it occurs together with *doulos*.

Concluding Remarks

I think the evidence surveyed above warrants the general conclusion that Jewish writers in the Second Temple period are using words for slaves as they know them to be used in their contemporary socio-cultural environment, that is, that the main terms for slaves can be roughly synonymous even though in individual uses some distinction of function might be intended. I want to emphasize at the beginning of this concluding section that this seems to me to be the best way to construe the use of these terms. On the other hand, several issues stand out as deserving special attention here.

First, Philo and Josephus demonstrate an intimate knowledge of Hellenistic-Roman slave systems. Many passages in their writings point to this fact. Philo certainly can be read in such a way that it appears as if he not only knows about slaves, but that he has personal interractions with slaves and masters; perhaps he even owned slaves. In addition, Philo's own attitudes

---

[46] The NRSV translates "servants," but Winston has "children."

towards slaves and slavery surface throughout his works, attitudes which reveal an acceptance on his part of the necessity and place of slaves in society. Josephus, as well, knows these systems from his involvement in the First Jewish Revolt and from his later relocation to Rome. Both of these authors' uses of slave terms would then seem quite consonant with the social realities that they experienced. Something of this may be what prompts both of these men to use the general word for slave, *doulos*, instead of the more ambiguous *pais* in several places where they discuss biblical passages that contain the latter term.[47] Like the papyri from this period and later, *pais* itself is not used a great deal for slaves, although its diminutives are, both in the papyri and in Philo and Josephus.

The glaring absence of *doulos* from the Greek Pentateuch remains somewhat of a mystery. The possible reasons that I adduced above for its absence, particularly the idea that the terms other than *doulos* connote a greater familiarity between slave and master, represent informed speculation, but may represent a different way of articulating what Zimmerli was trying to suggest and yet still account for the ambiguity inherent in the several cases of *doulos* that do occur. *Doulos*, of course, appears with great frequency in the later translations where all the major terms for slaves serve broadly as synonyms. Thus, the Jewish translations of the Bible witness the same process evidenced in the koine of the period, the increasing interchangeability of these terms for slaves.

When one looks to the metaphorical uses of the words for slaves, most of them can be seen in other Hellenistic literature. The use of these terms in the language of political subjection is not unique to Jews, and certainly Philo's utilization of this language to speak about domination by human appetites and desires draws on Hellenistic philosophy as does his notion that the wise person can never be a slave.

The one use that would seem to be drawn specifically from Jewish sources, the Bible in particular, is the notion of the "slave of God." Although the Greek term for slave can be any of those I have looked at in this essay, to be a "slave of God" is a good thing. Further, it does not seem to have ready sources in Hellenistic literature.[48] One other place where such an idea is prevalent is in the Greek magical papyri. One finds numerous examples like that in *PGM* XIII.637 where the supplicant says to Sarapis, "I am your slave and petitioner and the one who hymns your name."[49] Unfortunately, most of these papyri date from well after the first century CE, and, as a methodological

---

[47] Realizing, however, that they may have had texts that vary from what is now known as the Septuagint, and that they do not so in every case.

[48] See, Bartchy (1992). The more specific question of exactly what this term means is not the focus of this essay, but is, of course, critical for understanding its uses in Christian literature (see, for example, Jeremias).

[49] For the Greek text, see Preisendanz. For English translations of the Greek Magical Papyri, see Betz.

point, such use may have come to these magical texts via Jewish or Christian sources. It would seem, then, that this idea is unique to Jews, an idea that they drew from their scriptural traditions and their self conception as a nation of people who are "servants of God," as opposed to servants of human rulers.

Works Consulted

Attridge, H. W.
    1984   "Josephus and His Works." Pp. 185–232 in *Jewish Writings of the Second Temple Period*. Ed. Michael E. Stone. CRINT 2.II. Philadelphia: Fortress.

Bartchy, S. Scott
    1973   *First-Century Slavery and the Interpretation of 1 Corinthians 7:21.* SBLDS 11. Atlanta: Scholars Press.

    1992   "Slavery (NT)." *ABD* 6:65–73.

Betz, Hans Dieter
    1986   *The Greek Magical Papyri in Translation*. Chicago: University of Chicago Press.

Dandamayev, Muhammad A.
    1992   "Slavery (ANE)" and "Slavery (OT)." *ABD* 6:58–65.

Finley, M. I., ed.
    1960   *Slavery in Classical Antiquity*. Cambridge: Heffer.

    1987   *Classical Slavery*. Totowa, N.J.: Frank Cass.

Flesher, Paul Virgil McCracken
    1988   *Oxen, Women, or Citizens? Slaves in the System of the Mishnah*. Atlanta: Scholars Press.

Fuks, G.
    1985   "Where Have all the Freedmen Gone? On an Anomaly in the Jewish Grave-Inscriptions from Rome." *JJS* 36:25–32.

Garlan, Yvon
    1988   *Slavery in Ancient Greece*. Ithaca: Cornell University Press.

Gibbs, John G. and Louis Feldman
    1986   "Josephus' Vocabulary for Slavery." *JQR* 76:281–310.

Hengel, Martin
    1974   *Judaism and Hellenism*. Philadelphia: Fortress.

Horsley, G. H. R.
    1981–89   *New Documents Illustrating Early Christianity*. Vols 1–5. Macquarie University: The Ancient History Documentary Research Centre.

Jeremias, Joachim
1967   "*pais theou* in Later Judaism in the Period after the LXX." *TDNT* 5: 677–717.

Kraemer, Ross S.
1989   "On the Meaning of the Term 'Jew' in Greco-Roman Inscriptions." *HTR* 81:35–53.

1991   "Jewish Tuna and Christian Fish: Identifying Religious Affiliation in Epigraphic Sources." *HTR* 84:141–62.

Kraft, Robert A.
1975   *Septuagintal Lexicography*. SCS 1. Missoula: Scholars Press.

Kraft, Robert A. and Ann-Elizabeth Purinton
1972   *Paraleipomena Jeremiou*. Texts and Translations 1, Pseudepigrapha 1. Missoula: Society of Biblical Literature.

Levine, Baruch
1989   *The JPS Torah Commentary: Leviticus*. Philadelphia: Jewish Publication Society.

Llewelyn, S. R.
1992   *New Documents Illustrating Early Christianity*. Vol. 6. Macquarie University: The Ancient History Documentary Research Centre.

Martin, Dale B.
1990   *Slavery as Salvation: The Metaphor of Slavery in Pauline Christianity*. New Haven: Yale University Press.

Mendelsohn, Isaac
1949   *Slavery in the Ancient Near East: A Comparative Study of Slavery in Babylonia, Assyria, Syria and Palestine; From the Middle of the Third Millenium to the End of the First Millenium*. Oxford: Oxford University Press.

Patterson, Orlando
1982   *Slavery and Social Death*. Cambridge: Harvard University Press.

Preisendanz, Karl
1928   *Papyri Graecae Magicae: Die griechischen Zauberpapyri*. Berlin: Teubner.

Rahlfs, Alfred, ed.
1935   *Septuaginta*. Stuttgart: Württembergische Bibelanstalt.

Rengstorf, Karl
1967   "*doulos*" *TDNT* 2:261–80.

Skehan, Patrick W. and Alexander A. di Lella
1987   *The Wisdom of Ben Sira*. AB 39. New York: Doubleday.

Spicq, C.
1978   "Le vocabulaire de l'esclavage dans le nouveau testament." *RevBib* 85:201–26.

Stern, Menachem
    1976–84   *Greek and Latin Authors on Jews and Judaism.* Vols 1–3. Jerusalem: Israel Academy of Sciences and Humanities.

    1992   *Studies in the History of Israel in the Second Temple Period.* Jerusalem: Yitzchak ben Zvi (Hebrew).

Stone, Michael E. and Jonas C. Greenfield
    1993   "The Prayer of Levi." *JBL* 112:247–66.

Straus, J.-A.
    1976   "La terminologie de l'esclavage dans les papyrus grecs romaines trouvés en Egypte." Pp. 335–50 in *Actes du colloque 1973 sur l'esclavage.* Annales Litteraires de l'Université de Besançon, 182. Paris: Les Belles Lettres.

    1981   "La terminologie grecque de l'esclavage dans les papyrus de l'Égypte lagide et romaine." Pp. 385–91 in *Scritti in Onore di Orsolina Montevecchi.* Ed. Edda Bresciani, Giovanni Geraci, Sergio Pernigotti, Giancarlo Susini. Bologna: Editrice Bologna.

Tcherikover, Victor and G. Fuks
    1957–64   *Corpus Papyrorum Ioudicarum.* Vols 1–3. Cambridge: Harvard University Press.

Trebilco, Paul
    1991   *Jewish Communities in Asia Minor.* SNTS Monographs 69. Cambridge: Cambridge University Press.

Urbach, E. E.
    1964   "The Laws Regarding Slavery as a Source for Social History of the Period of the Second Temple, the Mishnah and Talmud." Pp. 1–94 in *Papers of the Institute of Jewish Studies London.* Ed. J. G. Weiss. Jerusalem: Magnes.

Vaux, Roland de
    1965   *Ancient Israel: Its Life and Institutions.* London: Darton, Longman & Todd.

Vogt, Joseph
    1974   *Ancient Slavery and the Ideal of Man.* Oxford: Blackwell.

Westermann, William L.
    1955   *The Slave Systems of Greek and Roman Antiquity.* Philadelphia: The American Philosophical Society.

Wiedemann, Thomas
    1981   *Greek and Roman Slavery.* Baltimore: Johns Hopkins University Press.

Winston, David
    1979   *The Wisdom of Solomon.* AB 43. New York: Doubleday.

Zimmerli, Walther
    1975   "*pais theou.*" *TDNT* 5:654–77.

THE DEPICTION OF SLAVERY IN THE ANCIENT NOVEL

Lawrence M. Wills
Episcopal Divinity School

ABSTRACT

To make a distinction between slavery in the Roman period of antiquity and slavery in the antebellum United States, the article begins with several basic definitions and distinctions ingredient to the complexity of social relations in Roman antiquity: 1) its vertical world view with a metaphysical presumption of inequality among deities, daimons and spirits in heaven and among human beings on earth; 2) its variety of overlapping deference entitlement determinants (such as *ordo*, class, wealth, gender, citizen, and family) all of which were governed by the aforementioned overarching dyadic hierarchy of relations; and 3) its denial of the slave's natal identity primarily through acts of deprivation (e.g., war or debt), not through distinctions based on race. Next, the article examines three categories of novels from the Greco-Roman period: 1) the ideal Greek romances 2) the satirical novels; and 3) the Jewish novels. All three novel categories presuppose the dyad and a negative view of slavery. In the case of the first two, the issue of slavery is used to represent the threat of the defilement of aristocratic station; in the case of the third, to represent the threat of destruction for a pious Jew or a whole group of Jews.

The novels of the Greco-Roman period constitute some of our best available evidence for the study of popular culture in antiquity, including prevailing attitudes (among the upper classes, at any rate) regarding slavery. Slavery is, indeed, a central part of the symbolic universe of the novels. I shall not attempt in this article to analyze in detail the depiction of slaves and slavery in the novel of the Greco-Roman period, but merely to make some observations that will constitute prolegomena for a hermeneutics of slavery in the novel genre in the ancient world. My choice of texts, though broad, will not be exhaustive, but will demonstrate the importance of the novels in illuminating our knowledge of the phenomenon of slavery in the ancient world.[1] This, in turn, will contribute to the interpretation of Jewish and Christian texts of the Greco-Roman period.

Before we turn to the novels, however, some basic definitions and distinctions are necessary to indicate more precisely the parameters of what we are

---

[1] Hopkins provides an excellent consideration of the role of slavery in *Life of Aesop*, but he does not address the depiction of slaves in the other novels, nor in the Jewish novelistic literature.

looking for and what we are likely to find. A constant theme in past studies of slavery in the Roman period has been the surprising complexity of social relations in this period, relative to the system of slavery in the antebellum United States. The complexity is not simply the result of the sudden expansion of the western world in the Hellenistic period, nor the mixing of cultures east and west. It is also found in the very nature of Roman social relations, which rest upon pillars very different from our own. In the Modern West, capitalism determines the economic sphere, while democracy determines the political. Both of these systems presume isolated, "equivalent" individual agents who exercise their economic rights to earn money and spend it as they choose, and to vote for whomever they want; it is, therefore, in theory a horizontal world view. To be sure, only some individuals are allowed the status of being a "generic agent," but that did not constitute sufficient reason to bring into question the social theory of horizontal equivalency. In fact, the gradual admission of women, former slaves, or the poor into the marketplace of equivalent agents tends to confirm in people's minds the essentially horizontal nature of social relations. This is very different from the Greco-Roman world, where a divinely ordained hierarchy pervaded the cosmos, part of a Great Chain of Being consisting of, in the heavens, a range of greater and lesser deities, daimons and spirits, and on earth, human beings arranged in an equally rigid hierarchy. The gradations on earth would also extend to animals, plants, and matter. Just as there is a "graduated divinity" in heaven, there is a "graduated humanity" on earth. All consideration of a social contract theory between individual agents, based on fairness in economic relations, would seem absurd in such a system. Our modern system is based on the *metaphysical* presumption of individuality and equality in the economic and political spheres, the Roman on the *metaphysical* presumption of inequality and hierarchy. Even though there can be found countless and persistent individual examples of inequality in our present economic order, and surprising social mobility and escape from these constraints in the Roman world, that does not negate the importance of the theoretical "nature of things" that undergirds each world view. There is an opposite ideological ethos in the two systems.

The surprising failure of philosophers in the ancient world to condemn slavery as an institution should be seen in light of this metaphysical principle of hierarchy. The whole universe, even the gods, were seemingly arranged according to this hierarchy; it would have seemed insane to the elite philosophers to deny it. Only Cynics, who dissolved all social distinctions, could dissolve the hierarchy of class as well, and even here this act of deviance only tended to reify the social distinctions left behind. Thus it is important to invoke as a hermeneutical principle that, whereas the actual social relations "on the ground" in the Roman world might have been irregular and complex, the *ideal* arrangement of social relations, grounded in fundamental metaphysical beliefs, was simple: the universe is hierarchical.

As far as the legal system was concerned, humanity could be cleanly divided into slave and free: "This is the basic division in the law of persons, that all men are either free or slaves" (Gaius, *Institutes* 1.9). In a number of important areas, the division carried symbolic and real implications of the greatest significance. Slaves were subject to a different, and much crueler, set of punishments. Masters possessed the rights of nearly unlimited sexual access to slaves (Finley: 95–96; Garnsey: 213–16). Despite the ability of slaves under some circumstances to attain de facto wealth and power, and the delimitation of a freed person in many cases to the status of "client" to the former master, manumission in Rome was considered the greatest possible change of condition, from object to subject in law. Citizenship might be conferred, and the person freed would no longer be kinless (Finley: 97). Thus the use in the New Testament of the term *apolytrōsis* (the purchasing of a slave for the purposes of manumitting him or her) for "redemption" is quite a potent metaphor. It has suffered from a pietistic and individualistic application, but it could easily be used as a key term for liberation theology. The purchase must be seen on its two levels, however. In practice, a slave thus purchased and manumitted would become a client to the one purchasing, and thus still be subservient; on the symbolic level, however, the change of status is fundamental.

If the principle of a hierarchical cosmos, ruled by dualities, was simple, whence the complexity? The complexity arises from the variety of status distinctions that would determine one's existence. A grid of overlapping determinants of one's social location might include *ordo* or class, wealth, gender, citizenship, and family. In addition, the patronage system created very well demarcated and even ritualized relations of patrons and clients. In addition to these overlapping distinctions, one must also consider the irregularities within them, that is, cases where people in supposedly restricted social categories attain greater power or status, or suffer a loss of status relative to their category (Garnsey: 99–100, 279–80; Weaver; Mohler). The complexity of Roman social relations results from the grid of multiple, overlapping categories on one hand, and the possible irregularities within each category on the other. Slavery could thus be viewed within this network as a social category that was not always restrictive of real gains in wealth or power, and not always marked by unrelieved despair at one's low social position (Martin). A discussion of slavery in the Greco-Roman world, therefore, must proceed along two lines, the real and the ideal. The real is the world in which people move and act, and the ideal is that set of categories by which they understand themselves and others, and their relation to the world.[2]

---

[2] Despite the many excellent observations of Martin on the real and symbolic meaning of "slave" in the Greco-Roman world and in Paul, he still overemphasizes the real gains of occasional slaves and freedpersons, and takes that as evidence that the symbolic meaning of slavery is ameliorated.

The grids and distinctions we are invoking—master/slave, male/female, citizen/non-citizen, rich/poor, patron/client—cut through Roman society in different ways, at different angles, but they are all dyadic, vertical relationships, that is, superior/inferior. Because the Greek word *kyrios* is used for the superior pole of this dyad in so many contexts—master, husband, sir, patron, and so on—Schüssler Fiorenza (8, 117, 122–25) has quite appropriately coined the term kyriarchy to describe the organization of society by these interrelated dyads. Although a male slave and a female slave may not experience equivalent social realities, the dualities are still operative, even if they involve continual interference and mutual modification. Nevertheless, in any given situation the average Roman probably understood very well what the implications were of being a master versus a slave, male versus female, citizen versus non-citizen, and so on. The hierarchical universe is essentially dyadic, even though there are many vertical levels, and many categories by which one may define relationships. Louis Dumont's analysis of the Indian caste system posits a similar order for *homo hierarchicus*: a multitude of vertical levels, governed (in India) by an overarching duality of pure/impure. No matter how complex, varied, and "manipulable" was the lifestyle of the slave in the Roman period, the concept was equally one of *homo hierarchicus*, and slavery involved an abject loss of identity.

The heights and depths of the perspective on human potential inherent in these dyads is reflected in the art of the Hellenistic and Roman periods, used in many cases to decorate the finer homes. On the one hand, we find the motif of the ladies at leisure: aristocratic, usually young women who are graceful and beautiful, depicted playing games together, gossiping, or riding piggy-back (Uhlenbrock; Fowler: 19, 58, 83; Havelock: #145). This is the ideal of aristocratic feminity that we also see in the heroine of the Greek novel. On the other hand, and contemporary with it, is the depiction of the "grotesque:" dancing dwarfs, hunchbacks, drunken old women, shriveled servants (Fowler: 66–78; Havelock: #105, 134–36). Side-by-side, these decorative sculptures make no sense (the apotropaic explanation for the grotesques seems weak), and yet surely we are to see a visual representation of the two levels of society for the aristocratic viewer: "my class" in the ladies at leisure, and "the other" in the degraded specimens of the poor and grotesque. Nowhere is the symbolic distinction in the dyadic hierarchy presented more graphically.

In 1982 Orlando Patterson attempted to arrive at a cross-cultural definition of slavery that would define its essence more sharply. His conclusions concerning the nature of slavery cross-culturally will be of great value in the present study. Slavery has generally been understood as the ownership of another individual as "property," which includes near-absolute control over that person, and the produce of that person. Enslavement is seen as the process of "enchattelization." Patterson, however, presents two criticisms of this definition: First, not all slavery involves the exploitation of the slave's labor. In some slave systems, slaves are not principally laborers and do not produce excess wealth for the use and dispensation of the master; slaves may instead be status symbols, available only to those who control great wealth and power. From this first criticism there follows a second: the true essence of the master/slave relationship is not so much exploitation, the appropriation of the value of the slave's labor, but a relation of ritualized humiliation and dishonor, a defining of the slave as less human in order to define the master as more human (Patterson: 11, 17, 23, 77–101). M. I. Finley, in fact, shows how the *humanitas* of a Seneca or a Pliny the Younger was linked to their ownership of slaves (Finley: 121). The term Patterson uses for this abject degradation of the slave, "natal alienation," strikes one at first as dry, detached, scientific. However, it gets at the heart of an important aspect of master/slave relations, in fact, to the essence of slavery: slaves are denied all means of *natal* identity. They are denied rights to kin or a special place, the choice of relationships, or any of the other factors that would define one by birth. They fall into what Patterson calls the "social death" of slavery:

> The real sweetness of mastery for the slaveholder lay not immediately in profit, but in the lightening of the soul that comes with the realization that at one's feet is another human creature who lives and breathes only for one's self, as a surrogate for one's power, as a living embodiment of one's manhood and honor. (78)

An important aspect of this alienation of the slave's own identity is the necessity for the identity-less slave to be defined by the super-identity of the master, which may include relations to family, to the city, to the gods, and so on.[3]

Patterson's definition of slavery may seem to partake too much of intellectual categories, unlike the more standard view of slavery as enchattelization and the slave as property. The latter would strike most readers as simple and self-evident.[4] But the "self-evidence" of the property theory may result from several other influences. First, modern capitalism provides very well developed categories of property, specifically private property, that are familiar concepts which may be used to understand what are now the alien concepts of slavery and enslavement.[5] We "understand" slavery if we assimi-

---

[3] This may indeed provide a key to the problem Martin sets for himself in trying to ascertain what "slave of Christ" could connote. Slave is a negative term, but if one accepts a relation of slavery to Christ, one acquires a head, an identity in the cosmos. Note especially in Judaism and Christianity the language of God as *kyrios* and even *despotēs*, for instance, at 2 Pet 2:1.

[4] Flesher, for example, has recently produced an excellent study of slavery in rabbinic literature which utilizes a definition of slavery as enchattelization. He is, however, intentionally not "comparative," and rejects Patterson's comparative agenda, on the grounds that it threatens to obscure the particular contexts of the various cultures in question (176). Wegner's work on the status of women in rabbinic Judaism touches on issues of the definition of slaves, but likewise eschews Patterson's comparative approach.

[5] Patterson (28–29) himself traces the focus on property to Roman law, which held to a notion of absolute ownership of property. This conception is doubtless related genetically to our

late it to concepts that we use: slaves are people who are like our private possessions, which we have the right to manipulate and exploit for private gain. Second, slavery in the American South was marked by a sense that one race was destined to be slaves and another destined to be masters, not that the slaves had been deprived of their free status through war or debt. This notion of the status of slaves would give rise not to the idea that slaves are people who have been enslaved, but to a category of permanent and inherent chattel. Thus here I shall utilize Patterson's notion of slavery as a form of ritualized degradation and natal alienation.

The Ideal Novel in the Ancient World

We turn now to the known novels from the Greco-Roman period. A recent and very important development in the study of the ancient novel is the division of this group of texts into those which depict a positive model of bourgeois domestic values—the establishment of the nuclear family and the containment of sexuality—and those which are satirical, often graphically overturning these values (MacQueen: 117–37). The ideal Greek romance promulgates a very strong ethic of domestic virtue, often tied to an identification with an aristocratic Greek versus a "barbarian" social order. In this category we find Chariton, *Chaereas and Callirhoe*, Xenophon of Ephesus, *An Ephesian Tale*, and Heliodorus, *An Ethiopian Story*. Other novels from the Greco-Roman period constitute obvious and deliberate attempts to satirize this genre. They belong to a counter-genre, what Gerald N. Sandy calls "accounts of low life . . . designed to shock moral sensibilities and conventional notions of decorum" (Sandy: 809). Here we would include the notorious examples of Petronius, *Satyricon*, and Apuleius, *The Golden Ass*, but also lesser known works such as the anonymous *Life of Aesop* (Winkler 1985:276–91; Hopkins), the fragments of *Phoenicica* and *Iolaus*, and also Greek novels which are not as ribald and offensive to aristocratic sensibilities as *Satyricon* and *The Golden Ass*, but which are now nevertheless considered rightly by some scholars to satirize the ideal genre: Longus, *Daphnis and Chloe*, and Achilles Tatius, *Leucippe and Clitophon* (MacQueen; Reardon). The lack of a travel motif in *Daphnis and Chloe* and its restrained, more pastoral eroticism may reflect a deliberate attempt to underplay ironically the usual presentation of sexuality. *Leucippe and Clitophon* also challenges the earnestness of the ideal Greek novels. It is not as obviously satirical as *The Golden Ass* and *Satyricon*, yet it nevertheless takes an arch view of bourgeois respectability.

This division of novels into ideal and satirical is nothing less than a hermeneutical key to the origin and essence of the novel genre. Bruce Mac-

---

own, but I am more interested at this point in establishing the more proximate sources of our point of view.

Queen suggests that the ancient novel arises as a means of realistically exploring domestic social relations, but from one of two possible perspectives, positively or satirically. The same has been argued in greater detail and in a more theoretical fashion regarding the modern novel as well (McKeon). The question then becomes, Is there a difference in the way slaves and slavery are depicted in each of the two types of ancient novel?

First, we shall consider the ideal novels. Dale Martin describes how, in the world of the Greek novel (and here his comments would refer to the ideal novels), the young, beautiful, and noble hero and heroine are dragged down into a horrifying underworld in which they are subjected to kidnappings, pirates, threats of rape, and most of all, slavery. Unlike the "true" slaves, our noble hero and heroine are *by nature* free and even superior, merely *trapped* in the condition of slavery.[6] The protagonists often rise within slavery, however, by ingratiating themselves to their masters (35–36). This perpetuates the slave-to-riches motif, which was often encountered in literature and inscriptions.[7] Chariton's *Chaereas and Callirhoe* can be considered typical of the ideal novels, where, for instance, we commonly encounter the notion that the protagonists undergo a descent into slavery. (See especially the protagonists' laments at *Chaereas* 1.14, 3.10, and 4.3). Chariton presents a common topos that the beauty of the hero and heroine indicates their nobility of birth and their true nature, even if they are by circumstances brought into slavery (1.10; 2.1,3, etc.). Parallel to this division of human nature is the notion also expressed that Greeks are inherently superior to barbarians (2.5, 7.3; cf. Xenophon 3.11). The superhuman nobility and beauty of the protagonists—in fact, they are likened to gods and goddesses—is exaggerated. In the scale of graduated humanity, the semi-divine beauty of the protagonists elevates them further above slaves, which effects the greatest possible distance—and irony—in their temporary fall into slavery.

In addition to these dualities of noble/slave and Greek/barbarian, other dualities operate in tandem. We note the image of the pirates, depicted as wild and threatening, unstable forces of chaos, who are by inference contrasted with citizens (1.9–14; cf. Xenophon 1.13–15; but interestingly, not always negative: Heliodorus 1.3–4). Vulgar and intemperate sex is opposed to the pure love (and sex) of the protagonists (Xenophon 2.1–4, 3.9–12). In

---

[6] It is not surprising that Terry Comito proposes an interpretation of the novels which compares the theme of entrapment of noble souls in a threatening world with gnosticism. The novels are not gnostic mystery texts, but at the same time, it is not coincidental that the theme of the "entrapment of a divine spark" in gnosticism could generate so much interest among different groups around the Mediterranean.

[7] Martin's evidence indicates that, especially for managerial slaves or slaves of important figures, a rise in power and wealth was possible even while still enslaved. That freedmen sometimes also attained great wealth was a common motif of the period, though it is difficult to ascertain how many may have actually risen to positions of significant power and wealth.

Xenophon, in fact, all the indignities that have been heaped upon the heroine are summarized in parallel when she is sold to a brothelkeeper: "Were the tombs, murders, bonds, and pirates' lairs not enough? But now, will I be made to stand up in a brothel . . . ?" (5.6; cf. *Apollonius King of Tyre* 33). Thus the horrible sufferings are all listed together, and what they have in common is clear: they are examples of the most degrading aspects of society, threats to the protagonists' aristocratic world view. A further extension of this, fascinating in its psychological interest, is the combination of two negative values in the notion of "slave to lust" (or the equivalent) in Heliodorus (5.26; 7.2, 21). The hero, it is to be noted by contrast, is, in his restraint when alone with the heroine, a "slave of love but a master of pleasure" (*erōtos mēn elattōn, hēdonēs de kreittōn*).[8] That is, his pure love, to which he is a slave, forces him to rein in and subordinate, even enslave, his lust. He is master, not slave, of lust.

Slavery, then, the binary opposite of free (or noble), is one of the negative values in the series of dualities mentioned above, but more concretely, how are actual slaves characterized or represented in the novels? In Erich Auerbach's classic study of the representation of social classes in literature, *Mimesis*, he presses the question, To what extent are characters of different classes depicted as real, three-dimensional agents, with their own articulated internal life and point of view? His strongly argued thesis is that in the premodern world, a view of human nature which is transparent to social class is practically non-existent. Although with the rise of the modern novel it becomes broadly accepted that characters from different social classes can be equally imbued with significant action and substance, this democratizing of "tragic potential" is not to be found elsewhere, according to Auerbach, except in the Christian gospels. In the novels we see that slaves only occasionally take on character (and names) as villains, for example, Kybele in Heliodorus Book 7. They are more often a mere extension of the master's will, or actively identify their will with their master's, and remain nameless (especially in *Apollonius* 25, 30; cf. Iamblichus, *Babylonian Story* 15). The insubstantiality of slaves in drama, which Joseph Vogt noted (7–19), generally applies here as well. They are socially invisible, not rendered at all as human beings (Pseudo-Lucian, *The Ass* 7, *Apollonius* 17). It is often presumed that the master has the right of sexual access to the slave (*Apollonius* 33, *Heliodorus* 7.26). This manner of depicting slaves is precisely what we would expect, and probably accords with the actual social relations of the period. The ideal novels do not all depict slavery in the same way, however. Although the dualities mentioned above all operate to the same effect—the threat of degradation for an aristocratic couple—they are like stops on an organ, not all to be pulled out to the same

---

[8] Heliodorus 5.4. On the theme of "slave of love" in general, and especially in Plautus, see Zagagi: 109–18. The treatment of slavery in the novels could also very profitably be compared to that in Plautus, but it would be beyond the scope of this essay.

extent in each novel. Chariton holds up to the audience the inherent contrast of the freeborn protagonists and slaves more than do the other novels. Xenophon emphasizes more the threat of barbarians and impure lust. *Apollonius King of Tyre* objectifies slaves as nameless extensions of the master or even as gifts more than do the others.

The Satirical Novel in the Ancient World

The satirical novels also take slavery as an important aspect of the social order, but everything is refracted through the lens of the satirical perspective. In the *Satyricon* of Petronius, for example, the ideal Greek novel is systematically inverted, as the hero and heroine of the aristocratic family structure become homosexual lovers, and all values of chastity and honor are reflected ironically in their inability to remain faithful. In the first pages of our fragments are found homosexual relations with a boy, a futile attempt by eunuchs to engage in an orgy, and forced sex between an underage boy and girl. The fragments end with a scene of cannibalism. Every boundary is violated, which should be kept in mind when the depiction of slaves is considered. Slavery is a major, even obsessive preoccupation in the *Satyricon*; Petronius's satirical agenda focuses principally on sex and class, as indeed do all the novels, both ideal and satirical. Through the course of the novel, the protagonists move in and out of slave and free personae, disguised constantly, in effect mocking class identity. They are uprooted, unmarked by any social community, unhinged psychologically. There is little for them to respect in the depiction of social mores in general, but we especially note the central episode of the *Satyricon*, which concerns the magnificent dinner party of the *nouveau riche* freedman Trimalchio and his freedmen-guests (26–78). The two themes of the long episode are the exaggerated opulence of the food—the economic surplus of Trimalchio's many estates is translated into the richest foods that can be provided—and the contrasting crassness of Trimalchio's true character, especially toward his slaves. Far from identifying with the critical perspective of slaves, however, the satire of the novel is directed against them as well. The irony of the scene is not that the slaves are more dignified than the rich guests, but that the wealthy ex-slaves erect such a distance between themselves and the class from which they have risen. Trimalchio's freedmen are proud of their rise from slavery and of their present attainments, even though Petronius's own perspective seems contemptuous of their pretense to high social standing. The freedmen lack any semblance of *urbanitas*. As Patterson notes, the degradation of slaves is a means of affirming the owner's enhanced status, and this we find highlighted in Petronius's presentation. The rough and peremptory treatment of slaves by Trimalchio is constant, even to the extent that after urinating, he cleans his fingers by dipping them in water and wiping them on the hair of a slave boy.

Martin addresses the question of the depiction of slavery in *Satyricon*, pointing out that although the author seems contemptuous of the *nouveau riche* Trimalchio and freedmen like him, the story does attest to the strength of the motif of the slave-to-riches story. The "myth of the upwardly mobile slave" is used by Petronius to satirize those slaves who became rich and powerful (Martin: 36–37). However, Petronius's depiction of the disdain with which the freedmen treat their own slaves is actually part of the satire: one step removed from slaves, these wealthy freedmen, utterly lacking in virtue, waste no time in degrading the very class from which they originated. The principle of raising one's own status by ritually degrading others' appears to be a second, very vibrant myth that lies behind the text.

The Golden Ass of Apuleius is, like *Satyricon*, a satirical novel, but accomplishes its satire in a different way. It is not simply a frenzied reversal of all accepted values; it attempts instead to provide a genuine social commentary which is sometimes quite subtle. The idealized values of the romance or epic are subverted by taking the first-person narratival perspective of a man-become-donkey (Winkler, 1985; Millar). Though based on the *The Ass* of Pseudo-Lucian, *The Golden Ass* introduces a much more profound theme of descent and ironic perspective. It is his incurable curiosity that gets the narrator, Lucius, into trouble, and it is also his curiosity which guides him throughout, and enlarges his character so that he becomes a truly interested and interesting observer of the parade of human life. The novel concludes with an initiation into the cult of Isis, and it is clear finally that his curiosity, and the adventure which it inaugurates, are metaphors for the life of the convert. Although Lucius does not explicitly compare his condition as a donkey to a form of slavery, it does suggest itself on a metaphorical level, and the connection is drawn in a humorous manner in the source-novel, Pseudo-Lucian's *The Ass* (42). As Fergus Millar also points out, Lucius's curiosity allows him during this sojourn to see people of different classes now from the underside, from the point of view of a donkey:

> (I)n narrating the adventures of the ass he is making a fictional journey which descends through all levels of society. . . . It is thus that Apuleius, looking through the eyes of Lucius transformed into an ass, can give his unique description of the slaves toiling in the mill (9.12), dressed in few rags, their half-naked bodies scarred with the marks of beatings, their foreheads branded, their heads half-shaved, their feet in fetters, all of them covered in a fine dust of flour. It is undeniable that the novel expresses a rare and distinctive level of sympathy with the working lives of the poor. (Millar: 65)

Millar does not go so far as to consider *The Golden Ass* a political critique of Roman society; rather, its agenda seems to be one of a metaphorical journey of discovery, which nevertheless includes a realistic depiction of society's lower classes. Auerbach's assessment of *The Golden Ass*, on the other hand, is very critical. He does not address the depiction of slaves as such, but condemns the emphasis on the bizarre and the flippant tone toward human relations in general, suggesting that *The Golden Ass* even borders on the sadistic (Auerbach: 60–63). At first sight, this appears to be too extreme, and one suspects that Auerbach's own need to force all ancient literature into a binary opposition with the Christian gospels may be in evidence. After all, could it not be that the satire is merely transparent to the inherent tensions and cruelties of Roman society, much as fables had communicated the cruelty of earlier society? However, underlying the "realistic" narrative of *The Golden Ass* is a continuing cynicism or disregard for the characters other than Lucius, as if to confirm the narrator in a permanent and impregnable egocentrism. Millar, for example, has too quickly seen Dickens in the pages of this novel. The passage Millar summarizes is indeed very moving—*to us*. But it is not clear at all that the narrator, or the author, or the audience were moved, for Millar does not mention what is narrated next. The narrator does not extrapolate from this pathetic scene of the marks of human misery in the backs of the slaves to the tragic potential of these people.[9] Lucius moves immediately to describe the equally pathetic condition of his fellow animals, but here draws a less than selfless conclusion:

> The dreadful condition of these poor beasts, whom I might soon be brought to resemble, so depressed me that I drooped my head like them and grieved for the degradation into which I had fallen since those far-off days when I was Lord Lucius.

What greater wisdom does Lucius gain from his position where he can observe all human and animal suffering?

> My only consolation was the unique opportunity I had of observing all that was said and done around me; because nobody showed any reserve in my presence. Homer was quite right to characterize Odysseus, whom he offered as an example of the highest wisdom and prudence, as one who had "visited many cities and come to know many different peoples" . . . . (M)y many adventures in ass-disguise enormously enlarged my experience, even if they have not taught me wisdom. It was at the mill that I picked up a story which I hope will amuse you as much as it amused me.

Lucius then recounts an uproarious tale of lust and revenge involving his owner's wife. His curiosity, which has led him on an odyssey of discovery of the human condition, has this as its proximate result: he has learned a good

---

9 Following Winkler 1985:135–79, I presume a relationship between Apuleius the author and Lucius the narrator which allows for a reflection of the former in the latter. The argument here is only strengthened by Winkler's consideration of how Apuleius enters into the persona in the text.

story about a "lady whore."[10] Is Apuleius making the ironic point here that the grand potential for observation and growth in wisdom is reduced to a good salacious tale? If we are to believe Auerbach, Apuleius and others like him are simply incapable of rising to a critical perspective concerning social strata.

Despite the fact that *Leucippe and Clitophon* by Achilles Tatius contains broad statements about slaves' cowardice (7.10; cf. Wiedemann: 62), it includes many characterizations of slaves that are much more even-handed. At 1.12 a slave is a crucial, reliable informant for the other characters. He remains nameless, and the "faithful servant" motif in itself is not unusual (Vogt: 129–45; Havelock: #120), but there are other positive depictions as well. At 1.16 two slave-lovers are introduced, Satyros and Kleio, who become real, almost equal characters to the two noble protagonists. Their roles are quite engaging, but it is the upstairs/downstairs parallelism of the two pairs of lovers which likely elevates the slaves to signifiers. The fact that parallel lovers from different classes are part and parcel of popular culture from Shakespeare to modern films as different as *Smiles of a Summer Night* and *Oklahoma!* should alert us to the fact that this construction may have been something of a popular topos then as well. It is interesting, however, that although the female slave in *Leucippe and Clitophon* runs away, this act is not treated as scandalous (2.25–27). Later, honest concern is also shown for the safety of the slave Satyros (3.5), and he is called a good friend of the protagonist (3.17). Thus the "class-bending" in this novel appears as a consistent theme, and slavery is not on the whole viewed as negatively as in Chariton. As noted above, the various dualities of positive and negative values are not all exploited equally in the different novels. Thus, whereas Achilles Tatius does allow room for the growth of slaves as characters, he portrays pirates and brigands very negatively (3.9–10, 5.7; Winkler, 1980).

The *Life of Aesop* is a popular novel told from the perspective of Aesop, who is "by chance, a slave." His experiences in this status are not wholly unlike those of Lucius in *The Golden Ass* (Winkler 1985: 276–91), told here from a point of view which satirizes the pretensions of Aesop's philosopher-owner and his class. The book does not, however, take up a true critique of slave-owning society, nor does it directly or indirectly condemn slavery. The true motive-force of the work seems to lie on other levels. Aesop is not simply a slave; he is "truly horrible to behold: worthless, pot-bellied, slant-headed, snub-nosed, hunchbacked, leather-skinned, club-footed, knock-kneed, short-armed, sleepy-eyed, bushy-lipped—in short, an absolute miscreant" (1).

---

[10] His odyssey of curiosity and story-acquisition is not without its interest from the point of view of a narrative satire; I do not wish to argue that *The Golden Ass* lacks literary merit, only that it does not seek to investigate the problem of class for an understanding of human nature. See especially Winkler 1985:165–68, 177–78.

Martin quite reasonably would take this novel to represent more of a slave's eye view of social relations, and to give a positive treatment of the slave-to-riches myth (Martin: 38-39). In this novel, unlike the others, the slave ascends not by shrewdly garnering the support of the master, but rises in spite of the master's opposition. To Martin, this novel may present the "hope among those frustrated with low-status positions, especially slaves. In any case, Aesop is a positive role model of the upwardly mobile slave" (39). Here, however, Martin misses a crucial aspect of the function of slavery within the narrative. It is not a critique of rigid class distinctions, nor an affirmation of the possibility of a slave beating the odds. It is important to recall Aesop's *double*-characterization as a slave *and a miscreant or grotesque* (Winkler, 1985: 279-91). This is constantly emphasized, in every possible way, and indicates that the force of this satire comes from the topos of the ugly or misshapen anti-social outsider who critiques the revered, heroic institutions (Nagy: 279-316; Compton). Other examples would be Thersites in the *Iliad*, or Socrates. Wherever Aesop goes, he is scorned not merely as a slave, but as a miserable specimen of humanity or subhumanity, who nevertheless ironically knows more and is more critically aware than anyone, including his famous philospher-owner. Recalling the powerful thesis of Auerbach that very little literature in the ancient, or indeed in the pre-modern world, could really view people of different classes as fundamentally equal in terms of their "tragic potential," we may question also whether *Life of Aesop* breaks from the typical mold. The appeal of its lampooning is approximately the same as that in the other satirical novels, although it does perhaps rise to a moral-philosophical concern for truth. Aesop carries through a critique of social appearances that would be consistent with Cynicism, but this is a gospel of individual philosophical perfection, not an ancient *Grapes of Wrath*.[11]

Longus's *Daphnis and Chloe* is gentler in its satire than the other novels addressed here, and it may be that "satire" is not the appropriate word. It does, however, convey an alternative world view to the ideal novels, creating a pastoral eroticism that lacks the charged tensions that arise from the containment of sexuality in the ideal novels. For our purposes, it is interesting to note that the alternative world view includes a classless society. Only with the coming of urban dwellers from the outside do we encounter slaves (2.12).

Having surveyed a number of ideal and satirical novels, we must pause to note a very peculiar characteristic of the latter category. Relative to the ideal novels, which presuppose a very rigid hierarchy of classes, the satirical

---

[11] Hopkins (21–22) correctly notes the probable function of aristocratic release in Aesop, but he is perhaps too one-dimensional (25) in emphasizing that Aesop is punished for his cleverness (true as that may be). Aesop's death is rightly seen by Nagy (279–316) as part of a cultic legend that will elevate Aesop to the category of cult-hero. The ignominious death is a necessary part of this process. See also Wills 1997:22–50.

novels press an alternative viewpoint. To one extent or another, they all enter into and take on the perspective of the slave. *Satyricon* explores the world of slaves and freedmen, confirming, to be sure, the upper-class perspective that the slave and freedmen class is base. *The Golden Ass* allows the reader, through the eyes of Lucius, to see the entire world through the eyes of a donkey, which levels all social distinctions. *Life of Aesop* is told through the slave's eyes, and a clever and successful slave at that. Achilles Tatius recounts the adventures of two sets of lovers, one free—customary in the ideal novel—and one slave—not customary at all. *Daphnis and Chloe* depicts a classless pastoral society. Although in each case I argued that the "revolution" was incomplete and that the perspective remained class-bound, the correlation of satirical novels with an investigation of life from the slave's point of view is very strong. It is a generic characteristic of the anti-genre "satirical novel."

Equally remarkable is the correlation of most of the satirical novels with negative views toward women. In the satirical novels mentioned, women are not a protected species of chaste heroines, but are more often sex-starved vixens. Even Achilles Tatius's *Leucippe and Clitophon*, which retains more of the trappings of the ideal novel, descends into a pornographic objectifying of women (and men) as sex objects (2.35–38), and remains the least convincing of the five main Greek novels regarding the central romance plotline. What we see in the satirical novels is not a simplistic exchange of perspectives, affirming slaves while denigrating women, but a more subtle satirical strategy. Class restrictions become muddled or overturned, allowing the fantasy of exploring the world from a slave's perspective, but at the same time women lose ground as a *protected* gender because it is *chastity* which is rejected. The positive values of class and chastity are dashed in this world turned upside down, an entertaining premise indeed for those who are kicking at the goads of a restrictive Roman social order. What ideal novels communicate is the wish-fulfillment of transcendence of all that slavery (or pirates, or prison, or illicit lust) stand for. The satirical novels engage the reader's blunt realization that we exist in a messy world that cannot be redeemed or transcended.[12] The "sphere" of slavery is generally just as messy, demeaning, and degrading in the satirical novel, but the reader enters into it willingly, through a sort of compulsive fascination.

Slavery in Jewish Novels

A number of Jewish writings from the Greco-Roman period can also be considered novels, although the basic plot complication of the separation of

---

[12] Again, the parallel to the world view of gnosticism should not be overlooked.

two lovers is lacking. The Jewish novels can be divided into novels proper (Greek Esther, Greek Daniel, Tobit, Judith, and *Joseph and Asenath*) and historical novels (*Tobiad Romance* and *Royal Family of Adiabene* from Josephus' *Antiquities* and 3 Maccabees; see Wills, 1994, 1995). The Jewish novels do not utilize slavery itself as a threat to the protagonists, a symbol of abject degradation, as do the Greek novels, but represent individual slaves in much the same way as do the ideal novels: slaves are in general faithful servants of the protagonists. Their will is identified with that of their masters. The Book of Esther in the Hebrew Bible describes the court servants who wait on Esther, but does not individualize them by separating them from the depiction of the court pomp and wealth, nor is there a need to. Esther is in the court, but not of the court, and the slaves pertain to the court as accoutrements. In the Apocryphal Additions to Esther, her maidservants also take on a more specific function: they bear her train and allow Esther a greater refinement as a true lady than is the case in Hebrew Esther. At the moment she enters in before the awesome King Artaxerxes, she faints, and the maidservants are there to catch her. The greater the distance between a lady and the untidiness of the everyday world, the more necessary are slaves to define the dualistic separation.

The same is true in Judith, but more specified. There is one faithful maidservant who accompanies Judith in her descent into threatened sexual improprieties and murder. This loyal servant has, in fact, been seen very positively by some scholars, an evidence of Judith's greater humanity in reaching beyond her class to create a special women's relationship. Further, Judith at the end of the book frees this maidservant and all of her other slaves. Still, the slaves are never described as characters; the maidservant is never named, and never acts independently of her mistress (Wills, 1995: 151; Glancy). Like the maidservants in Greek Esther, she serves to enhance Judith's graciousness. Tobit depicts slaves negatively in the narrative, but to the same end. At 3:7–9 the heroine, Sarah, despondent because each of her fiancés has died on their wedding night, is further humiliated by being reproached by her maidservant. The unusual passage clearly indicates the depth of her fall, since her maidservant can sum up public scorn for her, and make her feel it all the more sharply. Sarah immediately afterward prays for death.

The Jewish novel which most closely approximates the Greek ideal novel is *Joseph and Aseneth*, where a love-match of Joseph and the Egyptian woman Aseneth supplies the basic premise of the plot developments which follow. Here slaves appear in greater number, functioning much as they do in Greek Esther: to define in relief the greater purity and separation of the heroine. What is new here is the mystical overtone of the identity which they help to define in the lady:

> And seven virgins ... were waiting on Aseneth, and they were all of the same age, born in one night with Aseneth, and she loved them very much. And they were very beautiful, like the stars of heaven, and no man ever conversed with them, not even a male child. (2.6)

The lady/slave distinction, in its operation, is not unlike the sharper definition of the levels of purity that were introduced into the sacred precincts of the temple in the post-exilic period. Special, unapproachable, almost numinous qualities in the lady are being marked off by increasing the distance from the mundane world by the intermediation of slaves. This pushes to a further extreme Patterson's observation that owning a slave raises one's humanity by degrading another's. The story continues by depicting a split among the brothers of Joseph: those born of the maidservants Bilhah and Zilpah plot his death; those born of the free matriarchs Rachel and Leah remain loyal to him. The distinction in the evaluation of human character could hardly be more sharply drawn.

One Jewish historical novel is very illuminating on the issue of slavery. The so-called *Tobiad Romance* (preserved only in Josephus, *Ant.* 12.154–236) is a large fragment of a romanticized history of the Tobiad family, a wealthy dynasty of Jewish entrepreneurs (Wills, 1994, 1995). It probably dates from about 200 BCE. The novel fragment is a series of adventures of two members of that family as they establish themselves as the chief traders between Jerusalem, Samaria, and the Ptolemaic king. Their ability to rise from relative poverty (probably not true—the family was already established) to chief financiers is glorified, and told with a sense of bravado. The perspective of the wealthy class is reflected as a result, but one senses that it is the overcompensation of an entrepreneurial, rather than truly aristocratic class that motivates the narrative. Strongly emphasized is the heroes' natural *eutrapelia* (roughly equivalent to Latin *urbanitas*), contrasted with the rustic boorishness of their kinsmen.

This novel does not share the domestic values of the ideal novels, but contains interesting parallels to *Apollonius King of Tyre*. They both objectify slaves as a row of marionettes who are extensions, even decorations, of their masters' will. At one point in the *Tobiad Romance*, Hyrcanus ceremoniously bestows upon King Ptolemy a hundred male and female slaves, each bearing a talent of gold (*Ant.* 12.209, 217). The sense of vertical graduation, especially regarding the system of patron/client relationships (cemented through gifts) is very strong in *Tobiad Romance*, defined here by the degradation of slaves. An interesting parallel can also be drawn with *Satyricon*, where the same entrepreneurial spirit is portrayed. In *Satyricon*, or course, this spirit, displayed by social-climbers, is satirized mercilessly in the person of Trimalchio, the rich freedman. There such an act of ostentatious abundance would only reveal the crassness of the person orchestrating it, but in *Tobiad Romance*, the parade of slaves as gifts is a diplomatic success, proving Hyrcanus's inherent grace and munificence.

Conclusion

The Greek and Roman novels of antiquity can be divided into two categories, ideal and satirical, depending upon whether they idealize the social relations of the protagonists, or treat them from the more critical perspective of satire. The ideal novels reinforce rigid, hierarchical social categories by the utilization of a series of dualities: free/slave, rich/poor, Greek/barbarian, citizen/pirate, pure love/illicit lust, and so on. The tension and conflict in the narrative derives from the threat of degradation of the romantic protagonists, the threat of being subjected to the inferior element in each dyad. The dyadic, hierarchical relationship of masters and slaves must be seen in this context, but it is significant that the ideal novels generally bring slavery to the fore as one of the two principal obsessions: sex and class. These remain the principal obsessions in the satirical novels as well; the difference between the ideal and satirical novels is not whether these two issues will be central— they are in both cases—but whether they will be introduced in an earnest manner as the rigid hierarchical codes of the author and audience, or from a satirical perspective, to be dissolved and overturned. The satirical novels evidently provided an experience of release for the reader, a repudiation of chastity and heterosexual romantic love on one hand, and a temporary exploration of the world from the perspective of slaves on the other. In the readers' experience, this exploration did not lead to any fundamental revision of attitudes about the human potential of the lower classes, but merely reinforced the belief that one is fortunate to be stationed above them. In other words, the upper classes are temporarily brought down, the lower classes are not raised up.

The Jewish novels do not posit as the main plot complication the threat of the defilement of the aristocratic couple, but rather, the threat of destruction for a pious Jew or a group of Jews. Slavery still figures, either as a means of defining the heroine's "ritual separation" from the rest of the world (in the cases of Greek Esther, Judith, and *Joseph and Aseneth*), as the taint of depravity (the sons of the maidservants in *Joseph and Aseneth*), or as evidence of the hero's munificent giving in *Tobiad Romance*. Despite the differences in plot, the Jewish novels convey some of the same depictions and evaluations of slaves as do the Greek novels. Slavery is not as constant a theme in the Jewish novels, but it still constitutes a crucial element of the symbolic universe here as well, and is introduced in a way that is equally dualistic and negative.

Works Consulted

1. Ancient Novels

Life of Aesop
    1997   "Appendix: English Translation of the *Life of Aesop*." Pp. 180–215 in Lawrence M. Wills, *The Quest of the Historical Gospel: Mark, John and the Origins of the Gospel Genre*. London/New York: Routledge.

Apuleius
    1951   *The Golden Ass*. Trans. Robert Graves. New York: Farrar, Straus & Giroux.

Joseph and Aseneth
    1985   "Joseph and Asenath." Trans. C. Burchard. *OTP* 2.177–247.

Petronius
    1959   *The Satyricon*. Trans. William Arrowsmith. New York: Mentor.

2. Secondary Literature

Auerbach, Erich
    1957   *Mimesis: The Representation of Reality in Western Literature*. Princeton: Princeton University Press.

Comito, Terry
    1975   "Exile and Return in the Greek Romances." *Arion* (new series) 2:58–80.

Compton, Todd
    1990   "The Trial of the Satirist: Poetic *Vitae* (Aesop, Archilochus, Homer) as Background for Plato's *Apology*." *American Journal of Philology* 111: 330–47.

Daly, Lloyd
    1961   *Aesop Without Morals*. New York: Yoseloff.

Dumont, Louis
    1980   *Homo hierarchicus: The Caste System and Its Implications*. Rev ed. Chicago: University of Chicago Press.

Finley, M. I.
    1980   *Ancient Slavery and Modern Ideology*. Harmondsworth: Penguin.

Flesher, Paul Virgil McCracken
    1988   *Oxen, Women, or Citizens? Slaves in the System of the Mishnah*. Atlanta: Scholars Press.

Fowler, Barbara Hughes
    1989   *The Hellenistic Aesthetic*. Madison: University of Wisconsin Press.

Garnsey, Peter
    1970   *Social Status and Legal Privilege in the Roman Empire*. Oxford: Oxford University Press.

Glancy, Jennifer A.
  1996   "The Mistress-Slave Dialectic: Paradoxes of Slavery in Three LXX Narratives." *JSOT* 72:71–87.

Havelock, Christine Mitchell
  n.d.   *Hellenistic Art*. Greenwich, Conn.: New York Graphic Society.

Hopkins, Keith
  1993   "Novel Evidence for Roman Slavery." *Past and Present* 138:3–27.

MacQueen, Bruce D.
  1990   *Myth, Rhetoric, and Fiction: A Reading of Longus's "Daphnis and Chloe."* Lincoln: University of Nebraska Press.

Martin, Dale B.
  1990   *Slavery as Salvation: The Metaphor of Slavery in Pauline Christianity*. New Haven: Yale University Press.

McKeon, Michael
  1987   *The Origins of the English Novel* 1600–1740. Baltimore: Johns Hopkins University Press.

Millar, Fergus
  1981   "The World of *The Golden Ass*." *Journal of Roman Studies* 71:63–75.

Nagy, Gregory
  1979   *Best of the Achaeans*. Baltimore: Johns Hopkins University Press.

Patterson, Orlando
  1982   *Slavery and Social Death: A Comparative Study*. Cambridge: Harvard University Press.

Reardon, B. P.
  1994   "Achilles Tatius and Ego-Narrative." Pp. 80–96 in *Greek Fiction: The Greek Novel in Context*. Ed. J. R. Morgan and Richard Stoneman. London/New York: Routledge.

Sandy, Gerald N.
  1989   "A Phoenician Story." Pp. 809–12 in *Collected Ancient Greek Novels*. Ed. B. P. Reardon. Berkeley: University of California Press.

Schüssler Fiorenza, Elisabeth
  1992   *But She Said: Feminist Practices of Biblical Interpretation*. Boston: Beacon.

Tatum, James, and Vernazza, Gail M., eds.
  1990   *The Ancient Novel: Classical Paradigms and Modern Perspectives*. Hanover: International Conference on the Ancient Novel.

Uhlenbrock, Jaimee P.
  1990   *The Coroplast's Art: Greek Terracottas of the Hellenistic World*. New Paltz: College of New Paltz/New Rochelle: Caratzas.

Vogt, Joseph
    1975   *Ancient Slavery and the Ideal of Man*. Cambridge: Harvard University Press.

Weaver, R. P. C.
    1974   "Social Mobility in the Early Roman Empire: The Evidence of the Imperial Freedmen and Slaves." Pp. 121–40 in *Studies in Ancient Society*. Ed. M. I. Finley. London: Routledge.

Wegner, Judith Romney
    1988   *Chattel or Person? The Status of Women in the Mishnah*. New York/Oxford: Oxford University Press.

Wiedemann, Thomas
    1981   *Greek and Roman Slavery*. Baltimore: Johns Hopkins University Press.

Wills, Lawrence M.
    1994   "The Jewish Novellas." Pp. 223–38 in *Greek Fiction: The Greek Novel in Context*. Ed. J. R. Morgan and Richard Stoneman. London/New York: Routledge.

    1995   *The Jewish Novel in the Ancient World*. Ithaca: Cornell University Press.

    1997   *The Quest of the Historical Gospel: Mark, John, and the Origins of the Gospel Genre*. London/New York: Routledge.

Winkler, John J.
    1980   "Lollianus and the Desperadoes." *Journal of Hellenic Studies* 100:155–81.

Winkler, John J.
    1985   *Auctor & Actor: A Narratological Reading of Apuleius' Golden Ass*. Berkeley: University of California Press.

Zagagi, Netta
    1980   *Tradition and Originality in Plautus*. Göttingen: Vandenhoeck & Ruprecht.

SLAVE RESISTANCE IN CLASSICAL ANTIQUITY

Allen Dwight Callahan
Harvard University

Richard A. Horsley
University of Massachusetts Boston

ABSTRACT

New Testament scholars, following classical historians, have previously cited the relative paucity of slave rebellions in antiquity as reason to conclude that ancient Greek and Roman slavery was benign and the enslaved relatively content with their lot. More recent studies of the evidence from antiquity question such reasoning as wishful thinking. Comparative studies of slavery and slave resistance in the New World, moreover, have led historians of ancient slavery to a far more subtle sense of just how regularly, persistently, and sometimes extensively ancient slaves resisted and rebelled against the system that held them in bondage. This cross-cultural essay, drawing on James C. Scott's sensitivity to the slaves' own "hidden transcript," argues that slave resistance was far more serious and subtle than previously allowed, which has clear implications for how we read statements on slaves in Paul's letters.

> Quot servi, tot hostes.
> Seneca

> "If you roast me today, you cannot roast me tomorrow."
> Tony, a slave sentenced to be burned alive
> for his part in the 1675 slave revolt
> in Barbados

Slave resistance in Greek and Roman antiquity requires special treatment. It has been underestimated and downplayed by classical historians eager to defend the glorious ancient sources of modern humanism. Underestimated ancient slave resistance has then been used as a basis for arguing that ancient slavery was benign and/or that ancient slaves were content with their lot. Classical literature, which reflects the attitudes of slave-owners rather than slaves, finally, has been indefensibly used to argue for the psychology of those supposedly contented slaves. On the bases of (1) the analogy that Finley pioneered between the resistance of modern American slaves and that of slaves in antiquity, and (2) Patterson's theory of slavery as natal alienation, supplemented with (3) James C. Scott's recent reflections on hidden forms of resistance, a rather different picture of ancient slaves' resistance to their circumstances is now possible.

Developing a More Subtle Approach

Westermann was hardly unique in his argument that the absence of serious slave revolts in classical Greece was "a significant commentary on the generally mild treatment of slaves" (18; cf. Vogt). As noted at the outset of Horsley's article above ("Slave Systems . . ."), New Testament scholars picked up the corresponding generalization among classics scholars about slavery in the early Roman empire: the absence of slave revolts and other forms of resistance attests their degree of contentment and the mildness of their condition. Such simplistic historical reasoning has been coupled with, and is made possible by, ignoring the brutality of ancient Greek and Roman slavery and by interpreting facets of ancient Roman slavery such as the *peculium* and manumission only as mitigating factors rather than also as devices that made the slave system work (again, see Horsley's "Slave Systems . . ."). Such classical historiography of ancient slavery also tends to project simplistic psychological and behavioral alternatives onto the slaves themselves, despite the fact that extant ancient literature and inscriptions provide virtually no direct evidence whatever for the mentality of ancient slaves.

As Finley complained, however, "rigid behavioral alternatives have never existed in the history of slavery, and the stress on them [in historiography] stultifies any inquiry" (116). What is necessary, first of all, is to recognize that slaves have been placed into a humanly intolerable situation, one in which serious resistance would be simply suicidal. The vast majority of the enslaved seek some means of survival midst their intolerable dehumanizing situation. And that requires historians to summon some sense of ambiguity, ambivalence, and subtlety. The same masters could be both indulgent and cruel. The same slaves could be both obedient—"faithful"—and (potential) pilferers or fugitives. Both obedience and flight are means of survival. To deal with the ambivalence of the slave situation (and psychology) and to bring some subtlety into classical historiography of slavery, Finley drew analogies from the lively debate focused on slave resistance in modern America: "Brutally deracinated human beings seeking new ties, new psychological attachments, not infrequently turn to those in whose power they find themselves, in the case of slaves to their masters" (Finley: 104; cf. Patterson, 1970: 415). In a flawed and controversial work, Stanley Elkins had drawn an analogy between African-American slaves and Jews incarcerated in Nazi concentration camps. But the slaves were hardly so one-dimensional as Elkins suggested in their "personality-type." "Sambos" might also turn out to be rebels (Stampp, 1971:367–92). Slaves' attitudes have usually been ambivalent in one way or another, and their behavior has ranged from (at least ostensibly) obedient to intransigent to resistant (Frederickson and Lasch). At least a few classics scholars have pursued Finley's suggestion that historians of ancient Greek and Roman slavery attend to the vigorous debates during the 1960s and 1970s among historians of slave resistance in America (Cartledge; Bradley, 1989).

Orlando Patterson's theory of slavery as "natal alienation," which was designed to understand the condition into which slaves were placed, also serves to illuminate slave resistance. Slaves were violently removed from their families and communities of origin and forced into an alien household or *familia*. The Helots, subject to Sparta, who were kept in their native families and communities, were able to organize revolts; the atomized and more completely deracinated slaves in Athens were not (Garlan: 177–81). In ancient Greece and Rome, as advised in classical literature, slave masters purposely bought slaves of various origins precisely in order to "divide and conquer" once more as they forced their new slaves into a process of "resocialization."

This trick was used in the slave regimes of the New World to frustrate the solidarity of African slaves. The planters of Barbados, for example, purposely bought slaves from different West African regions and made of them mixed gangs so that tribal and language differences would impede conspiracies (Segal: 128–29). Slaves from Angola revolted against the French in Guadeloupe in 1656; they were not joined by other slaves on the island because the other slaves were not Angolans. After fifteen days of fighting the Angolans were finally subdued, their two leaders quartered, and the rest flogged, hanged, or torn to pieces alive (Segal: 128). The Cuban slave Estéban Montejo testified that masters shuffled slaves between plantations to foil disruptive slave rivalries and conspiracies of escape as well: "Many brawls were avoided because the masters changed the slaves around. They kept them divided among themselves to prevent a rash of escapes. That was why slaves of different plantations never got together" (Montejo: 24).

In his reflection on decades of his own study of peasant and other subordinates' resistance to the forms of their domination, James C. Scott has recently laid out a theory of "domination and the arts of resistance" that has crucial implications for historical investigation of slavery. Scott's reflections can be used to supplement Patterson's theory of slavery and to draw out its implications for understanding slave resistance. His starting point is the recognition that "powerless groups have ... a self-interest in conspiring to reinforce hegemonic appearances" (1990:xii). Those subject to elaborate and systematic forms of political-economic subordination, such as slaves, must engage in public performance in order to manage the impressions of those with power over them. Since historical sources such as texts, particularly attesting the voices of the powerless themselves, are so scarce, it is not surprising that he takes many of his illustrations from slave narratives from the U. S. South. For example, from the narrative of Lunsford Lane, published in 1848: "In every way I wore as much as possible the aspect of slavery.... I had never appeared to be even so intelligent as I really was. This all colored at the south, free and slaves, find it particularly necessary for their own comfort and safety to observe" (quoted in Scott, 1990:2). For slaves such as Lunsford Lane, it was "not just a question of masking one's feelings and producing the correct speech acts and gestures in their place. Rather it [was] often a question of controlling what would be a natural impulse to rage, insult, anger, and the violence that such feelings prompt.... The cruelest result of human bondage is that it transforms the assertion of personal dignity into a mortal risk" (Scott, 1990:37). Of course, in the same way as "subordination requires a credible performance of humility and deference, so domination seems to require a credible performance of haughtiness and mastery" (Scott, 1990:11). The latter is abundantly illustrated by ancient Roman writers' advice to slave-owners on how to appear and behave toward their slaves (some cited in the preceding essay above).

Since the dominant sense that their slaves' or serfs' deference and consent seem to be less than sincere, a "performance," they develop the view that their subordinates are "deceitful, shamming, and lying by nature" (Scott, 1990:3). The master class attributes slave behavior not to the effect of coercive power arbitrarily exercised, but to inborn character (Scott, 1990:35). In Aristotle's perverse "logic," some people were slaves *by nature*. Or in a Roman stereotype, Syrians, Jews, and other Asiatics were particularly well-suited for slavery. Moreover, since the dominant control the power relations, the resulting "public transcript" of their relations with their slaves or serfs effectively "scripts" social relations the way they would have them, including their own self-portrait as a higher type of humanity and their subordinates as a lesser breed or even sub-human. One important effect of this situation over time is that the faces of those obliged by domination to act a mask will grow to fit that mask, as the practice of subordination in effect produces its own legitimacy (Scott, 1990:10). But the antipode of this master-slave dialectic is equally true: the mask of slaveholder ideology grows to fit the face of the slave's defensive opacity and resignation.

Patterson has shown that the Sambo, and its ancient analogue in the Roman stereotype of the *graeculus* or Greek slave, is but an ideological projection onto the dishonored person of the slave, "no more realistic a description of how slaves thought and behaved than was the inflated conception of honor and sense of freedom an accurate description of their masters" (Patterson, 1982:96). It is a self-deception on the part of the master class, which slaves themselves played to their advantage.

> The slaveholder retaliated ideologically by stereotyping the slave as a lying, cowardly, lazy buffoon devoid of courage and manliness: the slave became, in the holder's mind, the "Graeculus" of ancient Rome, . . . the Sambo of the U.S. South. . . . The slave retaliated not only existentially, by refusing to be among his fellow slaves the degraded creature he was made out to be, but also directly on the battlefront of the political psychology of his retaliation with the slaveholder. He fed the parasite's timocratic character with the pretense that he was what he was supposed to be. Still, in his very pretense there was a kind of victory. He served while concealing his soul and fooling the parasite. As the Jamaican slaves put it in their favorite proverb, "Play fool to catch wise" (Patterson, 1982:338).

An effect of slave behavior that artfully reinforced the masters' stereotyped view of them as lazy or shiftless may well have been lowered expectations for their productivity, and a result of their good "performance" may well have been better treatment by their masters in terms of food allowance and demands (Scott, 1990:34).

The implications for historical investigation are not far to seek. If we rely on the usual sources, particularly ancient texts which, expressing the view of the dominant slave owners, form the "public transcript," we have only a superficial and one-dimensional view of historical social relations and behavior. Most previous studies of ancient Greek and Roman slavery, for example, as noted above, finding little evidence of slave resistance, take this to means that slaves were basically content with their lot, which must not have been particularly dehumanizing. The "public transcript" of Greek and Roman literature and inscriptions by its very character, however, is both ignorant of the "hidden transcript" of what the slaves were communicating among themselves when "off-stage," out of the hearing of their masters, and interested in denying, obscuring or distorting indications of resistance among the slaves—although it has expressions of paranoia aplenty about potential and imagined forms of insubordination and resistance.

Recognition that nearly all of our written sources express the "public transcript" and that there must have been also both a "hidden transcript" and hidden forms of resistance complicates the task of the historical investigator. To explain the incidence of publicly overt forms of resistance and why ancient slaves appeared to accept the inevitability of their slavery, we must search more critically for the ways in which slaves were coerced and/or socialized into accepting a view of their interests as propagated from above. In examining the "public transcript" of deference and consent, "how can we estimate the impact of power relations on action when the exercise of power is nearly constant?"—which it was in the conditions of ancient Greek and Roman chattel slavery. As noted in the essay on slave systems, domination took the forms of arbitrary whipping, sexual violation, and regular systematic humiliation and degradation. Those born into slavery would have been "socialized by their parents in the rituals of homage that [would] keep them from harm," a cruel paradox for slave mothers anxious to keep their children safe and by their side (Scott, 1990:24). Nevertheless, slaves' performance to please does not necessarily imply internalization of hegemony (Scott, 1990:85). "The goal of slaves . . . is precisely to escape detection; to the extent that they achieve their goal, such activities do not appear in the archives" (Scott, 1990:87). Compliance extracted under conditions of constant exercise of power and surveillance is unlikely to be a valid guide to slaves' "offstage" attitudes and actions. Just as subordinates such as slaves are not deceived by their own performance, there is no more reason for historians to take the performance at face value (89).

Scott has thus shown how the Sambo persona is a defensive mask donned by slaves as a matter of psychic and physical survival in the open interaction of dominant and subordinate that Scott calls the "public transcript": "At the very least, an assessment of power relations read directly off the public transcript between the powerful and the weak may portray a deference and consent that is possibly only a tactic. . . . Subordinates offer a performance of deference and consent while attempting to discern, to read, the real intentions and mood of the potentially threatening powerholder" (Scott, 1992:57). Therefore we must not read the absence of a great number of slave revolts in the early Empire as a register of slaves' contentment, even reconciliation to their bondage. All slave regimes hide the authentic sentiments of slaves from the compass of empirical scrutiny. To say that slaves were happy with their lot is to make a statement that may be criminally naïve, mendacious, or idiotic. But it is not and cannot be historical. Dissimulation makes the heart of the slave historically unverifiable until its hidden contents boil over in the heat of open warfare. Sometimes we may feel the heat, as it were, by applying a historical analysis to slavery that does not take the servile mask of the public transcript at face value. Once, in a fit of rage, the emperor Hadrian put out the eye of one of his slaves with a pen. Later the emperor offered the blinded slave anything he wanted. After a long silence, the slave asked for his eye back (Galen, *The Diseases of the Mind* 4). We do this story a disservice if we read it as illustrative of a slave's pathetic stupidity.

Given the real situation of the constant exercise of power in these highly effective forms of domination, what needs explanation is not that slave revolts were so infrequent, but that they—and the scores of plots that never came to fruition for every revolt that erupted—ever occurred at all. "How is it that subordinate groups such as [slaves] have so often believed and acted as if their situations were not inevitable when a more judicious historical reading would have concluded that it was?" (Scott, 1990:79). It would appear to be a testimony to slaves' resilient sense of personal dignity and justice, despite all appearances, and their determination to resist what appears inevitable that they have even plotted a revolt. Furthermore, since the overwhelming majority of slaves historically have had no knowledge of a social order founded on different principles and institutions than those of the dominant system to which they are subordinated, their revolts are unlikely to be revolutionary, but merely attempts to achieve personal relief from their slavery.

Scott's reflections on and analysis of subordinates' situations and the complexities of the dynamics of power relations require historians to detect hidden forms of resistance and to evaluate overt forms of resistance very differently than in previous accounts of Greek and Roman slavery. We will combine Scott's analysis with Patterson's incisive treatment of slavery in reviewing forms of slave resistance in Greco-Roman antiquity, supplementing with the kind of comparison with slave resistance in the New World that Finley pioneered.

Forms of Slave Resistance in Antiquity

Given the wide comparative material drawn on by Scott, it would be difficult to imagine that slaves in ancient Greece and the Roman empire did not engage in all the petty but pesky forms of resistance that subjected people have systematically mounted elsewhere (so also Finley: 110–11; Garlan: 193). It is likely that the ancient as well as the modern stereotype of slaves as lazy and dishonest reflects deliberate slave behavior such as working slowly or badly, pilfering crops or tools, and even sabotaging the work process or product. Historians of slavery in the U S South have gathered abundant evidence of multiple kinds of individual slaves' resistance, from the breaking of tools to work-slowdowns and theft to violent attacks against their masters (e.g., Stampp, 1956:86–140). Numerous examples of slave theft and violence and/or slave-masters' acute anxiety about it could be collected from the Greek and Latin "classics." The epitaph of Demetrius son of Pankrates from second century BC. Caria is telling testimony to both the reality and the cost of slave resistance: "overcome by draughts of the nectar of Bromios at a banquet, slaughtered at the hands of a slave and consumed in a great fire together with the house.... But as for the one who committed such actions, my fellow citizens crucified him alive, leaving him as prey for the beasts and birds" (in Robert and Robert: 259–63, n65).

A far more serious form of resistance was flight, running away. *Drapetēs* in ancient Greek meant specifically a "runaway" *slave*. In the fourth century BCE Antiphanes wrote a comedy entitled "The Slave-catcher" (*ho drapetagōgos;* in Athenaeus 4.161d), suggesting a typical phenomenon in the society. In Athens alone 20,000 slaves seized the opportunity of the Peloponnesian War to flee their servitude (Thucydides 7.27.5). Latin literature is virtually obsessed with fugitive slaves. In Plautus' plays, one of which was entitled *Fugitivi* and another *Captivi*, slaves are clearly characterized as likely to run away.

Chains and shackles simply make them all the more eager to escape. And first century Roman audiences are expected to understand that slaves would want to return to their country of origin as a matter of course (Bradley, 1989:36, n29). Most ancient slaves had the great advantage over African-American slaves of having roughly the same physical characteristics as the free population—except for obvious marks of previous beatings—so that they could easily merge with the rest of the population once they ran away.

Slave masters and the state devised various means to deal with this ubiquitous and persistent problem, which only escalated during times of social unrest or civil war. Antimenes of Rhodes, a contemporary of Alexander the Great, organized the first known insurance system backed by the state precisely to protect slaveowners against economic losses due to slaves running away, particularly during war (Pseudo-Aristotle, *Oeconomica* 2.2.34b). A large amount had to be paid out in premiums! But slaves who ran away in wartime usually did not get very far, since victors viewed them like any other property taken from the enemy as booty, and peace treaties usually provided for the return of fugitives (Garlan: 195). Even in peace-time city-states had treaties for the specific purpose of extraditing fugitive slaves, which suggests how serious a problem they posed for the slaveowners. Such treaties, for example between the Anatolian cities of Miletus and Heraclea of Latmos, involved "recovery fees" to be paid by the slave-owners and indicate that cities maintained "mountain guards" on their borders (Garlan: 196–97). Apprehended fugitives were subjected to escalated brutality and dehumanization. "They could expect a beating and chains and in many cases also to be branded or tattooed on the forehead with a word or symbol which made their degradation publicly known" (Garlan: 197).

From Roman times, archaeologists have unearthed slave collars, such as the one with the inscription: "I have escaped; arrest me; take me back to my master Zonimus and you will be rewarded with a gold piece" (*CIL* 15.7194). Professional "slave-catchers" (*fugitivarii*), who worked through "the keepers of less reputable inns, skippers engaged in contraband traffic, slave-dealers, actors, panders, gladiators and suchlike people" became a standard feature of Roman society from the late Republic on (Daube). Sellers of slaves were required to inform the prospective buyers of any tendency toward truancy. While it was not particularly effective in apprehending fugitives, the Roman state enacted increasingly ruthless laws of search and seizure (Bellen: Part I). Government officials boasted of their record in this matter that was all-important for an economic system based on slavery. A Senator recorded in an inscription that while serving as Praetor in Sicily he had captured and returned to their owners 917 fugitive slaves (Bradley, 1989:37 n30). Augustus himself boasted in his *Res Gestae* (25) that after the Civil War he had returned some 30,000 slaves to their masters for punishment (neglecting to mention that he had simply crucified an additional 6,000 for whom no master could be found, Dio 49.12.5).

Cicero's correspondence provides no less than three fascinating cases of successful flight from slavery, and some telling commentary on both the escapes and slave-masters' obsession with recapturing such fugitives through their network of friends and contacts in far-flung regions of the nascent empire. In 59 BCE he wrote to his brother Quintus, then Proconsul of Asia, about their friend Aesopus' slave Licinus, who had run away and posed as a free man in Athens with Patro the Epicurean. Later Plato of Sardis, having discovered that he was a runaway while on a visit to Athens, arrested him and placed him in custody in Ephesus. Quintus was supposed to find him in Ephesus and return him to Rome; for although he viewed the runaway as a worthless good-for-nothing, Aesopus was acutely distressed by his audacity in running away (Cicero, *Magistrates of the Roman Republic* 2.191; *Letters to Quintus* 2.14). While Cicero himself was Proconsul in Cilicia in 51 BCE he was asked by his friend T. Pomponius Atticus, known for using only homebred slaves (*vernae*), to search for his slave Amianus, who had fled all the way to the Taurus mountains in southern Asia Minor and taken refuge with a local chieftan named Moeragenes (Cicero, *Magistrates* . . . 2.243, 251–52; *Letters to Atticus* 108.3; 115.13). A few years later, in 46 BCE, Cicero requested the help of P. Sulpicius Rufus, a Roman official in Illyricum, in locating his fugitive "pilfering" slave librarian, Dionysius, who had told Cicero's friend M. Bolanus at Narona (in Illyricum) that his master had freed him. Like his friend Aesopus, Cicero did not place much value on the loss of a slave, but was "intensely vexed" that the slave had run away and wanted the satisfaction of recapturing him (Cicero, *Letters to his Friends* 212; Bradley, 1989: 32–33). Dionysius, however, had taken refuge among the tribe of the Vardaei along the Dalmatian coast that Rome had not yet completely controlled. Cicero's correspondence in these cases of "fugitive slaves" shows that slave-masters were obsessed with recapturing their runaways, as well as how they attempted to work through their extensive network of friends, who included Roman provincial officers, to do so. It also reveals how enterprising slaves could gain their freedom by fleeing to a distant area less under Roman control or attempting to disappear into the anonymity of a large city.

Runaway slaves would also often have joined or formed bands of brigands—an endemic phenomenon in agrarian societies—in the mountains and other remote areas of Italy or the provinces (Shaw). Those bands that became fairly large apparently resembled the maroons, communities of runaway slaves that formed in inaccessible areas in Jamaica and Brazil virtually from the beginning of slavery there. The governors of Jamaica continuously attempted to suppress the maroons with military action until, in 1739, a governor finally signed a fifteen point treaty with the maroon leader Captain

Cudjoe, recognizing their (semi-) independence (Patterson, 1970). A story in Athenaeus 6.6265d–266e, quoted from the earlier Nymphodorus of Syracuse, about a community of fugitive slaves from Chios bears remarkable resemblance to the historically well-attested maroons of Jamaica.

> The Chians' slaves ran away . . . into the mountains, where they gathered in large numbers and did a lot of damage to the country estates. The island is rough and covered with trees. . . . A certain slave [named Drimacus], a brave man who had a lot of luck when it came to fighting, led the runaways in the same way as a king leads an army. After the Chians had organised many expeditions against him which failed to achieve anything, . . . they made a treaty with him.

In the treaty Drimacus supposedly agreed to limit his raids on the storehouses of the estates and to welcome into his community only those fugitive slaves who made a credible case of having been treated intolerably. Despite their treaty with Drimacus, however, the Chians still put a price on his head and attempted to suppress his community of fugitives (see further Garlan: 181–82; Bradley, 1989:38–40). That this story was cited and recited for centuries, from Nymphodorus to Athenaeus, suggests that it resonated with audiences, i.e. that there may have been many such semi-independent communities of fugitive slaves in Greek and Roman antiquity. Indeed, Suetonius mentions that on his way to take up the governorship of Macedonia in 60 BCE, C. Octavius, the father of Augustus, attacked "a band of *fugitivi*, refugees from the revolts led by Spartacus and Cataline, who held the country about Thurii" (Suetonius, *Augustus* 3.1 [Loeb]; cf 7:1).

This pattern of resistance—that of fugitives slaves who repaired to inaccessible wilds, elected their own leaders, sustained themselves by carrying out raids on landed estates, and negotiated treaties with state armies that found them indomitable—is further illuminated by the maroon and quilombo bands of runaway slaves in the New World. In 1609 Spanish colonial authorities signed a treaty that granted amnesty and freedom to over one hundred marauding slaves in the Vera Cruz region of Mexico. After struggling intermittently with guerilla slave resistance in Surinam, the Dutch sued for peace and negotiated a treaty with rebel leaders in 1749. Devastating guerilla warfare continued until a general treaty was signed in 1762. The uneasy peace finally erupted in the largest slave revolt to date one year later (Segal: 96–97) Similar renegade communities of slaves troubled slave regimes throughout the Carribean in the eighteenth century. Perhaps the most trenchant guerilla resistance was encountered in Jamaica: its size, mountainous terrain, and lush were especially congenial to the formation of maroon colonies, which formed spontaneously after slaves fled to the hills following the British conquest of the erstwhile Spanish masters in 1655 (Segal: 131). The Maroons would wage full-scale war with the Britain in 1728, the First Maroon

War, and again, the Second Maroon War, in 1795. These treaties regularly included provisions for freedom and local autonomy in return for pledges not to raid estates and return future runaways. With the Maroons, however, we come to a form of slave resistance that could be called slave revolts.

SLAVE REVOLTS

On occasion, through much of Greek and Roman antiquity, these local bands of fugitive slaves escalated into what would then or now be classified as slave-revolts. Contrary to previous scholarly accounts that downplay the significance of slave revolts in antiquity, what is surprising is not the infrequency of such revolts, but that slaves were able to generate such widespread collective action at all. Despite the frequently desperate conditions of the peasantry in agrarian societies, peasants who remain organized in numerous local village communities are rarely able to mount widespread or sustained revolts. By definition, (except for the Helots subject to Sparta, on whose revolts see Garlan:176–80) slaves in the political-economic systems of Greek and Roman antiquity, like those in the modern Americas, had been removed from their supporting communities of origin and thrown into smaller or larger households in which they may not have been able even to communicate in the same language and in which they were under virtually constant surveillance. Communication and organization even within households, let alone across and among households, would have been difficult in the extreme. Thus it is not surprising that they so seldom generated revolts, but that they were able to make common cause at all. Even more astounding is that of the only four massive slave revolts in history that assumed the scale of a war, with thousands of armed men on both sides and pitched battles between armies, sieges, and occupation of cities, three occurred in Sicily and Italy between 140 and 70 BCE (the other in Haiti, in close connection with the French Revolution).

A late compiler, Polynaeus (*Strategems* 1.43.1) mentions a slave rebellion at Syracuse around 413–15 BCE, during the Athenian expedition there, put down when the leader, Sosistratus, was duped into trusting offers of negotiated settlement. Some would classify the case of the rebel slaves of Chios led by Drimacus in the third century BCE as a revolt (Garlan: 180–83; Cartledge). In the late second century slave revolts broke out at Athens, Delos, and other places in Greece (Diodorus 34.2.19), apparently at news of the success of the first massive slave revolt in Sicily in 134 BCE (discussed below). Again in response to the second great slave revolt in Sicily in 104–100, Athenian slaves rose in revolt: "Most of these Athenian slaves, counted in myriads, worked in the mines as prisoners. Poseidonius the philosopher says that they revolted, murdered the superintendants of the mines, seized the hill of Sunium and for a long time plundered Attica" (Athenaeus 6.272e–f). Large numbers of slaves were also apparently involved in wider revolts in Macedonia in mid-second century BCE and in Pergamum somewhat later (see Garlan's critical discussion: 184–91).

Extant Latin literature attests several slave revolts or widespread conspiracies in the centuries prior to the massive "slave wars," as the Roman slave system steadily grew in scope and severity. In the five attested prior to 200 BCE, the one in 419 involved an attempt to set fire to Rome and seize strategic points in the city, and the one in 259 involving 3,000 slaves was perhaps fomented by Carthage, then at war with Rome. Most of these came to little because betrayed from within, suggesting the extreme difficulty of organizing under constant surveillance in a system that promised rewards for "faithful" slaves.

This is perhaps the greatest danger facing slave conspirators. The risk of conspiracy was great and the emoluments for betrayal handsome, including freedom, preferential treatment, and material gain (see Wilmore on African American slave revolts: 32). A slave named Fortuna informed her master of the plans for the 1675 slave revolt in Barbados. The Governor was notified, slaves arrested and the alleged leaders executed. As a reward for her loyalty to the slave regime Fortuna was granted her freedom (Segal: 129). In the United States, the Gabriel Prosser Rebellion of 1800 and the Denmark Vesey Revolt of 1822, two of the largest and most famous slave revolts in American history, were both undone by the betrayal of slaves (Wilmore: 55, 61). Nat Turner, leader of the ill-fated slave revolt of 1831 that sent shock waves of violence and repression throughout the South, was apprehended in flight two weeks after being sighted by two slaves who reported his whereabouts to authorities (Wilmore: 70). On the other hand, slaves who forsook the emoluments of betrayal fell prey to the risks. In 1684 a slave of the Governor of Antigua was found guilty of inciting slave resistance. His tongue was cut out and one of his legs was chopped off to provide "a Living Example to the rest" (Segal: 131).

Slave revolts appear to have increased in frequency at the beginning of the second century BCE. In 198, former Carthaginian slaves acquired by slave-masters in Setia fomented revolt among slaves in Latium towns such as Norba and Circeii and the rebels actually captured Setia. A hastily raised Roman army came to the rescue and killed 500 of the insurgents (Livy 323.26.4–18; Bradley, 1989:42). Again in 196 Roman troops were required to suppress an even more widespread revolt in Etruria, returning the slaves who were spared to their masters (Livy 33.36.1–3). In Apulia, which had undergone the intensification of pastoral farming following the wars with Carthage, "there was a serious slave insurrection" in 185, "a conspiracy of shepherds who had endangered the highways and the public pasture-lands by their brigandage. [Lucius Postumius the praetor] condemned seven thousand men; many of them escaped, many were executed" (Livy 39.29.8–10). The endemic brigandage of fugitive slaves had escalated into what appeared as a revolt of serious proportions. Despite the troops deployed, total suppression was apparently not possible. Local slave revolts continued after the great "slave wars" as well. A close reading of accounts of the Cataline Conspiracy of 63 BCE (Esp. Sallust, *Catalina* 30.3,5; 56.5) suggests that slaves at least in Capua and Apulia and northern Etruria fled their households in revolt in response to the attempted insurrection led by Cataline. At least the Senate in Rome took the unrest seriously enough to dispatch troops to those areas (see Bradley, 1977). Tens of thousands of slaves, of course, fled their masters and joined one or the other side of combatants during the great civil wars after mid-first century BCE.

The three massive slave revolts during the late Republic (135–134, 104–100, and 74–73 BCE, respectively) all apparently began as local outbursts but spread rapidly until tens of thousands of slaves had joined in revolt and formed armies capable of holding their own against professional Roman armies. These major revolts all occurred during the dramatic expansion of the Roman slave system connected with prolonged wars of conquest in the late Republic. The rebels were largely agricultural slaves in Sicily and Italy, many of whom had only recently been enslaved by the Roman armies, for example, in the eastern Mediterranean. That these revolts so quickly escalated to such massive scale indicates just how eager the enslaved were to cast off their bondage. Most remarkable was that these massive movements could achieve and maintain such a degree of coherence and organization. Also striking were their collective discipline and longer-range planning. In the first Sicilian revolt, says Diodorus (34/35.2.30, 48), the rebels refrained from random destruction of farm equipment, buildings, and grain stores and did not attack the poor free peasants. Ironically, it was the latter, with their own long-standing grievances, who destroyed the wealthy landowners' "property." In the second Sicilian revolt, one of the leaders, Athenion, did not simply accept all rebel slaves into his burgeoning army but kept them at their agricultural tasks in order to supply the movement with food (Diodorus 34/35.9; 36.5.2, 3). Athenion's insistence on agricultural production is reminiscent of Toussaint-Louverture's revolutionary dictatorship of agrarian labor that was guided by identical reasoning (James: 155–56).

Bradley has made an admirable attempt to explain how the leaders of these revolts "attempted to foster a sense of community and unanimity among their adherents" by utilizing "existing modes of displaying authority" (1989:113–23). Besides requiring formulation more appropriate to the formation of such movements, however, his analysis would benefit from more adequate theoretical reflection. In dealing with ancient society and resistance movements, the religious dimension is hardly separable from the political;

such separation is a projection from modern Western societies. Ancient authors, writing from and for the ruling elite, almost certainly do not "record" events, particularly among movements of rebellion; they construct events according to certain conventional models and agenda. Moreover, the coherence and discipline generated and maintained by popular movements among peasants and/or slaves are hardly attributable to inherent personal qualities or symbols of authority possessed and exploited by leaders, but must be understood in more relational terms of the dynamic interaction between leaders and other participants in terms of cultural "scripts" current in the historical situation.

Diodorus portrays the first revolt in terms of a political-religious script long familiar (to both previous writers and to rebels who had been enslaved in Syria and elsewhere in the East) from Hellenistic kingship in the East. After the rebels, initial attack on the town of Enna, Eunus was "elected [acclaimed] king" and thereafter adopted the ceremonial-symbols-and-administrative-procedures that constituted the movement's power-relations and forms of its coherence, all familiar from Hellenistic kingship: "he put on a diadem and decked himself out as a king in every other respect, proclaimed the woman who was living with him . . . as his queen, and made those men who seemed to be particularly intelligent his councillors" (Diodorus 34/35.2.14, 16). That Hellenistic Syria was the source of this "script" is also clear from Diodorus' account: he took the royal name "Antiochus" (prominent particularly in the Seleucid dynasty in Syria, which also appeared on coins minted by the movement) and his followers were called "Syrians" (Diodorus 34/35.2.22–24). In the second great revolt in Sicily, similarly after an initial rebel victory in battle, says Diodorus:

> Many were deserting their masters every day. They were enjoying a quick and extraordinary increase in their numbers, so that after a couple of days there were more than six thousand of them. At this point they gathered together in a formal assembly, and when the proposal was put to them, the first thing they did was to elect someone called Salvius to be their king. (Diodorus 36.4.4)

Salvius supposedly adopted the royal name "Tryphon" (the name of a recent pretender to the Seleucid throne in Syria, which also appears on slingshots ascribed by archaeologists to the second revolt), appointed the most intelligent men as advisors in his council, and on ceremonial occasions wore a "purple-bordered toga and had "lictors with *fasces* to walk in front of him and had all the other things that constitute and symbolize the office of a king" (Diodorus 36.7.1, 4; 36.5.1–2). Athenion, the other principal leader of the second revolt, was also recognized as a king by his thousands of followers. After deferring to Salvius' kingship until the latter's death, Athenion then in effect "succeeded" him in a kingship symbolized with a purple robe, a silver scepter, and a diadem (Florus 2.7.10). While it is a gross exaggeration to claim that "there was at root little difference between the religious persona of the slave kings and that of the kings of the established Hellenistic dynasties" (Bradley, 1989:118; but see 168 n26), it is clear that, according Diodorus' and Florus' accounts, the great Sicilian slave revolts were following a particular "script" of social organization familiar to them presumably from the Syrian or other Eastern origins of many of their participants.

The "religious" dimension of these "kings'" leadership, whether it be their skill in divination (Salvius) or astrology (Athenion), their reputation for magical powers and prophecy (Eunus), or the general aura inherent in the dynamic relationship between leaders and followers, was inseparable from the "political" authority they exercised. Indeed, it was the dynamic political-religious relationship between leaders and followers that constituted the coherence of the movements and made possible the organization and discipline they manifested in their remarkably effective opposition to the military power brought against them.

Spartacus and his movement appear to have followed Roman political-religious patterns instead of those of Hellenistic kingship, such as those that might have been familiar from his native Thrace. Precisely in declaring their independence of the Roman system of slavery, they coopted the very Roman symbols of authority captured from Roman armies and their commanders: the rods and axes (*fasces*) that symbolized Roman magisterial power of coercion, Roman eagles, and legionary standards (Livy 31.11.11; Plutarch, *Crassus* 9.5; Florus 2.8.7–8). Appian (*Civil Wars* 1.116) suggests that his appointment of Crixus and Oenomaus as subordinate officers proceeded on the model of *legati* of Roman commanders.

Instances of violent slave resistance were points of convergence of the variables and constants of all slave regimes. Rebelling slaves harbored within their hearts an alternative tableau of retribution. Sometimes this tableau was no more than seething resentment and the lust for revenge. To this contingency was joined opportunity for reprisal. Such reprisal was so real a threat under the Roman slave regime that the jurists of the Digest were constrained to formally treat the problem of slaves killing their masters (29.5.14, Maecianus; 29.5.13, Venuleius; 29.5.16, Marcellus). Motivation was steeled by some especially egregious violation. Clearly the slave uprising in 70 CE sought to take advantage of the imperial interregnum that preceded the rise of the Flavian house. Tacitus suggests that Pedanius was murdered by one of his slaves because he had reneged on a promise of manumission. Often rebellion was directed by the bold leadership of especially courageous—or especially desperate—slaves who, perhaps due to the recent vintage of servitude or special intelligence, had not reconciled themselves to the indignities to which they were subject. These leaders took advantage of the solidarity that might be forged in the shared environment of execrable treatment, be it the common conditions of the rural latifundia or the urban household.

This powderkeg of contingencies was kept dry by the constant violence of the slave regime itself. It was an intimate violence the corporal punishments etched on the slave's body, and its terror was the tissue of the slave's imagination just as its torture was the tissue of the slave's memory, for terror is but the anticipation of torture and torture the realization of terror.

In his modern classic of historiography *The Black Jacobins*, C. L. R. James recounts the story of the Haitian revolution, "the only successful slave revolt in history" (James: ix). James describes in vivid detail the attempted siege of Crête-à-Pierrot, by the French generals Leclerc, Boudet, and Lacroix, an island fortress.

> Dessalines, naked to the waist, with dirty boots, a hole in his hat where a bullet had passed through, patrolled the ramparts, glasses in hand. He had thrown small detachments of scouts right round the fortress, awaiting the approach of the French reinforcements. Getting the news from Debelle, Leclerc knew that Crête-à-Pierrot had to be taken as quickly as possible, and ordered a concentration there of all his forces. Dessalines, on the ramparts, placed a barrel of powder next to where he stood, and with a lighted torch in his hand invited those of the garrison who wished to become slaves of the French to leave. "We are going to be attacked. If the French put their feet in here, I shall blow everything up." With one voice the garrison replied, "We shall die for liberty." Boudet sent a herald to the fortress, but Dessalines wanted no lying messages and shot him down, whereupon Boudet engaged one of the outposts. The blacks retreated before him until they reached the ditch; then they jumped in, and a terrific fire of artillery and musketry cut the French to pieces. The French broke, Boudet was wounded, and Lacroix gave the command to retreat, leaving the ground covered with dead and wounded. (315)

Though Toussaint had been the mastermind of the revolution, it was Dessalines who led the rebel slaves to independence from France and nationhood. To explain the different psyches of these two monumental heroes of the world's only successful slave revolt is beyond history. Such an explanation is not, however, beyond reason. Patterson has helped us to explain what James in riveting prose has helped us to know. Toussaint, liberal in his dealings with the white overlords he so brilliantly overthrew, had enjoyed a relatively easy life under the *ancienne régime*: "There was a small privileged caste, the foremen of the gangs, coachmen, cooks butlers, maids, nurses, female companions, and other house-servants.... Toussaint-Louverture also belonged to this small and privileged caste" (James: 19). James suggests that "he had probably never been whipped as so many slaves had been whipped" (92). Unlike Toussaint, who remained a loyal subject of Mother France even as he languished and expired in one of Napolean's dungeons, Dessalines knew not only the pain of the whip but its ineluctability in the establishment and maintenance of slavery. Indeed, James refers to Dessalines throughout *Black Jacobins* with reference to his whip-scarred body: "Dessalines, unable to read or write, his body scarred with strokes from the whip" (130); "this old slave, with the marks of the whip below his general's uniform" (301); "the fierce and uncultured Dessalines, though with the marks of the whip on his skin" (373). Dessalines knew that to yield to the French would mean a return to slavery, and thus a return to the whip, that instrument of terror and torture that had permanently marred his body. It was this scarred body that was exposed to the waist on the ramparts of Crête-à-Pierrot, where he gladly embraced death and invited his comrades to do so rather than countenance a return to the whip. Early in *Black Jacobins*, James describes the torture that was quotidian in the colony of Saint-Domingue.

> The torture of the whip . . . had "a thousand refinements," but there were regular varieties that had special names, so common were they. When the hands and arms were tied to four posts on the ground, the slave was said to undergo "the four post." If the slave was tied to a ladder it was "the torture of the ladder"; if he was suspended by four limbs it was "the hammock," etc. the pregnant woman was not spared her "four-post." . . . the blowing up of a slave had its own name—"to burn a little powder in the arse of a nigger": obviously this was no freak but a recognized practice. (James: 13)

Dessalines stands on the ramparts next to a powderkeg with "a little powder" for every French soldier that would breech the fortress. Though James does not explain the details of his narrative, they become clear through Patterson's phenomenological lens. Dessalines knew the whip with a somatic intimacy, and this knowledge informed his resolve to make the whip impossible in what was to become Haiti. Therefore it was Dessalines, not Toussaint, who made the break with France and led his troops to independence. Dessalines knew that the white, whip-wielding master class itself would have to be extirpated from the island: "then I shall make you independent," he promised in the speech to his troops before the battle at Crête-à-Pierrot, "There will be no more whites among us" (James: 315).

At one point in the war with Napoleon's forces in Saint Dominique when the prospects of the revolutionary army looked especially bleak, James writes: "the few thousand who remained faithful to Toussaint were the advance-guard of the revolutionary army fighting a revolutionary war. They were for the moment outnumbered. . . . But the liberty and equality which these blacks acclaimed as they went into battle meant far more to them than the same words in the mouths of the French. And in a revolutionary struggle these things are worth many regiments" (James: 306). James recognizes that the bitterness of slavery and the sweetness of freedom are themselves motives forces in history. Without giving these forces their due, the history of slavery and slave resistance remains improbable, opaque, hidden behind the mask.

Works Consulted

Bartchy, S. Scott
    1973   ΜΑΛΛΩΝ ΧΡΗΣΑΙ: *First Century Slavery and the Interpretation of 1 Corinthians 7:21.* Missoula, Mont.: Scholars Press.

Bellen, Heinz
    1971   *Studien zur Sklavenflucht im römischen Kaiserreich.* Wiesbaden: Steiner.

Bradley, Keith R.
    1977   "Slaves and the Conspiracy of Catiline." *Classical Philology* 73:329–36.

    1989   *Slavery and Rebellion in the Roman World 140 BC to 70 BC.* Bloomington: Indiana University Press.

Cartledge, Paul
    1985   "Rebels and Sambos in Classical Greece: A Comparative View." Pp. 16–46 in *Crux: Essays in Greek History.* Ed. P. Cartledge and F.D. Harvey. London: Duckworth.

Daube, David
    1952   "Slave-catching." *Juridical Review* 64:12–28.

Elkins, Stanley M.
    1959   *Slavery.* Chicago: University of Chicago Press.

Finley, Moses I.
    1980   *Ancient Slavery and Modern Ideology.* New York: Viking.

Frederikson, G. M., and C. Lasch
    1967   "Resistance to Slavery." *Civil War History* 13:315–29.

Garlan, Yvon
    1988   *Slavery in Ancient Greece.* Ithaca, N.Y.: Cornell University Press.

Hopkins, Keith
    1978   *Conquerors and Slaves.* Cambridge: Cambridge University Press.

James, C. L. R.
    1963   *The Black Jacobins.* New York: Vintage Books.

Montejo, Esteban
    1995   "A Cuban Slave's Testimony." Pp. 11–28 in *Slavery and Beyond: The African Impact on Latin America and the Carribean.* Ed. Darien J. Davis. Jaguar Books on Latin America, 5. Wilmington, Del.: Scholarly Resources.

Patterson, Orlando
- 1970 "Slavery and Slave Revolts: A Sociohistorical Analysis of the First Maroon War, 1665–1740." *Social and Economic Studies* 19:289–325. Reprinted in *Maroon Studies: Rebel Slave Communities in the Americas*. Ed. R. Price. Garden City, N.Y.: 1973.
- 1982 *Slavery and Social Death: A Comparative Study*. Cambridge: Harvard University Press.

Robert, J, and L. Robert
- 1983 *Fouilles d'Amyzon en Carie 1*. Pariside Boccard.

Scott, James C.
- 1990 *Domination and the Arts of Resistance*. New Haven: Yale University Press.
- 1992 "Domination, Acting, and Fantasy." Pp. 55–84 in *The Paths to Domination, Resistance, and Terror*. Ed. Carolyn Nordstrom and JoAnn Martin. Berkeley: University of California Press.

Segal, Ronald
- 1995 *The Black Diaspora*. New York: Farrar, Straus and Giroux.

Shaw, Brent D.
- 1984 "Bandits in the Roman Empire." *Past and Present* 105: 5–52.

Stampp, Kenneth M.
- 1956 *The Peculiar Institution: Slavery in the Ante-Bellum South*. New York:.
- 1971 "Rebels and Sambos: the Search for the Negro's Personality in Slavery." *Journal of Southern History* 37:367–92.

Vogt, Joseph
- 1974 *Ancient Slavery and the Ideal of Man*. Oxford: Oxford University Press.

Westermann, William L.
- 1955 *The Slave Systems of Greek and Roman Antiquity*. Philadelphia: American Philosophical Society.

Wilmore, Gayraud
- 1983 *Black Religion and Black Radicalism*. 2nd ed. Maryknoll, N.Y.: Orbis.

PAUL AND SLAVERY:
A CRITICAL ALTERNATIVE TO RECENT READINGS

Richard A. Horsley
University of Massachusetts Boston

ABSTRACT

Modern scholarly interpretation of Paul continues to understand the apostle as a "conservative" in his stance toward social issues and social relations, as exemplified in recent handbooks. This judgment about Paul's social attitudes in fact is based on one or two passages in which Paul is understood to advocate slaves remaining in their condition because of the short time before the parousia. Recent studies arguing that metaphorical slave/slavery language was central to Paul's discourse tend to reinforce the general picture of a socially "conservative" Paul. In reviewing these recent studies, which rely upon a portrayal of ancient Greek and Roman slavery standard in classical studies until recently, this review essay begins from the more comprehensive and more precise picture emerging from more recent classical studies and comparative sociology, as sketched in the previous studies in this volume. After dealing with the procedural problems entailed in adapting sociology of knowledge to Paul's counter-imperial mission, this article critically reviews the metaphorical use of "slave-slavery" in Paul's discourse and then attempts to assess the way(s) in which his statements thought pertinent to slavery can be understood in the context of the slave-holding society under the Roman empire. Throughout, attempts are made to avoid or adapt the standard conceptual apparatus of Pauline studies that are so heavily influenced by Christian theology and to understand Paul's statements and mission in the multicultural context of the early Roman empire.

Historically the canonical Paul has proven very useful for the legitimation of slavery as well as for the subordination of women. In a now widely cited illustration, the great theologian and mystic Howard Thurman tells of how his grandmother

> would not let me read any of the Pauline letters [except 1 Corinthians 13]. "During the days of slavery the master's minister would occasionally hold services for the slaves.... Always the white minister used as his text something from Paul. At least three or four times a year he used as a text: 'Slaves, be obedient to them that are your masters . . . , as unto Christ.' Then he would go on to show how it was God's will that we were slaves and how, if we were good and happy slaves, God would bless us. I promised my Maker

that if I ever learned to read and if freedom ever came, I would not read that part of the Bible." (Thurman: 30–31)

Not surprisingly, many African Americans, including distinguished theologians, have little use for the Apostle responsible for the divine sanctioning of slavery (Cleage; Cone). Similarly, the consistently critical and highly-articulate "non-traditional" women students in my courses in biblical studies have what can only be described as visceral reaction against Paul, not only for what he wrote but for the manner in which he wrote it. And I must admit my own discomfort at Paul's seeming megalomania and authoritarian insistence on his own ways at several points in his letters.

On the issue of slavery and, to a degree, that of gender-relations as well, academically established scholarly biblical studies relieved Paul himself of the statements in which he most dramatically and explicitly called for submission and obedience. Yet even after modern "critical" scholarship separated Paul's authentic seven letters from the deutero-Pauline epistles that had assimilated to the established Roman imperial order based on the slave-holding patriarchal family, the view of Paul as a conservative supporter of the established social-political order persisted in biblical scholarship. Scholarly understanding of Paul in general has been heavily determined by modern Western bourgeois theology, particularly the Lutheran theology in which Pauline scholarship was so deeply rooted. Paul, the hero of faith, was the great apostle of a new, universalistic and spiritual religion breaking with the particularistic, overly political religion of Judaism. Salvation was for the introspective individual *homo religiosus*, and had little or nothing to do with the social order, which belonged to a different "kingdom." Paul's letters were read to abstract his theology in its various doctrines. For such a theological assimilation of Paul, social relations were virtually irrelevant and not for Paul or the interpreter to question. Yet even in widely read handbooks on Paul and paperback books on his ethics the view of Paul as a "conservative" or "quite conservative" stance, or a "quite conservative, even quietistic, social posture" has persisted among those who were by no means perpetuating the traditional Lutheran theology of which Paul was the hero (Keck: 94–95; Sanders: 107; Sampley: 113). The reason given for why Paul supposedly insisted that his readers not change social roles is the imminence of the parousia, but the social-political implications of the latter go unexplored.

It is remarkable, moreover, the degree to which the generalization about Paul's conservative stance toward social roles and relations is based on his ostensible statement about slavery in 1 Cor 7:21, with his brief letter to Philemon sometimes adduced in further support. 1 Cor 7:21 and its immediate context 7:21–24 are still being read in connection with what Luther called the Pauline *Haustafeln* and *Standestafeln* the principal examples of which occur in the deutero-Pauline epistles, e.g., Col 3:18–4:1; Eph 5:22–6:9; 1 Tim 2:8–15

(Jones: 32–38), which presupposed and provided solid support for the slave-holding patriarchal household that formed the building block of ancient Greco-Roman society. Standard commentaries continued to conclude that in 1 Cor 7:21–24 Paul was indeed instructing slaves to remain in the condition in which they were called (Barrett; Conzelmann). That both Paul's supposed stance on slavery in particular and his supposed social conservatism was based on such limited textual evidence seems astounding when we realize that the advocates of a socially conservative Paul simply assume a particular paraphrase of 1 Cor 7:21, usually without so much as acknowledging that "translation" of this passage is conjectural and (at least in some circles) highly contested. The standard scholarly reading of Philemon, moreover, is not based on information derived from the text itself. That the NRSV—undertaken partly to provide contemporary churches with "inclusive language" translations of Paul's and others' patriarchal language—reversed the RSV, reestablishing the "make use of your present condition [slavery]" option in the "translated" text of 1 Cor 7:21 suggests that the conservative reading of Paul is still dominant or resurgent in established scholarly and publishing circles. That Paul's social conservatism depends so heavily on his attitude toward slavery, which in turn rests on such utterly insecure textual evidence, the principal "prooftext" of which is conjectural and contested, invites some critical review of the issues.

On the issue of Paul's discourse there is a second reason for review. Some recent studies of Paul's (metaphorical) use of the terms slave/slavery in his letters, one of which argues the case for a more liberal Paul on master-slave relations, appear problematic in certain ways. They appear to be based on an understanding of ancient Greek and particularly Roman slavery that is heavily dependent on older classical studies that have been superceded by more critical recent investigations (as summarized in my essay above [19–66]). And they represent Paul as employing "slave/slavery" terms in a far more prominent and positive way than is warranted by a critical review of pertinent passages and arguments in his letters. In the one study, a sophisticated adaptation of recent social science has the ironic effect of reinforcing the standard "conservative" reading of Paul. Paul's use of "slavery" in his discourse is an important issue in itself. But it is indirectly relevant to assessing his stance toward slavery itself, particularly given the paucity of his direct statements on the issue.

HISTORICAL RECONSTRUCTION AND A CRITICAL SOCIOLOGY OF KNOWLEDGE

The Promise and Problems of a Social Scientific Approach

Partly in order to break through the problems and limitations of the previous theological determination of New Testament studies, along with its generally conservative perspective, many scholars experimented with newer forms of literary analysis and borrowed certain social scientific approaches. An important effort on this front specifically focused on the epistle to Philemon and Paul's use of the language of slave/slavery was Petersen's analysis of Paul's "symbolic universe." This analysis offered both the possibility of moving closer to the way Paul's discourse may connect with patterns of meaning inherent in Paul's letters and the possible interplay between the Pauline symbol system and the social system of the communities he established. Indeed, as the result of his elaborate analysis of Paul's "symbolic universe" as he applied it to the brief epistle to Philemon, Petersen concluded that being "in Christ" "is a state of social being that governs the relationships between believers even outside the spatial and temporal boundaries of the church . . . [and] therefore excludes all other forms of social being for those who are 'in' him." Thus, in contrast to the previous "conservative" readings that tended to divide sharply between "spiritual" (religious) life and worldly (political-economic) life, Petersen interpreted Paul as having shaped his argument to Philemon and the church meeting in his house in such a crafty way that Philemon has no choice but to proceed with Onesimus's manumission (Petersen: 133, 135, 290). Of course we are left wondering why this implication of the Pauline symbol system for the social system was not as clear when Philemon and his household were converted and became clear only when Onesimus (generally assumed to have been a slave) was converted.

As an approach to Paul's letters, however, Petersen's analysis of the epistle to Philemon exhibits some of the same problematic features as the standard older theological interpretation, in two major respects. While attempting to move beyond analysis primarily in theological terms, it still depends heavily on many of the standard assumptions, concepts, and approaches of Pauline studies. And while arriving at an interpretation of the epistle to Philemon that is less conservative than the traditional one, the use of a social science oriented to the maintenance of the established social order has the effect of further consolidating the conservative construction of Paul with regard to slavery in particular and to political affairs in general.

Previous Pauline scholars treated the letters as if they were theological treatises expounding doctrines. In pursuing an analysis of Paul's symbolic universe one cannot simply read the symbol system directly off of Paul's frequently theologizing arguments, but must critically discern the key symbols in and behind them. Petersen carefully confines his analysis to Philemon and the other authentic letters of Paul, constructing the Pauline narrative world and symbolic universe (like a reader-response critic) without resorting to extrinsic information from other literature or historical data that might influence interpretation. Along with others in the field, including other applications of sociology (e.g., Meeks), however, he in effect assumes that the recipients of Paul's letters shared the same symbolic universe with Paul—a remarkable assumption for an analysis supposedly building on the sociology of knowledge of Berger and Luckmann, which includes a critical discussion of complications and changes in symbol system such as religious conversion (but cf. Petersen: 273n11).

The new analysis in terms of symbolic universe, moreover, pays no more attention to Paul's letters as letters—i.e., *ad hoc* communications of Paul with particular communities—than the old theological approach. The problem is readily apparent. Petersen takes the determinative step, understandable for his focus on the Epistle to Philemon read according to the standard assumptions, of focusing on kinship and master-slave terminology. That leads to the claim that among the fundamental features of Paul's symbolic universe two of the most stable symbol systems we find are the kinship and the master-slave systems; indeed that these are "organizing metaphors" in Paul's symbolic world, and that the relations between Christ and believers "often represents typical and even ideal master-slave relations" (Petersen: 240, 242). Since, as Petersen acknowledges, Paul simply does not refer to believers as slaves of Christ, he must use Pauline texts referring to Christ as *kyrios*, which he takes as meaning "slave-master," as the principal basis for claiming that the relation between believers and Christ is a master-slave relation. Petersen focuses on 1 Cor 8:1–6 in particular because there God is referred to as Father in conjunction with Christ as *kyrios*. Such an analysis, however, does not consider what lies behind Paul's "theologizing" in particular arguments in particular letters. Paul does not use language like this anywhere else in his letters. As should be readily evident particularly in 1 Corinthians, where the key language is so different from that in other letters, Paul has run into misunderstanding rooted apparently in different ways of thinking (Horsley, 1976; 1978b; 1998). Far from providing a good text for a symbolic universe supposedly shared by Paul and his communities, 1 Cor 8:1–6 provides a case study of a conflict between two different symbolic universes. As is evident in his quotation and qualification (or even contradiction) of theological principles, apparently from the Corinthians, in 1 Cor 8:1, 4, he is theologizing here in response to a perceived threat from the Corinthians to his own symbolic universe. Far from representing Paul's symbolic universe, the formulaic predicates in 1 Cor 8:4 and 6, which are so atypical of Paul, may in fact obscure it (Horsley, 1978a; 1980).

Not only is each of Paul's letters an *ad hoc* communication with a particular "assembly" he and his co-workers had recruited, dealing with particular issues that had emerged in that assembly. Paul was also attempting to persuade the particular addressees to take a particular course of action and/or to assume a particular viewpoint, as recently rediscovered rhetorical criticism has made clear. In attempting to discern Paul's symbolic universe, it is not clear which if any of his *ad hoc* letters might serve as key; certainly the tiniest, Philemon, provides the least discourse or "narrative world" to work from.

Given both the *ad hoc* and rhetorical character of his letters, Paul's own symbolic universe would have to be ferreted out of his arguments through more comprehensive critical analysis of his whole corpus, with critical analysis of the rhetoric and the rhetorical situation of each. To explore Paul's letters and/or early Christian communities adequately, moreover, we must take into account the multiple symbolic universes operative in the pluralistic Roman empire which were informed by diverse social-cultural histories, particularly among recently subjected and resistant peoples such as the Jews. In order adequately to assess how particular symbols (in this case the slogans in 1 Cor 8:1, 4 and the philosophical "causes" formulae appearing in 1 Cor 8:6) may have been functioning in a symbolic universe operative in Corinth in particular, we must be aware of the diverse Hellenistic cultural currents that may have been flowing through this cross-roads of Roman Greece at the time (in this case, school philosophy and Hellenistic Jewish mysticism; Horsley, 1978a; 1978b; 1980). Moreover, insofar as Paul successfully communicated with certain Corinthians by adapting some key components of their symbolic universe in his theologizing, a new symbolic universe may have been emerging in the Corinthian community—and beyond, insofar as 1 Corinthians was read more widely in the ensuing consolidation of Pauline Christianity in the direction indicated in Colossians, Ephesians, and the Pastoral Epistles (Horsley, 1998).

The application of established Western social science of the last generation to Paul's mission and letters also tends further to consolidate the conservative construction of Paul by previous New Testament studies. Most influential in this regard has been Meeks's (cf. Stowers) and Theissen's use of structural-functional sociology, including the latter's projection of deutero-Pauline "love-patriarchalism" back onto Paul himself. Petersen's treatise, which borrows heavily from Berger and Luckmann, tends to do the same with regard to Paul and slavery in particular.

Like the structural-functional sociology of Parsons and others, Berger and Luckmann's intellectualistic sociology of knowledge was focused on the institutionalization and legitimation of complex, large-scale established societies. "Symbolic universes, . . . the fourth (most comprehensive) level of legitimation [of the institutionalized social order] are bodies of theoretical tradition that integrate different provinces of meaning and encompass the institutional order in a symbolic totality. . . . *all* the sectors of the institutional order are integrated in an all-embracing frame of reference . . ." (Berger and Luckmann: 95–96). The focus and organizing conceptualization for understanding Paul is thus not the theology or rhetoric of his letters or the particular situations to which they are addressed but his "symbolic universe" as a "comprehensive system of shared knowledge that legitimates institutions and individual identities" (57) and "encompasses the social order in a symbolic totality" (59). Paul is thus made to appear accepting of and concerned about the symbolic universe that legitimates the established institutional order. It is simply assumed, not argued, moreover, that Paul's symbolic universe included as one of its "organizing metaphors" (Petersen: 206) a "system" of master-slave relations, slavery being one of the principal institutions of the ancient Hellenistic-Roman social order.

Compounding this concern for the equilibrium of the established order, however, are serious problems of the applicability of the concept "symbolic universe" to Paul. As developed by Berger and Luckmann, the concept applies readily to the dominant Roman imperial culture in which Paul worked, at least by the time he came to Corinth and Ephesus. In Roman imperial society, in a way at least somewhat analogous to a complex modern society, "various sectors of the institutional order" and "different provinces of meaning" became integrated to some extent "in an all-embracing frame of reference." Like the modern United States and, to a degree, other modern societies, the Roman empire was pluralistic, with many local and regional variations in culture. There would have been significant historically-rooted cultural differences between, say, Galatia, Thessalonika, and Corinth. Such pluralism and cultural variations made all the more important the operations of the "conceptual machineries of universe maintenance" such as the mythology, theology, and philosophy (104–12). Philosophy, of course, originated in classical antiquity, where thinkers such as Aristotle provided rational legitimation for basic institutions such as the hierarchical state and the patriarchal slave-holding household: "(just as) it is natural for the body to be governed by the soul ... so the male is by nature ruler and the female subject. ... and [some people] are by nature slaves for whom to be governed by authority is advantageous" (*Politics* 1.1254b). There was no equivalent in Western antiquity to established social science, perhaps one of the most important "machineries of universe-maintenance" in modern Western societies, left unmentioned by Berger and Luckmann (see Foucault, e.g., 78–108). But certainly in Roman imperial society, as in complex modern societies, naive mythologies among the masses and sophisticated "theologies" among "an elite of theoreticians" worked in tandem to maintain an overarching symbolic universe (Berger and Luckmann: 112).

The role of mythology and philosophy in maintaining the symbolic universe of Roman imperial society makes specially relevant one further aspect of the concept as developed Berger and Luckmann. As illustrated by the Aristotle quotation just above, "because these products of human consciousness present themselves as full-blown and inevitable totalities ("by nature"), it is all the more important to recognize that symbolic universes are "social products with a history" (Berger and Luckmann: 97). This recognition should lead us to investigate ways in which the "maintenance machineries" worked to legitimate (for example) the new institution of the emperor and the growth of the slave system and the corresponding impoverishment of the peasantry in the late republic and early empire. One of the principal sets of symbols that emerged at the very center of the Roman imperial symbolic universe in the

Greek cities was the emperor as *Sōtēr* and *Kyrios*, which of course meant the political-religious Lord who ruled ultimately over people's lives. Classical historians have now delineated how this aspect of the imperial symbolic universe developed historically (Price; Zanker; Horsley, 1997:20–24, 47–86). Once we are aware of the historical development of the symbolic universe of the Roman imperial order, however, we can hardly ignore the question of Paul's historical relationship to both the imperial society and its symbolic universe (including its local variations). In the generation or two after Paul, even "Pauline" writers were using Christ as *Kyrios* to maintain the symbolic universe that legitimated slavery and patriarchy (e.g., Col 3:18–4:1; Eph 5:21–6:9). Paul himself, however, insists upon his own exclusive devotion to the cause of Christ as his *Kyrios* and represents that Lord both as having been ignominiously and torturously executed as a rebel or slave by the imperial order and as exalted by God as the true ruler of the universe who will subject every rule and authority. It thus seems highly doubtful that the totalizing concept of "symbolic universe," developed to understand how "bodies of theoretical tradition" integrate "all sectors of the institutional order in an all-embracing frame of reference" is directly applicable to what are discerned as key terms in the rhetorical arguments of his *ad hoc* letters to newly established communities in various cities of the empire. Presumably a method and its concepts should fit the subject matter. Structural-functional sociology and "symbolic universe" may well help us understand the *Res Gestae* of Augustus, but are of questionable utility for understanding Paul's epistle to Philemon.

A Less Theologically Determined Historical Construction of Paul's Perspective and Agenda

Understanding Paul's letters and his mission rather requires a painstaking dialectical process. We must move critically back and forth between analysis of his particular arguments in their respective rhetorical situations and historical contexts, on the one hand, and comparative analysis of information about the broader historical situation of Roman Palestine, Asia Minor, and Greece, in which he worked, on the other. Throughout we must discern Paul's overall perspective and agenda in which particular arguments and practices can be comprehensible. In cutting through the heavy overdetermination of Pauline studies by Christian theological concerns, as well as avoiding premature borrowing of inappropriate social scientific concepts, perhaps it would be well to resort to the standard discourse of historical analysis and reconstruction. In attempting through theological determination we can also attempt to avoid determination by some other interrelated modern agenda (in their theological variations): a "universalism," surprisingly Western European in its complexion, that is often projected onto ancient

"Hellenistic" culture by biblical studies; enlightenment individualism, including its theological variations of "conversion" and "justification" of the individual; and liberalism, which is now seeking multi-ethnic, multi-cultural and multi-gender extension and application. Paul must rather be examined in his particular orientation in his own peculiar historical context, both of which were hybrids in a multi-cultural imperial situation.

Paul was a Hellenized diaspora descendant of Israel, of the tribe of Benjamin (Phil 3:4–6). Even if we trust the book of Acts that he came originally from Tarsus on the southern coast of Asia Minor, we must be sceptical about his Roman citizenship because of the clear indications in Acts of Luke's overall apologetic agenda (Roetzel: 19–22). From the combination of his own patterns of thought that resemble those of Judean apocalyptic literature (e.g., in 1 Thessalonians and 1 Corinthians 15) and his own references to both his earlier fanaticism and his heavenly apocalyptic experiences (e.g., Gal 1:13–18; Phil 3:4–6; 1 Thess 4:14–18; 2 Cor 12:1–5), it seems almost certain that he had been decisively shaped by and involved in Judean scribal circles with an apocalyptic perspective on their current situation, that of subjection to Roman rule (more generally, see also Roetzel: 5, 37–38, 61–63, 146–47). In contrast with the Judean apocalyptic literature that assumes a reactive anticipatory and/or reflective posture over against an oppressive empire, however, Paul the apostle was convinced that God's action to bring the final historical crisis to resolution had already begun; indeed he had been commissioned according to a prophetic paradigm as the apostle to implement part of the fulfilment of history.[1]

Paul was not "converted," i.e., changing from one religion to another, nor did he start or found another religion, called Christianity, for neither "Judaism" nor "Christianity" existed yet as what could be called religions. He rather understood his mission as part of the fulfilment of promises to Abraham, in which Israel's distinctive historical destiny was finally being implemented. The *ioudaismos* in which he (a "Hellenistic" diaspora Jew) was involved, including his persecution of early Jesus-followers (Gal 1:13–14; Phil 3: 6), must have been some sort of program to maintain Judean-Israelite culture with rigorous group discipline over-against a Roman-backed dominant cultural program of *hellenismos* (perhaps combined with some sort of *romanismos*), while simultaneously avoiding any overt provocation of the Romans— a struggle in which Judean intellectuals and diaspora Jews had been engaged since the time of the Maccabean Revolt in the second century BCE. The reve-

---

[1] As these deliberate formulations may indicate, the standard synthetic construct of Jewish "apocalypticism" is virtually inapplicable. Rather comparisons with particular Judean (and other) documents and passages assessed in historical context may prove helpful in illuminating particular visionary and counter-imperial aspects of Paul's letters and mission, as suggested with regard to Jesus-traditions in Horsley, 1987:129–46.

lation of Jesus Christ that he refers to in Gal 1:15–16 led him to join the equally fanatical popular movement of the renewal of Israel that he had previously persecuted as dangerously disruptive. His prophetic commission from his *apocalypsis* directed him to devote his considerable energy toward building that movement among the other peoples of the world, since the leadership of the mission to the "circumcised" was already in the hands of Cephas (and James, brother of Jesus). The movement, whose expansion into Asia Minor and Greece he spearheaded, along side of or in competition with other "apostles," understood itself to be involved in the fulfilment of God's promises to Abraham (Galatians 2–3). As is evident in his arguments in Galatians, both Paul and Cephas, James, and other leaders of the movement believed that in the crucifixion and resurrection of Jesus the promises to Abraham were being fulfilled not only to Israel but to the other peoples who were also to receive blessings. The disagreement was only with regard to how the other peoples were to be included in the movement of historical fulfilment: whether by joining Israel, in effect, by becoming circumcised and otherwise observing the Law, or simply by responding to the gospel of the fulfilment through Christ in faith and receipt of the Spirit (Galatians 3–5).

Theologically determined Pauline study has focused on the crucifixion and resurrection aspects of his gospel. But once God had inaugurated the fulfilment of history in the crucifixion and resurrection of Christ, Paul himself was oriented toward the third key aspect of his gospel, the *parousia* or the "day of the Lord," when the fulfilment already inaugurated would finally be completed. Because of the "structural differentiation" in modern Western societies and thinking, whereby religion has become a distinct sphere of life separated from others, with "church" separated from "state" and economic enterprise, modern Western biblical scholars have often overlooked the social and political dimensions that are inseparable from the religious dimension in Paul's message and mission. We have been reminded recently how much of Paul's key "symbols" are parallel to, perhaps borrowed from, Roman religio-political ideology: *euangelion, pistis, dikaiosyne, kyrios, sōtēr,* etc. (Georgi; Horsley, 1997). That should lead us to take more seriously what Paul says about "what is happening" in the historical situation in which he sees himself playing an important role. As Paul the visionary now knew, in God's apocalyptic plan for the fulfilment of history (and the promises to Abraham), in their crucifixion of Christ "the rulers of this age" had unwittingly sealed their own doom (1 Cor 2:6–8). At his resurrection-exaltation, Christ had become, in effect, the emperor of the world—or, given the context in the Roman empire, the *counter*-emperor. At "the end"/ the *parousia*/ day of the Lord, along with the completion of the resurrection of the dead, when every imperial earthly ruler and authority and power were destroyed, God would finally come to reign directly (1 Cor 15:24–28, etc.; presumably the destructive violence was somehow being managed in heavenly places!). Meanwhile, "the present form of this world is passing away," as "the appointed time has grown short" (1 Cor 7:31, 29). Paul is vague in the extreme in his symbolization of the future (e.g., Romans 8). He apparently imagines a future with some sort of social contours, e.g., with embodied persons in social interaction. This is sometimes partly obscured because he has borrowed language from the addressees of the letters for his peculiar formulations, such as the mortal body putting on "immortality" (an oxymoron in certain Hellenistic Greek cultures, 1 Cor 15: 53; Horsley, 1998). Yet it is clear that he understands the assemblies he is helping organize as, in effect, beachheads of the new age that will replace "the present evil age" (Gal 1:4), of the imminently to be realized "kingdom of God" (1 Cor 6:9–10; 15:51; Gal 5:21; 1 Thess 2:12). He thus insists that the assemblies he founded not only maintain solidarity among themselves, but avoid dealing with institutions of the dominant imperial order, such as the civic courts (1 Thess 5:1–11; 1 Cor 6:1–9; 7:29–31).

Another Try at an Historical Sociology of Knowledge

In the light of this provisional sketch of Paul's perspective and agenda, about the only component of Berger and Luckmann's scheme of "symbolic universe" that might pertain to Paul is that of "an intellectual . . . whose expertise is not wanted by the society at large" and who could be understood to have been leading "a religious sect" or a (non-violent) "revolution." "His social marginality expresses his lack of theoretical integration within the universe of his society. He appears as the counter-expert in the business of defining reality" (126). In Berger and Luckmann's terms Paul would appear to have helped generate a "subsociety" within which "all significant relationships" occurred between fellow-members, who supported each others' deviant conception of reality. Whether he would have been leading a "sect" or a "revolution" depends on the degree to which he was attempting "to realize his design for society *in* society—i.e., to have the local assemblies of the overall assembly embody some sort of *alternative* society still living in the dominant social order that Paul expected to disappear at the parousia.

In terms of the sociology of knowledge, however, Paul's relationship with the symbolic universe of Roman imperial society does not really fit into Berger and Luckmann's scheme. The latter did not extend their analysis and conceptual apparatus to include imperial situations, in which a dominant society controls subordinate peoples and in varying degrees either assimilates them into the dominant symbolic universe or impacts their indigenous symbolic universes. Hellenistic Jewish intellectuals such as Philo of Alexandria had simply assimilated to the dominant symbolic universe, recasting the Jewish biblical tradition in terms of the Hellenistic philosophies that helped maintain the legitimacy of the dominant order. The intellectuals who produced Judean apocalyptic literature, on the other hand, attempted to reaffirm their own traditional symbolic universe as well as the (future) independence of Judean society by projecting a future divine judgment of imperial rule and a restoration of Israel.

Thus, if we want to pursue an historical sociology of knowledge, Paul's letters and mission to the peoples would have to be understood in connection with Jewish and other reactions to Hellenistic-Roman imperial domination. Seen in the broader context of an imperial situation, Paul cannot be understood to be helping legitimate the Roman institutional order, intentionally or unintentionally. Even though he writes in standard Hellenistic Roman rhetorical conventions and uses numerous "symbols" in the language of the dominant culture, his letters indicate an opposition to the dominant order. Indeed, if passages such as 1 Thess 4:14–18 or 1 Cor 7:29–31 and 15:20–28 or Rom 8:18–25 and 11:25–26 are any indication, Paul himself expected the dominant order to be terminated soon, with the imminent *parousia* of his Lord. Insofar as Paul knew the symbolic universe of Roman imperial society, he appears to have been using it in order to subvert and replace the institutions it legitimated.

Understanding the communities Paul helped organize in the few years of his mission in Galatia, Macedonia, Corinth, and Ephesus (and which he addresses in his letters), poses problems very different from understanding Paul's letters and his sense of his mission. In this connection Berger and Luckmann's sociology of knowledge may well be appropriate, although in a very different way than suggested by Petersen or Meeks. As explained above "symbolic universe" refers to the integrating, all-embracing frame of reference of a whole society, not that of only a "subsociety," much less that of a tiny movement or a dissident individual intellectual. Even if we adapted the concept so as to speak of the symbolic universe of a movement or subsociety, it would still be extremely problematic with reference to Paul's communities and addressees because the acquisition and emergence of a symbolic universe requires what Berger and Luckmann call "socialization." Most people born into an established institutional order acquire the legitimating symbolic universe by a long process of primary socialization, as significant others such as parents mediate the social world in an emotionally intense atmosphere of family, neighborhood, school, peer-group, etc. To put it most graphically perhaps, nascent persons internalize identities, roles, and *the* social world even as they learn language and interact with immediate family (Berger and Luckmann: 131–37). Built on the base of the primary social order acquired through primary socialization most people are then integrated into institutionalized (i.e., often role-specific occupational, associational, educational) "subworlds" in a less emotionally charged process of "secondary socialization" (138–46). New cultural contents and identifications with certain roles are superimposed on already formed selves and an already internalized social world. In a highly diverse and plural social order such the United States, this can involve relatively greater emotional intensity and personal commitment, as in the training of religious specialists (clergy) who are not part of the central maintenance machineries of the dominant order or the training of the military officers who are.

There are cases, however, in which people, in effect, switch worlds. This requires a more complete, intensive, transforming process of "resocialization" (Berger and Luckmann: 157–63). The latter replicates to a considerable degree the process of primary socialization, with the strong emotional attachment to significant others characteristic of childhood. It also requires the dismantling of the world being left behind. A religious "conversion" may or may not be an example of resocialization. "To have a conversion experience is nothing much. The real thing is to be able to keep on taking it seriously, to retain a sense of its plausibility." A community, a whole supportive, reinforcing network of significant others and beyond, all committed members of the same new "world," is necessary. Otherwise the previously internalized subjective reality cannot be transformed. Moreover, the old reality must be reconfigured within the legitimating (emergent) conceptual-symbolic apparatus of the new reality.

Obviously, the process of resocialization does not happen overnight. It is a far more sustained and complex process than a simple "conversion experience." Recognition of the difference between "secondary socialization" and the more transforming process necessary for "resocialization" should give us pause about speaking in facile fashion about "Paul's symbolic universe" or about using Paul's letters as direct evidence for the communities of people to whom he was writing. He had been in Corinth for eighteen months and presumably even less time in Galatia, Thessalonika, and Philippi, teaching, sharing the Lord's Supper," and otherwise interacting in relatively intensive ways with the small communities of people who formed the assemblies (*ekklesiai*). Paul himself understood the resulting relationship in intimate familial "reproductive" terms, as his having become the believers' "father in Christ Jesus" or the mother giving birth to them (1 Cor 4:15; Gal 4:19). But prior to his arrival, there was no community and symbol system already formed into which individuals could be resocialized. These had to be developed "from scratch." It is thus not surprising, as the relatively extensive Corinthian correspondence indicates, for example, that serious conflicts over focal symbols, behavior issues, and relations with outsiders ("the world") prevailed both within the Corinthian assembly and between Paul and a sizeable number of the Corinthian believers (Wire; Horsley, 1976; 1978b; 1998). Those conflicts must have been rooted in the different "socializations" (into different "symbolic universes") that the Corinthians and Paul had undergone.

The people who comprised the membership of the assemblies Paul "founded" appear to have been predominantly "gentiles," as Paul indicates at points in his letters (e.g., 1 Thess 1:9). He clearly understands his mission and gospel as directed to gentiles (Galatians 1–2). Yet his orientation towards the future judgment and parousia of Christ was clearly rooted in a Palestinian Jewish apocalyptic world-view. His gospel, moreover, was not only received in an apocalyptic experience (Gal 1:13–17; 2 Cor 12:1–4), but featured as central "organizing metaphors" (or focal symbols) such things as "the resurrection of the dead (body)" and Israelite scriptural figures and stories understood as concrete historical people and events (1 Cor 10:1–13; Galatians 3). Such were alien to the dominant world-view or symbol system of Hellenistic-Roman culture and probably to many local cultures as well. Thus, even though he spent a year and a half in Corinth attempting to "father" a process of resocialization of those who formed the new assembly there, that was nowhere near a sufficient time to effectively dismantle the symbolic universe firmly implanted in the Corinthians through their primary socialization and to effectively internalize the principle symbols and the new orientation that Paul was apparently pressing upon them.

In fact, far from Paul's arguments in his letters being evidence for what "early Christians" (no such thing as Christianity existed yet!) believed and practiced, they are rather additional instruments of the ongoing process of resocialization which Paul was apparently attempting to accomplish. Again judging from the Corinthian correspondence, Paul repeatedly attempted to explain key aspects of his gospel in the Corinthians' own Hellenistic terms, reconfiguring some of their symbols in his attempts at persuading them to his view or the behavior he was recommending (Horsley, 1998). The different letters compiled to form 2 Corinthians indicate that his rhetorical efforts in 1 Corinthians, for example, were not particularly effective. If Colossians and Ephesians are any indication of the result of Paul's mission and letter-writing, then the resulting "sect" or "subsociety" constituted by one branch of the early Christian movement settled back into the institutional patterns of the dominant social order and at least some deutero-Pauline intellectuals were articulating theological and ethical expressions rooted as much in the dominant Hellenistic-Roman symbolic universe as in Paul's apparent conviction of the divine transformation of the dominant social order. The result could hardly be described as an effective process of resocialization. It appears rather to have been what Berger and Luckmann call a "secondary socialization," in this case into a new "religion" that accepted and itself reinforced the dominant institutional order.

Thus, neither during Paul's own mission nor in the "Pauline" churches one or two generations later can his "genuine" letters be used as sources for a "symbolic universe" that was (supposedly) effectively shared by the communities who read those letters (*contra* Meeks, Petersen, and many in the field). Far from being records of an already established "early Christianity," Paul's letters were among the instruments which influenced the long process of community formation, presumably from the incipient stages. Paul's letters must rather be read, in the first instance, as attempts to persuade particular communities about certain matters of belief and/or behavior. We can to a considerable degree discern what Paul was driving at. But then we must examine later evidence to discern the results of the process of community formation and social behavior (probably more one of secondary socialization than of resocialization) that Paul's letters may have influenced. And we must recognize that Colossians, Ephesians and the Pastoral Epistles provide information only on certain branches of the Pauline and other "early Christian" movement.

"Slave/Slavery" and "Free/Freedom" in Paul's Letters

Recent studies of Paul's use of the terms "slave" and "slavery" conclude that such language is central and/or important to his discourse or "symbolic universe," indeed was an "organizing metaphor" in his mission. Such studies would seem to reinforce the general sense in Pauline studies, which is so heavily determined by Protestant/Lutheran theology, that Paul took a "conservative" stance on social relations, such as slavery. A critical review of Paul's letters, however, indicates that "slavery" language is not prominent in the ways claimed in recent studies and that the use of "slave" language is more complicated than allowed.

In approaching Paul's use of the language of slave/slavery (and free/freedom), we cannot simply focus on the key terms and take them at face value—as if, for example, *doulos* automatically referred to a chattel slave (see the articles by Callender and Wright above). We must take several interrelated factors into account. Any conclusions about the significance and prominence of symbols of slave/slavery (and freedom) in Paul's symbolic universe, to start with, must be based on a critical survey of Paul's rhetoric, including the complex multi-cultural background of his discourse. We cannot simply assume a basic and consistent meaning of a given term such as *doulos*. As classics scholars at least since Finley have repeatedly cautioned, there were different forms of dependent labor in the ancient Mediterranean world (e.g., the Helots of Sparta as well as the chattel slaves of Athens; the *laoi basilikoi* or "royal peasants" of areas of Asia Minor as well as household slaves in most cities and courts), on the one hand, and different terms for the same form of dependent labor (e.g., *pais, oikētes, doulos*, etc.) on the other. In discerning the meaning of terms in context, moreover, New Testament scholars must be cautious in using previous narrowly focused word-studies overdetermined by anachronistic theological distinctions, such as "religious" language separate from political-economic language, conducted without adequate attention to social relations and historical social context. In dealing adequately with the historical context of Jewish and "Christian" texts of the Hellenistic-Roman period, we need to take into account the imperial situation of a subject people, some of whom had been slaughtered and others enslaved in the very establishment of Roman imperial power relations, and how they were responding to the imperial situation. Finally, since Jewish authors such as Paul were coming from a subject society with social relations and cultural traditions different from those of the dominant imperial society, we need to take into account the discourse of Israelite-Jewish tradition (even after its translation into Greek terms) which originated in and was shaped by ancient Near Eastern political-economic-religious patterns.[2]

One suspects that the latter is particularly important in the case of figures such as Paul, whose attitudes and language were decisively shaped by Judean scribal circles that cultivated an apocalyptic perspective in their struggle to maintain their own indigenous cultural traditions (in anticipation of regaining their people's independent sovereignty!) over against the dominant imperial culture. A thorough investigation of this matter would require a monograph. Only a broad sketch of the cultural background from which Paul appears to be coming is possible here. In the ancient Near Eastern societies from which ancient Israel emerged, the people generally were understood as the "servants/slaves" of the gods and/or of the human regents of the gods (i.e., the "great ones," "kings," or "high priests") These "servants" owed their lords goods and labor services, but they were not chattel slaves in the same sense as those of the Roman or the later American slave systems (see essay by Callender above). The structure and dynamics of such an ancient Near Eastern system can be seen in the story of Joseph's shrewd manipulation of royal power in Egypt in Genesis 47. Israel understood its origins, in the book of Exodus and elsewhere, as its God's redemption from the "house of bondage/slavery" (*oikos douleias*) in Egypt. In maintaining its freedom from servitude to any human rulers such as the Egyptian Pharaoh or a potential domestic strong-man, Israel committed itself to Yahweh as its (literal) king and lord. Its Mosaic covenantal loyalty and service to Yahweh were therefore correspondingly exclusive. The concrete social-economic-political-religious (we must re-combine dimensions that are separated in the modern West) dynamics of Israelite tradition can be seen in the laws concerning slavery (see esp. Exod 21:2–6; Deut 15:12–18; Lev 25:39–43). Like most other ancient societies, Israel practiced debt-slavery. But Israelites were not to enslave fellow Israelites on a permanent basis as chattel slaves or to sell indebted Israelites as

---

[2] The standard European-American field of New Testament studies has been relatively uninterested in such issues as colonial and imperial relations. As academic biblical studies is broadened to include previously unaccepted voices (e.g., the essays in Sugirtharajah, 1998; *Semeia* 73, 75, 78), it will be better equipped to understand this major determining factor in the life of diaspora as well as Palestinian Jews in the Roman empire and in the Pauline mission. For an attempt to address the imperial situation of Jesus' ministry, see Horsley, 1987; Crossan; and for a preliminary attempt to sketch the imperial context of Paul's mission, see Horsley, 1997.

slaves to foreigners. Debt-slaves had to be released after six years of service. Why? Because you/they who were slaves in Egypt are now God's/my slaves, "whom I brought out of the land of Egypt" (Deut 15:14; Lev 25:43). Once Israel itself reverted to the usual ancient Near Eastern political-economic-religious structure of monarchy (and later a monarchic temple-state headed by a high priesthood), the officers and support staff of the king (high priests) were also considered "servants" of the king. One can still discern this meaning of *doulos* in Luke's version of the "parable of the talents" (Luke 19:11–27), in which the first two servants of the nobleman who receives royal power are given political-economic "authority" over ten and five "cities" (respectively), while in Matthew's version (Matt 25:14–30) they appear simply as the slaves of a wealthy man who goes on a journey, i.e., more conformed to the Greco-Roman patterns of slavery.

It would appear to be in continuity with this Israelite and ancient Near Eastern pattern that Paul refers to himself at two or three points (Rom 1:1; Gal 1:10; Phil 1:1) as a "servant of Christ," probably as a designation of his own relation with Christ as a specially designated apostle (as "commissioned," Gal 1:15–16), perhaps even in a semi-titular sense. The reference to Paul and Timothy as "servants of Christ Jesus" in Phil 1:1 may be original, with the reference to "bishops and deacons" a secondary addition to the text. In Rom 1:1, Paul's reference to himself as "a servant of Jesus Christ" is followed immediately by "(called to be) an apostle (of Jesus Christ)," which was the standard opening in other letters (1 Cor 1:1; 2 Cor 1:1; Gal 1:1). There is no justification for reasoning backwards historically from the opening of the later letters 2 Pet 1:1; Jude 1:1 and James 1:1, but the fact that other apostles are referred to as "slave/servant of Christ" in all these cases is suggestive. In fact, the background of the reference to James as "a servant of God and of the Lord Jesus Christ" in James 1:1, addressed to "the twelve tribes in dispersion," is clearly not Greco-Roman slavery but Hebrew Biblical usage of "servant of God" for one with a special calling or role as an officer or prophet or other envoy of God. Thus "servant of Christ" in Rom 1:1 would appear rather similar to Paul's self-designation in Gal 1:10 as "a servant of Christ" in direct connection with his prophet-like commission as a special apostle (Gal 1: 15–16; cf. Isa 49:1 and esp. Jer 1:5). Since these are Paul's own distinctive self-references, however, they provide no evidence that "slave of Christ" was a more general term for members of Paul's assemblies or believers in Christ (cf. Martin, 1990:65). Nor does 1 Cor 7:22 support the contention that "slave(s) of Christ" was a general term for believers. There Paul is simply making a rhetorical contrast between "whoever was called in the Lord as a slave" who is now "a freedperson of the Lord," and "whoever was free when called," who is now "a slave of Christ." We shall explore below the larger argument of which this rhetorical contrast was a part.

Paul twice refers to himself as "a slave/enslaved" to the people he is evangelizing (1 Cor 9:19; 2 Cor 4:5). In 2 Cor 4:5, it is part of his increasingly desperate rhetoric in defense of his ministry. In the context of 1 Corinthians 8–10 he is using his self-"enslavement to all" as an illustration of his exhortation not to use one's *exousia* (liberty/authority, to eat idol meat) if it would offend another member of the assembly. Over against some enlightened Corinthians who apparently believe themselves to be authorized, to be "free," in their newfound theological *gnōsis*, to engage in any mundane activity without consequence, Paul insists that although he is "free" with respect to all, he has not used his freedom, but "enslaved himself to all" in his "commission" to win/save as many as possible. Both of these references to himself as "a slave/enslaved" to the people appear to be specific to his argument against the enlightened Corinthians, and do not indicate a standard way of understanding apostleship, let alone of symbolizing the believer's relationship to Christ (see further Horsley, 1998:124–33).

Since, as Petersen acknowledges, Paul does not write of believers as "slaves of Christ," his claim that for Paul "believers know themselves to be slaves of Christ," indeed that the relations between Jesus Christ and believers "often represents typical and even ideal master-slave relations" (240, 242) appears to rest on a reading of *kyrios* in reference to Christ as lord in the sense of slave-master. But that reading would also appear to be unwarranted, at least in the vast majority of cases. *Kyrios* is, at base, the title of Jesus, and that title has the primary sense of political ruler, not of slave-master. That Jesus' title of Lord means political ruler can be seen again and again in the letters, whether in credal/confessional contexts or in reference to the parousia (e.g., Rom 1: 3–4; 10:9,12; 1 Cor 2:8; 8:5–6; 12:3; 2 Cor 4:5; 13:10; Phil 2:11; 3:20; 1 Thess 3:13; 4:6, 15–18). Particularly interesting in this regard may be Phil 3:20, where *sōtēr* as well as *kyrios* has explicit political ruler connotations in connection with believers' "citizenship," and Rom 10:9, 12 where Jews and Greeks have the same *kyrios*, or ruler. It is also noteworthy that in passages where "slavery" is used metaphorically for the human predicament under Sin, the Law, and Death (Romans 6–7, on which see below), Christ does not appear as a new or better or alternative "slave-master". Perhaps also telling is that in 2 Cor 4:5, where the apostle(s) proclaim(s) Jesus Christ as *kyrios* (= Lord/ruler, not slave-master), and the apostle(s) as slave(s), the latter are *your* slaves, not Christ's. Finally, in other apparently typically Pauline language usage, the *kyrios* comes in his *parousia* with all his *saints*, not his slaves (1 Thess 3:13); and the counterpart of the Lord in the present time is not slave but *brother* (1 Thess 4:6). Even in Philemon, *saints* is the term corresponding to the Lord (5) and "in the Lord" corresponds to "in the flesh," not to "slave" (16). Thus, if *kyrios* should be understood primarily in the sense that Christ is exalted as the true (if temporary) ruler or regent of God, then it is difficult to find any evidence for "master-slave relations in Paul's symbolic universe," let alone that master-slave was an organizing metaphor therein.[3]

In his exhortation to the Philippians to be of one mind, putting the interests of others above their own, he sets forth the pre-Pauline credal hymn portraying Christ Jesus as having become a slave, with no will of his own ("emptied himself"), obedient to the point of death, even death by the humiliating form of crucifixion used for slaves as well as rebellious provincials (Phil 2:1–11; on which see Briggs). However powerful a paradigm of slave-like humiliation the hymn communicated, Paul's ethical deployment of Christ as a slave in the humiliation of his crucifixion in Philippians 2 does not indicate that Paul thought of the status or role of believers as that of a slave of Christ. As we shall see below, Paul avoids just such a concept in Galatians 3–4, one of two principal passages in which he uses the language of slavery.

In contrast to his pointed "self-enslavement" in 1 Cor 9:19, Paul uses the verb *douleuō* metaphorically in other places where its meaning is not so pointedly "to be enslaved," but rather "to serve." In these texts the primary, denotative meaning does not appear to be "slavery," although in a Greek-speaking urban context the overtones of the term would be present. Timothy has "served me in the work of the gospel" (Phil 2:22). In commending the Thessalonians' faith Paul repeats reports that they had "turned to God from idols to serve a living and true God" (1 Thess 1:9). That is, the emphasis is on their turning from idols to God, repeated in "living and true God," with *douleuein* as a subordinate, unemphasized verb.[4] Paul uses the phrase "to serve the Lord or Christ" at three points toward the end of Romans, all in the context of exhortation concerning community order and solidarity: once in the middle of a series of several phrases, once in connection with refraining from eating food that might offend another, and once in exhortation not to cause dissensions (12:10–12; 14:13–23; 16:17–18). Such service of the Lord in maintaining community solidarity derives from the biblical tradition of Israel as servants of God, hence observing the covenantal mutuality that main-

---

[3] Petersen is surely right that Paul knows about and draws on the terminology of "the economic master-slave system of the world outside the church" (241). But all of those metaphors such as "purchase" and "redemption" and "buying" do not constitute evidence for a symbolization of the believer-Christ relation as that of "master-slave."

[4] *Pace* Martin (62), I see no basis in this section or the rest of 1 Thessalonians for *douleuein* being read as "to become slaves" and lending to idols and God the character of slave-masters. Aside from the lack of evidence that "slavery" is in focus in 1 Thess 1:9, to claim that conversion "could be represented as the prudent choice to enter into the more profitable relationship" "because of the relative benefits of slavery to a different master" appears to read a kind of modern economic rationalism back into a dynamic and perhaps dramatic change of life-orientation and emotional psycho-social transformation which the Thessalonians had undergone. In its dominant focus on cognitive meaning, NT exegesis generally tends to ignore or underestimate the presence and importance of emotion or "desire."

tained its group solidarity—although again the overtones of "slavery" would be present in the context of a slave-holding society. That this community solidarity as covenanted servants of the one Lord is the sense in 14:13-23 in particular is all the more evident by comparison with the one passage in which Paul clearly uses the metaphor of "(household) slave-and-master" (*oiketēs-kyrios*) for the believer-Christ relationship, earlier in the same discussion, at Rom 14:4 (although that also may have had a biblical background for Paul himself—sees Wright's survey of varying Greek translations for ʿ*bd* above).

By far the two most prominent passages in which the imagery of slavery (and freedom) plays a dominant role are the climax of Paul's sustained argument about how the fulfilment of the promise to Abraham has superceded the Law in Galatians 3-5, and the climax of his sustained argument of Romans 1-8 in chs. 6-8. In both of these passages slavery characterizes that from which Christians have been delivered. As a quick check in a concordance indicates, Gal 3:28 through 5:13 has the greatest concentration of the word complexes of slave/slavery and free/freedom in Paul's genuine letters; and Romans 6-8 is a close second. In Galatians 3-5 the "slavery" to which people are subjected is the minority status of still being under the Law or Sinai covenant and/or the subjection to the *stoicheia tou kosmou* (Gal 4:1-8). The gentile Galatians, born according to the Spirit, have received adoption as children and heirs in the fulfilment of the promise to Abraham now made possible by the redemption in Christ. He could have made his point simply by contrasting the situation of the underage son in the Roman (and Hellenistic?) family with that of the son who finally became the heir. His introduction of the slave serves to emphasize just how hopeless the Galatians' situation was under the "elemental spirits of the world" to which they had been enslaved—and would be under those "weak and beggarly elemental spirits" or the Law, if they reverted. Under Roman law and customs, the *paterfamilias* held all power and property until he took action to endow the son (or adopted son) as his heir. Thus the position of the heir to be was "no different from and/or better than that of the slave" over whom the slave-master not only held but often exercized the power of death. If we in any way mitigate the desperate situation of the slave in the patriarchal slave-owning household, we miss how Paul is attempting to portray to the Galatians the extremity of the danger they were in if they yielded to circumcision, etc. Paul's portrayal of the Galatians' previous situation as slavery to the elemental spirits—and their current danger of reversion—as slavery sets up his dramatic rhetorical climax to his argument focused on freedom, by way of an allegory on the classic biblical example of slave woman and slave son versus free woman and free son. His concluding statement is an almost ecstatic exultation in their newfound freedom over against their previous (and potential future) "slavery": "For freedom Christ has set us free! Stand firm, therefore, and do not submit again to a yoke of slavery.... For you were called to freedom!" For Paul, of course, in contrast with Greek philosophical thought based on the contrast between free master and constrained slave, that was not freedom in a formal, abstract, and individual sense, but freedom to join the new society and to express that freedom in love as "slaves to one another" (Gal 5:1, 13), in sharing one another's burdens" (6:2). Paul's argument for "freedom" here, of course, comes at the cost of a degrading treatment of the "slave-woman," Hagar, used as an allegory for the historical Jerusalem—a treatment very different from the more sympathetic narrative in Gen 16:1–16; 21:1–21.

It is conceivable that this whole extensive conceptualization of salvation focused on "liberation" or "freedom" from slavery to the Law emerged only in Paul's struggles with the Galatians, after which he utilized some of the same conceptual apparatus in the climax of his argument in Romans 1–8. This appears unlikely, however, for three reasons. First, his argument in Galatians has all the appearance of a reassertion of his message in response to what he sees as a misunderstanding or reversion by the Galatians. Second, twice elsewhere he uses "freedom" in passing in a way that sounds like a standard symbol in his "symbolic universe": the "freedom" he has "in Christ Jesus" which others are secretly spying out referred to in Gal 2:4, and what appears almost like one of his own special "Pauline proverbs" thrown into his argument about the unveiling of the old covenant in 2 Cor 3:18: "Where the spirit of the Lord is, there is freedom." Third, in Paul's discussion of eating idol meat in 1 Corinthians 8–10, "freedom" (9:1, 19; 10:29) is his own term for his own status in Christ, as can be seen from his use of the Corinthians' "buzz-word" *exousia* in 8:9 and their slogan *panta moi exestin* in 6:12. Freedom appears to be an important and central soteriological concept or symbol for Paul. And the most prominent uses of "slavery" in Paul's letters appear precisely to characterize that from which one has been redeemed. Paul's brief statement in 1 Cor 7:23 makes the same point, except that the implication is that by Christ they have been freed from slavery in the concrete human sense, not simply in the figurative sense.

In the second prominent passage Paul uses slavery or enslavement as the key metaphor for people's subjection to sin in Romans 6 and to the Law in Romans 7 and freedom for the climactic redemption at "the revelation of the sons of God" when even the creation groaning in travail would be transformed as well (Romans 8). To suggest that slavery in Romans 6–7 is a "salvific image ... recalling the benefits a slave might expect from a good master as opposed to a bad one" (Martin, 1990:62) quite literally *domesticates* Paul's sweeping salvation-historical argument. It risks making a subordinate image (slavery) into the dominant emphasis in the overall argument, and misses the background of Paul's way of thinking in the Israelite biblical tradition. Paul has just been articulating a grand scheme of human history, caught in a struggle for domination between the grace of God now manifested in the death and resurrection of Christ and the superhuman forces Sin, the Law and Death (5:12–21). In the struggle for control over human life and history, Sin had ruled in Death, but because of Christ's act of obedience, Grace is now ruling through justification for eternal life. Paul, however, is uneasy about the potential (logical) ethical implications of his exclamation that "as Sin increased, Grace abounded all the more" (5:20): "Does that mean that we should continue in Sin in order that Grace may abound?" (6:1). "By no means!" he insists, and then continues with images of the life-and-death struggle for control over human life. The struggling forces are still the same: Sin, Death, the Law *versus* God and righteousness in chs. 6–7, with the Spirit and God's Grace becoming more prominent in ch. 8. The dominant imagery is of political rule and domination by the superhuman forces of Sin, Death, and the Law *versus* God/ righteousness/ Spirit (*basileuein* 6:12, continuing 5:14, 17, 21; *kyrieuein*, 6:9, 14; 7:1) and the corresponding political subjection and servitude of people (*doulouein* 6:6; 7:6). In portraying this struggle for domination of human life, Paul features images of political violence such as military weapons, terrorizing execution by torture on the cross (crucifixion), and subjection/enslavement, on the one hand, and setting free by acquittal and liberation, on the other. Paul's use of the imagery of slavery/servitude here does not refer to the relations of master and slave in the household, but to the broader Roman imperial conquest, subjection, and enslavement of peoples such as the Jews/Israel. This is an argument formulated by a member of a people who had been subjected by the overwhelming military might of Rome and whose perspective had surely been formed in the apocalyptic mentality of frustrated Jerusalem scribal circles before he received his distinctive evangelical commission from his Lord, Jesus Christ. And it is an argument that he trusts will be appreciated by a Roman community of Christ-believers, some of whom (or some of whose ancestors) had likely been forcibly taken to Rome as "natally alienated" enslaved subjects (see my essay above [19–66] on the violence by which the Romans generated the slave system).

In Romans 6, in which Paul's concern is not soteriological but ethical, he indeed writes of "liberation" from Sin, but he now juxtaposes this "freedom" imagery with that of "slaves" to righteousness or "enslavement" to God (6:19, 22). In Romans 7, where Paul is at pains to avoid the implication that the Law actually caused sinning, he juxtaposes images of being free or discharged from the Law with being now enslaved in the new life of the Spirit (7:3,6). Although Paul ends his convoluted argument about the Law in 7:25 with the image of a dual slavery, the intentional one of the mind in struggle with the compulsive one of the flesh, he launches immediately into his climactic concluding argument on the highly positive note of liberation already underway: "For the law of the Spirit of life in Christ Jesus has set you free from the law of sin and death" (8:2). From that point, the rest of the argument in Romans 8 builds, through emphasis on the enlivening presence of the

Spirit (8:4–17), to an ever more dramatic climax (8:18–25, 26–39). He opposes the "spirit of slavery" with the "Spirit of adoption" which makes believers "children" and "heirs of God" and "joint heirs with Christ" (reminiscent of the argument in Galatians 4) about to be glorified with him (8:14–17). "Slavery" is now left behind in the almost ecstatic emphasis on the anticipated eschatological "freedom": "the creation itself will *be set free* (*eleutherōthēsetai*) from its bondage (*douleias*) to decay and will obtain the *freedom* (*eleutherian*) of the glory of the children of God" (Rom 8:21). Finally, the imagery at the very end of Romans 8 is, in effect, a rehearsal of God's apocalyptic mystery, i.e., the plan for the eschatological fulfilment of history that has run through Israel and not through but against Rome (cf. 1 Cor 2:7–8; 15:24–28, 51–56; Rom 11:25–27). The climactic "freedom of the glory of the children of God" is thus the eschatological resolution of God's (and Israel's and now Christ-believers') historical struggle against those superhuman forces that have held people in "slavery," including (the imperial) rulers (*archai*) as well as the more spiritual forces such as Death and angels, the struggle that Paul has been discussing throughout the argument from Romans 5–8, indeed throughout Romans 1–11.

This survey of Paul's use of slave/slavery and free/freedom suggests that some influential recent studies, like traditional Pauline interpretation, have overemphasized the importance of slavery metaphors and inappropriately valorized slave language in Paul's "theology" and "symbolic universe." Martin (1990:65), for example, argues that in many Pauline passages "slavery is functioning ... as a positive metaphor for Christian salvation as upward mobility." As he points out, however, there was precious little "upward mobility" in the Roman empire. In fact, about the only manifestation of it was a distinctive type of men, the *novi homines* most of whom, ironically, were products of the Roman slave system and the manumission that made the whole system work (see above, 48–53), for they acquired their wealth as freedmen clients of wealthy Roman patrons. The *novi homines* could rise only to a certain level, however, since their wealth could not buy *dignitas*. Petronius made art imitate life in the *Satyricon* (which was hardly an expression of "popular culture," but of elite, literate cultural attitudes) with his ridiculous figure of Trimalchio (see Wills's article above). As Martin himself points out (148), his thesis about slavery as a metaphor of upward mobility depends on the non-elite not sharing the Roman and Greek elite's utter disdain of all slaves. Stereotyped and ritualized sentiments in inscriptions, some of which may have been sponsored by the slaves' masters, hardly provide adequate evidence. And it seems generally doubtful that the low status free population felt much solidarity with slaves, the very persons in the social order that defined them as at least free-born. The very concept of upward mobility (apparently from Meeks), of course, derives from an individualistic sociological worldview that accepts and presupposes the dominant social system (without fundamental critique let alone challenge) and then focuses on how individuals may be upwardly or downwardly mobile within it. As argued below, however, far from facilitating upward mobility in imperial society, Paul proclaims a radical challenge to the dominant social system of the Roman world.

Although Paul refers to himself in a semi-titular way as a "slave of Christ," it is simply not true that he refers to believers generally as "slaves of Christ" or conceives of the God/Christ-human relationship in terms of master-slave relations. Nor does he use "slavery" as a positive soteriological image. In the two principal passages which focus on slavery and freedom imagery, "slavery" refers to people's subjection to super-human powers such as Sin and Death, Law and "elemental spirits" in the situation prior to Christ. The Christ events, however, have brought about (the possibility of) "freedom" for those who believe. Paul, however, did not understand "freedom" in a formal abstract individualistic sense. For Paul freedom was a contingent historical shift from servitude to dehumanizing superhuman forces to obedience to God. In that sense, he stands in the Israelite tradition that understood its historical liberation from bondage to human rulers (in Egypt, etc.) as involving a continuing commitment in service of God, who required obedience to fundamental covenantal principles of social cooperation and solidarity. The dominant note in Paul's arguments, particularly in Galatians 3–5 and Romans 6–8, however, is that "slavery" characterizes that bondage to superhuman forces to which people/believers have been historically subjected, while "freedom" characterizes the deliverance that God has inaugurated and will soon complete in the crucifixion, resurrection, and parousia of Christ.

Paul's Stance towards Slaves in the *Ekklésia*

The brief examination of the information Paul provides about himself and his understanding of his mission made above indicated that he was evidently attempting to establish communities of what was, in effect, an international counter-imperial (alternative) society. It was international (and multicultural) insofar as assemblies were established in a number of cities and peoples, and as the assemblies in particular cities involved people of various and/or hybrid ethnic and cultural background. It was counter-imperial insofar as it owed its loyalty to Christ, who was enthroned in heaven as the true emperor or *kyrios* of the assemblies, indeed of the world (1 Cor 2:6–8; 15:24–28; Phil 3:17–21). And it was an alternative society insofar as the assemblies were to conduct their own affairs, without interacting with the civil and other aspects of the dominant society while recruiting and expanding their movement (esp. 1 Corinthians 5; 6:1–11; 7:29–31; 10:14–22) during the time remaining before the parousia of their Lord. The key text for determining Paul's stance on slaves and slavery, as for assessing his position on social relations generally, is the baptismal formula he cites at the climax of his explanation of his gospel and mission in Galatians 3 (Schüssler Fiorenza). It should be possible to move beyond anachronistic understandings, such as the purely spiritual or the liberal individualistic, abstracted from the historical context of Paul's Galatian, Thessalonian, Corinthian, etc. *ekklēsiai* in the Roman imperial order.

Depending on how concretely we take the language of the baptismal formula, the sacred words pronounced at the initiation of people into the new society ("there is no longer Jew or Greek, there is no longer slave or free, there is no longer male and female," Gal 3:28), it can be read to mean that the principle forms of social domination that prevailed in Roman imperial society were supposedly transcended in the new alternative society. Presumably this formula expressed at least the ideal social relations in the new movement, the *ekklēsia*, for Paul in his own mission. By scholarly consensus, Paul was adamant that there be "no longer Jew or Greek" in the assemblies he helped organize among the peoples of Asia Minor and Greece. That is, in contrast to the ideology of the Roman imperial order, for Paul history had been run toward its fulfilment not through Rome but through Israel. The promises to Abraham included blessings not just for Israelites but for the other peoples of the world as well. Yet Paul insisted, over against Peter and James and others, that to receive those blessings the Jews/Israelites had no pride of place other than historical priority in God's plan. The Galatian people and others could now become heirs of God's blessings in their own right, as whoever they were, without having to become Jews, without having to join Israel by being circumcised (Galatians 3–4; cf. Romans 9–11, esp 9:22–26, 10:12–13). Paul's principle for all the particular assemblies of "remaining in the condition in which you were called" (into the *ekkēsia*) applied well in the case of the circumcised and the uncircumcised, so that precisely as their ethnic-cultural differences remained intact, there would no longer be any distinction between Jew and Greek in the determination of blessings and membership in the assemblies.

Debate currently rages, however, over whether Paul himself compromised on the issues of slave or free and male and female, regressing toward the prevailing patterns of traditional social relations when push came to shove in certain local assemblies such as the one in Corinth. Within a generation or two, of course, some early Christian writers who saw themselves as the heirs of Paul had simply assimilated to the dominant imperial order, reverting to the usual domination of Jews by Gentiles, slaves by free, and females by males (Ephesians, Colossians, the Pastorals). Modern Western Christian theology, rooted in scriptures that included these deutero-Pauline letters, has done somewhat the same, by reading Paul's statements as only religious/theological (e.g., the institution of slavery or patriarchal marriage continues, but there is no longer slave and free, male and female *in the eyes of God*). Whether there is a warrant for this in Paul's own letters on the issue of male and female depends heavily on whether certain passages such as 1 Cor 11:3–16 and 14:34–36 are accepted as written by Paul himself (Wire) or are taken as later interpolations (Horsley, 1998). While relevant to the issue of slave and free, however, the issue of male and female cannot be explored here. To explore the issue of slave and free the next step is to examine critically Paul's few statements about slaves/slavery to determine how concretely Paul may have understood the baptismal formula. In the following section we can then assess evidence for the way in which early Christian communities acted with regard to slaves who had joined the movement, which may also shed some light on what Paul may have been urging on his newly founded assemblies at the inception of the movement in Greece and Asia Minor.

As noted at the outset, once the deutero-Pauline letters were separated from Paul's own letters, the standard view of Paul as an advocate of slaves remaining in their slave status—and as a social conservative generally—focused on only two principal texts, 1 Cor 7:21 and the letter to Philemon. This has involved a misreading in both cases. Recent studies have made clear that the letter to Philemon is not about a runaway slave, perhaps does not concern a slave at all, and that there are compelling reasons to read 1 Cor 7:21 as instructing a slave to take the opportunity of freedom if presented rather than to remain in slavery.

The Letter to Philemon

The traditional scholarly interpretation of Philemon could not have been more helpful for pro-slavery arguments, even for legitimation of the fugitive slave law. Onesimus was a runaway slave and Philemon his master. Bishop Lightfoot's commentary on Philemon reveals how much this view depends on the stereotype of the irresponsible lying and stealing slave:

> He was a thief and a runaway. His offence did not differ in any way, so far as we know, from the vulgar type of slavish offences. He seems to have done just what the representative slave in the Roman comedy threatens to do, when he gets into trouble. He had "packed up some goods and taken to his heels." Rome was the natural cesspool for these offscourings of humanity. In the thronging crowds of the metropolis was his best hope of secrecy. In the dregs of the city rabble he would find the society of congenial spirits. (310)

Having encountered Paul (or having sought him out) in prison in Rome or Ephesus, Onesimus was converted to Christ, whereupon Paul sent the fugitive slave back to his owner Philemon with remonstrance that the latter receive him back as a "brother," without the expected whipping or other standard punishment.

Without questioning the traditional assumption that Onesimus was the fugitive slave of Philemon, and building on more recent literary criticism and a sensitivity to the narrative implied in the letter, Petersen argues that in fact Paul is, with subtle rhetorical skill, leading Philemon to the decision to manumit Onesimus. Petersen makes sure we realize just how serious a situation this is, both for the "worldly" social relations of slavery and for the "churchly" social relations of ostensible siblings in Christ. "Onesimus' action, therefore, poses a threat both to the institutionalized social system and to the [social] structures it serves, and it is in this light that we can best appreciate the state of tension that surrounds the relationship between Onesimus and Philemon and encompasses people like Paul who have gotten involved with the guilty party" (Petersen: 94). Meanwhile, in the church that meets in Philemon's house, the pressure is on Philemon, both from Paul's letter and from the rest of the church, co-addressees of the letter. "It is now [Philemon's] responsibility to act in such a way as to bring *his* social relations with Onesimus into conformity with both their structural ground and the social systems that function to preserve the structures" (98). The pressure is on also partly because the community needs to have its problem solved, needs to have its social relations brought into conformity with its social structure and social system. "We can safely assume that this message was understood by all concerned, certainly after the reception of Paul's letter" (99). For Paul has subtly but clearly and in a highly public manner insisted on "the structures and relationships of equality" (101). Thus, even on the traditional assumption that Onesimus was Philemon's runaway slave, an appropriate reading of Paul's rhetoric leads to the recognition that Paul is here advocating the emancipation at least of a slave who had joined his movement by his master who was also a member of the movement.

Unfortunately this argument, however attractive it makes Paul appear as an ostentible liberationist within his own movement, is flawed in its dependence on an unwarranted assumption. It assumes that, in writing the Letter to Philemon *et alii* and sending Onesimus back, Paul can count on the addressees sharing not only the same symbolic universe but a corresponding social structure and social system of equality (brother- and sisterhood) as well. Then how can it be that it was not until Onesimus was converted that the problem arose for the first time? Why had the problem not come up when Philemon had been converted. Was there no problem with a member of the siblinghood remaining a slave-master as long as the slave himself did not belong? But the assembly consisting only of a dozen or so "siblings" was meeting in the relatively intimate atmosphere of Philemon's own household (Petersen: 100). If he had been a household slave, Onesimus had probably been involved in waiting on the other members of the congregation when they held meetings at Philemon's house. If the problem of Onesimus being

Philemon's slave had not arisen both for Philemon himself and for the siblinghood when Philemon was converted/joined—i.e., if there was no serious sense of the social implications of the baptismal formula of no longer slave or free, etc.—then what grounds do we have for believing that it was a problem when Onesimus was converted? Perhaps there would have been an embarrassment involved. But if we take evidence for the pervasive acceptance of slavery in the Hellenistic-Roman world and for the general paternalism involved in household relations, then the point about the church meeting in Philemon's household would play the other way, i.e. in the "relatively intimate atmosphere" of Philemon's own house, it would be all the more difficult to make a decisive departure from long-established and widely-accepted patterns into which all concerned had been thoroughly "socialized." For evidence we need only note that the "assemblies" addressed in the "Pauline" letters to the Colossians, the Ephesians, and the pastorals apparently simply presupposed that addressees were members of patriarchal slave-holding households that formed the basis of the Roman imperial order as well as the classical city-states (Schüssler Fiorenza).

While Petersen carried out his innovative new reading of Philemon without questioning the traditional assumption of Onesimus as a runaway slave, others were simultaneously questioning that assumption. Independently, both Sara Winter and Peter Lampe, building on the much earlier work of John Knox (1935), established that Onesimus was not a fugitive. According to Roman jurists, a slave such as Onesimus seeking out a friend of his master's such as Paul was not considered a fugitive (Lampe). The introductory "thanksgiving" section of a letter such as that to Philemon, moreover, ordinarily informs the recipient of important events that have happened since the last communication, yet Paul does not mention the circumstances of Onesimus' arrival. This means that the recipients of the letter, Philemon, Apphia, and Archippus, already knew that Onesimus was with Paul, indeed probably that they had sent him, just as the Philippians had sent Epaphroditus to minister to Paul in prison (Phlm 2:25–30; Winter 1984; 1987). In fact, far from sending Onesimus back to his servitude under Philemon, Paul is petitioning Philemon (in the legal language of Philemon 8–14) to permit Onesimus to remain with him in the service of the gospel, and Onesimus is no longer to be considered a slave in the Christian community (Winter 1987:5–9, 10–11).[5]

Either of these readings that eliminate the "fugitive" aspect of Onesimus' presumed slave status would fit better into the historical situation of

---

[5] Barclay attempts to rehabilitate the runaway slave hypothesis, involving Paul in a violation of Deut 23:15–16 (164–65). In a highly speculative reconstruction, he pictures Paul as addressing well-established churches such as those evident in the deutero-Pauline letters: "Paul could not imagine how the wealthier members of his churches could retain their social status or their houses without the ownership of slaves; and he and his churches depended on such people as financial supporters and hosts of the Christian movement" (166, 176, 184).

Paul's mission, which would have involved the necessary "re-socialization" or "secondary socialization" that Petersen did not take into account. Following Lampe's reading of the letter, one could imagine that Onesimus, having heard about or experienced Paul's message and the baptismal celebration of "no longer slave or free," had appealed to Paul for assistance in leading Philemon to bring the relations in his household more into accord with what had happened in the crucifixion-resurrection of Christ and believers' baptism into Christ. Similarly, following Winter's reading of the letter, one could imagine how Paul, using an ad hoc letter as an instrument in the "re-socialization" of Philemon and his "house-assembly," skillfully led his "beloved co-worker" to release Onesimus from his domestic servitude for service in the gospel ("knowing that you will do more than I ask"). Like Petersen's approach to Paul's letter to Philemon, Lampe's and especially Winter's interpretation of the letter reconstruct Paul as an active advocate of freedom for a slave in one of the communities he had helped catalyze, a reading diametrically opposed to the traditional understanding of both this letter and Paul in general.

An even more decisive challenge to the traditional assumption about Onesimus and Philemon has come in Allen Callahan's recent work (1993; 1995; 1997). Not only was Onesimus not a runaway slave; he was not a slave. None of the components of the traditional stereotyped view of Onesimus as a fugitive slave and thief is indicated in the text of the letter itself. Callahan reinforces his own acute observations regarding what is contained or implied and what is not contained or implied in the text of the letter with earlier readings that were not constrained by what became the traditional Christian interpretation. Driven to question the "Pro-slavery Perversions of the New Testament" such as the traditional claims about Onesimus and Philemon, abolitionists took a closer look at the text. "A slight examination of the epistle assures us that . . . there is not a particle of evidence in it to prove that [Philemon] was a slaveholder, but the reverse. . . . Nor is there any evidence that Onesimus was a slave, but the reverse." (Bourne: 82; Callahan 1997:11). Indeed, "there is evidence in the epistle [v. 16] that Onesimus was a natural brother to Philemon. . . . Paul calls him "a brother beloved, especially to me, but how much more unto thee both IN THE FLESH and in the Lord'" (Fee, 1848:112; Callahan 1997:11). Callahan himself points out incisively that in the decisive passage, the only place where "slave" (*doulos*) appears, the key word is "as (if)" (*hōs*), since it indicates a virtual, not actual, state of affairs. In the next sentence (17b) Paul urged Philemon to receive Onesimus *hōs emē*, "as (you would) me" (and note in v. 14: *hōs kata anagkēn*, "as though by constraint"). "Likewise, in verse 16a *hōs* indicates that Paul is speaking not of Onesimus's actual status, but of Philemon's attitude toward Onesimus and thus of Onesimus's virtual status in Philemon's eyes" (1993:362). Callahan further dismantles and dismisses arguments adduced from supposedly parallel letters used as evidence in support of Onesimus' slave status and/or

Paul's message to Philemon. The supposed parallels, however, only serve to illustrate that what we would expect to find in the letter to Philemon on the fugitive slave interpretation are in fact missing (Callahan 1997:6–8; *contra* Lohse: 196–97 ; Nordling: 100–101). Newly discovered inscriptions from the Roman imperial period, moreover, invalidate previous arguments (by Lightfoot and others) that the name "Onesimus" was an indication of servile status (G. H. R. Horsley, 1982:4 #96; Callahan, 1997:10, 34–35).

Callahan's research, furthermore, has ferreted out the source of the fugitive slave interpretation of the letter to Philemon (see esp. Callahan, 1993; 1995; cf. Mitchell). Callahan has examined the manuscript history and the reception-history of the letter more thoroughly and critically than previously done. Until the late-fourth century Christians apparently either ignored the letter or considered it insignificant, unedifying, and/or non-Pauline, as indicated in comments by church fathers such as Jerome, John Chrysostom, and Theodore of Mopsuestia. Then, in the late-fourth century, beginning with and primarily in the writings of John Chrysostom, explicitly over against the widespread denigration of the letter, appears a virtual topos of the stereotyped "runaway-slave-who-absconded-with-his-master's belongings" illustrated by Onesimus. Indeed, slavery is one of Chrysostom's favorite topics. In fact, it is evident at points that Chrysostom, in attempting to rehabilitate the letter to Philemon on the (supposedly original) runaway slave reading, was attempting to counter the subversive disestablishmentarian reputation of the Christianity of his day: "many are saying Christianity has been introduced into life for the subversion of everything, masters having their servants taken from them, and it is a matter of violence" (Chrysostom in Callahan, 1997:14). Thus the runaway slave reading of the letter to Philemon that appears toward the end of the fourth century in Chrysostom, Jerome, Theodore and other church "fathers" "perhaps can best be understood in the context of the conservative reaction that gripped elites in the late empire. This conservatism called for a biblical hermeneutics of domestication, an appeal to "traditional values" to shore up the crisis-ridden Roman order." (Callahan, 1997:15).

Besides further exposing the "Pro-Slavery Perversions of the New Testament" begun by abolitionists over a century and a half ago, Callahan's research effectively eliminates Philemon as a text pertinent to Paul's attitude or practice toward slavery. Among the material cited by Callahan is a report by a white missionary to slaves in antebellum Georgia that his audience had the critical sense to reject the epistle to Philemon in his pro-slavery interpretation. The letter to Philemon, far from providing evidence that Paul acquiesced in or even advocated slavery, turns out to be irrelevant to the issue of slavery.

1 Corinthians 7:21

Apparent ambiguities in the text of 1 Cor 7:21b provided an opportunity for advocates of slavery and defenders of power and privilege to develop the traditional "conservative" interpretation of Paul as defender of differential power-relations. Key is Paul's "brachylogy," his rhetorical omission of an object in the last, imperative clause: "rather use [it]" (*mallōn chrēsai*). Correspondingly, the *ei kai* in the preceding apodosis can be read either as "even if" or as "if indeed." The standard established interpretation simply inserted "slavery" as the object and read Paul to say: "Were you called as a slave? Do not worry about it. But even if you can become free, rather make use of your slavery." The continuing confusion and indecisiveness among established scholars is evident in the switches made in the Revised Standard and the New Revised Standard Versions. The RSV committee went against the traditional interpretation, choosing "use freedom," while indicating the alternative translation "use slavery" in a footnote. Then, as noted above, the NRSV committee, while substituting "inclusive language" for Paul's patriarchal terms such as "brothers," reverted to the traditional "use slavery," albeit cloaking the severity of the translation with the euphemistic "your present condition," while relegating the alternative "choose freedom" to a footnote.

The fourth-century theologian John Chrysostom, whose influence contributed decisively to the establishment of the traditional pro-slavery interpretation, knew very well that this passage had been understood in the opposite sense. "Now I am not ignorant that some say that the words 'rather use it' are spoken with regard to freedom, interpreting it: 'if you can be come free, become free.' But...." (*Hom. 19 in epist. I ad Cor.* 5 [PG 61.164]; further discussion in Harrill: 77–78). In his exegetical writing, Luther broke with the traditional interpretation: "'But,' St Paul says, 'if you can gain your freedom, avail yourselves of the opportunity'," reassuring the serfs of his day that they were not "to interpret the words of St. Paul, when he says that everyone should remain in the estate in which he was called, to mean that [they] must remain a serf" (Luther 28:42–43)—although he reverted to the traditional interpretation of 1 Cor 7:21 in his adamant opposition to the "Twelve Articles of the Peasants in Swabia" and the German peasants' revolt of 1525 (Luther 46:146–47). Abolitionists, like Luther in his exegetical mode, discerned that 1 Cor 7:21 could be claimed for the emancipation of slaves. But established biblical scholarship reverted to the traditional pro-slavery reading, with the estimable Adolf von Harnack declaring authoritatively that "it is a mistake to suppose that any 'slave question' occupied the early church" (Harnack: 192; Harrill: 83–93). Underlying the traditional interpretation, besides the general conservative stance of established biblical studies, was a dualistic theological stance separating the spiritual realm from the concrete social or worldly realm and the well-known tendency to read biblical statements or pericopes in isolation from their literary and historical contexts. As noted in recent studies, modern scholars who followed the traditional interpretation usually justified it on theological grounds or (ironically) because the "context" of the general argument in 1 Cor 7:17–24, that everyone should remain in the condition in which they were called required it (e.g., Barrett: 170; Conzelmann: 130).

Lexical and syntactical considerations require the "choose freedom" reading. In an elliptical (brachylogical) sentence such as 1 Cor 7:21b, "one would ordinarily supply a word from that sentence—in this case 'freedom'—not a word from an earlier sentence," i.e., "slavery" from 7:21a (Fee 1987:317). Moreover, although Paul uses the combination *ei kai* (or *ean kai*) in a concessive sense ("although/even if . . ." e.g. in 2 Cor 4:16, he also uses it with emphatic effect ("if indeed"), for example in 1 Cor 4:7; 7:11 and 7:28. Used together with *alla* ("But . . .") here, the sense is unmistakably an emphatic contrast with the preceding statement ("Were you called as a slave? Do not be concerned about it."): "*But if indeed you can become free. . . .*" (Fee 1987:317; Dawes: 692). Even more decisive, it has recently been shown that "the force of the adverb *mallōn*, when used with the deponent verb *chraōmai*," while occasionally appearing intensive, "is usually adversative," so that it has the sense of "instead" or "preferably" rather than of "more" (Harrill: 109–19). The many comparative texts adduced, moreover, suggest that the "rather use [it]" in 1 Cor 7:21b contrasts not with "if you can become free" immediately preceding it but with the previous question-and-command, i.e., being called as a slave and not worrying about it, in 7:21a.

Contrary to the arguments of its defenders, considerations of literary context do not support the traditional interpretation of 1 Cor 7:21. Even within the limited literary context of 1 Cor 7:17–24, far from being a second example parallel to that of the circumcised and uncircumcised in 7:18–19, which illustrates the general principle in 7:17, 20, 24, Paul's address to slaves and others in 7:21–23 breaks the pattern and offers an exception to the general principle. In 7:18–19 Paul is following a standard rhetorical ("diatribal") pattern in which a statement of fact is given in the form of a rhetorical question, followed by an imperative and an explanation. 1 Cor 7:18 (cf. 7:27) consists of a pair of corresponding rhetorical questions plus imperatives, and 7:19 (cf. 7:26a, 29a) the explanation ("[un]circumcision is nothing, but obeying . . . is everything . . ."). In 7:21–23, however, both 21b and, in effect, 22–23 interrupt the pattern begun in 21a. On analogy with 7:18a and b followed by 7:19 we would expect 7:21a to read "do not seek your freedom," 7:21b to read "Were you free when called? Do not . . . ," followed by a 7:22 reading "For slavery is nothing and freedom is nothing. . . ." The latter would provide the *theological* explanation necessary for the instruction in 7:21a to fit and illustrate the principle articulated in 7:17, 20, 24. Instead we find the more consolatory "do not be concerned about it" in 7:21a, then the strong adversatives "But . . . rather" in 7:21b, and Paul's rhetorical playing with the respective new relationships of believers with Christ in terms of slave/freedperson in 7:22, followed by the strong general exhortation (to all) not to become slaves of human masters in 7:23. Nothing in 7:22–23 explains why a slave who is offered freedom should nevertheless remain a slave. His command is precisely the opposite: "Do not become slaves. . . ." The slave and free "conditions" are not analogous to the circumcised-uncircumcised and the married-unmarried, and Paul's address to slaves is an exception to his "rule in all the assemblies" (7:17, 20, 24). "Either Paul added 7:21b to turn up the volume, so to speak, on an already shrill pattern of rhetoric"—a further slap in the face for one who was a slave when called!—"or he intended to mute its shrillness, so as to avoid being led by this diatribal pattern into saying something that he really did not mean" (Deming: 136). Further considerations below will indicate that he obviously wished to mitigate, not increase, the possible rhetorical impact of his attempted condolence of 7:21a.

Moreover, the recent recognition that Paul makes sustained arguments in his letters and the related recent rediscovery of rhetorical criticism have led to the realization that 7:17–24 is not a separate discussion of Jews and Gentiles and slaves and free in their own right but a pointed "digression" or illustration by analogy as an integral step in the larger argument on marriage and sexual relations in 1 Corinthians 7 as a whole (Dawes; Deming). Throughout the argument on marriage and sex in 1 Corinthians 7, Paul includes exceptions in his advice to various kinds of relations. In 7:1–7 he inserts a temporary exception, 7:5a, into his general exhortation to spouses to engage in regular conjugal sexual relations. 1 Cor 7:9 offers an exception to the general advice to the unmarried and widows in 7:8. 7:11a provides an exception to his command to married people not to separate or divorce. 7:15 interrupts the advice to those married to unbelievers in 7:12–16 with an exception. And 7:28 (and 7:35) interrupts with an exception Paul's general counsel for the single to remain so in 7:25–31(-38). 7:21–23 can therefore be seen as the corresponding exception in his presentation of his general rule that "each remain in the condition in which s/he was called" in 7:17–24. He easily illustrates his rule with the directly analogous conditions of those who were circumcised or uncircumcised when called in 7:18–19. Someone who was a slave when called, however, is an exception to the rule of remaining in the condition in which one was called, requiring special instruction and exhortation. And in providing that exception to his general rule in 7:17–24, Paul's "digression" parallels all of the preceding and succeeding instructions/advice to the various categories of married or unmarried in 1 Corinthians 7.

The historical context, finally, virtually requires the "choose freedom" reading, since the traditional interpretation would have been simply unintelligible. In the context of the early Roman empire, in which even social conservatives such as Cicero or Seneca both advocated and practiced manumission of their household slaves, it would have been utterly reactionary for Paul to have commanded slaves who had a chance of manumission to remain in slavery. As discussed in the essay on ancient slavery above, a credible prospect of manumission was one of the principal factors that made the Roman system of slavery work. To advise slaves to refuse manumission would hardly have been an advocacy of the established order/*status quo*. Are we to imagine that Paul was either particularly hostile to slaves or, on the other side of the spectrum, that he had some strange scheme to build up slave resentment to the point of explosion as part of "the end" when "every rule and every authority and power" would be destroyed (cf. 1 Cor 15:24)? That he encouraged slaves who could become free to use the opportunity would appear to be the only historically intelligible reading of 1 Cor 7:21b in the context of the Roman empire.

From all of these interrelated and overlapping factors that impinge on the reading. Interpretation of 1 Cor 7:21, it is clear that slaves were a special case not parallel with or comparable to married and unmarried and circumcised and uncircumcised. Except possibly for an adamant non-believing spouse, no external forces in the dominant society would have prevented wives and husbands or Jews and Gentiles from the various courses of behavior mentioned in 1 Corinthians 7 and basically left up to each person to decide for her/himself. Because slavery was constituted and supported by institutionalized violence and coercion, however, slaves had no comparable freedom of ethical choice. In contrast to circumcision and uncircumcision, which are each "nothing" (7:19), slavery is indeed "something" that matters, presumably because it is contrary to the freedom that God has brought by means of the Christ events. So Paul makes a significant exception for slaves to his "rule in all the churches" about remaining in the condition at the time of one's call: if you can gain your freedom, by all means do so. In 7:22 he then reinforces that instruction with an argument that relativizes the standing of slaves and free in the *ekklēsia*, i.e., "in Christ," in a way that corresponds to the erasure of the differences between married and unmarried and circumcised and uncircumcised. Indeed, the slave who has become the "freedperson of Christ" now has (as it were) a standing higher and freer than the free person who has become the "slave of Christ" (and both have obligations to their Lord). "Slave of Christ" here is clearly part of Paul's rhetorical word-play, of course, and can hardly be taken as referring to a general status or role of all believers.

Finally, we should note what is not included in the argument of 1 Corinthians 7 with regard to slaves/slavery. Many interpreters of 1 Cor 7:21 and/or of Paul on slavery take Paul's insistence that "the appointed time has grown short . . . the present form of this world is passing away" (1 Cor 7: 29–31), together with his rule about remaining in one's condition when called, as the literary context that determines the meaning of 1 Cor 7:21b. Their arguments are usually variations on how, in the face of the impending end of the world, there is no point in altering institutionalized social relations such as slavery. Rigorous application of rhetorical criticism, however, would require recognition that Paul's point about the time having grown short is part of his argument addressed to men who are contemplating marriage to a "virgin" (1 Cor 7:25–38). The general "rule" from 7:17, 20, 24 is repeated in 7:26. But Paul had just made the situation of slaves an exception to that general rule. Considering the structure of the overall argument of 1 Corinthians 7, therefore, the point about the time having grown short does not apply directly to the situation of slaves. If we were to speculate how it might apply indirectly to the situation of slaves, we would have to consider that slaves would be an exceptional case considering the shortness of time just as they were to the general rule about remaining in one's condition. This would appear to be the implication of the principle of "as if not . . ." which Paul derives from the shortness of the time, if we draw the analogy with the particular case of "possessions" and the general case of "dealings with the world" (7:30–31). Since the form of this world is passing away, believers are to deal with worldly institutions and relationships as if they were not. Thus, just as those with possessions are to act as if they did not have them, so presumably those in slavery are to act as if they were not. It is pertinent to remember that this argument comes shortly after others in which Paul insists that the *ekklēsia* in Corinth act in independence of the dominant society in handling its own internal conflicts (1 Corinthians 5 and 6:1–11). Thus, if there are any implications for slaves in the shortness of time argument, it would appear to be in the direction of "rather choose/use [freedom]"!

Also worth noting are two other ways in which arguments made with respect to marital relations elsewhere in 1 Corinthians 7 have no counterpart with respect to slaves in 7:21–23. Paul urges wives and husbands to remain in marriage, including regular sexual relations, as a means of preventing *porneia* (1 Cor 7:1–5). But he does not urge slaves to remain in slavery as a means of counteracting some corresponding threat to the ekklēsia. He also encourages the believing wife to remain in marriage with an unbelieving husband because she just might save him (7:13–16). But he does not encourage a slave to remain in her or his present condition because s/he might save the slave-master.

Implications for Galatians 3:28

The conclusions reached in the preceding examinations of Paul's use of the language of slavery and freedom and his statements pertinent to slaves lead to a more precise sense of what Paul understood as the implications of the baptismal formula with which he concludes his argument about fulfilment of the promise to Abraham in Galatians 3. Some previous theological readings understood the new relations that had resulted from the Christ events as strictly spiritual, in terms only of believers' relationship with God, with no implications for social relations, even within the church. But it has become clear that Paul's phrase "in Christ" was not purely spiritual; it included the social dimension, meaning "in the assembly(ies)" under the Lordship of Christ. That the whole formula has implications for social relations is clear at least from Paul's insistence that differential standing of Jew and Greek be transcended in the assemblies. As noted above, his insistence that the Galatians did not have to join Israel (by being circumcised) in order to become heirs of the promises to Abraham indicates just how concretely he understood this aspect of the ideal enacted in the baptismal ritual of entry into the assembly (Galatians 3–4). Similarly the uncircumcised in Corinth (and Philippi and Thessalonikē, etc., as stated in 1 Cor 7:18, 20, 24) did not have to change their ethnic-cultural identity to receive the blessings promised through Abraham's seed. Although God had worked through the history of Israel to fulfil his plan (mystery) for humankind, the peoples were included with their ethnic-cultural differences intact, and did not have to meet some particular requirement. "No longer Jew or Greek" can hardly be reduced to a merely spiritual matter or to only *coram deo*, although those dimensions are included.

The traditional interpretation of Philemon and 1 Cor 7:21 in terms of Paul's advocating that slaves remain in their condition, however, led interpreters to think either that Paul was inconsistent, implementing the "no longer Jew or Greek" but not the "no longer slave or free," and/or that Paul meant the new situation only in spiritual terms. Once we recognize that Paul represents the deliverance accomplished in the Christ events as meaning believers' freedom over against their previous slavery to superhuman forces, that Philemon is either irrelevant to the issue or should be read to argue in favor of Onesimus' manumission, and that 1 Cor 7:21 must be read as Paul's encouragement of a slave to choose freedom if it were offered, it becomes not only possible but necessary to entertain a far more socially concrete reading of Gal 3:28. Another look at 1 Corinthians 7 and a general observation about interpreting Paul reinforce this conclusion.

Although it often goes unrecognized by interpreters of 1 Cor 7:21, Paul's arguments in both 1 Corinthians 7 and 1 Corinthians 12 refer to and build on the baptismal formula cited in Gal 3:28 (albeit in different ways). His reference to the baptismal formula is explicit in 1 Cor 12:13. But why does he omit the third pair, "male and female," there? Recent investigations of Paul's arguments in 1 Corinthians and the rhetorical and historical situations they address have solidified the conclusion that it was precisely because the baptismal formula had implications for concrete social relations of people in the assemblies. That is, some of the Corinthians had taken the liberty of becoming independent of traditional patriarchal marriage, including sexual relations, perhaps precisely on the grounds stated in their baptism, i.e. that for believers traditional patriarchal marriage had been transcended (Schüssler Fiorenza; Wire). While not explicitly referring to baptism, 1 Cor 7:18–19, 21–23, in the context of an argument about marital-sexual relations, is clearly referring to the same three problematic traditional social relations which were declared transcended in the baptismal formula. Paul's argument and points in 1 Corinthians 7, moreover, indicate that he considers those problematic traditional relations transcended in regard both to "male and female" (married and unmarried) and to circumcised and uncircumcised. The latter were now "nothings" with clear implications for concrete relations and behavior in the assemblies (do not seek circumcision, etc). With regard to "male and female" Paul writes in a "rhetoric of equality" (7:1–16) that includes the statement unheard of under patriarchy, that a woman has authority over her husband's body just as he has authority over hers (7:4)— although this rhetoric may well be manipulative of the women who are its primary addressees (Wire: 79–90). When he comes to the third case, that of slaves and free, where institutionalized violent coercion still constrained the behavior of slaves, he makes the appropriate exception to his "rule in all the assemblies": rather than remain in their condition, they should take the opportunity of becoming free if offered.

Because Paul's letters have been interpreted primarily for edification of faith and the spiritual life, which has been reinforced by the historically peculiar modern Western separation of religion from the political-economic dimensions of life, Paul's orientation to the social, political, and even economic aspects of life have simply gone unrecognized. Whether the issue be the collection for the poor among the saints in Jerusalem (1 Cor 16:1–4; 2 Corinthians 8–9), support for his own mission (1 Corinthians 9; Phil 4: 15–18), the threat of *porneia* (1 Cor 6:12–20), marriage and sexual relations (1 Corinthians 7), eating food offered to idols (1 Corinthians 8, 10), physical suffering and persecution (1 Thessalonians 1–2, 5), becoming circumcised (Galatians 2–6), the resurrection of the dead (body! 1 Corinthians 15; 2 Corinthians 5), or the relationship of members within the assemblies (e.g., 1 Corinthians 1–4, 5, 12; 1 Thess 4:9–12), much of Paul's writing focuses on concrete aspects of political-economic-social life. Indeed, as indicated briefly above, it appears that Paul's overall agenda in his mission was to build a new international society alternative to Roman imperial society, organized in local *ekklēsiai* which he insisted stand over against the institutions of the dominant order (1 Cor 6:1–11).[6] It is in that context that the baptismal formula

---

[6] See further the argument in Horsley, 1997: chap. 14. Jennifer Glancy has recently called attention to a fundamental reality of ancient Roman slavery that has been more or less ignored in New Testament studies: not only was slavery tantamount to forced prostitution for many slaves, particularly women and boys, but slaves in general were subject to the sexual predations of their masters, his friends, and family members (483–90). This does not mean that slaves would have been excluded from Paul's *ekklēsiai* because they would supposedly corrupt the "body." As pointed out below, slaves were clearly included in the congregations; indeed there is evidence that the congregations often attempted to get them freed. Baptism was a rite of personal transformation as well as entry into a new people/society that was now "in Christ," and Paul himself argued that the strength of the new existence was such that believing partners could, in effect, "save" unbelieving partners (1 Cor 7:16). That slaves were often prostituted and otherwise sexually available to their masters, however, does suggest another close connection between Paul's argument in 1 Corinthians 6 and 1 Corinthians 7, one that hinges precisely on the last statement

for admission of new members into the *ekklēsia* must be understood and that the application of that formula in 1 Corinthians 7 must be understood. It may be disappointing to modern interpreters that Paul did not speak in direct opposition to institutionalized slavery, or at least its dehumanizing effects. But he was caught up in a commission and engaged in a program far more radical than opposition to particular abusive aspects of an otherwise acceptable system. He was convinced that "the present form of this world" was passing away imminently, its rulers being subjected by/to Christ, and that he had been commissioned to organize communities as beachheads of the alternative society that would come fully into existence at the parousia of Christ.

THE REDEMPTION OF SLAVES BY THE EARLY CHURCHES

It would be very surprising if the assemblies Paul helped organize had quickly implemented and embodied the arguments Paul laid out in his letters, for two major reasons.

The dominant symbolic universe of Hellenistic-Roman culture was so well established, with powerful media such as the shrines and festivals honoring the emperor, legitimating major social institutions such as slavery, and determining individuals' roles and identities. It would have been difficult for any small new movement effectively to oppose the prevailing system even in running its own affairs. Moreover, from the underside, it would have been difficult in the extreme for a few travelling missionaries to catalyze, "from scratch," a set of congregations that could embody a serious and sustained alternative to the dominant order because genuine resocialization into an alternative symbolic universe, identity, and set of social relations would have been virtually impossible without an already existing network or community of "significant others" (as discussed above). Because it was so important

---

in 1 Corinthians 6. Arguing against the hypothetical implications of the Corinthian "spirituals'" principle "all things are lawful/possible for me" (6:12; 10:23), Paul rhetorically poses the shocking hypothetical possibility (logically implied by the Corinthians spirituals' principle) of "members of Christ" becoming in their bodies "members of a prostitute" (6:15–16). Insofar as *pornē* would carry connotations of a slave, it makes all the more intelligible the concluding step in Paul's argument in 6:12–20. Picking up on his previous reference to the community ("you" plural) as the temple of God in which the Holy Spirit is dwelling (3:16–17) he now focuses on the collective (again "you" plural) "body" as the temple . . . , and thus "you are not your own" (6:19). The reason given, in language borrowed from the slave-market, is that "you were bought with a price" (6:20a). In a metaphor alluding to the slave system central to Roman imperial society, Paul completes a second argument insisting on the *ekklēsia*'s solidarity over against the dominant order that parallels the first argument insisting on separation from that order in the treatment of conflicts within the new community. This is what Paul then has in mind when he addresses the slaves' situation directly in 7:21–23, where he repeats the principle "you were bought with a price," and in 7:29–31 where he places decisions on behavior within the frame of eschatological fulfilment in which believers are to behave "as though they had no dealings with this world which is passing away."

both to the economic basis and to the honor system of the dominant social order, and because it was maintained by institutionalized coercion, slavery would have been particularly difficult to counteract. As evident in Gal 3:28, a new ideal was articulated and baptismally embodied in the Pauline and other assemblies. In fact, precisely through Paul's letters we can see how difficult it must have been for a new symbolic universe and corresponding patterns of social relations to take hold and to "determine behavior" in the first few years of the Pauline mission and its impact. Thus it is also not surprising to find in the deutero-Pauline letters Colossians, Ephesians, and the Pastorals a reversion to the basic hierarchical social relations of the imperial order embodied in the slave-holding patriarchal household. Yet those deutero-Pauline letters do not tell the whole story of early Christian assemblies. A surprising amount of evidence indicates that at least some of those assemblies in fact attempted to implement the principle of "no longer slave...."

Several important second-century Christian documents indicate that redemption of their enslaved brothers and sisters from slavery was standard practice among early Christian communities, usually by using the common funds of the community. We have considerable evidence from early in the second century, only two generations after Paul's mission, ranging from Antioch in Syria to Smyrna in Asia Minor to Corinth to Rome for the practice of corporate, ecclesial manumission of slaves (on this practice, see Callahan, 1989–90). "We know that many among ourselves have given themselves to bondage that they might ransom others; many have delivered themselves to slavery, and provided food for others with the price they have received for themselves" (*1 Clem.* 55:2). This statement is offered by a writer in the Christian community in Rome to that in Corinth as an example of noble self-sacrifice for the sake of others or the general good of the community as if it were common knowledge (like the heroism of Judith and Esther, *1 Clem.* 55:3–6) of a frequent practice ("many among us").

Somewhat later, another writer from the church in Rome twice exhorts the faithful, or perhaps the better-off members of the community, "to minister to widows, to look after orphans and the destitute, and to redeem from distress (*ex anankōn lutrousthai*) the servants of God" and "instead of lands, to purchase afflicted souls and to look after widows and orphans" (Herm. *Mand.* 8:10 and Herm *Sim.* 1:8). Those to be "redeemed from distress" probably included prisoners as well as slaves (Osiek: 372–73). These exhortations constitute basic economic measures to be taken by community members who currently dwell in a "strange land/city," since their true "city," with "fields and houses," i.e., their true political-economic order, is that of God. Hermas' understanding of the community's situation and "polity" can be seen to stand directly in the tradition not only of Judean apocalyptic perspective but of Israelite covenantal exhortation (including the "two-ways" scheme). In that tradition, of course, the purchase of people out of slavery was the original meaning of redemption: God had redeemed Israel from the house of bondage in Egypt, and Israelites, correspondingly, were to redeem each other from debt-slavery. Justin Martyr, at mid-second century, further attests the same tradition and practice among the early churches: "Those who are wealthy and willing give what each thinks fit; and the collection is deposited with the president, who supports the orphans and widows and those who are in want, through any sickness or any other cause, and those who are in chains . . ." (1 *Apol.* 67.6).

The sharp prohibition of some action is almost certainly solid evidence that it was being practiced. Thus the martyr-bishop Ignatius of Antioch, who expresses the standard early Christian concern to provide concrete aid to the widow, orphan, the distressed and imprisoned (*Smyrn.* 6:2) has some pointed instruction to his fellow bishop Polycarp regarding slaves that resembles the tone of the deutero-Pauline and Pastoral letters: "Do not be haughty to slaves, either men or women; yet do not let them be puffed up, but let them rather endure slavery to the glory of God, that they may obtain a better freedom from God. Let them not desire to be made free from the common fund, that they not be found the slaves of desire" (*Pol.* 4:3). Ignatius makes no allusion to 1 Cor 7:21–23 here, although in another passage where he does make such an allusion (comparing himself to an enslaved captive who will become a freedman of Jesus Christ if he suffers martyrdom, Ign. *Rom.* 4:3), he dramatically transforms Paul's understanding of the relation of believer to Christ as well as of death and resurrection (cf. Harrill: 185). Despite the prohibitions of Bishop Ignatius of Antioch, the practice of redeeming slaves and others from their desperate circumstances must have continued in the Syrian and other churches. The fourth-century *Apostolic Constitutions*, which contains much earlier material and is usually located in Antioch/Syria, includes the exhortation to Christian communities to provide corporate assistance to people in various difficult political-economic circumstances. "Therefore, maintain and clothe those who are in want from the righteous labor of the faithful. And such sums of money as are collected from them . . . appoint to be laid out in the redemption of the saints, the deliverance of slaves (*rhuomenoi doulous*) and of captives and of prisoners, and of those that have been condemned by tyrants to single combat and death in the name of Christ" (4.9.2; cf. 5.1–2). Furthermore, the only reason for Christians to be found at public meetings was "to purchase a slave and save a soul/life" (*Const. App.* 2.62.4). Such Christian manumission of slaves lasted through the time of St. Augustine (Chadwick: 432–33).

The textual evidence for early Christian ecclesial manumission of slaves is made all the more credible by the parallel evidence for diaspora Jewish congregations (synagogues) and comparative evidence for Hellenistic and Roman associations (now gathered in Harrill). Inscriptions and documents from the Black Sea to Egypt attest Jewish congregations' redemption of fellow

Jews from slavery (required by Exod 21:2–6; Deut 15:12–18). In third century C.E. Oxyrhynchos, a brother and sister, Aurelius and Aurelia, manumitted their forty-year-old house-born slave Paramone (note the nick-name; cf. Patterson: 54–58) and her ten-year-old and four-year-old children (the latter named Jacob), relinquishing all their rights to them, for fourteen talents of silver paid through two intermediaries by the synagogue of the Jews (P. Oxy. 1205 = CPJ 3.473). Earlier inscriptions from Panticapaeum on the north shore of the Black Sea also attest manumissions to slaves by/to congregations (*synagōgai*) of Jews. An inscription dated to the second century reads: "I release in the congregation Elpia the son(?) of my slave, bred in my house; he shall remain undisturbed and unassailable by any of my heirs, except for [his duty] to visit regularly the prayer-house (*chōris tou proskarterein tē proseuchē*); the congregation of the Jews and the God-fearers (?) will be guardian (*epitropeuousēs tēs synagōgēs tōn Loudaiōn kai theōn sebōn*)" (CII 683a). Elpia appears required to give *paramōnē*-like service to the prayer-house of the synagogue in return for its patronage of the freedman (Harrill: 177). It seems unclear whether the slaves in these inscriptions were Gentiles who joined the Jewish community and also unclear whether the *paramōnē*-like obligations they have to the congregation and its prayer-house were part of a legal financial arrangement by which Jews were redeeming fellow Jews (Westermann: 126, n100; Nadel: 217; Harrill: 174–77).

The model for both Christian and Jewish corporate manumission of slaves with common funds of the churches or congregations may have been certain customs in Athens and Hellenistic cities as well as the practices of Greek and Roman associations. It is clear that both Greek and Roman associations, like temples and civic "corporations," held common property and set up and drew on common funds for a variety of purposes, usually for the benefit of members, often the poorer ones. It is also evident that slaves were members of some associations and that others collectively owned slaves, and that some associations manumitted their slaves on occasion (Harrill: chap. 3). Athenian documents attest non-interest-bearing *eranos*-loans from *ad hoc* groups that were used for various purposes, including ransom, tax payments, or manumission of slaves (Finley: 105; Millett: 153–55; Harrill: 167–68). In connection with the Delphic manumission inscriptions and their *paramōnē* obligations of the freedperson to remain in service to the former owner, it appears that in the Hellenistic East corporate manumission paid from a common fund was accepted (Harrill: 169). The varieties of comparative evidence for corporate manumission from a common fund suggest certain possible facets of the various scenarios in which Christian communities redeemed slaves. They must have paid, out of their common fund, individual slave masters to manumit slaves who had joined their communities, and perhaps other slaves as well. In some cases, suggested by the Jewish cases, the former owners may well have relinquished their rights to the continuing services that freedpersons were ordinarily expected to provide. Furthermore, as suggested by both Hellenistic and diaspora Jewish evidence, the Christian churches may have constituted a public assembly that witnessed as well as facilitated the ceremony of manumission (cf. Harrill: 188–89).

It has already been recognized in the field that the Pastoral epistles and other deutero-Pauline letters are not the only continuation of Paul's legacy and certainly not the primary or at the time dominant line of early Christianity (e.g., MacDonald). Those letters may have been included in the canon of the church that became established after Constantine and Ignatius' letters may have become highly regarded components of the "Apostolic Fathers," but they represent a literate elite's attempts to control the churches and to lead them into accommodation and assimilation to the prevailing imperial social order. The very way in which Ignatius appeals to a fellow bishop, in attempting to consolidate ecclesial power in the monarchical episcopate, to check the practice of ecclesial manumission from the community fund, seen in the context of other evidence for the practice, suggests just how common and widespread the practice was and how distinctively "out-of-step" the bishop's prohibitions were. In regard to the churches' stance toward slaves as well as other issues, it is thus simply inappropriate historically to continue to read Paul exclusively through the reactionary branch of "Paulinism" articulated in the Pastorals, other canonical deutero-Pauline letters, and Ignatius.

The conclusion that seems warranted from this survey of the early Christian practice of ecclesial manumission is that some of the congregations established through the Pauline mission and other missions came to act upon the fundamental principles of their faith, the central baptismal declarations of social relations to be embodied in the new communities. It would be a reasonable surmise that the pre-Pauline and Pauline symbolism that included the repeated baptismal experience that solemnly proclaimed "no longer slave and free, etc." came to have some re-socializing effect on the members' social behavior, not simply within the assemblies, but in their dealings with the institution of slavery in the dominant imperial society.

Conclusions on Paul and Slavery

It makes no sense to discuss Paul and slavery or Paul and social issues generally in modern terms such as "conservative" or "liberal" or "reform." Such concepts presuppose at least tacit consent to and acceptance of the continuation of the basic social system in which one lives. Paul, however, adamantly rejected the "world" he lived in as standing under God's imminent judgment. The gospel he was commissioned to preach focused on how "the rulers of this age" had outwitted themselves by crucifying "the Lord of Glory," for in the crucifixion, resurrection, and parousia of Christ, God was finally implementing the establishment of a new age ("kingdom of God," etc.), while "the form of this world is passing away." His use of "slave/slavery" imagery is tied up with the particular scheme of his gospel. As one who received a special prophetic commission to take the gospel given him by Christ in his *apokalypsis*, Paul is a "servant of Christ," just as previous Israelite prophets had been special envoys or "servants" of God. (But he does not regularly speak of believers in general as "slaves of Christ.") A prominent way of articulating the process that is happening to believers who appropriate the crucifixion and resurrection of Christ in faith, as seen in Galatians 3–5 and Romans 6–8, is that they are gaining "freedom" from their previous "slavery" to debilitating and dehumanizing superhuman forces such as Sin. The believers who have joined the international movement have become "slaves of God" or "slaves of righteousness," but such obedience to God in the new social life they have gained is really "freedom" in the Spirit, as they receive adoption as "children of God" and heirs of the promises to Abraham. Believers are not characterized regularly as "slaves of God," but primarily as "children of God" and "saints."

What is more, believers are not individual free agents in the modern sense, but integral members of local communities or "assemblies" which are components of an international "assembly." These local communities were apparently to embody an alternative society in the sense that, while recruiting additional members, they were to have little or no dealings with "the world" and its institutions such as the civil courts. They were to maintain their own community solidarity, including handling their own internal conflicts (1 Corinthians 5, 6, 7; 1 Thess 5:1–11). Many sections of Paul's letters deal with issues of concrete social interaction within the assemblies he and others had helped establish in the cities and towns of the empire. With regard to slaves and slavery, Paul was clearly not a "conservative" advocating acceptance of slavery. Nothing in the letters of Paul himself suggests this. Simply from the way Paul uses language, we can sense that he was aware of the institution of slavery as inseparable from the dominant society. Depending on how the baptismal formula in Gal 3:28 is taken, the dichotomy of slave *versus* free that permeated ancient society was declared transcended in the new movement ("in Christ").

How this may have been implemented we simply do not know, since we have only seven pieces of Paul's "mail." His approach in the two possible cases in which he addresses the issue of slavery are *ad hoc*, as was his approach to concrete issues in general. Depending on how we read his letter to Philemon and the rest of that assembly, the letter did not have to do with a slave in the first place or Paul is persuading Philemon to free his "brother" Onesimus. 1 Cor 7:21–23, on the other hand, is a fairly clear case, once we read the Greek text appropriately and get a sense of the rhetorical pattern of 1 Corinthians 7 as a whole and 7:17–24 in particular. In the course of appealing apparently to the celibate women in the Corinthian assembly to help control their men's potential for *porneia*, Paul reaches for analogies from the other two social dichotomies declared transcended in the baptismal formula. The circumcised-uncircumcised works fine as an analogy for married-unmarried (a shift from the "male and female"). But precisely in order to be consistent with the freedom proclaimed in his gospel, Paul must make an exception to his "rule in all the assemblies" that persons remain in the condition in which they were called. This principle cannot apply to slaves! If one is a slave (in the "world"), it does not make any difference to God and in the assembly. Paul's rhetorical play on slave/freedperson/free language in 7:22 reinforces this, suggesting that indeed the slave has a higher status than the free person in relation to Christ/the Lord. But, if slaves should get a chance for freedom, they should by all means "take it." Finally, 7:23 seems to indicate Paul's fundamental position: "You were bought with a price; do not become slaves of human masters!" In the subsequent life of the assemblies established by Paul and others, some of them appear to have gathered resources to free some of their members from slavery. Others, those better known because of the deutero-Pauline letters, simply accepted the fundamental social form of the Roman imperial order, the slave-holding patriarchal household.

Works Consulted

Barclay, John M. G.
    1991   "Paul, Philemon, and the Dilemma of Christian Slave-Ownership." *NTS* 37:161–86.

Barrett, C. K.
    1968   *A Commentary on the First Epistle to the Corinthians*. London: Black.

Bartchy, S. Scott
    1973   ΜΑΛΛΟΝ ΧΡΗΣΑΙ: *First-Century Slavery and the Interpretation of First Corinthians 7:21*. SBLDS 11. Missoula, MT: Scholars Press.

Berger, Peter L., and Thomas Luckmann
    1966   *The Social Construction of Reality*. Garden City, NY: Doubleday.

Betz, Hans Dieter
    1994   "Paul's Concept of Freedom in the Context of Hellenistic Discussions about the Possibilities of Human Freedom." Pp. 110–25 in *Paulinische Studien: Gesammelte Aufsätze III*. Tübingen: Mohr (Siebeck).

Bourne, George
    1845   *A Condensed Anti-Slavery Bible Argument*. New York: S. W. Benedict.

Briggs, Sheila
    1989   "Can An Enslaved God Liberate? Hermeneutical Reflections on Phil 2:6–11." *Semeia* 47:137–53.

Caird, G. B.
  1976   *Paul's Letters from Prison*. Oxford: Oxford University Press

Callahan, Allen Dwight
  1989–90 "A Note on 1 Corinthians 7:21." *JITC* 17:110–14.
  1993   "Paul's Epistle to Philemon: Toward an Alternative *Argumentum*." *HTR* 86:357–76.
  1995   "John Chrysostom on Philemon: A Response To Margaret M. Mitchell." *HTR* 88:149–56.
  1997   *Embassy of Onesimus: The Letter of Paul to Philemon*. The New Testament in Context. Valley Forge, PA: Trinity Press International.

Chadwick, Henry
  1983   "New Letters of St. Augustine." *JTS* 34:425–52.

Cleage, Albert B., Jr.
  1968   *The Black Messiah*. New York: Sheed and Ward.

Cone, James H.
  1969   *Black Theology and Black Power*. New York: Seabury.

Conzelmann, Hans
  1975   *1 Corinthians*. Hermeneia. Philadelphia: Fortress.

Crossan, John Dominic
  1991   *The Historical Jesus*. San Francisco: HarperCollins.

Dawes, Gregory W.
  1990   "'But If You Can Gain Your Freedom' (1 Corinthians 7:17–24)." *CBQ* 54:681–97.

Deming, Will
  1995   "A Diatribe Pattern in 1 Cor. 7:21–22: A New Perspective on Paul's Directions to Slaves." *NovT* 37:130–37.

Elliott, Neil
  1994   *Liberating Paul: The Justice of God and the Politics of the Apostle*. Maryknoll: Orbis.

Fee, Gordon D.
  1987   *The First Epistle to the Corinthians*. NIC. Grand Rapids, MI: Eerdmans.

Fee, John Gregg
  1848   *An Anti-Slavery Manual*. Mayville, KY. Reprint: New York: Arno, 1969.

Finley, Moses I.
  1951   *Studies in Land and Credit in Ancient Athens, 500–200 B.C.: The Horos Inscriptions*. Social Science Classics Series. Reprint 1985. Brunswick, NJ: Rutgers University Press.

Foucault, Michel
  1980   *Power/Knowedge*. New York: Pantheon.

Garlan, Yvon
    1988   *Slavery in Ancient Greece*. Ithaca: Cornell University Press.

Georgi, Dieter
    1991   *Theocracy in Paul's Praxis and Theology*. Minneappolis: Fortress.

Glancy, Jennifer A.
    1998   "Obstacles to Slaves' Participation in the Corinthian Church." *JBL* 117:481–501.

Harnack, Adolf von
    1924   *Die Mission und Ausbreitung des Christentums in den ersten drei Jahrhunderten*. 4th ed. 2 vols. Leipzig: J. C. Hinrichs.

Harrill, J. Albert
    1995   *The Manumission of Slaves in Early Christianity*. Tübingen: Mohr (Siebeck).

Horsley, G. H. R.
    1982   *New Documents Illustrating Early Christianity. Vol. 4: A Review of the Greek Inscriptions and Papyri Published in 1977*. North Ryde, Australia: Macquarie University.

Horsley, Richard A.
    1976   "*Pneumatikos vs Psychikos:* Distinctions of Spiritual Status Among the Corinthians." *HTR* 69:269–88.

    1978a   "The Background of the Confessional Formula in 1 Kor 8:6." *ZNW* 69:130–35.

    1978b   "How Can Some of You Say 'There is No Resurrection of the Dead'? Spiritual Elitism in Corinth." *NovT* 20:202–31.

    1980   "Gnosis in Corinth: 1 Corinthians 8:1–6." *NTS* 27:32–51.

    1987   *Jesus and the Spiral of Violence*. San Francisco: Harper & Row.

    1997   *Paul and Empire: Religion and Power in Roman Imperial Society*. Harrisburg, PA: Trinity Press International.

    1998   *First Corinthians*. Abingdon New Testament Commentaries. Nashville: Abingdon.

Jones, Amos, Jr.
    1984   *Paul's Message of Freedom: What Does It Mean to the Black Church?* Valley Forge: Judson Press.

Keck, Leander E.
    1979   *Paul and His Letters*. Philadelphia: Fortress.

Knox, John
    1935   *Philemon among the Letters of Paul*. New York: Abingdon.

Koester, Helmut
    1991   "Writings and the Spirit: Authority and Politics in Ancient Christianity." *HTR* 84:353–72.

Lampe, Peter
    1985   "Keine Sklavenflucht des Onesimus." *ZNW* 76:135–37.

Lightfoot, Joseph B.
    1875   *Saint Paul's Epistle to the Colossians and Philemon.* London: Macmilan.

Lohse, Eduard
    1971   *A Commentary on the Epistle to the Colossians and Philemon.* Philadelphia: Fortress.

Luther, Martin
    1955   *Luther's Works.* Ed. Jaroslav Pelikan. 55 vols. St. Louis: Concordia.

MacDonald, Dennis R.
    1983   *The Legend and the Apostle: The Battle for Paul in Story and Canon.* Philadelphia: Westminster.

Martin, Clarice J.
    1991   "The *Haustafeln* (Household Codes) in African American Biblical Interpretation: 'Free Slaves' and 'Subordinate Women'." Pp 206–31 in Cain Hope Felder, ed. *Stony The Road We Trod: African American Biblical Interpretation.* Minneapolis: Fortress.

Martin, Dale B.
    1990   *Slavery as Salvation: The Metaphor of Slavery in Pauline Christianity.* New Haven: Yale University Press.

Meeks, Wayne
    1983   *The First Urban Christians: The Social World of the Apostle Paul.* New Haven: Yale University Press.

Meyer, Heinrich A. W.
    1880   *The Epistles to the Ephesians and Philemon.* Edinburgh: T&T Clark.

Millett, Paul
    1991   *Lending and Borrowing in Ancient Athens.* Cambridge: Cambridge University Press.

Mitchell, Margaret M.
    1995   "John Chrysostom on Philemon: A Second Look." *HTR* 88:135–48.

Moule, H. C. G.
    1893   *Colossians and Philippians Studies: Lessons in Holiness and Faith.* London: Revell.

Nadel, Benjamin
    1976   "Slavery and Related Forms of Labor on the North Shore of the Euxine in Antiquity." Pp. 195–234 in *Actes du colloque 1973 sur l'esclavage.* Annales littéraires de l'Université de Besançon 182. Paris: Les Belles Lettres.

Nordling, John G.
    1991   "Onesimus Fugitivus: A Defense of the Runaway Slave Hypothesis in Philemon." *JSNT* 41:97–119.

Osiek, Carolyn
    1981   "The Ransom of Captives: Evolution of a Tradition." *HTR* 74:365–86.

Patterson, Orlando
    1982   *Slavery and Social Death: A Comparative Study.* Cambridge: Harvard University Press.

Petersen, Norman
    1985   *Rediscovering Paul: Philemon and the Sociology of Paul's Narrative World*. Philadelphia: Fortress.

Price, S. R. F.
    1984   *Rituals and Power: The Roman Imperial Cult in Asia Minor*. Cambridge: Cambridge University Press.

Roetzel, Calvin
    1997   *Paul: The Man and the Myth*. Columbia, S.C.: University of South Carolina Press.

Sampley, J. Paul
    1991   *Walking Between the Times: Paul's Moral Reasoning*. Minneapolis: Fortress.

Sanders, Ed P.
    1991   *Paul*. Past Masters. New York: Oxford University Press.

Schüssler Fiorenza, Elisabeth
    1983   *In Memory of Her: A Feminist Theological Reconstruction of Christian Origins*. New York: Crossroad.

Stowers, Stanley K.
    1985   "The Social Sciences and the Study of the Early Christianity." Pp. 149–81 in *Approaches to Ancient Judaism*. Ed. W. S. Green. Atlanta: Scholars.

Sugirtharajah, R. S., ed.
    1998   *The Postcolonial Bible*. The Bible and Postcolonialism 1. Sheffield: Sheffield Academic Press.

Theissen, Gerd
    1982   *The Social Setting of Pauline Christianity*. Philadelphia: Fortress.

Thurman, Howard
    1949   *Jesus and the Disinherited*. Nashville: Abingdon.

Westermann, William L.
    1955   *The Slave Systems of Greek and Roman Antiquity*. Philadelphia: American Philosophical Society.

Winter, Sara C.
    1984   "Methodological Observations on a New Interpretation of Paul's Letter to Philemon." *USQR* 39:203–12.

    1987   "Paul's Letter to Philemon." *NTS* 33:1–15.

Wire, Antionette C.
    1990   *The Corinthian Women Prophets: A Reconstruction Through Paul's Rhetoric*. Philadelphia: Fortress.

Zanker, Paul
    1988   *The Power of Images in the Age of Augustus*. Ann Arbor: University of Michigan Press.

Part II

"I Consider the Days of Slavery as the Darkest Days of the World": The Pauline Corpus and Modern Slavery

"Somebody Done Hoodoo'd the Hoodoo Man": Language, Power, Resistance, and the Effective History of Pauline Texts in American Slavery

Clarice J. Martin
Colgate University

ABSTRACT

This essay examines the strategic hermeneutical uses, function, and effects of Pauline texts about slavery within the American slave system of the seventeenth through the nineteenth centuries. This overview of the effective history of Pauline texts is centrally focused on the uses of language and discourses to "create worlds" and encode reality with either emancipatory or death-dealing effects. Three central rubrics are explored: (1) "Hoodooing the Hoodoo Man: Discourses Enabling Transformations of Identity, Space, and Place"; (2) "Pauline Statements in American Slavery: Discourses of Domination, Social Control, and Social Death"; and (3) "Say It's Not So! Discourses of Resistance, Empowerment, and Liberation."

I. "Hoodooing the Hoodoo Man:" Discourses Enabling Transformations of Identity, Space, and Place

The police hear so much about Marie Leveau that they come to her house in St. Anne Street to put her in jail. First one come, she stretch out her left hand and he turn round and round and never stop until someone come lead him away. Then two come together—she put them to running and barking like dogs. Four come and she put them to beating each other with night sticks. The whole station force come. . . . She did her work at the altar and they all went to sleep on her steps. (Hurston: 193)

Acclaimed anthropologist, folklorist, and novelist Zora Neale Hurston includes the fictional account of Marie Leveau in her book, *Mules and Men*, a collection of stories, songs, "hoodoo" and voodoo customs, and humor and wisdom (193). Hurston's narration of the triumph of Marie Leveau's ability to "put to confusion" the police who were resolved to arrest her for being a renowned "hoodoo doctor" in nineteenth-century New Orleans ("The City of New Orleans had a law against fortune tellers, hoodoo doctors, and the like . . . and people come from the ends of America to get help from her" [192]) represents one of her many fictive narrations of the importance of conjure traditions in the African diasporic community. Leveau's rout of the police force is an example of turning intended "bad will" or "evil intent" back upon those who intended to extend or inflict "bad will" or "evil" upon others.

While the police were not themselves literal "conjurers," they could be viewed as those who contributed to the exploitative conditions of a dominating society through the "sorcery of white America" (Baker: 95). Leveau was able to thwart this sorcery, in effect, outwitting her opponent, or "hoodooing the hoodoo man." The ability to "turn the trick back upon the one who set it" in hoodoo practice, or to "change things around" *through the wisdom of words* demonstrates the poetics, efficacy and vitality of conjure in African diasporic communities.

The Leveau story is reminiscent of traditions about "High John the Conqueror," a fictional, human character in the stories of black folk culture during slavery in the American South. High John helped the slaves to endure, often providing nearly divine assistance to the slaves by helping to trick or overcome the machinations and brutality of slave masters. The effect of his appearance among the slaves was a radical transformation of the slave's identity and place: "No longer were they bounded by Old Massa's plantation. In the mighty battle between oppression and justice, John realized a new kingdom, a new realm where marginalized people could name themselves and determine their own direction . . . and struggle on toward the future" (D. Hopkins: 112–13).

It is important to distinguish between Hurston's terminology of *"hoodoo"* and practices called *"conjure,"* conjuring, and *"voodoo."* The terms "hoodoo" and "conjure" (conjuration), the preferred vernacular terms, refer to North American religious traditions that had definable African antecedents; that is, they were a variant of African religious "retentions" or "survivals" found in the New World. "Voodoo" is usually traced to practices of the Yoruba peoples on the West Coast of Africa, and refers more broadly to traditional West African religions and (or) Caribbean and South American developments. Hoodoo and conjure practitioners are less likely to engage in the worship or summoning of spirits or deities than their Haitian, Caribbean, and South American counterparts who use voodoo. What the conjure of the United States and the voodoo of Haiti have in common is their common African origin, enduring appeal, and their relationship to "workings of the spirit" and the spiritual, including the limitless cultural repertoire of efficacious, life-sustaining, and liberatory practices (T. Smith: 48–49; Baker: 76–77, 80–81).

Theophus Smith has shown that "conjure" is a metaphor for describing black people's ritual, figurative, and therapeutic transformations of culture (T. Smith: 4). But more than a mere metaphor, it is a magical means of transforming reality, a way in which humanity maps and manages the world. As a primordial, yet enduring, system of communication in all cultures (and not merely a so-called "irrational" or "marginal" phenomenon in some, nor as synonymous with the unorthodox or the occult), it is, in fact, *a form of language*. As language which employs ritual speech, "it also evinces a performative aspect, with actions performing what is expressed" (T. Smith: 4).

As a normatively constructive part of the religious folk traditions of black North Americans, conjure practices within African-American contexts are usually distinguished from English or European conjure traditions. While Eurocentric conjure traditions and assimilations tend to focus on conjuration and sorcery or witchcraft, conjure figures in the African diasporic communities advanced the work and efforts of enslaved Africans to build a culture, to resist acculturation, domination, and oppression against the "black magic" of white oppression (T. Smith: 5; Wilmore: 26).

An analysis of Marie Leveau's conjure work reveals that it is consistent with that of other "hoodoo doctors": enemies are repaid with punishment (retributive justice), grievances are remedied, faith yields the fruit of good luck and "found" love, the ailing are renewed, communal disharmony is mediated and replaced with restored harmony (Baker: 9). The thaumaturgical component of the conjure doctor's work is effective (the use of conventional and unconventional substances to effect medicinal healing, health, or other benefits) for both body and spirit.

The phrase "Somebody Done Hoodoo'd the Hoodoo Man" is taken from the title of one of the acclaimed writer Al Young's essays featuring that title (59–63). Young, a celebrated novelist, poet, screenwriter, and educator, uses "Somebody Done Hoodoo'd the Hoodoo Man" to expose the roots of his lifelong love affair with the mystery and power of words, syllables, and language. Recalling family "verbal jam sessions" where the old folks enjoyed "marbling the fat of our utterance with lean strips of proverbial wisdom" (59), Young bears witness to the mystery and power of language, including its function as "actualized speech." According to Young, words and language as actualized speech can bring a created order and world into being ("And God said, 'Let there be light'; and there was light" [Gen 1:3, the Priestly account of creation]), solidify family cohesion, effect profound curative effects, and transmute perception, consciousness, and empirical reality (as with hoodoo or conjure traditions).

In "Somebody Done Hoodoo'd the Hoodoo Man," Young recalls a childhood memory of age seven or eight where his grandmother, called affectionately, "Mama," uses the term "hoodoo"—a term whose precise meaning had long been shrouded in mystery for Young.

Coming in fresh from her garden "with an apronful of fresh cut okra, snapbeans, and tomatoes" one day, Mama encountered a smiling, tattered hobo who had just approached their home. Claude, the sleek black farm dog who would normally have reacted with fervid and vigorous protectionism "didn't stir," and, moreover, "didn't let out so much as a low growl"

(Young: 60). Declaring of the hobo,"that old rascal must have hoodoo'd that dog," Mama launched into a brief overview of the how's and why's of hoodoo to her young, inquisitive grandson. Young concludes: "This was the same woman who moaned and hummed and sang spirituals all day long while she worked, and who taught me table blessings and the beautiful Twenty-third Psalm" (61).

The comfortable alliance between the Hebrew Bible, Christian Scriptures, and conjure discourses uttered by "Mama" has long and historic roots within African diasporic communities. In fact, the religion of black slaves, and the distinctive African-American form of Christianity that evolved from this rich synthesis of traditions, attest to the slaves' very gradual appropriation of Christianity into their existing African cosmological framework. The African cultural past not only remained efficacious in reinforcing their devotion to the supreme transcendent being in whom they believed *before* their forced advent to American soil during the Trans-Atlantic Slave Trade (Paris, 1995; Wilmore); as we shall see, elements of the African cultural past also provided them with the ideological and moral resources and determination to reject the Christianity of their white slave masters and to resist the profound injustices to which this particular expression of the Christian faith gave rise.

II. Pauline Statements in American Slavery: Discourses of Domination, Social Control, and Social Death

Prolegomenon: A Genealogy of the Metalanguage of Racial Domination in Western Culture

To speak at all of the "effective history" of Pauline texts in American slavery is to acknowledge the fundamental veracity of observations by philosopher Hans-Georg Gadamer and religion scholar Daniel Patte that: "'Understanding is never subjective behaviour toward a given "object," but towards its *effective history*,' and thus, a classic text such as the Bible is always interpreted in terms of the history of its *effects*" (Patte: 55, quoting Gadamer: xix; italics mine). An assessment of the effects of the usage of Pauline texts in the legitimation and perpetuation of American slavery, one of the most brutal slave systems in human history, bears witness, anew, to the power of the performative aspects of language as actualized speech to "bring into being a created order," and to legitimate a new or existing created order with the intention of transmuting perception, consciousness, and empirical reality (Young: 63). In this instance, the language of "sacred texts," the Pauline texts, were pressed into service of the protocols of domination, social control, social inequality, and social death.

Theologian Robert Farrar Capon describes the language of theology as a "pack of foxhounds," with the theologian as the "master of the hunt in search of the Divine Fox" (for Capon, the Divine Fox is God). His more "masculinist imagery" of hunting is nonetheless relevant here for the light it sheds on the effective use of Pauline texts in the legitimation and perpetuation of American slavery. Capon observes:

> I mean only to suggest that every word—and, particularly, every image—used in theology be examined with the greatest care and handled with as much judiciousness as we can manage. The language of theology is a pack of foxhounds, and the theologian is the master of the hunt. His [sic] job is to feed, water and exercise his dogs so that they will be in peak condition for the hunting of the Divine Fox—and to keep them, if possible, from biting defenseless Christians.... (164)

A review of the effective use of Pauline texts in American slavery reveals that the "foxhounds of theological language" in proslavery discourse are anything but benign. In fact, Pauline texts were used in service of a larger "metalanguage" of domination endorsing the enslavement of black peoples in America. It is appropriate to first review very briefly the existential anxiety that gave rise to the white supremacist rationalism about the inferiority and sub-humanity of black peoples, an anxiety which contributed to an ideological climate in which the dogmatic use of Pauline texts in slavery could wield their greatest and most pernicious effects.

In his discussion and overview of American civil religion, Charles H. Long, a renowned historian of religion, has observed that while the American national community offers salvation to all in its ideals and history, takes pride in itself as a community that includes people from all over the world, and proffers a history in which religious meanings and sacred symbols are intrinsically rooted in the founding documents of the American Republic—The Declaration of Independence and the Constitution (with civil religion constituting a parallel structure alongside the revealed religion of Christianity)—American religion, and writings on American religion, have been decidedly myopic with reference to the religious experiences of non-Europeans (Long: 148–49).

According to Long, writers of the American religious experience have tended to mean by the term "American" primarily European immigrants and their progeny—overlooking Native Americans and African Americans (among others). Hence, many of the writings about, and discussions on "American religion" have been "ideological" (consciously or unconsciously), serving to enhance, justify, and "render sacred" the history of European immigrants to America (149).

A notable corollary to the traditional modes of orientation of American civil and religious history is "American cultural language." The American cultural language is not a recent creation:

> It is a cosmogonic language, a language of beginnings: *it structures the American myth of the beginnings* and has continued to express the synchronic

dimensions of American cultural life since that time. It is a language forged by the Puritans and the Jeffersonians and carried on by succeeding generations. (Long: 150; italics mine)

The "American cultural language" of which Long speaks, while often resonating with strains of the possibilities of creating a truly free society in the United States, has retained those characteristics which reveal it to be a language rooted in the physical conquest of space (to the detriment of Native Americans), and a language resonant with the strains of conquest, marginalization, and oppression (for both Native Americans and peoples of African descent). It is an insidiously hegemonic discourse which reifies the deeds and accomplishments of persons of European descent above all others. Its paradoxical dimensions are evident in that the American cultural language is used, on the one hand, to render black peoples *invisible* or marginal when it comes to such matters as equitable access to power, civil rights, and even respect for the intellectual contributions, knowledge claims, and knowledge production of peoples of African descent. On the other hand, the hegemonic discourses of white supremacy and racism in American cultural language have rendered black peoples *quite visible* when advancing the myth of the so-called sub-humanity of the darker races of the world. This discourse, which portrays (and seeks to actualize) black peoples as "natural hewers of wood and drawers of water" entrenches and reinforces the structural mechanisms of racism.

As texts which were "pressed into service" of a larger and continuing myth of American beginnings in which peoples of African descent were deemed to be ontologically inferior but functionally utilitarian, the *Pauline texts functioned as the linguistic, ideological, and religiously sanctioned lynchpins in the stolid and death-dealing institution of American slavery.* To use Capon's foxhunting metaphor, proslavery apologists fed, watered, and exercised the "dogs" or words and language of Pauline texts about slavery not only to "bite" defenseless Christians; the "doggedly" aggressive architects of the "peculiar institution" of American slavery used the religious language and imagery of Pauline texts about slavery to entrench the colonialist empire-building of the southern plantation economy, to undergird the ideology and myth of white supremacy, and to provide steady hermeneutical grist for a seemingly inexhaustible theological mill which ratified slaveholders and proponents as the divinely appointed, solely legitimate, and authoritative gate-keepers and interpreters of the Hebrew Bible and Christian Scriptures.

It is important to remember that the incubator for white supremacist thinking in Western culture predated the horrors of the full scale Transatlantic Slave Trade with its woeful and torturous sale and bartering of human cargo in the seventeenth century (of the more than 11.5 million Africans transported to the Americas from the seventeenth through the nineteenth centuries, however, the vast majority came during the eighteenth and nineteenth centuries [Patterson, 1982:118]). "Ethnocentrism," the tendency to valorize one's cultural or ethnic group above others, has been documented in antiquity, with Aristotle arguing that "barbarians"—any group of persons who were not Greek—were "natural slaves." The Hellenistic Greeks deemed themselves privileged donors of enlightenment to "lesser breeds," (Davies: 14).

While Greco-Roman culture was generally relatively less preoccupied with color prejudice (Snowden), it is interesting to note that intermarriage between white and black peoples was rare, and especially in Greek and Roman upper classes. The classicist Grace Beardsley (119) has traced the earliest negative attack on black peoples in Roman literature to Cicero (106–43 CE), who calls Ethiopians stupid ("*cum hoc homine an cum stipite Aethiope*"). This generic designation may have been uttered of other peoples whom the Romans deemed to outside the pale of their ethnocentric identity. But Juvenal's barb about Ethiopians exhibits greater contempt: "Let the straight-legged man laugh at the club-footed, the white man at the Ethiopian (*derideat Aethiopem albus*)." The reference to the Ethiopian's color is unmistakable here (Hood: 40; see also Martin, 1993).

Robert Hood and others have traced the encroaching development of blackness as synonymous with evil in early Christian thought. In fact, visual metaphors equating whiteness with "good" and blackness with "evil" abounded in Christian literature (Snowden). The Patristic literature quite frequently records the sentiment that Christ makes "black" bodies "white" in the regenerative process of salvation and sanctification. The Devil is personified as the "Black One" in the *Epistle of Barnabas* 4:9 (written between 70–117 CE). *The Acts of Peter*, written in approximately 180–200 CE, describes Satan as black and an enemy of Christ (Lake: 14; Hennecke and Schneemelcher: 291). Jerome, the "First Theological Critic of Blackness," equated blackness to sin and evil, and is one of the first theologians to link blackness to carnal lust and sexual prowess (Hood: 82–84). Of the equation of blackness with sin, Jerome comments:

> *People of the Ethiopians* means those who are black, being covered with the stain of sin. In the past we were Ethiopians, being made so by our sins and vices. How? Because sin has made us black. But then we heeded Isaiah (1:16)—"Wash yourselves, be clean"—and we said, "Thou shalt wash me, and I shall be made whiter than snow" (Ps 50[51]:9). Thus we, Ethiopians that we were, transformed ourselves and became white. (Courtès: 27)

The Middle Ages witnessed the rise of a largely white European Christendom imagining itself encircled by "menacing pagan realms" both literally and figuratively darker. As religious historian Alan Davies has observed: "In one sense, colonial expansion at the end of the medieval period was a kind of final crusade against the children of darkness—an outburst of the European cultural, racial, political and social 'superiority-complex'" (14).

Medieval Christian beliefs about blacks and blackness were influenced by attitudes toward the Muslims and the Turks," dark-skinned" heathen infidels, and the Moorish occupation of parts of Christian Europe such as Spain, Sicily, southern Italy, and Rhodes (Brooke and Brooke: 46–62, 146–55; Hood: 92). The Medieval Antichrist figure was often depicted as black, with Negroid features. A twelfth-century painting shows John the Baptist being beheaded by an executioner with Negroid features and black skin. Even torturers of Christ were depicted as black with African or Negroid features (Hood: 94).

In time, whiteness was assumed to be the "normative" human condition, and darker skin colors were attributed to sickness, degeneracy, environmental factors, or religious causes (the Hamitic hypothesis, which attributed the racial subordination of black people to Gen 9:20–27, was advocated here). The retention and tenacity of the tendency to denigrate and trivialize black peoples would gain intellectual legitimacy and momentum, and both philosophical and scientific sanction, by the early eighteenth century. Philosopher and historian David Hume (1711–76), one of the leading neo-skeptics of the early modern period, reveals an ethnocentric and white supremacist bias that continued to set the ideological stage, context, and climate for the full flowering of proslavery ideologues in the later eighteenth and nineteenth centuries when he observed:

> I am apt to suspect the Negroes, and in general, all other species of men [sic] (for there are four or five different kinds) to be naturally inferior to the whites. There never was a civilized nation of any other complexion than white, nor even any individual eminent either in action or speculation. No ingenious manufactures amongst them, no arts, no sciences....
>
> In Jamaica indeed they talk of one Negro as a man of parts and learning; but 'tis likely he is admired for very slender accomplishments, like a parrot, who speaks a few words plainly. (Quoted in West: 62)

Social Control and Social Death

A critical and comprehensive analysis of the use of Pauline texts in American slavery should not only situate the discussion within the larger epistemological and conceptual framework of the genealogy and evolution of the metalanguage of white (Eurocentric) supremacy and domination (with the countervailing discourses of the dehumanization and denigration of black peoples), on the one hand; it is also essential to address the ideological supposition that the institutions of ancient and modern slavery were relatively benign, for the presumably "happy slave," on the other hand.

I have argued elsewhere that the pervasive perception of ancient slavery as only moderately or sporadically stressful for the slave is historically naive and ideologically presumptive (Martin, 1990); and yet, the promulgation of this view by American proslavery apologists would be advanced as philosophically—if polemically—defensible.

In his book *The Social Context of the New Testament*, Derek Tidball says the following about Paul's posture toward slavery:

> In the first place, the institution of slavery was such an integral part of the social fabric in Paul's day that it would have been difficult for Paul or others to conceive of social organization without it.... By the time of Paul it was not a severe and cruel institution. Of course there were exceptions ... but the experience of most slaves was different. *In Carcopino's memorable phrase, "with few exceptions slavery in Rome was neither eternal, nor, while it lasted, intolerable...."* There was no widespread discontent about slavery. So, to the early church the question of the abolition of slavery was probably insignificant.... What Paul offers to Christian slaves is a totally new appreciation of their value as persons. They are no longer "things" but people who have standing and status before God (1 Cor 7:20). In Christ the slave is a free man.... If only, Paul argues, they grasp this greater fact, slavery becomes inconsequential. *A slave can remain happily a slave and still serve the Lord in spite of his social limitations.* (114–16; italics mine)

In order to adequately address Tidball's idyllic notion of the "happy slave" in the first century of the Common Era it is necessary and appropriate to document the fact that the institution of slavery was not, in fact, as innocuous as he wants to portray it. Such a task is easily undertaken, and there is no dearth of literature on the subject (Bellen; Finley; Patterson; Watson). While a full-scale discussion of Greco-Roman slavery is not possible here, I would make a few brief observations about Greco-Roman slavery pertinent to the present discussion.

First, that slavery was an integral part of the social fabric of Paul's day is not in dispute, but the thesis that it was not a "severe and cruel institution" has been challenged in recent years. In *Slaves and Masters in the Roman Empire*, Keith R. Bradley argues that while harmonious relationships may have existed between masters and slaves, one must be cautious about concluding that such intimacy was necessarily *characteristic* of the master-slave relationship. While "simple, constant animosity between slave and slave master is too naive a concept to have had universal applicability or meaning," the less human side of Roman slavery should not be romanticized:

> But although the harmonious relations attested between some slaves and their masters should not be lost sight of, they were not in all likelihood characteristic of the Roman slave system as a whole.... The essential brutality of the slave experience in the Roman world and especially the kind of harsh pressures in which slaves were constantly exposed as a normal part of their

everyday lives ... must be understood. ... it is vital to understand something of the less elevated, less humane side of Roman social relations, of which the depressed conditions under which most slaves lived provide abundant illustration. (13–14)

Roman slave owners may have treated their slaves generously, but generosity alone did not, in Bradley's words, "secure the elite ideal of servile *fides* and *obsequium* that is to guarantee social stability. ... *Generosity had to be tempered with either force or the threat of force in order for control to be maintained, and a climate of fear over those of subordinate social position had to be created* ... 'Fear in the slaves produced greater loyalty,' so it was said" (113). Slaves were subjected to a number of indignities: capricious sexual abuse (slaves could be used as or sold for prostitutes, and they could be sexually exploited for as long as the master wished); flogging was a "widespread" punishment for which little justification was required; agricultural and mining slaves, domestic slaves and children were all subject to the same violence: "servile distinctions of status, function, age or sex gave no protection against arbitrary punishment" (123; italics mine; cf. 116–19).

Second, even if some slaves in Greco-Roman society were treated with less severity than others, and could, indeed, become freedmen or freedwomen, psychosocial aspects of the institution itself were less than salutary. In his groundbreaking book, *Slavery and Social Death*, the distinguished sociologist Orlando Patterson analyzes the structure and dynamics of slavery based on a study of tribal, ancient, premodern, and modern slavery in sixty-six societies (including Greece, Rome, medieval Europe, China, Korea, the Islamic kingdoms, Africa, the Caribbean islands, and the American South). *He describes three distinctive constituent elements of slavery that typify master-slave relationships in all of these societies.* Aspects of these three elements have been shown to be present within American slave systems (Grant, Harding, Lincoln, Parker, Raboteau, Williams, Wilmore). Patterson argues that in anatomies of power in human relationships of inequality or domination, slavery is distinctive as a relation of domination in three ways.

1. *Slavery is unusual in the extremity of power involved.* That the master exercised total domination over the slave was normative, and a constituent feature of the relationship was the use of some forms of coercion. Force, violence and might both maintained and perpetuated slavery. When slaves were manumitted or died, it became necessary to "repeat the original, violent act of transforming the free man into slave. ... Whipping was not only a method of punishment. It was a conscious device to impress upon the slaves that they were slaves; it was a crucial form of social control particularly if we remember that it was very difficult for slaves to run away successfully." (Patterson, 1982:2–3).

2. *The slave relation is characterized by what Patterson calls the slave's "natal alienation."* The slave, however recruited, is a socially dead person. "Alien-

ated from all 'rights' or claims of birth, he ceased to belong in his own right to any legitimate social order. All slaves experienced, at the very least, a secular excommunication" (Patterson 1982:5).

> Slaves were "genealogical isolates." They had a past, but they were not allowed freely to integrate the experience of their ancestors into their lives, to inform their understanding of social reality with the inherited meanings of their natural forebears, or to anchor the living present in any conscious community of memory. That they reached back for the past, as they reached out for the related living, there can be no doubt. Unlike other persons, doing so meant struggling with and penetrating the iron curtain of the master, his community, his laws, his policemen or patrollers, and his heritage. (Ibid)

The slave may have reached out to the "related living," but the slave's own community and social relations were not usually recognized as legitimate and binding, as the cavalier selling of children and family members, refusal to respect marriage bonds, and rampant disregard for ancestral, family, and communal traditions attests (6).

3. *Slaves were persons who had been dishonored in a general way—their status held no honor; indignity, indebtedness, and the absence of an independent social existence reinforced the sense of dishonor.* The slave was without power, except through another; she or he had become "imprintable" and "disposable," the "ultimate human tool" (7).

Proslavery Apologists: Texts and Practices

It has never escaped the notice of serious students of history that Christianity has been at once the religion of enslaved black peoples, slaveholders, and abolitionists. Even if the particular forms and functions of the Christian faith were nuanced through different existential prisms for each of these three groups, the first-century biblical writers who penned the precepts about relations between slavemasters and slaves could never have imagined or envisioned the nefarious ways in which those narratives would be used *en masse* in the confraternity of religion and chattel slavery centuries later. *Texts in the Hebrew Bible and Christian Scriptures were the southern church person's major defense of slavery.* From 1772 until 1850 Scripture comprised *the* primary source of authority and legitimization for the enslavement of black peoples. Not surprisingly, proslavery advocates used the Christian Scriptures to emphasize the ethical mandates of slaves, with little comment about masters. Proslavery hermeneutics neither jeopardized the privileged status of the slavemaster, nor altered the social condition of the slave (H. S. Smith: 129; Faust: 1–20; Evans: 39).

As noted earlier, the so-called "Pauline texts" about slavery served as the ideological and religious "lynchpins" in the stolid and death-dealing edifice of American slavery. In fact, the defenders of human bondage were more comfortable and "at home" in the letters of Paul than in any Christian Scripture text (H. S. Smith: 134). The particular appeal of the Pauline texts was their *specific* injunctions to the duties of masters and slaves. "In fact, virtually every proslavery tract of any consequence explored the Pauline epistles far more exhaustively than any other portion of the New Testament" (134).

The pantheon of premier texts regularly cited in support of slavery included primarily six Christian Scripture texts:

1. 1 Corinthians 7:20–21
2. Ephesians 6:5–9
3. Colossians 3:22, 4:1
4. 1 Peter 2:18–25
5. Philemon 10–18
6. 1 Timothy 6:20–21

The roster of Pauline and other Christian Scripture texts, it was argued, supported slavery in two ways. First, Paul had admonished both masters and slaves to fulfill their obligations to one another without ever intimating that it was problematic that one human being owned another. Paul, it was argued, never suggested that slavery was sinful, and, like Jesus, Paul was quite aware of the cruelties of the slavery practices in the Roman Empire. Governor Hammond, of South Carolina, advanced this argument in "Hammond's Letters on Slavery," presented to the Virginia legislature in 1831–32:

> It is vain to look to Christ or any of his Apostles to justify such blasphemous perversions of the word of God. Although Slavery in its most revolting form was everywhere visible around them, no visionary notions of piety or philanthropy ever tempted them to gainsay the LAW, even to mitigate the cruel severity of the existing system. On the contrary, regarding Slavery as an established, as well as an inevitable human condition of human society, they never hinted at such a thing as its termination on earth, any more than that "the poor may cease out of the land," which God affirms to Moses shall never be.
>
> It is impossible, therefore, to suppose that Slavery is contrary to the will of God. It is equally absurd to say that American Slavery differs in form or principle from that of the chosen people. We accept the Bible terms as the definition of our Slavery, and its precepts as the guide of our conduct. (Elliot: 107–108).

A second argument invoking Pauline authority in support of slavery noted that slaveholders (like Philemon) were members of churches founded by Paul and other apostles, hence, neither Paul *nor* the early church considered slavery sinful *per se*.

In proslavery apologia, then, Christian faith was viewed as consistent with slavery, as shown by (1) the specific biblical injunctions to slaves and masters, and (2) the argument that the first-century church provided an enduring paradigm of not interfering with the political and economic realities of the institution of slavery. George D. Armstrong, pastor of the Presbyterian Church in Norfolk, Virginia, held this conviction, as recorded in his book, *The Christian Doctrine of Slavery*, published in 1857: "Master and slave are, alike, the creatures of God, the objects of his care, the subjects of his government: and, alike, responsible to him for the discharge of the duties to their several stations" (64).

Charles B. Hodge, a distinguished Princeton Seminary professor, echoes the sentiments of Armstrong in his treatise, "The Bible Argument On Slavery": "These external relations . . . are of little importance, for every Christian is a freeman in the highest and best sense of the word, and at the same time is under the strongest bonds to Christ" (848).

Both Armstrong and Hodge allow one concession: the apostles approved of the *institution* of slavery, but not its *abuses*.

> . . . they [the apostles] did not shut their eyes to the abuses of these several institutions—civil government, marriage, the family, slavery; nor did they affect an ignorance of them, but carefully distinguishing between the institutions themselves and the abuses which had become attached to them, they set themselves to work with zeal and faithfulness . . . to correct the abuses (Armstrong: 57; cf. Hodge: 852; Swartley: 31–64).

The fact that some of the texts about slavery attributed to Paul were not actually Pauline (Colossians,[1] Ephesians, and 1 Timothy) mattered little to proslavery rhetoricians in a time which had only just begun to see the rise of historical biblical criticism. *The fact is, defenders of human bondage were "hermeneutical contortionists," striving to make the round blocks of selected, and historically conditioned first-century biblical traditions fit the square holes of seventeenth, eighteenth, and nineteenth-century discourses of "domination" and "subjectivity" designed to reinforce a construction of reality that rendered some "natural" lords, leaders and masters, and others the ruled, the dominated, and the enslaved.* The use of Pauline, or other Christian Scripture texts to legitimate racist dogma helped immensely to frame a discourse whose power and effects would insure the hegemony of white supremacy, with the horrific abuses that attended it, including a slaveocracy which supported the plantation capitalists of the South, and many merchants and industrial capitalists in the North.

The Presbyterian clergyman Robert L. Dabney of Virginia argued that a *biblical* doctrine of slavery would effectively lead to the conversion of a significant number of northern Christians to the proslavery agenda: "Here is our policy, then, to push the Bible argument continually, drive abolitionism to the

---

[1] In fact, the authorship of Colossians is still disputed. See Martin, 1991a:206–207, and notes 1–3).

wall, to compel it to assume an anti-Christian position. By so doing, we compel the whole of Christianity of the North to array itself on our side" (quoted in Johnson: 129). While Dabney's assertion is overly simplistic and idealistic, it does corroborate a widely held perception that "biblical warrant," or justification for slavery as rooted in "God's word," and especially at the helm of one of Christianity's most influential and illustrious figures, Paul the Apostle, comprised the strongest and most convincing apologetic rationales for slavery. Here a thoroughgoing biblical literalism would be exploited for its full effect.

Five additional observations may be made about the texts, practices, and effects of Pauline texts (or texts attributed to Paul) during American slavery.

First, white Southern clergy were in the forefront of those who justified slavery, and who called for secession from the North to retain it. Challenging the thesis that all people have a right to an equal share of personal liberty, they argued, instead, that each government should establish those regulations "which promote the good of the population" (Cheseborough: 11). The household morality codes in Col 3:18–4:1, Eph 5:21–6:9, and 1 Pet 2:18–3:7, were centrally used to argue that people were placed in different social arrangements by God's providence: "some are rulers, some subjects; some are rich, some poor; some are fathers, some children; some are bond, some free. And if a man is justly and providentially a ruler, he has the rights of a father; and if a slave, only the rights of a slave" (Loveland: 201–202).

The historian Donald G. Matthews, in his book, *Religion in the Old South*, reveals the ways in which a literalist interpretation of the household codes served the patriarchal interests of white males with reference to both women and enslaved black peoples. Matthews argues that in order to establish the doctrine of human inequality, many southern evangelical preachers

> insulted and demeaned a majority of their own constituency with the same . . . insensitivity which they usually reserved for talking about black people. In tract upon tract, male writers emphasized the subordination of women as built into the very nature of human society by God himself, citing Scripture to that effect and rewarding the submissiveness of women with elaborate praise for her grace, "passive fortitude," and "enduring love." (169–70)

Frederick Ross, a clergyperson from Huntsville, Alabama, makes a case for honoring the biblical injunctions regarding slaves and women, as recorded by Donald Matthews:

> "Do you say," asked Ross, "the slave is held to involuntary service? So is the wife. Her relation to her husband, in the immense majority of cases, is made for her, and not by her." He reminded the wives that they, like the slaves, were "under service," and "bound to obey their husbands." Ross continued:

"Do you say the slave is sold and bought? So is the wife the world over." Ross, along with many other southern clergy, spoke and wrote about the inequality of women to justify their stances on the inequality of Blacks. (Matthews: 12; see Ross: 55–58, 124–25)

The religious world view of proslavery apologists was constructed upon a combination of a self-serving biblical literalism, patriarchal ideology, and conservative political theory in service to the economic interests and class structure of the American South (and in some instances, the North as well). Proslavery apologists argued that since slavery was sanctioned in the Hebrew Bible and Christian Scriptures, it represented "orthodox religion." As such, proslavery advocates perceived the abolitionist attack on slavery as motivated by "unorthodox religion"; hence, the argument was more than "proslavery versus antislavery," it was a struggle between true religion and false religion, between orthodoxy and heresy, and between a "biblically revealed" religion and a "man-made" religion. Those who opposed slavery were construed to be anti-God, anti-Bible, anti-Constitution, heretics, and infidels. James Henley Thornwell, an eminent South Carolina preacher, publisher, and educator, charged in one of his sermons (delivered in 1850): "The parties in this conflict are not merely abolitionists and slaveholders—they are atheists, socialists, communists, red republicans, Jacobins, on the one side, and friends of order and regulated freedom on the other. In one word, the world is the battleground—Christianity and Atheism the combatants; and the progress of humanity the stake" (quoted in Cheseborough: 12–13).

Second, Paul's letter to Philemon (esp. vv. 8–21) illustrates the tension between a discourse of equality (Gal 3:26–29) and the reality of social hierarchy. This tension emerges in some Pauline traditions about women (1 Cor 11:2–16; Gal 3:26–29).

The fact is, Paul's intention in the letter to Philemon, and his general views about slavery, betray some ambiguity. Many Eurocentric scholars have favored an interpretation which suggests that Paul wanted Philemon to receive Onesimus as a Christian brother who remained a slave (Meyer; Moule; Caird; Ridderbos). A majority of African-American biblical interpreters (and many others) have shown that Paul intended that Onesimus be received as a "brother in truth" who was no longer a slave, in accord with the sentiment of 1 Cor 7:21, 23, and Gal 3:26–29 (Bruce; Hinks; Paris, 1982; Patterson, 1991:320; Perkins; Petersen; Schüssler Fiorenza; Thomas; Winter).

I have argued elsewhere that Paul used the conventions of Greco-Roman rhetoric masterfully to advocate for Philemon's full-scale emancipation, with the commercial language in verse 18 functioning figuratively and not literally (in short, there is no evidence that Onesimus had "absconded with the silver" because he was a morally bankrupt person). Further, the evidence that Onesimus is a runaway *at all* is to be questioned:

> Paul's stated readiness to share his economic resources shows the boundless character of his concern for Philemon. The commercial allusions function, then, as a quintessential illustration of the fact that Paul would utilize all resources at his disposal to prevent possible economic barriers, or any hindrances from forestalling the full granting of his request, for Paul's rhetorical offer of a "promissory note," a kind of *cheirographon* (Col. 4.18), an autographed "I.O.U.," has fully opened the door for Philemon's full cooperation. (Martin, 1991b: 335)

It is *possible* that Onesimus was a runaway slave, but that is not stated in any definitive sense. There are a number of other reasons which could account for his presence with Paul: he could have been sent to Paul by Philemon for a particular purpose, and decided to remain with Paul. John Knox questions whether Philemon had sent Onesimus to Paul with some message or gift for Paul or one of Paul's companions in prison. Was he simply overdue in his absence from Colossae on Philemon's business? (Martin, 1991b:336).

It is not insignificant that this most personal of Paul's letters is addressed to a large audience: Philemon, Apphia, and "the church in your house" (v. 2), for Paul expects Philemon's response to his plea to be positive and paradigmatic for others.

Paul's passionate appeal on behalf of Onesimus does not fully forestall the argument that Paul appears to tolerate chattel slavery (1 Cor 7:21–24), particularly as he views the duration of the social order through eschatologically-tinged spectacles (7:29–31). The suggestion that enslaved persons remain in the condition in which they were called within the context of 1 Corinthians 7 may be construed as a disincentive against radical social change by some (7:24), and, moreover, a minimalist attempt to subvert aspects of the existing social order.

Third, Pauline texts were used in plantation missions as part of a formal programme of religious instruction to require enslaved black peoples to conform to the creation of a "Christian social order" based on duty—that of slave to master.

A chief aim of plantation missions was to "show forth from the Scriptures that slavery is not forbidden by Divine Law." One of the leading theorists and proponents of plantation missions, Charles Colcock Jones, explained the reason for plantation missions in his *Catechism* published in 1834. Jones's *Catechism* enjoined slaves

> to count their Masters "worthy of all honour," as those whom God has placed over them in this world; "*with all fear*," they are to be "*subject to them*" and obey them in all *things*, possible and lawful, with good will and endeavour to *please them well*, . . . and let Servants serve their masters as faithfully behind their backs as before their faces. God is present to see, if their masters are not. (Quoted in Crum: 204–205)

Jones would later be surprised when a congregation of enslaved black peoples walked out upon hearing him justify slavery on the "authority of Paul." The now famous incident occurred in 1845:

> I was preaching to a large congregation on the *Epistle of Philemon*: and when I insisted upon fidelity and obedience as Christian virtues in servants and upon the authority of Paul, condemned the practice of *running away*, one half of my audience deliberately rose up and walked off with themselves, and those that remained looked any thing but satisfied, either with the preacher or his doctrine. After dismission, there was no small stir among them; some solemnly declared "that there was no such an Epistle in the Bible"; others, "that they did not care if they ever heard me preach again!" ... There were some too, who had strong objections against me as a Preacher, because I was a *master*, and said, "his people have to work as well as we." (Quoted in Raboteau: 24–25)

Fourth, the Pauline texts functioned as a central actor in the theater of proslavery drama, one which sought to reinforce the rituals of subordination which left enslaved black peoples on a daily precarious tightrope walk between punishment and humiliation, life and death. In an interview recorded in Canada in 1863, Mrs. Joseph Smith, formerly enslaved in Maryland, narrates her experience of biblical texts enjoining subordination and the concomitant brutality of Christian slavemasters:

> I was born and brought up on the Eastern shore of Maryland. I didn't have a hard time, but a pretty easy one; but I was a slave, any how. I never see none of the cutting and slashing that I have heard of. I came away because I wanted to be free. I was tired of working for somebody else, and I knew they might sell me whenever they'd a mind to. The ministers used to preach—"Obey your masters and mistresses and be good servants"; I never heard anything else. I didn't hear any thing about obeying our Maker. Those who were Christians & held slaves were the hardest masters. A card-player and drunkard wouldn't flog you half to death. Well, it is something like this—the Christians will oppress you more. For instance, the biggest dinner must be got on Sunday. Now, everybody that has got common sense knows that Sunday is a day of rest. And if you do the least thing in the world that they don't like, they will mark it down against you, and Monday you have got to take a whipping. Now, the card-player & horse racer won't be there to trouble you. They will eat their breakfast in the morning and feed their dogs, & then be off, & you won't see them again till night. I would rather be with a card-player or sportsman, by half, than a Christian. (Blassingame: 411)

Slavemasters often functioned as "acrobats without safety nets": suffused with the confidence of those in positions of power who have "no fear of falling," they feared no accountability for their actions. Fueled by claims of "biblical sanction" for their slaveholding prerogatives, they acted with full impunity toward enslaved men and women. Enslaved women and men often viewed the misfortunes of slave masters and slave mistresses as an act of divine justice or retribution, as was the case with James Curry, enslaved in Georgia in the early nineteenth century:

> When my master's family were all gone away on the Sabbath, I used to go into the house and get the great Bible, and lie down in the piazza, and read, taking care, however, to put it back before they returned. There I learned that it was contrary to the revealed will of God, that one man should hold another as a slave. I had always heard it talked among the slaves, that we ought not to be held as slaves; that our forefathers and mothers were stolen from Africa, where they were free men and free women. But in the Bible I learned that "God hath made of one blood all nations of men to dwell on all the face of the earth." While I worked in the house and waited upon my mistress, she always treated me kindly, but to other slaves, who were as faithful as I was, she was very cruel. At one time, there was a comb found broken in a cupboard, which was worth about twenty-five or thirty-seven and a half cents. She suspected a little girl, 9 or 10 years old, who served in the house, of having broken it. She took her in the morning, before sunrise, into a room, and calling me to wait upon her, had all the doors shut. She tied her hands, and then took her frock up over her head, and gathered it up in her left hand, and with her right commenced beating her naked body with bunches of willow twigs. She would beat her until her arm was tired, and then thrash her on the floor, and stamp on her with her foot, and kick her, and choke her to stop her screams. Oh! it was awful! and I was obliged to stand there and see it, and go and bring her the sticks. She continued this torture until ten o'clock, the family waiting breakfast meanwhile. She then left whipping her; and that night, she herself was so lame that one of her daughters was obliged to undress her. The poor child never recovered. A white swelling came from the bruises on one of her legs, of which she died in two or three years. And my mistress was soon after called by her great Master to give her account. (Blassingame: 131)

Finally, while the range of topics which explore the full spectrum of the effects of Pauline texts in American slavery cannot be examined here, it should be noted that the nation's system of American jurisprudence was often complicit with, and reinforced, proslavery religious dogma and precepts which safeguarded the institution of slavery, with its material benefits to slaveholders. Here, Pauline texts or sentiments were usually less explicit; however, the assumption that Christianity could be mined as a legal resource for a typology of attitudes supporting slavery was a given.

A. Leon Higginbotham, the esteemed jurist, advocator, and historian on race and the American legal process in the Colonial period, has observed that the causal factors for the legislated and adjudicated arguments for the legalization of black suppression were multifaceted. Moreover, he notes many Americans still find it too traumatic to study the true story of racism as it has existed under the "rule of law." Higginbotham comments: "Generally, neither the courts nor the legislatures seemed to have been any more sensitive about commercial transactions involving slaves than they were about sales of corn, lumber, horses, or dogs" (12). An advertisement for the sale of one hundred and twenty slaves illustrates the "casual" affectation of the advertisements:

> One hundred and twenty Negroes for sale—The subscriber has just arrived from Petersburg, Virginia, with one hundred and twenty likely young Negroes of both sexes and every description, which he offers for sale on the most reasonable terms. The lot now on hand consists of plough-boys, several likely and well-qualified house servants of both sexes, several women and children, small girls suitable for nurses, and *several small boys without their mothers*. Planters and traders are earnestly requested to give the subscriber a call previously to making purchases elsewhere, as he is enabled to sell as cheap or cheaper than can be sold by any other person in the trade. —Hamburg, South Carolina, Benjamin Davis. (Goodell: 54–55)

The legion of documented slave advertisements for runaway slaves likewise corroborates Higginbotham's point regarding the "casualness" of trafficking in human lives. They also document the daily and unrelenting efforts of enslaved peoples to secure their freedom. In his book, *Stealing A Little Freedom: Advertisements for Slave Runaways in North Carolina, 1791–1840*, Freddie L. Parker compiled notices for more than 2,600 enslaved persons. One sample illustrates the cavalier attitude of slavemasters seeking to recover their "property."

> 635. May 3, 1816
> **TWENTY DOLLARS REWARD.**
> RAN AWAY from the subscriber, living near Charlotte, N.C. night of the 7th inst. FOUR likely NEGROES, viz. TOM & THREE CHILDREN.
> Tom is about 47 years of age, dark complected, stout made, grey headed, has a remarkable white spot on the side of his neck, and scars of white across his breast.
> Stephen is about 20 years of age, stout made, has a scar in his under lip cut with a penknife.
> Puggy is about 14 years of age.
> Ellick is about 12 years of age, some of his jaw teeth are rotten.
> They are all middling well clothed, and took with them a number of good clothing. They also took a shot Gun and two Pistols.
> I purchased the above Negroes some years ago of the estate of Wallis Alexander, Esq. deceased, of Lincoln county, N.C.
> I will give the above reward and pay all reasonable expences to any person who will apprehend said Negroes, and deliver them to me in Charlotte, or secure them in any Jail, so that I get them.
> April 11, 1816   ZENAS ALEXANDER
>   (Parker: 212)

As early as 1667, colonial jurisprudence in Virginia legislated that baptism did not affect the bondage of black peoples and Native Americans, decreeing that "baptism does not alter the condition of the person as to his bondage of freedom" (Higginbotham: 19–40).

The notion that the conversion and baptism of slaves had no effect on their status was echoed in South Carolina law: "it shall be, and is hereby declared, lawful for any negro or Indian slave, . . . to receive and profess the Christian faith, and be thereinto baptized; that notwithstanding . . . he or they shall not thereby be manumitted or set free . . . (Higginbotham: 200).

Arguments have been advanced in support of the thesis that baptism encouraged slavemasters to regard enslaved persons with greater compassion, as advocated in Quaker abolitionist rhetoric (Higginbotham: 201, 293); however, many states continued to join legal precept to religious precept in forbidding literacy, mobility, and emancipation to the enslaved. The Pauline texts so eagerly embraced and wielded to both undergird and legitimate the discourses of domination, social contra, and social death, were firmly buttressed by formal, legal prescriptions to entrench *fides* and *obsequium* to slave masters, and the continuation of the American slave in perpetuity.

III. "Say It's Not So!"
Discourses of Resistance, Empowerment, and Liberation

James Gronniosaw, a young African teenager sold to a Dutch trader in the 1730s, recorded one of the first five slave narratives published in England in the eighteenth century. He recalls his reaction to his first exposure to the written word:

> My master used to read prayers in public to the ship's crew every Sabbath day; and when I first saw him read, I was never so surprised in my life, as when I saw the book talk to my master, for I thought it did, as I observed him to look upon it, and move his lips. I wished it would do so with me. As soon as my master had done reading, I followed him to the place where he put the book, being mightily delighted with it, and when nobody saw me, I opened it, and put my ear down close upon it, in great hope that it would say something to me; but I became very sorry, and greatly disappointed, when I found it would not speak. (Cornelius: 16)

Gronniosaw was not the first enslaved African to mention the "voice in the text." Of those first five slave narratives published in England, four mentioned this notion of the "voice in the text," attesting to both the popularity of the story, and perhaps the frequency of the experience in the lives of some enslaved persons. Ultimately, the desire and ability to achieve literacy, to read and write, would become a major preoccupation of many enslaved Africans. The unquenchable desire and ability to read the Bible (often by stealth and at great personal cost, since slavemasters and others forbade literacy and schooling for slaves) would function as one more instrument of effective political resistance and liberation for black peoples (Cornelius: 16).

The fact is, whether literate or not, enslaved African-Americans did not hear the same "voice in the text" as their slavemasters. When, upon hearing Charles Colcock Jones's sermon about the Pauline endorsement of slavery fully one half of the congregation "rose up" and "walked off with themselves," questioning whether such an epistle was even found in the Bible (see above), they were rejecting with "head" (intellect), heart, and "feet" alike what they believed to be a deliberate distortion of Christian doctrine. The point should escape no one that one-half of the congregation walked out, and the other half who remained disputed Jones's theological argument. Their "hermeneutics of critical suspicion" yielded a response of incredulity to the idea that God endorsed a construction of reality in which some human beings became the "property" of other human beings—a response conveying the sentiment, "Say It's Not So!" or "It Can't Be So!" Implicit in the slaves' walking out of Jones's religious assembly was unqualifiable rejection of the morally bankrupt philosophy of white racist supremacy, with its twin corollaries, racial denigration and rampant injustice.

Enslaved African peoples brought with them to North America a distinct perception of God, one who was transcendent, immanent, and impartial, the universal parent of all of humankind (Acts 17:26-28). The distinct monotheism at the heart of African traditional religions focused on God as the power which unites the realms of nature, history, and spirit (Paris, 1995:28).

Structural similarities between Christianity and African cosmologies made conversion to Christianity easier for African slaves, but it never meant the wholesale exchange of their indigenous religion for a new one. "When Africans embraced the Christian God they simultaneously *extended* rather than *transcended* their own particular practice" (Paris, 1995:28-37; cf. Genovese: 211; Wiredu: 155).

Since religion pervaded every dimension of African life (there was no notion of the modern Western distinction between sacred and profane in African cosmological thought), the theological and *moral* implications of faith were always pivotal, including one's relationship to community, society, and nature. Africans who desired to be Christians sought to "Africanize" Christianity, enculturating Christianity with African moral virtues such as beneficence, the promotion of an appreciation for the integrity of all human personhood, community, and the preservation of freedom and justice (Paris, 1995:27, 117, 136).

The Christianity of enslaved Africans was distinct from that of proslavery apologists, with black folk religion advancing a decisive moral critique of slavery, an embrace of the legitimation of slave resistance, and a resounding affirmation of the integrity, beauty, and value of black humanity. Black slave theology was rooted in an understanding of God as one who hears the cries of those in bondage (as in the Exodus traditions in the Hebrew Bible), a God who is just, and compassionate, and who vindicates the oppressed. This God also punishes the wicked. African-American Spirituals are but one of many cultural venues through which these themes were mediated and reinforced. The pre-Civil War hymn below, which describes the end of slavery as God's liberating act, is but one example:

> Slavery chain done broke at last, broke
>   at last, broke at last,
> Slavery chain done broke at last,
> Going to praise God till I die.
> Way down in-a dat valley,
> Praying on my knees;
> Told God about my troubles,
> And to help me ef-a He please.
>
> I did tell him how I suffer,
> In de dungeon and de chain,
> And de days I went with head bowed down,
> And my broken flesh and pain.
>
> I did know my Jesus heard me,
> 'Cause de spirit spoke to me,
> And said, "Rise my child, your chillun,
> And you shall be free.
>
> "I done 'p'int one mighty captain
> For to marshall all my hosts,
> And to bring my bleeding ones to me,
> And not one shall be lost."
>
> Slavery chain done broke at last, broke
>   at last, broke at least,
> Slavery chain done broke at last,
> Going to praise God till I die. (Cone: 41–42)

If God is Just and the Divine Liberator in black folk religion, Jesus is the "Dying Lamb" who became the Hero, the Conquering King, and the Friend who not only provides salvation, but who "fights your battles and rolls away all of Satan's blocks" (D. Hopkins: 30–31). Moreover, the significance of Jesus is not his maleness, but his humanity. He is known as one who empowers the weak and frees them from bondage, who signifies freedom from the sociopsychological, economic, and political oppression of black peoples (Grant: 215; Douglas).

In contradistinction to white proslavery apologists, black peoples found within the Hebrew Bible and Christian Scriptures a "voice within the text" which recognized the reality of evil in human person and institutions, and they provided a sustained prophetic witness and unyielding, active resistance against all that dehumanized black men and women made in the image of God (Williams: 1–33). Seeking diligently to reveal the contradictions in the life of the nation, to clarify the moral dimension of those contradictions, and to urge their reasoned and just resolution (Paris, 1982), black peoples rejected the carefully packaged interpretations of an uncritical Pauline "slaveholding religion" which they believe to be disconsonant with both God's divine intention for the human family, and God's justice. The voice they "heard in the text" was one which was consonant with a nonracist interpretation and appropriation of the Christian tradition and Christian faith, which was free from the racist overlays and entanglements of legal and systemic oppression, and which recognized the universal kinship of humanity. This fundamental hermeneutic perspective which recognized the universal parenthood of God and the kinship of humankind would always mandate a disavowal of any hermeneutic or interpretation of Scripture which would seek to legitimate and perpetuate racism, slavery, or any other form of human bondage (Paris, 1982:134–35).

Part I of this essay illustrated the fact that the rich synthesis of "hoodoo" and biblical traditions could be used in service of wide-ranging discourses enabling personal and (or) communal transformations of identity, space and place. These discourses could be used to transmute the "sorcery of white racism" in ways that circumvented the persistent onslaught of injustice, denigration, and humiliation. Language could thus be used as a stratagem of political resistance against the hegemonic discourses of domination.

African-American peoples have always used language as a conveyor of religious, cultural, and moral meaning and values. One of the most powerful and poignant examples of discourses enabling pragmatically affirmative, transformative, and ennobling effects during the antebellum period of American slavery is found in the celebrated novelist Toni Morrison's Pulitzer Prize-winning novel, *Beloved*. This fictional account of a gathering of black slaves in a clearing in the woods to engage in a ritual of the worship of God, and especially the celebration of the integrity of Black personhood, was not uncommon.

> Whether in bushes, fields, cabins, or at night under the canopy of a star-studded sky, enslaved African Americans took the remnants of their traditional religious structures and integrated them with their interpretation of the Bible. All of this occurred in the "Invisible Institution" of the black church far away from the watchful eyes of white peoples. Only in their own cultural idiom and political space could black slaves truly exercise some control in a world where they often lacked control over their present and future. While white masters attempted to force their Christianity onto their slaves, slaves secretly worshiped God. Their practical and sacred world view evolved into an institutional worship setting under bondage. (D. Hopkins: 18)

James C. Scott was correct when he observed in his book, *Domination and the Arts of Resistance: Hidden Transcripts*, that "Most of the political life of subordinate groups is to be found neither in overt collective defiance of power holders nor in complete hegemonic compliance, but in the vast territory between these two polar opposites" (136).

The map of that vast territory between the two opposites contains multiple strategies for survival and resistance against the forces of domination and oppression. Morrison's imaginative narration of the preacher Baby Suggs's sermonic discourse provides a stirring example of what Scott calls a "discourse of dignity," a form of "Public, Declared Resistance" in a more private setting. The "discourse of dignity" is a response to ideological negation and indignity, often shared by a social circle of family, friends, neighbors, and peers, and it provides a partial refuge from the humiliations of domination. As a collective hidden discourse, a "discourse of dignity" shared with others in a concealed site provides an opportunity for the group to elaborate affirmatively a constructive hidden script in comparative safety (Scott: 113–14). Morrison narrates the drama with telling and gripping clarity:

> When warm weather came, Baby Suggs, holy, followed by every black man, woman and child who could make it through, took her great heart to the Clearing—a wide-open place cut deep in the woods nobody knew for what at the end of a path known only to deer and whoever cleared the land in the first place. In the heat of every Saturday afternoon, she sat in the clearing while the people waited among the trees.
>
> After situating herself on a huge flat-sided rock, Baby Suggs bowed her head and prayed silently. The company watched her from the trees. They knew she was ready when she put her stick down. Then she shouted, "Let the children come!" and they ran from the trees toward her.
>
> "Let your mothers hear you laugh," she told them, and the woods rang. The adults looked on and could not help smiling.
>
> Then "Let the grown men come," she shouted. They stepped out one by one from among the ringing trees.
>
> "Let your wives and your children see you dance," she told them, and groundlife shuddered under their feet.
>
> Finally she called the women to her, "Cry," she told them. "For the living and the dead. Just cry." And without covering their eyes the women let loose.
>
> It started that way: laughing children, dancing men, crying women and then it got mixed up. Women stopped crying and danced; men sat down and cried; children danced, women laughed, children cried until, exhausted and riven, all and each lay about the Clearing damp and gasping for breath. In the silence that followed, Baby Suggs, holy, offered up to them her great big heart.
>
> She did not tell them to clean up their lives or to go and sin no more. She did not tell them they were the blessed of the earth, its inheriting meek or its glorybound pure.
>
> She told them that the only grace they could have was the grace they could imagine. That if they could not see it, they would not have it.

"Here," she said, "in this here place, we flesh; flesh that weeps, laughs; flesh that dances on bare feet in grass. Love it. Love it hard. Yonder they do not love your flesh. They despise it. They don't love your eyes; they'd just as soon pick em out. No more do they love the skin on your back. Yonder they flay it. And O my people they do not love your hands. Those they only use, tie, bind, chop off and leave empty. Love your hands! Love them. Raise them up and kiss them. Touch others with them, pat them together, stroke them on your face 'cause they don't love that either. *You* got to love it, *you*! And no, they ain't in love with your mouth. Yonder, out there, they will see it broken and break it again. What you say out of it they will not heed. What you scream from it they do not hear. What you put into it to nourish your body they will snatch away and give you leavins instead. No, they don't love your mouth. *You* got to love it. This is flesh I'm talking about here. Flesh that needs to be loved. Feet that need to rest and to dance; backs that need support; shoulders that need arms, strong arms I'm telling you. And O my people, out yonder, hear me, they do not love your neck unnoosed and straight. So love your neck; put a hand on it, grace it, stroke it and hold it up. And all your inside parts that they'd just as soon slop for hogs, you got to love them. The dark, dark liver—love it, love it, and the beat and beating heart, love that too.

More than eyes or feet. More than lungs that have yet to draw free air. More than your life-holding womb and your life-giving private parts, hear me now, love your heart. For this is the prize." Saying no more, she stood up then and danced with her twisted hip the rest of what her heart had to say while the others opened their mouths and gave her the music. Long notes held until the four-part harmony was perfect enough for their deeply loved flesh. (Morrison: 87–89)

This "discourse of dignity" affirmed a constructive self-love of bodies too often shackled in chains, or overworked, or underfed, or undernourished, or beaten, or mutilated, or torn, or lynched—but certainly disregarded—in slavery. A discourse like the one uttered by Baby Suggs in the Clearing, and safely away from the ever watching eyes of slavemasters and slave mistresses, functioned as a discourse of celebration, resistance, empowerment, and liberation for men and women whose physical and material humanity, and very ontological being, were in constant jeopardy in slavery.

The rhetorical discourses of enslaved persons in sermon and song, poetry and speeches, autobiographies or as dictated reminisces, would document black peoples' refusal to accept the notion of their inhumanity and the terms of their structural subordination even when advanced under the auspices of Pauline authority.

Like Baby Suggs's sermon, many of these antebellum discourses would be rhetorically eloquent, poignant, revolutionary (e.g. Nat Turner, Sojourner Truth), life-giving, and life-sustaining, and they would often be uttered within contexts that were participatory and communal, as was that of Baby Suggs. Such discourses would "thwart," "hoodoo," or nullify the pernicious sorcery of white racism—temporarily at least—which sought ever to crush and destroy black minds and bodies and spirits. Such discourses of resistance would forestall evil and create those healing and empowering ideological, epistemological, and existential "safe places" which provided some reprieve from the constant onslaught and battery of the proslavery apologia which regularly trafficked in the full-scale exploitation of Pauline traditions.

Works Consulted

Armstrong, George D.
    1857   *The Christian Doctrine of Slavery*. Repr. 1969. York: Negro University Press.

Baker, Huston, Jr.
    1991   *Workings of the Spirit: The Poetics of Afro-American Women's Writings*. Chicago: University of Chicago Press.

Beardsley, Grace Hadley
    1929   *The Negro in Greek and Roman Civilization: A Study of the Ethiopian Type*. Baltimore: Johns Hopkins University Press.

Bellen, Heinz
    1971   *Studien zur Slavenflucht im römischen Kaiserreich*. Wiesbaden: Steiner.

Blassingame, John W., ed.
    1977   *Slave Testimony: Two Centuries of Letters, Speeches, Interviews, and Autobiographies*. Baton Rouge: Louisiana State University Press.

Bradley, Keith R.
    1987   *Slaves and Masters in the Roman Empire: A Study in Social Control*. Oxford: Oxford University Press.

Brooke, Rosalind, and Christopher Brooke
    1984   *Popular Religions in the Middles Ages: Western Europe 1000–1300*. London: Thames and Hudson.

Bruce, F. F.
    1981   *Paul: Apostle of the Heart Set Free*. Grand Rapids: Eerdmans.

Callahan, Allen
    1997   *Embassy of Onesimus: The Letter of Paul to Philemon*. Valley Forge, Penn.: Trinity Press International.

Capon, Robert Farrar
    1974   *Hunting the Divine Fox. Images and Mystery in Christian Faith*. New York: Crossroad.

Cheseborough, David B.
    1996   *Clergy Dissent in the Old South, 1830–1865*. Carbondale and Edwardswille: Southern Illinois University Press.

Cone, James H.
    1991   *The Spirituals and the Blues*. Maryknoll, N.Y.: Orbis.

Cornelius, Janet Duitsman
    1991   *When I Can Read My Title Clear: Literacy, Slavery, and Religion in the Antebellum South*. Columbia, S.C.: University of South Carolina Press.

Courtès, Jean Marie
    1979   "The Theme of Ethiopia and Ethiopians in Patristic Literature." *Images of the Black in Western Art*. Volume 2/i. New York: Morrow.

Crum, Mason
    1940   *Gullah: Negro Life in the Carolina Sea Islands*. Durham, N.C.: Duke University Press.

Davies, Alan
    1982   "The Ideology of Racism." In *The Church and Racism*. *Concilium* 151. Ed. Gregory Baum and John Coleman. New York: Seabury.

Douglas, Kelly Brown
    1994   *The Black Christ*. The Bishop Henry McNeal Turner Studies in North American Black Religion 9. Maryknoll, N.Y.: Orbis.

Elliot, E. N., ed.
    1860   *Cotton is King, and Pro-slavery Arguments: Comprising the Writings of Hammond, Harper, Christy, Stringfellow, Hodge, Bledsoe, and Cartwright on This Important Subject*. Repr. 1969. New York: New York Universities Press.

Evans, James H.
    1992   *We Have Been Believers: An African-American Systematic Theology*. Minneapolis: Fortress.

Faust, Drew, ed.
    1981   *The Ideology of Slavery*. Baton Rouge: Louisiana State University Press.

Finley, M.I.
    1983   *Ancient Slavery and Modern Ideology*. New York: Penguin.

Gadamer, Hans-Georg
    1975   *Truth and Method*. Trans. G. Barden and J. Cumming. New York: Seabury.

Genovese, Eugene
    1974   *Roll, Jordan Roll: The World the Slaves Made*. New York: Pantheon.

Goodell, William
    1853   *The American Slave Code in Theory and Practice*. Repr. 1969. New York: American Library.

Grant, Jacquelyn
    1989   *White Women's Christ and Black Women's Jesus: Feminist Christology and Womanist Response*. AAR Academy Series 64. Atlanta: Scholars Press.

Harding, Vincent
    1981   *There is a River: The Black Struggle for Freedom in America*. New York: Harcourt Brace Jovanovich.

Hennecke, Edgar and Wilhelm Schneemelcher, eds.
    1976   *New Testament Apocrypha*. Vol. 2. Philadelphia: Westminster.

Higginbotham, A. Leon
    1978   *In The Matter of Color: Race and the American Legal Process: The Colonial Period*. New York: Oxford University Press.

Hinks, Peter P.
    1997   *To Awaken My Afflicted Brethren: David Walker and the Problem of Antebellum Slave Resistance*. University Park: Pennsylvania University Press.

Hodge, Charles B.
    1860   "The Bible Argument on Slavery." See E. W. Elliott, "Cotton is King and Pro-slavery Arguments." Pp. 841–77 in *This Important Subject*. New York: Negro University Press, 1969.

Hood, Robert E.
    1994   *Begrimed and Black: Christian Traditions on Blacks and Blackness*. Minneapolis: Fortress.

Hopkins, Dwight
    1993   *Shoes That Fit Our Feet: Sources for a Constructive Black Theology*. Maryknoll, N.Y.: Orbis.

Hopkins, John Henry
    1864   *A Scriptural Ecclesiastical and Historical View of Slavery from the Days of the Patriarch Abraham, to the Nineteenth Century*. New York: Pooley.

Hurston, Zora Neale
    1990   *Mules and Men*. Repr. of the 1935 ed. New York: Harper Collins.

Johnson, Thomas Cary
    1903   *The Life and Letters of Robert Lewis Dabney*. Richmond (publisher not stated).

Lake, Kirsopp, ed.
    1959   *The Apostolic Fathers*. Volume 1. Loeb Classical Library. Cambridge, Mass.: Harvard University Press.

Lincoln, C. Eric
    1984   *Race, Religion, and the Continuing American Dilemma*. New York: Hill and Wang.

Long, Charles H.
    1986   *Significations: Signs, Symbols, and Images in the Interpretation of Religion*. Philadelphia: Fortress.

Loveland, Anne C.
    1980   *Southern Evangelicals and the Social Order, 1800–1860*. Baton Rouge: Louisiana State University Press.

Martin, Clarice J.
    1990   "Womanist Interpretations of the New Testament: The Quest for Holistic and Inclusive Translation and Interpretation." *Journal of Feminist Studies in Religion.* 6/2: 41–61.

    1991a   "The Haustafeln (Household Codes) in African American Biblical Interpretation: 'Free Slaves' and 'Subordinate Women.'" Pp. 206–31 in *Stony the Road We Trod: African American Biblical Interpretation.* Ed. Cain Hope Felder. Philadelphia: Augsburg/Fortress.

    1991b   "The Rhetorical Function of Commercial Language in Paul's Letter to Philemon (Verse 18)." Pp. 321–37 in *Persuasive Artistry: Studies in New Testament Rhetoric in Honor of George A. Kennedy.* JSNTSup 50. Ed. Duane F. Watson. Sheffield: Sheffield Academic Press.

    1993   "A Chamberlain's Journey and the Challenge of Interpretation for Liberation." Pp. 485–502 in *The Bible and Liberation: Political and Social Hermeneutics.* Revised Ed. Ed. Norman K. Gottwald and Richard A. Horsley. Maryknoll, N.Y.: Orbis.

    1999   "Womanist Biblical Interpretation." Pp. 655–58 in *Dictionary of Biblical Interpretation*, Vol. 2. Ed. John H. Hayes. Nashville: Abingdon.

Matthews, Donald G.
    1977   *Religion in the Old South.* Chicago: University of Chicago Press.

Morrison, Toni
    1987   *Beloved.* New York: Knopf.

Paris, Peter
    1982   "The Bible and the Black Churches." In *The Bible and Social Reform.* Ed. Ernest R. Sandeen. Philadelphia: Fortress.

    1995   *The Spirituality of African Peoples: The Search for a Common Moral Discourse.* Minneapolis: Fortress.

Parker, Freddie L., ed.
    1994   *Stealing A Little Freedom: Advertisements for Slave Runaways in North Carolina, 1791–1840.* New York: Garland.

Patte, Daniel
    1995   *Ethics of Biblical Interpretation: A Reevaluation.* Louisville: Westminster/John Knox.

Patterson, Orlando
    1982   *Slavery and Social Death: A Comparative Study.* Cambridge, Mass.: Harvard University Press.

    1991   *Freedom in the Making of Western Culture.* Vol. 1. New York: HarperCollins.

Perkins, Pheme
    1992   "Philemon." Pp. 362–63 in *The Women's Bible Commentary.* Ed. Carol H. Newsom and Sharon H. Ringe. Louisville: Westminster/John Knox.

Petersen, Norman R.
   1985   *Rediscovering Paul: Philemon and the Sociology of Paul's Narrative World.* Philadelphia: Fortress.

Raboteau, Albert J.
   1978   *Slave Religion: The "Invisible Institution" in the Antebellum South.* New York: Oxford University Press.

Ridderbos, Herman
   1975   *Paul: An Outline of His Theology.* Grand Rapids: Eerdmans.

Ross, Frederick A.
   1859   *Slavery Ordained of God.* Philadelphia: Lippincott.

Schüssler Fiorenza, Elisabeth
   1985   *In Memory of Her: A Feminist Theological Reconstruction of Early Christian Origins.* New York: Crossroads.

Scott, James C.
   1990   *Domination and the Arts of Resistance: Hidden Transcripts.* New Haven: Yale University Press.

Smith, H. Shelton
   1972   *In His Image, But . . . : Racism in Southern Religion, 1780–1910.* Durham, N.C.: Duke University Press.

Smith, Theophus
   1994   *Conjuring Culture: Biblical Formations of Black America.* New York: Oxford University Press.

Snowden, Frank M.
   1970   *Blacks in Antiquity: Ethiopians in the Greco-Roman Experience.* Cambridge: Harvard University Press.

Swartley, Willard M.
   1983   *Slavery, Sabbath, War and Women: Case Issues in Biblical Interpretation.* Scottdale, Penn.: Herald.

Thomas, Latta R.
   1976   *Biblical Faith and the Black American.* Valley Forge, Penn.: Judson.

Thornwell, James Henry
   1850   *The Rights and the Duties of Masters.* Charleston, S.C.: Walker and James.

Tidball, Derek
   1984   *The Social Context of the New Testament: A Sociological Analysis.* Grand Rapids: Academic Books.

Watson, Allen
   1987   *Roman Slave Law.* Baltimore: Johns Hopkins University Press.

West, Cornel
   1982   *Prophesy Deliverance.* Philadelphia: Westminster.

Williams, Delores S.
  1993   *Sisters in the Wilderness: The Challenge of Womanist God-Talk.* Maryknoll, N.Y.: Orbis.

Wilmore, Gayraud
  1989   *Black Religion and Black Radicalism: An Interpretation of the Religious History of Afro-American People.* 2nd ed. revised and enlarged. Maryknoll, N.Y.: Orbis.

Winter, S.C.
  1994   "Philemon." Pp. 301–12 in *Searching the Scriptures: A Feminist Commentary.* Vol. 2. Ed. Elisabeth Schüssler Fiorenza. New York: Crossroad.

Wiredu, K. (J. E.)
  1984   "How Not to Compare African Thought With Western Thought." In *African Philosophy: An Introduction.* Ed. Richard A. Wright. 3rd ed. Lanham, Md.: University Press of America.

Young, Al
  1996   "Somebody Done Hoodoo'd The Hoodoo Man." In *African American Literature.* Ed. Al Young. New York: Harper Collins.

"BROTHER SAUL":
AN AMBIVALENT WITNESS TO FREEDOM

Allen Dwight Callahan
Harvard University

ABSTRACT

Most contemporary African Americans read Paul as an anti-emancipatory biblical witness. But in the beginning it was not so: there is a venerable tradition of the emancipatory appropriation of Paul in which both his life and letters are enlisted in the struggle for African American freedom. This emancipatory appropriation of Paul, sometimes reading against the grain of his canonical correspondence and sometimes reading into the canonical account of his career rendered in the Acts of the Apostles, suggests a theologically fruitful *via media* for contemporary Pauline theology between a dogmatic privileging of the Pauline legacy with its anti-emancipatory elements on the one hand and the thoroughgoing rejection of Paul along with his emancipatory proclamation on the other.

In African American life and letters the Apostle Paul's emancipatory insights and enormous prestige were acknowledged with a careful reverence, even as his words were interpreted with canny qualification. Though touted as the apostle of freedom, Paul's letters were used to legitimate American slavery. Antebellum pro-slavery apologists called the Epistle to Philemon, supposedly a cover letter attending the return of a runaway slave to his angry master, "the Pauline Mandate." The letter was their biblical sanction for the return of fugitive slaves (Callahan: 1). Pauline exhortations to servile obedience in the Pauline epistles became the raw material for the catechesis of slaves in early nineteenth century plantation missions (Callahan: 10–12). Thus Paul became, in the minds of slave and master alike, the patron saint of the master class. The freedom the Apostle proclaimed in some of his letters was overshadowed in pro-slavery propaganda by the penumbra of accommodation to the slave regime signaled elsewhere in the Pauline corpus.

It is not remarkable that African Americans found Paul an ambiguous witness to the Gospel proclamation. It is remarkable that very few African American intellectuals have openly rejected that apostolic witness as hopelessly anti-emancipatory. Quite the contrary: rejection of Paul, the Paul of the so-called deutero-Pauline epistles and Pastoral epistles, the Paul who exhorts slaves to be obedient to their masters and recommends oppressive governments as God-ordained, has been rare among African Americans. Some have found in Paul a compelling voice of freedom that articulates their own *cri de coeur*. A consideration of how they heard that voice, how they heard the voice of freedom in some ostensibly anti-emancipatory tones, suggests a creative, complex, and sometimes contradictory African American hermeneutics, with its own vagaries of suspicion and retrieval appropriate to the creativity, complexity, and contradictions of the Divine Apostle himself.

Some slaves found in Pauline patriarchy and subordinationist parenesis a check on the ubiquitous powers of the master class. In a 1774 petition to the Massachusetts House of Representatives, a group of colonial slaves enlist the words of Paul to argue against their status of perpetual servitude. It is slavery's conflict with Pauline commandments of family and communal life, they contend, that shows the institution to be inherently incompatible with Christianity.

> ... our lives are embittered to us ... By our deplorable situation we are rendered incapable of shewing our obedience to Almighty God. How can a slave perform the duties of husband to a wife or a parent to his child? How can a husband leave master to work and cleave to his wife? How can the wife submit themselves to their husbands in all things? How can the child obey their parents in all things? There is a great number of us sincere ... members of the Church of Christ. How can the master and the slave be said to fulfil the command Live in love let brotherly love continue and abound, Beare ye one anothers Burdens? How can the master be said to Bear my Burden when he Bears me down with the heavy chains of slavery and oppression against my will? And how can we fulfill our part of duty to him whilst in this condition as we cannot serve our God as we ought in this situation? (Aptheker: I.8–9, modified)

The petitioners claim that they cannot serve the Master because of their service to the masters, because in slavery they cannot obey the orders of the apostolic slave for Christ's sake, Paul. It is the Apostle who instructs believers to bear one another's burdens in Gal 6:2, and enjoins the submission of wives to husbands and children to parents in Eph 5:22, 24, and Col 3:20. Here the injunctions of the Pauline household codes are given an emancipatory application. The patriarchal household was the norm for the master class of American colonial society, and it was as fervently sought after by African Americans as it was unavailable to them. That parents might retain possession and control of their own children and that a husband might command the honor of and exclusive sexual access to his own wife were troubled desiderata for black folks under the American slave regime. For the petitioners, Paul's patriarchal commandments gave these desiderata the sanction of Holy Scripture.

Some slaves and former slaves found wise counsel even in the quietist virtue advocated in the Pastoral Epistles. The slave poet Jupiter Hammond, who lived his entire life in bondage without hope of living otherwise, saw obedience as an investment in peace in the present world and eternal life in the world to come. He introduces his 1786 Address to the Negroes of the City of New York by troping the Apostle's lament in Rom 9:1. "With a view to promote your happiness," writes Hammond, "I can with truth and sincerity join with the apostle Paul, when speaking of his own nation the Jews, and say: 'That I have great heaviness and continual sorrow in my heart for my brethren, my kinsmen according to the flesh'" (Sernett: 33). Hammond's first piece of advice is for slaves to obey their masters, citing with approval Eph 6:5–7, the part of the Ephesian household code that enjoins slaves to obey their masters as they would obey Christ, adding, "Here is a plain command of God for us to obey our masters. It may seem hard for us, if we think our masters wrong in holding us slaves, to obey in all things, but who of us dare dispute with God!"(35). His counsel to obedience is nevertheless both principled and strategic. "This should be done by us," he continues, "not only because God commands, but because our own peace and comfort depend upon it" (35). Hammond's counsel is also qualified: slaves are to faithfully carry out "all . . . lawful commands, and mind them [i.e., their masters] unless we are bid to do that which we know to be sin, or forbidden in God's word" (35). He thus makes limited space for some discrimination, some moral discernment and agency for his hapless addressees. Hammond exhorts his addressees to acquire literacy and devote themselves to reading the Bible, for in its sacred oracles they discover the comforting revelation, "for such ignorant creatures as we," that Paul first commended to his status-anxious Corinthian correspondents: "For God hath not chosen the rich of this world. Not many rich, not many noble are called, but God hath chosen the weak things of this world, and things which are not, to confound the things which are" (40). Hammond concludes his address with an exhortation to free blacks to abide by the Pauline parenesis of 1 Tim 2:2, "to lead quiet and peaceable lives in all Godliness and honesty" (41).

African Methodist Episcopal Bishop Daniel Alexander Payne's 1863 address to the newly emancipated African Americans of the District of Columbia, "Welcome to the Ransomed," encourages freedmen to labor for their living, pray for their magistrates, and mind their own business. Payne begins his welcome with instructions on civic obedience found in the Pastoral Epistles. For Bishop Payne, the prayer offered on behalf of ruling authorities that Paul commands is the only permissible and the only truly effective weapon of Christian warfare. Prayer is the proper politics for Timothy and his Ephesian charges, and it is proper post-Emancipation politics in the United States as well, especially for the recently liberated but politically and economically marginal freedmen.

> Now, then, although weak, few, despised and persecuted, we can aid all these departments of government by our daily supplications, prayers and intercessions.

> In doing this service, we can accomplish what we could not if we were leading the van of battle; for conquering armies are preceded and succeeded by anguish, misery, and death, but our service brings nothing but blessing upon all.
> They are also weapons, "not carnal, but mighty through God, to the pulling down of strongholds;" even casting down principalities and powers—the moving of heaven and earth.
> ... When Israel fought against the five kings of the Amorites, Joshua prayed and the sun stood still upon Gibeon, while the moon hung over the valley of Ajalon, till Israel had conquered. (Sernett: 224)

Even Joshua, that paragon of biblical jihad, is reinterpreted in the light of the metaphor of spiritual warfare that Paul puts forth in 2 Cor 10:4–5. With this warfare of prayer Payne couples the warfare of pious praxis. It is through "habits of thrift and industry ... duties of religion and piety" and obedience to divine and human law that the former slaves achieve complete liberty.

> We entreat you to never be content until you are emancipated from sin, from sin without, and from sin within you. But this kind of freedom is only attained through the faith of Jesus Christ, love for Jesus Christ, obedience to Jesus Christ. As certain as the American Congress has ransomed you, so certain, yea, more certainly has Jesus redeemed you from the guilt and power of sin by his own precious blood.
> As you are now free in body, so now seek to be free in soul and spirit, from sin and Satan. The noblest freeman is he whom Christ makes free. (Sernett: 219)

By his discovery of a pragmatic politics, Bishop Payne provided emancipatory readings of the ostensibly reactionary exhortations of the Pauline corpus and by such readings Payne, Jupiter Hammond, and the signatories of the above-mentioned 1774 petition sought to use Paul's hard sayings to make servitude and subjugation easier loads for black people to bear.

The hard sayings of the Pauline corpus were also sometimes rendered less so by reading them in the light of other, more emancipatory declarations of the Apostle. In her memoir published in the last quarter of the nineteenth century, Holiness preacher Julia A. J. Foote bids her Christian sisters not to be bound "by those who say, 'We suffer not a woman to teach,' thus quoting Paul's words [1 Cor 14:34], but not rightly applying them" (Andrews: 227). Foote laments that her vocation to preach was disparaged even in Holiness churches. She marshals a scriptural defense of her calling, and the scriptures she cites, with exegetical finesse, are the Pauline epistles themselves.

> The Bible puts an end to this strife when it says: "There is neither male nor female in Christ Jesus" [Gal 3:28]. ... Paul called Priscilla, as well as Aquila, his "helper," or, as in the Greek, his "fellow-laborer." Rom. xv. 3; 2 Cor. viii.23; Phil. ii.5; 1 Thess. iii.2. The same word, which, in our common translation, is now rendered a "servant of the church," in speaking of Phebe (Rom.

xix.1 [sic]) is rendered "minister" when applied to Tychicus. Eph. vi.21. When Paul said, "Help those women who labor with me in the Gospel," he certainly meant that they did more than to pour tea. In the eleventh chapter of First Corinthians Paul gives directions, to men and women, how they should appear when they prophesy or pray in public assemblies; and he defines prophesying to be speaking to edification, exhortation and comfort. (209)

For Foote, the Apostle Paul vindicates and affirms the ministry of preaching women in both word and deed.

A different, double inversion is embodied in the biblical figure of Hagar that sculptor Edmonia Lewis appropriated in stone. While a young art student at Oberlin College just before the Civil War, Lewis was involved in a scandal that resulted in her expulsion. Binding the wounds of her rejection and humiliation she continued to pursue a career as a sculptor in Boston and Rome. Lewis's determination is expressed in the pose of her most famous work, "Hagar of the Wilderness." The figure of Hagar is strident, with upturned gaze, encouraged, indeed emboldened the voice of God from heaven that tells her, "Do not be afraid" (Gen 21:17b). Hagar is confident, "very plucky," which is how the articulate, forthright Lewis herself was described. The artist hacked her sculptures directly from marble, wore clothes with a manly cut, and spoke with intensity and directness. Lewis survived the 1867 cholera epidemic in Rome, she later claimed, with a Bible and a bottle of whiskey at her bedside so that if one gave out she could turn to the other. Which of the two was her first recourse she left unclear.

Lewis, as Hagar and countless other expatriate African women, had overcome humiliation and rejection, had struggled and suffered, had come to know the wilderness as a place of tears and promise. God himself calls to her in the wilderness and grants to her issue a compensatory covenant. It is this compensatory covenant that Paul declares hopelessly servile in the fourth chapter of his epistle to the Galatians. Paul gives an allegorical reading to the patriarchal narrative of struggle for inheritance between Ishmael, the son of the slave Hagar, and Isaac, the son of Abraham's wife Sarah. Isaac is the son of promise. But Paul's tortured typology leaves off precisely where the implicit, lapidary exegesis of Lewis begins. The center of gravity in Lewis's representation is in the concluding verses of Hagar's story.

> Arise, lift up the lad, and hold him in thine hand; for I will make him a great nation.
> And God opened her eyes, and she saw the well of water, and she went, and filled the bottle with water, and gave the lad drink.
> And God was with the lad; and he grew, and dwelt in the wilderness, and became an archer.
> And he dwelt in the wilderness of Paran, and his mother took him a wife out of the land of Egypt. (Gen 21:19–21)

In one verse of scripture Hagar moves from abandonment to agency: in verse 19 alone she is the subject of no less than four verbs. The slave woman Hagar receives a promise from God that bestows dignity on her posterity. She re-establishes her Egyptian ancestry by selecting a wife for her son from her native land and secures her progeny. In other words, Hagar gains for herself honor, family, and power, the three elements of full humanity the absence of which, as sociologist Orlando Patterson has taught us, is constitutive of slavery. "The slave . . . could have no honor because he had no power and no independent social existence" (Patterson: 10). Yet Hagar's repudiation ends in her honor, empowerment, and social independence: Hagar emerges from her ordeal in the wilderness a free woman. The denouement of her drama, and Lewis's faithful representation of it in stone, has turned Paul's allegory on its head: Hagar has her freedom, and her issue has a divinely ordained heritage. The freedom and heritage that God grants Hagar are clearly affirmed in the plain sense of the text even as they are plainly denied in Paul's exegesis. Lewis takes Paul's text and implicitly denies the denial of his exegesis. Lewis's alternative focus on the biblical text challenges the Pauline interpretation of a story about a slave woman and her issue.

With a alternative focus on the Pauline corpus, slave women and their issue challenged the Apostle's interpretation. They also challenged the interpretation of the Apostle. In the last quarter of the nineteenth century and the first of the twentieth, the African American women of the forerunner of the National Baptist Convention, USA, crafted an emancipatory interpretation of Paul. Lay biblical exegetes such as Mary Cook and Virginia Broughton, leaders of the national convention of black Baptist women, founded as an auxiliary of American National Baptist Convention in 1900, contextualized Pauline texts used to hinder the full participation of women in the affairs of the church and the world. Mary Cook, born a slave in Kentucky in 1862, graduated from State University at Louisville in 1883, and later taught Latin and literature there. Virginia Broughton's father bought the freedom of himself, his wife, and his children. She graduated from Fisk in 1857, perhaps the first woman ever to graduate from a southern college. Cook argued that an analysis of the historical context of Paul's statement revealed that his words were addressed specifically "to a few Grecian and Asiatic women who were wholly given up to idolatry and to the fashion of the day." Therefore the passage was not universally applicable (Higginbotham: 132). Both Cook and Broughton argued that Paul praised the work of various women and, at times, depended upon "quite a number of women" and delegated important apostolic responsibilities to them (ibid.)

African American women were thus able to carefully heed the Apostle by carefully and selectively hearing him. The grandmother of theologian and Christian mystic Howard Thurman was loathe to hear the words of the Apostle Paul, and allowed young Thurman to read to her only, and on rare occasion, Paul's paean to love in 1 Corinthians 13. Howard Thurman's grandmother shuts her ears to the entire Pauline corpus except this one text, and so tunes out the anti-emancipatory accent that she heard and hated as a slave.

> "During the days of slavery," she said, "the master's minister would occasionally hold services for the slaves. Old man McGhee was so mean that he would not let a Negro minister preach to his slaves. Always the white minister used as his text something from Paul. At least three or four times a year he used as a text: 'Slaves, be obedient to them that are your masters ... as unto Christ.' Then he would go on to show how it was God's will that we were slaves and how, if we were good and happy slaves, God would bless us. I promised my Maker that if I ever learned to read and if freedom ever came, I would not read that part of the Bible" (Thurman: 30–31).

This oft-quoted passage from Thurman's *Jesus and the Disinherited* is remarkable for what it does not say. Though psychically scarred by pro-slavery parenesis from the Epistles, Thurman's grandmother does not reject Paul completely. Her reading of Paul, or, more accurately, her hearing of Paul is not reductive but corrective. She tries to hear Paul's Corinthian voice more often and more intensely than she heard his Ephesian and Colossian counsels to obedience and in the parenesis of his pastoral epistles to Timothy and Titus. And it is the radically selective register of the Apostle's voice that is the impetus for Thurman's essay on the historical Jesus. "Since that fateful day on the front porch in Florida," writes Thurman in the first chapter of *Jesus and the Disinherited*, "I have been working on the problem her words presented" (31). Thurman begins his study of Jesus with a study of Paul. Taking as his point of departure the claim of Roman citizenship Paul is made to make for himself in Acts, Thurman offers an analysis of "a peculiar twist in the psychology of Paul," a security and stability based on his privileged status as a Roman citizen. "The stability of Paul's position in the state," reasons Thurman, "was guaranteed by the integrity of the state. One is not surprised, then, to hear him tell slaves to obey their masters like Christ, and say all government is ordained of God" (32). Thurman's diagnosis of Paul's comfort with Roman hegemony is, nevertheless, as qualified and as discriminating as his grandmother's reading practice. Though it is in part because of Paul "that too often the weight of the Christian movement has been on the side of the strong and the powerful and against the weak and oppressed," (30) the Apostle must not be completely dismissed. "It would be grossly misleading and inaccurate to say that there are not to be found in the Pauline letters utterances of a deeply different quality—utterances which reveal how his conception transcended all barriers of race and class and condition" (33).

Thurman's psychohistory accounts for this "deeply different quality," the contrast between Paul's universalistic liberalism and his accommodationist conservatism, by recourse to the Lukan narrative of the Apostle's career in the latter half of the Acts of the Apostles. It is there, in Acts 22:25, that Paul owns his Roman citizenship. In his exegesis and historical reconstruction Thurman does explicitly what his grandmother does implicitly in her directed reading of the Bible: he hears the voice of Paul in the canonical chorus of others in the New Testament, that of Jesus on the one hand and Luke on the other. Acts and Epistles, Jesus and Paul, inform each other in canonical correlation that moves backwards and forwards through the New Testament.

In one direction of canonical correlation, Black folks' reverence of Paul was occasionally qualified by prior allegiance to that great Apostle, as the quasi-Pauline Epistle to the Hebrews uniquely refers to him, the High Priest and Advocate Jesus. When Paul's anti-emancipatory pronouncements threatened to compromise the freedom he proclaimed in Christ Jesus, the words of the Christ trumped those of the servant for Christ's sake. African American women were constrained to use Scripture against Scripture to overcome the Pauline mandates that served as gag rules against their witness to the truth of Gospel. In the early nineteenth century, African Methodist Episcopal preacher Jarena Lee corroborates her contested call to preach with the witness the Gospel witness.

> If the man may preach, because the Saviour died for him, why not the woman, seeing he died for her also? Is he not a whole Saviour, instead of a half one, as those who hold it wrong for a woman to preach, would seem to make it appear? Did not Mary first preach the risen Saviour, and is not the doctrine of the resurrection the very first climax of Christianity? Hangs not all our hope on this, as argued by St. Paul? (Sernett: 169)

The concluding rhetorical question is telling. Lee alludes to Paul's synopsis of the Gospel proclamation in 1 Cor 15:1–11, a résumé of witnesses to the Resurrection notorious in contemporary critical scholarship for its omission of women. Lee has read against the grain of Paul's omission, and implicitly undermines the force of his counsel to silence enjoined on the women of Corinth, the scriptural basis of the prohibition against women preachers. Here the words and deeds of the Lord show that there is no condemnation of women preachers in Christ Jesus, the words of Paul notwithstanding. Indeed Paul's Corinthian text and the silences it recommends in 1 Cor 14:33–36 and 15:1–7 are subverted and transcended by Lee's exegesis. Lee even expresses the ineffable joy of her experience of personal sanctification by likening it to Paul's account of ineffable revelations of the third heaven which he recounts in 2 Cor 12:1–4. She articulates her inarticulateness through her own articulation of Paul's inarticulateness. And yet Lee argues for her own sanctified voice by overturning Paul's silencing and silences. She concludes her autobiographical account of her vocation as she has expressed it and defended it—with the words of Paul. Lee is finally confident in her calling because, she writes, "I have never found the Spirit to lead me contrary to the Scriptures of truth, as I understand them. 'For as many as are led by the Spirit of God are the sons of God'" (Sernett: 178). Lee here quotes, in the gender-exclusive parlance of the King James Version, Rom 8:14. Paul's declaration of the Spirit's victory over fear becomes Lee's declaration of the Spirit's victory over her fear—fear of damnation, fear of her own vocation, fear of condemnation even by the words of him who has said that "there is now no condemnation in Christ Jesus."

Essayist, orator, and political philosopher Maria Stewart bucked the convention of female public silence to speak out against slavery and racial discrimination in the second quarter of the nineteenth century. Like Jarena Lee before her, Stewart too had initial misgivings about her vocation to proclaim what she called "the pure principals of religion." "I found that sin still lurked within; it was hard for me to renounce all for Christ, when I saw my earthly prospects blasted" (Richardson: 66). And like Jarena Lee, she found solace in the words of Rom 8:38–39. "Thus ended these mighty conflicts, I received this heart-cheering promise, 'That neither death, nor life, nor principalities, nor powers, nor things present, nor things to come, should be able to separate me from the love of Christ Jesus, our Lord'" (66). Stewart's vocation as a lay preacher of Christian virtue met fierce resistance from men in the public square. The argument wielded by hostile interlocutors to silence her was biblical: the Apostle Paul had said that women should be silent; though he had enjoined this silence on women in public worship, the principle was readily extended to silence women in all public spaces. Stewart's defense of her transgressive speech, however was itself biblical. She argues that the weightier matters of justice and mercy required as a moral imperative that she, though a woman, lift up her voice as a trumpet in Zion.

> What if I am a woman; is not the God of ancient times the God of these modern days? . . . Did not . . . Mary Magdalene first declare the resurrection of Christ from the dead? . . . St. Paul declared that it is a shame for a woman to speak in public, yet our great High Priest and Advocate did not condemn the woman for a more notorious offence than this; neither will he condemn this worthless worm. . . . Did St. Paul but know of our wrongs and deprivations, I presume he would make no objections to our pleading in public for our rights. Again, holy women ministered unto Christ and the apostles. . . . Again; why the Almighty hath imparted unto me the power of speaking thus, I cannot tell. 'And Jesus lifted up his voice and said, I thank thee, O Father, Lord of Heaven and Earth, that thou hast hid these things from the wise and prudent, and has revealed them unto babes: even so, Father, for so it seemed good in thy sight.' (Richardson: 68)

When outraged white men insisted that Maria Stewart should not be speaking in public and cited the Apostle Paul as sanctioning the silence of women, Stewart, as had Jarena Lee a half century earlier, cited the example of Mary Magdalene as the first preacher of the Resurrection. Stewart's adversaries had quoted Scripture against her; Stewart responded by quoting Scripture against Scripture, trumping the Apostle Paul with the Apostle and High Priest Christ Jesus. And had the Apostle Paul only known of the enormities of slavery, Stewart argued, he himself would have insisted that she speak out against the racism that made American Christianity a mockery of the Gospel he had preached. The Apostle became, in Stewart's hermeneutic inversion, her ally against the forces that claimed his sanction of both women's silence and African slavery. Though the objection to Stewart's preaching begins with the words of Paul, her rejoinder ends with the words of Jesus, and it is the words of Jesus that are for Stewart the end of the matter.

In the peculiar context of the Peculiar Institution, Paul is an ambiguous figure in the biblical imagination of African Americans. This ambiguity is also a feature of canonical correlation with the Apostle's narrative portrait in Acts. There are two canonical versions of Paul available for reflection and appropriation: one, the hero in the second half of the Acts of the Apostles; the other, the apostolic author of the Epistles. Modern historical criticism has further distinguished the purportedly authentic voice of Paul's Roman, Galatian, Corinthian, and Philippian epistles from the secondary and perhaps subapostolic voice of his Asian correspondence with Ephesus, Colossae, Timothy, and Titus. Similarly, African Americans have made a tacit distinction between these divergent Pauline registers, but making a difference with a difference. Whereas German higher criticism has tended to privilege Paul's European correspondence over the Lukan portrait of Acts and the Asian letters, some black folks have given Luke's narrative profile pride of place. They have concurred with the Lukan insight that Paul was, after all, a man of suffering acquainted with grief. In this way, Luke is profoundly faithful to Paul's self-presentation in his own letters as a sojourner, a visionary, a praying man who preached the gospel to Jew and Gentile, barbarian and Scythian, slave and free. The faithfulness of Luke's depiction of Paul to the trials that the Apostle recounts in his own letters is echoed in the convergence of these features of sojourn, vision, and prayer in the story of the encounter of the then Saul with the Risen Lord on the road to Damascus. The Damascus Road encounter, related in the ninth chapter of Acts, has subsequently become the locus classicus of the conversion experience in Western religion and literature. Activist, educator, and presidential advisor Mary McLeod Bethune tropes Acts 9 in describing her childhood awakening to her own self-worth. When her teacher reads aloud to her the proclamation of God's love in John 3:16, Bethune describes her revelation using the Lukan language of Paul's blinding revelation on the Damascus Road.

> The whole world opened to me when I learned to read.... My teacher had a box of Bibles and texts, and she gave me one of each for my very own. That same day the teacher opened the Bible to John 3:16, and read: "For God so loved the world, that He gave his only begotten Son, that whosoever believeth in Him should not perish, but have everlasting life."
>
> With these words the scales fell from my eyes and the light came flooding in. My sense of inferiority, my fear of handicaps, dropped away. "Who-

soever," it said. No Jew nor Gentile, no Catholic nor Protestant, no black nor white; just "whosoever." It meant that I, a humble Negro girl, had just as much chance as anybody in the sight and love of God. These words stored up a battery of faith and confidence and determination in my heart, which has not failed me to this day.... (Lerner: 136)

Like Paul, the scales fall away from the eyes of Bethune upon hearing the words of Jesus, and, like Paul, from that moment on her life and her mission are one. For the incarcerated hustler Malcolm Little, later to be known as Malcolm X, the sudden insight into his own soul and all of history came with the inarticulate intensity of "a blinding light."

"The true knowledge," ... was that history had been "whitened" in the white man's history books, and that the black man had been "brainwashed for hundreds of years." ... Many a time, I have looked back, trying to assess, just for myself, my first reactions to all this. Every instinct of the ghetto jungle streets, every hustling fox and criminal wolf instinct in me, which would have scoffed at and rejected anything else, was struck dumb. It was as though all of that life merely was back there, without any remaining effect, or influence. I remember how, some time later, reading the Bible in Norfolk Prison Colony library, I came upon, then I read over and over, how Paul on the road to Damascus, upon hearing the voice of Christ, was so smitten that he was knocked off his horse, in a daze. I do not now, and I did not then, liken myself to Paul. But I do understand his experience....

Not for many weeks yet would I deal with the direct, personal application to myself, as a black man, of the truth. It still was like a blinding light. (Malcolm X: 77–78)

Only in the Bible does the Muslim find words to adequately articulate his revelation. He reads his own painful encounter with truth into and out of the Apostle Paul's Damascus Road experience, the dazzling light of an epiphany that is no epiphany at all. Malcolm X reads his experience into Acts 9, when Paul's encounter with Jesus Christ becomes intelligible even as does Malcolm's own biblically articulated crisis, for he too has had to reassess his whole life in a flash of blinding light.

Sojourn, vision, and prayer also punctuate the drama, danger, and deprivations of Paul's summons to Europe and subsequent Philippian imprisonment in Acts 16. The Spirituals know Paul almost exclusively as a man of prayer. Based on the account of the jailhouse prayer meeting in Acts 16:25–35, the second verse of the Spiritual "Blow Your Trumpet, Gabriel," reminds us, "Paul and Silas, bound in jail, / No one can work like Him; / The Christians prayed both night and day, / No one can work like Him." In Acts 16, the singing and prayer of the imprisoned preachers resulted in an earthquake that shook their shackles loose and their cells open. To "pray like Paul," as a verse of the Spiritual "Balm in Gilead" puts it, is to pray with the force of an earthquake. The interest of the Unknown Bards in Paul was the Lukan portrayal of his sufferings at the hands of Europeans and miraculous deliverance from their cruel imprisonment.

Martin Luther King imitates the form as well as the content of Paul's epistles in his "Letter to American Christians," though Acts informs the narrative time of King's faux-epistle. Even in his homiletic imitation of Paul's epistolary style, King has not taken the words that he has chosen as the basis of Paul's anti-discriminatory ethos from the Epistles but from Paul's Athenian declaration of the familial bond uniting all humanity in Acts 17:26: "God . . . hath made of one blood all nations of men." King introduces this imaginative homiletic experiment as a long-lost epistle of Paul; the Pauline quotations, however, hang together in King's distinctive style. This much King admits at the outset in his preface, albeit tongue-in-cheek. "If the content of this epistle sounds strangely Kingian instead of Paulinian, attribute it to my lack of complete objectivity rather than Paul's lack of clarity" (King: 127). "Paul" urges his addressees to continue to struggle for their rights. He exhorts them not to "sell your birthright of freedom for a mess of segregated pottage" (131), biblical phrasing more reminiscent of King's parlance than anything to be found in the Acts of the Apostles or the Pauline Epistles. The letter, however, is laced with self-quotations, as it were, from 1 Corinthians, Galatians, and Romans. Like Maria Stewart, "Paul" is comforted by the revelation of Rom 8:38–39 "that neither death nor life, nor angels, nor principalities, nor things present, nor things to come . . . shall . . . separate us from the love of God, which is in Jesus Christ our Lord" (King: 132). "Paul" concludes his letter from Troas as King himself had begun his letter from Birmingham jail. "I must bring my letter to a close . . . and I must take leave for Macedonia, from which an urgent plea has come requesting help" (133). Paul's answer to the Macedonian summons results in his abusive imprisonment, just as King's own response to the call for aid in the Birmingham struggle against racial segregation was similarly greeted: "I am in Birmingham," wrote King from prison, "because injustice is here. . . . Just as . . . the Apostle Paul left his little village of Tarsus and carried the gospel of Jesus Christ to practically every hamlet and city of the Graeco-Roman world, I too am compelled to carry the gospel of freedom beyond my particular hometown. Like Paul, I must constantly respond to the Macedonian call for aid." The final exhortations of "Paul's Letter to American Christians," however, tropes the praise of charity in an updated version of 1 Corinthians 13.

> American Christians, you may master the intricacies of the English Language and you may possess the eloquence of articulate speech; but even if you speak with the tongues of men and of angels, and have not love, you are like sounding brass or a tinkling cymbal.

> You may have the gift of scientific prediction and understand the behavior of molecules, you may break into the storehouse of nature . . . so that you have all knowledge . . . but, devoid of love, all these mean absolutely nothing.
>
> But even more, Americans, you may give your goods to feed the poor, you may bestow great gifts to charity, and you may tower high in philanthropy, but if you have not love, your charity means nothing. . . .
>
> The greatest of all virtues is love. (King: 133–34)

Occasionally, traditional reverence for Paul did not sustain the apparent contradictions between the proclamation of the Master and that of his apostolic servant. In *The Fire Next Time,* James Baldwin chronicles what he calls "the slow crumbling of my faith, the pulverization of my fortress" (48). In this essay, at once an autobiography of his early life and obituary of his early vocation as a Holiness Pentecostal preacher, Baldwin shows himself to be American literature's most distinguished backslider. His adolescent crisis of faith was attended by a crisis of confidence in the Bible itself. "I realized," concluded the young Baldwin, "that the Bible had been written by white men" (50), and the religion of the Bible was the property of white men. Baldwin became excruciatingly mindful of what he claimed white Christians had conveniently forgotten. "[T]he religion that is now identified with their virtue and their power . . . came out of a rocky piece of ground in what is now known as the Middle East before color was invented, and that in order for the Christian church to be established, Christ had to be put to death, by Rome, and that the real architect of the Christian church was not the disreputable, sun-baked Hebrew who gave it his name but the mercilessly fanatical and self-righteous Saint Paul" (58). Baldwin drives a wedge between Jesus, "the disreputable, sun-baked Hebrew" (ibid.), and Paul, dismissing the latter with a repudiation that became *au courant* in the wake of Black Theology.

In the echo of cries of "Black Power" outside and inside African American churches, Black Christian nationalist Albert Cleage coined a contemporary christology of Jesus as Black Messiah, God's agent of deliverance for black people. Cleage argues that "when we go to the Bible, we must search for the religion of Jesus, the Black Messiah. We must separate it from these Pauline interpretations which tend to make us think that Jesus was something which he was not, and that he taught something that he did not teach" (93).

> [W]e also find in the Epistles of Paul, a religion addressed primarily to persons who are seeking an individual escape from death and punishment for sin. These individuals found in the Resurrection an individual assurance that after death their lives would take on a new meaning. The Resurrection Faith, as preached by the early evangelists, took on a definite form in no way related to the teachings of Jesus. This is not the religion of Jesus. This is not the religion of Israel (92).

Paul's influence corrupts thereby the entire New Testament witness. "We can understand Jesus more fully by looking at Moses and the Maccabees than by looking at the Apostle Paul with his pagan concept of blood redemption" (1972:3).

Both Baldwin and Cleage reject Paul as a corrupter of the religion of Jesus. But in the last instance they reject not only the person of Paul, but his proclamation as well, and so the entire New Testament which is so deeply informed by that proclamation. Christology, in the form of the "the sun-baked Hebrew" or "Black Messiah," is purchased at the cost of kerygma. As goes Paul, so goes the proclamation.

In the wake of Black Theology, however, other theologians insisted that the emancipatory message of Paul must be recognized and recuperated. Hubert Danford Maultsby argues that "Black theologians like Cleage and Cone have 'used' the N.T. in their hermeneutic but . . . not as creatively as they might have, thereby underestimating (and in the case of Cleage, rejecting altogether!) the resources available in Pauline theology" (51). Maultsby proposes that Black theologians "translate Paul's view of *Hamartia*, 'Sin', as a cosmic power by means of the contemporary analogue: 'Racism' as that cosmic power" (51). Paul's "expression of the problem of Sin and Law in Romans 7" holds promise as a useful language to express "the contemporary struggle with institutional and personal racism." Biblical scholar Latta Thomas argues that 1 Cor 7:20–21 shows "that in spite of Paul's advice that for the short time remaining Christians ought to suspend or freeze all general plans, he found the achievement of human freedom important enough to be made an exception to the interim ethic" (Thomas: 38). New Testament biblical theologian Amos Jones argues that "Paul . . . has been misrepresented, corrupted, perverted and misused by the white church of the pre-Civil War era in America and, to a large degree, by the white church of today . . . he is misrepresented, perverted, corrupted, and misused by the white church to perpetuate institutional racism" (31). Jones proposes that "Paul offers something viable and dynamic in his understanding of Christian freedom, something powerful enough to destroy the idea and institution of slavery and every vestige of bondage" (Jones: 31). The churches that Paul founded constituted "an underground movement" that "came under attack and suffered flagrant persecution because of its theological tenets that amounted to serious aberrations from conventional Roman religion and posed a threat to the common political good of the Empire" (47). And though New Testament scholar Cain Felder has pointed out the problems of the Pauline legacy, he offers an emancipatory reading of Paul's epistle to the Galatians, in which "Paul alerts his readers to the social implications of freedom's call" (109). Galatians, asserts Felder,

> can easily be directed to the Black Church, for it serves as a reminder of the need on the part of Blacks to reclaim the call to freedom. In still another an-

cient community, Paul had occasion to write his summary commentary on the divine call to freedom. In 2 Cor 3:17, he says simply but profoundly, "where the Spirit of the Lord is, there is freedom." As in the past, the Black Church must open herself afresh to God's Spirit in our midst.... (116–17)

All these emancipatory, revisionist readings of Paul, in the face of traditional African American suspicion, are purchased at the cost of dissociating the "authentic" Apostle from the canonical accretions of the Lukan narrative on the one hand and the deutero-Pauline and Pastoral epistles on the other. Contemporary New Testament critics make emancipatory appropriations of Paul by appropriating less of him, cropping his portrait with the tools of New Testament higher criticism and seconding the judgment of European liberal Protestant scholarship.

In the modulation of activism and accommodation African Americans appreciated with ambivalence, and, rarely, with hostility, Paul's canonical ambiguity. Paul was a man beckoned by a Spirit that illumined him in his darkness, led him in his sojourn, and vindicated him in his suffering. That same Spirit moved him to write of freedom, and of love, freedom's greatest exercise, in words that speak and have always spoken to the enslaved and the unloved. But that same Spirit on occasion recommended accommodation to the powers of a world that Paul believed was passing away. Paul's ambiguity is captured for posterity in the Bible: in the stories told about Paul in Acts and the stories he struggled to tell about himself in the Epistles, in the occasional conservatism of his Asian letters and the occasional recklessness of his European correspondence, and in the radical proclamation of freedom by a man who often referred to himself as a slave. It is this profound ambiguity that black folks have not only appreciated in Paul, but, perhaps, have shared with him as well.

Works Consulted

Andrews, Williams L.
    1986   *Sisters of the Spirit*. Bloomington: Indiana University Press.

Aptheker, Herbert, ed.
    1951   *A Documentary History of the Negro People in the United States*. 2 vols. New York: Citadel.

Baldwin, James
    1963   *The Fire Next Time*. New York: Dial.

Callahan, Allen Dwight
    1997   *Embassy of Onesimus*. Valley Forge: Trinity Press International.

Cleage, Albert
 1968   *The Black Messiah*. New York: Sheed and Ward.

 1972   *Black Christian Nationalism*. New York: Morrow.

Dett, R. Nathaniel, ed.
 1927   *Religious Folk-Songs of the Negro*. Hampton, VA: Hampton Institute Press.

Felder, Cain Hope
 1989   *Troubling Biblical Waters: Race, Class, and Family*. Maryknoll, N.Y.: Orbis.

Higginbotham, Evelyn Brooks
 1994   *Righteous Discontent: The Women's Movement in the Black Baptist Church 1880–1920*. Cambridge, Mass.: Harvard University Press.

Jones, Amos
 1984   *Paul's Message of Freedom: What Does It Mean to the Black Church?* Valley Forge: Judson Press.

King, Martin Luther, Jr.
 1963   *Strength to Love*. New York: Harper and Row.

Lerner, Gerda, ed.
 1973   *Black Women in White America*. New York: Vintage.

Lewis, Edmonia
 1875   "Hagar of the Wilderness." [Sculpture]

Little, Malcolm, see Malcolm X

Malcolm X [Little, Malcolm]
 1992   *The Autobiography of Malcolm X*. New York: Ballantine.

Maultsby, Hubert Danford
 1976   "Paul, Black Theology, and Hermeneutics." *Journal of the Interdenominational Theological Center* 3:49–64.

Patterson, Orlando
 1982   *Slavery and Social Death*. Cambridge, Mass.: Harvard University Press.

Richardson, Marilyn, ed.
 1987   *Maria Stewart: America's First Black Woman Political Writer*. Bloomington and Indianapolis: Indiana University Press.

Sernett, Milton, ed.
 1985   *Afro-American Religious History*. Durham, N.C.: Duke University Press.

Thomas, Latta
 1976   *Biblical Faith and the Black American*. Valley Forge: Judson.

Thurman, Howard
 1981   *Jesus and the Disinherited*. Richmond, Ind.: Friends United Press.

Putting "Paul" Back Together Again: William Wells Brown's *Clotel* and Black Abolitionist Approaches to Paul

Abraham Smith
Andover Newton Theological School

ABSTRACT

This article examines the "Pauline hermeneutics" of the first African American novel, William Wells Brown's *Clotel*. Written as an abolitionist novel, *Clotel* draws on the conventions of earlier black abolitionist writings to counter the hegemonic arguments of pro-slavers, especially their use of the apostle "Paul" to endorse slavery. Reconstructing the apostle to serve abolitionist ends, the novel proffers a critique of slavery's hegemonic claims; a portrayal of the abolitionists in the image of the apostle; and an exposure of pro-slavers' limited canon of the apostle.

Introduction

The struggle against slavery's hegemony could not have been fought through physical resistance alone. As Antonio Gramsci has shown, hegemony's most insidious forms of destruction owe as much to civic formation as to coercion, as much to consent as to physical force.[1] Thus, along with the cries of freedom that echoed through the camps of slave conspiracies, revolutions and insurrections in the 1800s, a different voice of righteous and persuasive rage was spoken against the din and noise of arguments claiming "presumably unimpeachable authorities" for the legitimation of slavery (Wood, 1968:5).

Through several early African American novels (William Wells Brown's *Clotel*, Frank Webb's *The Garies*, Martin R. Delany's *Blake*, and Harriet Wilson's *Our Nig*), that voice of rage spoke vividly, starkly at times, and always persuasively against the naturalizing of slavery. Incorporating yet extending

---

[1] Gramsci defined hegemony as the domination of one social group over others not through coercion, but through civic formation (to which the dominated groups give consent). Furthermore, Gramsci avers that subjugated people must create a new hegemony against the dominant class (Buttigieg: 1–32).

the traditional forms of abolitionist writings,[2] these novels emerged when pro-slavery ideologues mounted a vigorous campaign against the abolitionist movement. On the one hand, the anti-abolitionist struggle was waged through physical force: riots from the mid-1830s to the 1850s, destruction of abolitionist publications, and even the capture and enslavement of free Negroes. On the other hand, the anti-abolitionist campaign was also fought with an arsenal of propagandistic tools, including the Christian bible.

Among these novels, Brown's *Clotel* is particularly striking—not simply because it was the first but because its de-naturalizing of slavery repeatedly resorted to a biblical figure that constituted the heart and soul of the pro-slavers' hegemonic efforts: Paul.[3] Brown, however, used a "Paul" reconstructed from the undisputed Pauline letters, the disputed ones, the epistle to the Hebrews, and even Acts to expose and counter the mystification and dehumanization techniques of slavery's colonizing regime. To see Brown's strategies for putting "Paul" back together again, however, it is necessary to explore three factors in the struggle: 1) Pro-slavery's Biblical Arguments; 2) Black Abolitionist Uses of "Paul"; and 3) Brown's Adaptation of Black Abolitionist Uses of "Paul.

Pro-Slavery's Biblical Arguments

According to Katie Cannon (119–28), pro-slavers resorted to three mythological structures which gave ideological support for the perpetuation of slavery: the denial of black humanity; a "reconstruction of history" to support racialized discourse; and the use of legal codes to sanction slavery. For the denial of black humanity, pro-slavers frequently turned to pseudo-scientific discourse. Some banked on the American School of ethnology (Samuel Morton, Josiah Nott and George Gliddon) and the Harvard naturalist Louis Agassiz whose composite efforts compared cranium types; insisted that culture-rich Egyptians were Caucasoids, thus denying Africans the possibility of contributing to the world's culture; and advocated a theory of *polygenesis*, that is, that blacks evolved from a different species than whites (Wood, 1968:8). Other pro-slavers agreed with those scientists who maintained a *monogenesis* thesis (that all human beings evolved from the same species) along with a degeneracy theory. Thus, they asserted that "all of the world's societies had degenerated from their original state of purity during the time of Eden and that the inferior peoples [among whom they presumed Indians and Africans

---

[2] One abolitionist writing during this period—not written by a black person—was Harriet Beecher Stowe's *Uncle Tom's Cabin* (1850). The work spoke of the cruelty of slavery and of the radical divide between the North and the South over the issue of slavery.

[3] Brown: 55. All citations are taken from the 1969 reprint edition of *Clotel*.

to be prime examples] were simply the most conspicuous products of such decay" (100).

As for the reconstructions of history, a telling case developed in the wake of Napoleon's 1798 expedition to Egypt (Sanders: 524–25). When Napoleon's explorers discovered that the beginnings of civilization were in Egypt as opposed to Rome and Greece, a flurry of scholarship was created with the purpose of distinguishing the Egyptians and other "culture-rich" Africans from the "Negroes" who were presumed to have been inferior and thus incapable of making a contribution to world civilization (524–32).[4]

As for the legal codes, pro-slavers used both civil and biblical sanctions. Beyond the horrors of the "watery, rocking tombs" of the Middle Passage, the civil codes brought a fresh torrent of abuses: assigning children born of a slave to the same status; granting masters the power to maim, to abuse sexually or otherwise torture their "chattel" real estate; and limiting the traveling, educating and corporate assembling of the African captives (Johnson, Smith and the WGBH Series Research Team: 60–76). As if the civil codes that supported the degradation of black subjectivity were not enough, however, at least three types of biblical tropes or texts were summoned for the assault as well: 1) the Garden of Eden myth; 2) the Hamite hypothesis; and 3) "Paul."

The Garden of Eden trope was first exploited in the pre-Columbus European imagination (Greene: 16), later adopted by seventeenth century Europeans (Clinton: 28), and incorporated into the thinking of Puritan colonial settlers whose Calvinistic doctrine of election supported their efforts to create a New Eden and to look on others, e.g., Africans and Indians, as the non-elect (Greene: 14). Fashionable as early as the sixteenth century, the Hamite hypothesis interpreted Noah's curse against Canaan as a curse from God (Genesis 9),[5] banked on the rabbinic assignment of the color black to Canaan or to all of his descendants (Copher),[6] and thus decreed an entire race of people (black people) to servitude on the basis of fifty-one verses (Wood, 1990:87, 89). Pro-slavers turned to "Paul" as a part of a larger body of texts which seemed to support slavery. Though pro-slavers sometimes resorted to Hebrew bible texts on servitude (e.g., Exod 12:43–45; 20:17; 21:2–6; 21:20–21;

---

[4] Thus, the American School of Ethnology could fuse their polygenesis thesis to the story of Ham because they claimed that the story about Ham did not apply to blacks at all.

[5] On the problems of the hypothesis, see Wood (1990:92).

[6] According to Charles Copher (111), the first connection between servitude and a specific color did not appear in written form until it did so in rabbinical material—in the Midrash Rabbah-Genesis (200–400 CE) and the Babylonian Talmud (500 CE). In the case of Rabbah-Genesis (36:7–8), Copher argues, the curse comes to "Ham, not directly but through Ham's fourth son, Canaan, who will be ugly and dark-skinned (the degree of color being dependent upon the translator of the original)." In case of the Babylonian Talmud (Sanh 108b), Ham emerges "from the Ark black, having been turned that color because, contrary to prohibitions, he, along with the dog and the raven, had copulated while aboard the Ark."

Lev 25:44–46; Deut 23:15–16)[7] or to an argument from silence, when they noted that Jesus did not explicitly forbid slavery (Snay: 26), "Paul's" letters, "together with selected passages from some of the other epistles, constituted the most important—and extensively quoted—biblical weapon in the arsenal of the Christian slaveholder" (Wood, 1990:67). Why? On the one hand, the pro-slavers cherished Paul because, on the basis of their interpretation of Romans 13:2, Paul supported obedience to earthly institutions. On the other hand, pro-slavers cherished "Paul" because specific passages attributed to Paul unequivocally endorsed slavery. Whatever the motivation, pro-slavers drew on religion in general and "Paul" in particular as "contingent alliances" to naturalize slavery.[8]

Black Abolitionist Uses of "Paul"

Brown's novel is replete with scriptural citations and allusions, from the Pentateuch, the Psalms and the prophets in the Hebrew bible to the Synoptics, James and "Paul" in the New Testament. Yet, an appeal to scripture alone could not prove convincing inasmuch as slavery's advocates, as we have seen, could also so appeal. As Gladys Sherman Lewis (231) has noted, "The [Christian] Bible's bane and blessing lies in its ambiguity, in its capacity for furnishing proponents from either side of an issue with ammunition to fuel their attacks." Nor could Brown, uninfluenced by historical criticism, use the distinction between the Paul of the undisputed Pauline letters on the one hand and the "Paul" of the disputed letters or the "Paul" attributed the authorship of Hebrews or the "Paul" portrayed in Acts on the other as a strategy in his critique of slavery. That is, Brown does not suggest that the slavers' use of Colossians and Ephesians (as in the case of the character known as missionary Snyder, 93–99) renders their pro-slavery biblical arguments suspect because the real Paul did not write these letters—as if the letters, once deemed not written by Paul, suddenly lost their authoritative status. So, how does Brown put "Paul" back together again?

Critical for understanding Brown's (re-)construction of "Paul" is a consideration of the approaches to "Paul" which Brown adopted from black abolitionist circles. It is well known that Brown drew heavily on the literary conventions of the abolitionists (Bell: 39). Not examined, however, are the approaches the black abolitionists took toward "Paul" and Brown's adoption of these approaches in his writings. Examples of these approaches—of which there are three major types—appear in the speeches, papers and slave narra-

---

[7] The list comes from Robert Allen Dunne (191, n. 5).

[8] Gramsci argued that the dominant class's hegemony is powerful over the masses because hegemony connects itself to other ideological agencies (or "contingent alliances") which perpetuate the thought of the dominant class. On "contingent alliances" in Gramsci, see Lucente (361).

tives of J. W. C. Pennington, Henry Highland Garnet, Frederick Douglass, David Walker and Maria W. Stewart all of whom sought to demystify the assumption of slavery as natural and "commonsensical" (Gramsci: 419–25).

One approach of the black abolitionists was the use of "Paul" to critique slavery's mythological structures. That is, some black abolitionists used texts from "Paul" to dismiss more directly hegemony's claims that blacks were inferior, that blacks were without a substantial origin and that blacks were decreed by scripture to be slaves. In a speech at Exeter Hall (London, England, 1843), J. W. C. Pennington (132) relegates all persons—whether black or white—to the common bondage of sin and exploits Gal 3:27 to support his claim of the common humanity of all persons despite the societal labels of bond persons and free persons. In the same speech, he uses Paul's imagery of the body and its members (1 Corinthians 12) to acknowledge the need for society to recognize blacks as members of the human family (130). The cause of society's fragmentation, he concludes, "originates in the dismemberment of those portions of the human family who have been long and cruelly disfranchised. The human family, taken as a whole, are [sic] like the body. Each class is a limb; every limb sustains its appropriate relation. Strike off a limb, and you injure the whole body" (130). In his speech to the House of Representatives, Henry Highland Garnet alludes to the universal parentage of God as asserted by the "Paul" of Acts 17:26 to indicate the moral contradiction of Christians supporting slavery (Garnet: 189). In his speeches, Frederick Douglass denounces the claim that the Christian bible supports slavery. To the contrary, Douglass frequently alludes to the "Paul" of 1 Tim 1:10 to illustrate the Christian bible's pronouncements against "menstealing," a term he equated with slavery (Douglass: 49, 50, 109, 115, 155, 230, 235, 247, 256, 286, 297, 298, 315, 363, 459, 451, 427, 448). As well, when others sought sympathy for slaveholders, Douglas alluded to the "Paul" of Heb 13:3 to cast sympathy rather toward "those in bonds as bound with them" (382, 427). Thus, with this approach, the abolitionists used "Paul" to deconstruct the "commonsensical" myths about the origins or the divinely decreed status of blacks.

A second approach to "Paul" was to assume a typological correspondence between the life, words or experiences of Paul on the one hand and that of an abolitionist speaker or narrative character on the other. In doing so, the abolitionist speaker or character would endow himself or herself with "Pauline" authority over and against the negative *dramatis personae* of a speech or story. Even before the black abolitionist tradition dawned, this typological approach to "Paul" had seen the light of day among Africans in the American diaspora. John Marrant's *Journal* (1790) depicts his life "in the missionary role of St. Paul who spread Christ's teachings" (Costanzo: 103). Gronniosaw speaks of a light as a critical component in his conversion, as does the "Paul" of Acts 9. George White not only preaches sermons on Paul and exploits Paul's "labor in vain" (1 Thess 3:5; 1 Cor 15:58; Gal 4:11) and "armor" (2 Cor 6:7; Rom 13:2) imagery, but adopts the farewell speech form given by "Paul" to the Ephesian elders of Acts 20. John Jea likewise quotes "Paul" extensively and adopts the same aforementioned Pauline imagery. In addition, Jea reads his boldness in a dangerous sea journey against the backdrop of a similar self-control exhibited by "Paul" in his near-death, horrific voyage narrated in Acts 27.

Among the black abolitionists who picked up the mantle of this approach to "Paul," one could place David Walker. In his famous *Walker's Appeal*, Walker's "four articles" as noted by Houston Baker, Jr. (69) "are similar to the Pauline Epistles. Each article begins with a didactic statement addressed either to 'My Beloved brethren,' or 'my brethren.'" Maria Stewart's "Farewell Address to Her Friends in the City of Boston," like the farewell addresses given by George White and John Jea, adopts "Paul's" farewell speech form of Acts 20. As well, the speech begins with a citation from the "Paul" of Acts (Acts 14:22) and an allusion to the "Paul" of Ephesians (Eph 2:8). Throughout the speech, moreover, Stewart draws liberally from Paul (Rom 8:38, 39; 9:21 15:29; 1 Cor 3:6), even evoking the famous "labor in vain" imagery (Richardson: 66, 67, 73). A similar tack was taken by Frederick Douglass. In speaking of the commitment of the abolitionists, Douglass (108) assumes they can speak with the "Paul" of 2 Timothy who labors "in season and out of season" (2 Tim 4:2). In his slave narrative *The Fugitive Blacksmith*, moreover, J. W. C. Pennington individualizes Paul's statement in Rom 7:21 to describe his life as a slave (Swift: 207). Thus, the abolitionists typologically aligned Paul with their own struggles in order to deconstruct the pro-slavers' exclusive claim to "unimpeachable authorities."

Yet a third approach to "Paul" was a quest for the general "spirit" of Paul as opposed to a specific enactment which could be easily contradicted by an opposing enactment. Accordingly, black abolitionists recurrently questioned readings of Paul which limited the assumed canon of "Paul" or even failed to consider the general historical or literary context of a specific "Pauline" verse. In one of his speeches, Douglass shares with the British public a sample of a pro-slavery preacher's sermon. The sermon is based on the dictum "Servants be obedient to your masters," an expression drawn from the "Paul" of Eph 6:5. Then, with characteristic wit, Douglass (404–405) adds: "This is the Alpha and Omega, the beginning and ending of the religious teaching received by the slaves of the United States."

Douglass's wit was matched by his boldness in his critique of a famous biblical scholar's analysis of Paul's letter to Philemon. Responding to the scholar's suggestion that Onesimus was "sent back to Philemon for life," Douglass examines both the historical and the literary contexts of the letter. With respect to the historical context, Douglass (115–16) doubts that Onesimus could have been sent for life because, as he asserted, "there was no such thing known among the Jews as slavery for life, except it was desired on the part of the servant himself."⁹ With respect to the literary context, Douglass (116) examines other portions of the letter and argues that Paul "sent back Onesimus greater than a servant; and told Philemon to receive him as he would receive him, Paul; not as a slave who could be sold in the market, but as a brother beloved" (Philem 10–19). Thus, with this approach, Douglass and other abolitionists adopted a hermeneutics of suspicion and averred that the pro-slavers used a limited canon. That is, the pro-slavers' use of "Paul" did not entail a comprehensive accounting of "Paul's" views.

In all of these ways, black abolitionists (re-)constructed "Paul" as a useful resource against slavery. Not satisfied with hegemony's (re-)constructions of "Paul," these abolitionists denied the pro-slavers' use of the Christian bible and "Paul" as "contingent" alliances, questioned the civic formation that rested on the pro-slavers' views of "Paul" and developed literary strategies to put "Paul" back together again.

Brown's Adaptation of Black Abolitionist Uses of "Paul"

When Brown shifted his attention from the slave narrative genre to novelistic fiction, he did not abandon many of the conventions which had helped him to make a convincing appeal for the abolition of slavery in the earlier genre. As *Clotel* follows and gives commentary to the travels, encounters and fates of several female protagonists who suffer the physical, psychological and legal constraints of North American slavery, one can see several of the conventions of the earlier genre: a slave narrative preface, tales of slave trickery, repartee jokes, newspaper and journal notices and borrowed verse from Shakespearean plays or popular poets. Brown's slave autobiography prefaces the novel and, along with notices from newspapers and journals, certifies the authenticity of the slave experiences found within it.[10] Tales and jokes by minor characters contrast the seriousness of the main characters (Loggins: 166–67). And borrowed verse heads virtually every chapter—foreshadowing the contents of riveting scenes, highlighting the inconsistencies of America's principles and practices, and resounding the moral degradation of slavery's cultural economy.

In addition, however, Brown also draws on some of the black abolitionist demystification approaches to "Paul" for the service of resistance to slavery. As noted before, these methods include: 1) the use of "Paul" to critique slavery's mythological structures; 2) typological correlation between "Paul's" life,

---

⁹ According to Woods (1990:70), many abolitionists "saw the Philemon story as a clear argument against slavery."

10 *Clotel* is prefaced by Brown's own autobiography. On Brown's use of several techniques (e.g., mistaken identity, the imprisoned princess, literary borrowings, the tragic octoroon and authentic documentation), see Richard O. Lewis (130).

words and experiences and those of the abolitionists; and 3) a quest for "Paul's" spirit.

A. Clotel's *Use of "Paul" to Critique Slavery's Mythological Structures*

Because pro-slavers used the Christian bible in general and "Paul" in particular to support their mythological claims, Brown's novel puts scripture, especially "Paul," in the service of exposing slavery's dehumanizing contentions. The Reverend Peck's daughter, Georgiana, for example, responds to each of the pro-slavers' ideological supports in her use of "Paul." Against the denial of black humanity and a reconfiguration of history to support a racialized discourse (best exemplified in the Reverend Peck, 88), Georgiana cites an expression from "Paul's" Areopagite speech: "God has created of one blood all nations" (115). Against the claim that the New Testament lacks any legal catalogues denouncing slavery, moreover, she repeatedly notes "Paul" in 1 Tim 1:9, 10. In describing slave traders, she avers: "The Christian religion is opposed to slaveholding in its spirit and its principles; it classes menstealers among murderers; and it is the duty of all who wish to meet God in peace, to discharge that duty in spreading these principles" (115). Later, she actually cites the passage, stating: "The law is not made for a righteous man, but for the lawless and disobedient, for the ungodly and for sinners, for unholy and profane, for murderers of fathers and murderers of mothers, for manslayers, for whoremongers, for them that defile themselves with mankind, for menstealers, for liars, for perjured persons" (118–19).

Like Georgiana, *Clotel*'s narrator also critiques the mythologies of slavery. The narrator closes the book with allusions to Paul in Galatians and "Paul" as portrayed in Acts. That is, the narrator's suggestion that there is a "common salvation which knows no distinction between the bond and the free" (245) alludes to Gal 3:28 ("There is no longer Jew or Greek, there is no longer slave or free, there is no longer male and female; for all of you are one in Christ Jesus"), and the narrator's assertion that both the British reading public and the slaves are persons "whom God has made of one flesh" (245) appears to be an allusion to Paul's Areopagus speech in Acts (cf. 17:26).

In having Georgiana and the novel's narrator use "Paul" in this counter-hegemonic fashion, then, Brown suggests that the hegemonic naturalizing of slavery need not be accepted.[11] With carefully chosen biblical citations designed to point out the fallacy of hegemonic mythologies, it is possible to challenge slavery rather than to acquiesce to its commonsensical constructs. Thus, according to Brown, good people—like Georgiana and the British reading public—have the power to question the moral ground of slavery and they must not stand in complicity with evil.

---

[11] It should be noted that after her father's death, Georgiana frees her father's slaves.

B. Clotel's *Typological Correlation with Paul's Life, Words and Experiences*

Clotel's typological identification with "Paul" appears in two forms: 1) in the adventurous narration of several enslaved female characters; and 2) in the dramatization of the life and thought of the fictional abolitionist character, Georgiana Peck. *Clotel* depicts the struggles of several enslaved women: Currer, the mother of Clotel and the assumed former mistress of Thomas Jefferson; Clotel, the key protagonist; Clotel's sister, Althesa; Althesa's daughters, Ellen and Jane; and Clotel's daughter, Mary. All endure travail because of the separation of Currer from her daughters but the story reads like an adventure tale, especially in the case of Mary who faces a number of near-death scenes on her way from slavery to freedom. The adventure motif itself may be fashioned on the form of Acts, for some protagonists in Acts are whipped; others are killed; and yet others escape near-death scenes. Of course, the story of "Paul" in Acts is also an adventure tale as Paul himself faces a number of trials and near-death scenes.

Just as critical for Brown's novel is the typological correlation between Georgiana and Paul. Upon her death, the narrator quotes from Paul's letter to the Philippians (2:4) to describe Georgiana's beneficent character: "Look not every man on his own things, but every man also on the things of others" (185). Quoting the "Paul" of 2 Timothy, the narrator extends the eulogy for Georgiana, saying that she "fought the faith" and that she "wears the crown," an allusion to 2 Tim 4:7–8 (189). Thus, because she is dramatized as a modern "Paul," Georgiana is given "Pauline" authority, a direct blow to the pro-slavers' exclusive claim to "unimpeachable authorities."

C. Clotel's *Quest for "Paul's" Spirit*

In *Clotel*, Brown argues that the Christian slavers who use "Paul" to support slavery are not reasonable or logical in their deductions because they overlook the spirit and principles of the Christian bible or of "Paul" himself. In quoting extensively from "Paul" through one of the novel's characters or through the narrator's voice, Brown shows, by comparison, the limited canon of both the Reverend Peck and Snyder. In chapter ten, Peck's daughter, Georgiana, quotes extensively from "Paul" and elsewhere, even alluding to Ephesians without mentioning the "Servants be obedient to your masters" passage. Speaking of Jesus' life as a "living testimony against slavery," Georgiana alludes to Philippians 2:7, saying, "When he [Jesus] designed to do us good, he took upon himself the form of a servant" (120). In the same chapter, she speaks of "prayer and supplication," perhaps an allusion to Philippians 4:6 (116). In her description of slave traders, she cites a Pastoral passage, namely 1 Tim 1:9,10 (118–19). Later, in the same chapter, she describes how the early church's prayer prepared them for "the great and glorious enterprise of preaching the unsearchable riches of Christ to a lost and perishing world" (116), a line reminiscent of Eph 3:8.

Thus, the use of other texts from "Paul"—whether from the undisputed letters, the disputed ones or from Acts—suggests the truth of a remark given by Uncle Simon, the novel's black preacher who questions the limited canon of the missionary Snyder: "thars more in de Bible den dat" (100). In quoting more extensively from "Paul," Brown shows that the pro-slavery biblical arguments lacked a wider frame of interpretation for understanding "Paul" or the entire Christian bible. Thus, the pro-slavers' limited frame of interpretation allowed them to perpetuate the peculiar institution—to perpetuate the vicious cycle of slavery and its detriment on one Currer family after another. For Brown, however, the pro-slavers' limited frame of interpretation could perhaps expose the motivation of the pro-slavers' interpretation. The goal for the pro-slavers was not to produce a fuller picture of "Paul" in which "Paul" might speak to a *variety* of challenges and concerns in antebellum times. Rather, the goal for them was to bring premature closure to "Paul" as an endorser of slavery.

Conclusion

Brown's *Clotel* is a remarkable story which uses the Christian bible, particularly "Paul," in a narrative about purportedly good people's complicity with evil. In this article, I have shown Brown's hermeneutics of suspicion about pro-slavery biblical hermeneuts as well as his insistence that slavery continued because supposedly religious people condoned it. Brown's novel draws heavily on black abolitionist literature to challenge hegemonic ideas about the naturalness of slavery; to demonstrate the utility of a Pauline hermeneutics in support of abolition; and to widen the discourse on "Paul" beyond a mere prooftexting support of slavery. Thus, with other abolitionist writings, Brown's novel puts "Paul" together again by proffering a "war of position" or a cultural confrontation with the hegemonic constraints of slavery.[12] For whatever forces of hegemony we may have to face today, Brown's novel challenges us to become voices of righteous rage against any claims of "unimpeachable authority," to examine the cultural practices of biblical hermeneutics, and to raise questions about the origins and implications of the interpretive models we use.

---

[12] On "war of position" as a Gramscian term used to describe a cultural war against the prevailing ideas of hegemony, see Gramsci (239).

Works Consulted

Baker, Houston A., Jr.
    1990   *Long Black Song: Essays in Black American Literature and Culture.* Charlottesville, VA: University Press of Virginia.

Bell, Bernard W.
    1987   *The Afro-American Novel and its Tradition.* Amherst: University of Massachusetts Press.

Brown, William Wells
    1969   *Clotel.* New York: Arno.

Buttigieg, Joseph A.
    1995   "Gramsci on Civil Society." *Boundary* 2:1–32.

Cannon, Katie
    1995   "Slave Ideology and Biblical Interpretation." Pp. 119–28 in *The Recovery of Black Presence: An Interdisciplinary Exploration.* Ed. Randall C. Bailey and Jacquelyn Grant. Nashville: Abingdon.

Clinton, Catherine
    1995   *Tara Revisited: Women, War, & the Plantation Legend.* New York: Abbeville.

Copher, Charles
    1989   "Three Thousand Years of Biblical Interpretation with Reference to Black Peoples." Pp. 105–28 in *African American Religious Studies: An Interdisciplinary Anthology.* Ed. Gayraud S. Wilmore. Durham: Duke University Press.

Costanzo, Angelo
    1987   *Surprising Narrative: Olaudah Equiano and the Beginnings of Black Autobiography.* New York: Greenwood.

Douglass, Frederick
    1979   *The Frederick Douglass Papers, Series One: Speeches, Debates, and Interviews.* Vol. 1: 1841–46. Ed. John W. Blassingame. New Haven: Yale University Press.

Dunne, Robert Allen
    1992   "Protestant Backlash: The American Dream Myth and Marginalized Groups, 1820–1860." Ph.D diss., Lehigh University.

Garnet, Henry Highland
    1972   "Discourse Delivered in the House of Representatives." Pp. 187–203 in *Let Your Motto Be Resistance: The Life and Thought of Henry Highland Garnet.* Ed. Earl Ofari. Boston: Beacon.

Gramsci, Antonio
    1972   *Selections from the Prison Notebooks of Antonio Gramsci.* Ed. Quintin Hoare and Geoffrey Nowell Smith. New York: International Publishers.

Greene, J. Lee
    1996   *Blacks in Eden: The African American Novel's First Century*. Charlottesville, VA: University Press of Virginia.

Johnson, Charles, Patricia Smith and the WGBH Series Research Team
    1998   *Africans in America; America's Journey through Slavery*. New York: Harcourt Brace.

Lewis, Gladys Sherman
    1994   *Message, Messenger, and Response: Puritan Forms and Cultural Reformation in Harriet Beecher Stowe's* Uncle Tom's Cabin. Lanham, MD: University Press of America.

Lewis, Richard O.
    1985   "Literary Conventions in the Novels of William Wells Brown." *CLA* 29: 129–56.

Lucente, Gregory L.
    1994   "Antonio Gramsci." Pp. 360–63 in *The Johns Hopkins Guide to Literary Theory & Criticism*. Ed. Michael Groden and Martin Kreiswirth. Baltimore: Johns Hopkins University Press.

Pennington, J. W. C.
    1985   "Speech by J. W. C. Pennington, Delivered at Exeter Hall, London, England, 21 June 1843." Pp. 129–33 in *The Black Abolitionist Papers*, vol. I, The British Isles, 1830–1865. Ed. C. Peter Ripley. Chapel Hill, NC: University of North Carolina Press.

Richardson, Marilyn, ed.
    1987   *Maria W. Stewart, America's First Black Woman Political Writer: Essays and Speeches*. Bloomington: Indiana University Press.

Sanders, Edith R.
    1969   "The Hamitic Hypothesis; Its Origin and Function in Time Perspective." *Journal of African History* 10:521–32.

Snay, Mitchel
    1993   *Gospel of Disunion: Religion and Separatism in the Antebellum South*. New York: Cambridge University Press.

Swift, David E.
    1989   *Black Prophets of Justice: Activist Clergy before the Civil War*. Baton Rouge: Louisiana State University Press.

Wood, Forrest G.
    1968   *Black Scare: The Racist Response to Emancipation and Reconstruction*. Berkeley: University of California Press.

    1990   *The Arrogance of Faith: Christianity and Race in America from the Colonial Era to the Twentieth Century*. New York: Knopf.

PAUL, SLAVERY AND FREEDOM:
PERSONAL AND SOCIO-HISTORICAL REFLECTIONS

Orlando Patterson
Harvard University

I. INTRODUCTION

It was wise of the editors to confine the contributors' comments to my earlier work, *Slavery and Social Death* (Patterson, 1982). This provides me with the opportunity to compare my own interpretation of early Christianity and Paul's theology in *Freedom in the Making of Western Culture* (Patterson, 1991), published nine years later, to those of the contributors. I am heartened by the degree to which my interpretation dovetails with so many of their own. There are, to be sure, important differences, as my treatment of Paul in *Freedom* indicates, but the extent to which our ideas converge is quite striking.

The contributors to this collection may not know it, but I write in a tradition of historical and cultural sociology that is at variance with what prevails in sociology today. Most historical sociologists are structuralist: that is, they are concerned with cultural objects, including ideas and beliefs, mainly, and often only, to the degree that they can be explained or discussed in social terms. This is especially true of the sociology of religion, which is now a thriving field. Thus the typical sociologist of religion is interested in issues such as the class background of religious Americans, the way different denominations vote, the degree of conservatism or radicalism of different faiths or different levels of religious attendance, the social and political consequences of fundamentalism, and the like (for a good general review, see Billings and Scott; see also Hamilton).

However, sociologists rarely attempt to understand the doctrinal meaning of the modern Christian religion they study. At most, sociologists will explore in national surveys the attitudes of respondents to certain broad questions of values and religious beliefs—"Do you believe in a life after death?" "Have you ever had a born-again experience" and so on—but stay clear of any exploration of the textual or expressed meanings of the people they study, unless the culture being studied is in some exotic land. Thus it is perfectly acceptable to explore the hidden meanings of a Balinese cockfight or Islamic rite, and every sociologist of religion will cite the works of Clifford Geertz approvingly, but any attempt to do the same thing with Christian ritual and doctrine invites professional suspicion or worse.

It was not always so. The monumental figure to whom all sociologists of religion, myself included, trace their intellectual ancestry is Max Weber. However, there were at least three Webers: a structuralist Weber concerned with the social aspects of religion and religious behavior, and especially with the influence of the former on the latter; a more idealist Weber who explored the effects of religious ideas on social and economic organization, most famously in *The Protestant Ethic and the Spirit of Capitalism;* and an interpretive Weber who advocated *Verstehen*—the intersubjective understanding of people's meanings—and boldly examined the nature of religious doctrine in the light of the cultures in which they developed (see Bendix, Part 2; Weber, 1963, 1952). Modern sociologists of religion now wholly embrace, and have virtually made an icon of the structuralist Weber. For a long time, sociologists agonized over the idealist Weber of *The Protestant Ethic,* but have turned against this tradition in recent decades, especially following the collapse of Parsonian sociology in the early seventies. The interpretive Weber was never popular with the generality of American sociologists although an important group of social theorists continue to work in, and extend this tradition.[1]

Although I work primarily in this last mentioned tradition, my own perspective tends to be more comparative and to emphasize the interaction of meanings and structure more than others in this area of cultural sociology. Ideas, beliefs and other cultural creations emerge, in the first place, from people's attempts to make sense of their social worlds, especially in times of change and struggle. In doing so, they not only invent new ways of viewing the world, but draw upon and reinterpret previous patterns of thought and culture. The new creations, especially if embodied in texts, then acquire a life of their own and, in turn, interactively influence social action, including even the action that may have generated them. There is a mutual causal interplay between structure and culture, at any given moment in time and over time. It is easy to see the operation of this interactive process in the history of Christianity, slavery and freedom.

II. History, Society and Biography in the Making of *Slavery and Social Death*

Slavery and Social Death did not begin as a book with any special concern for religion. I labored over that work for twelve years and only toward the end of writing it did it become clear what I was subliminally engaged in, and hence the reason for taking so long over it. *Slavery and Social Death,* I eventually realized, was my route to an understanding of the most formative

---

[1] The works of Robert Bellah, Clifford Geertz, Peter Berger and Robert Wuthnow still pursue this line of Weber's sociology of religion. For a good assessment of where things are now, see Wuthnow, esp. chs. 1–2.

forces in my past, and of my deepest intellectual preoccupation. The formative forces were slavery and Christianity, the first operating on the collective level, the second individually; the intellectual preoccupation was my passion for freedom and the need to understand it.

There is no comprehension of the rural Jamaican society in which I grew up without an understanding of its slave past and the post-emancipation order which it overshadowed. Jamaica had what was, arguably, the most brutal and all-encompassing system of slavery in the modern world. Indeed, its closest parallel in world history is the Roman slave system near the end of the second century BCE. As I tried to show in my first academic book, *The Sociology of Slavery: Jamaica, 1655–1838* (1967), and my third novel, *Die the Long Day* (1972), it came as close to the Hobbesian state of nature as was socially possible. For both slaves and masters, life was literally nasty, brutish and short. It left a terrible imprint on nearly all aspects of Jamaican life—its dependent plantation economy, its vicious color-class hierarchy, its deeply fraught gender and familial relations, its chronic lack of discipline, and its endemic violence.

But there were two other influences which not only lingered but grew with the decades, and was to have a direct impact on my own individual development. One of these was an almost anarchic commitment to freedom; the other, a fervent belief in Christianity. The zest for freedom grew directly out of the brutalities of the slave system and the sustained resistance to it. Jamaican slaves began a guerrilla war against the British almost from the moment the latter seized the island from the Spaniards. Slave revolts continued throughout the period of slavery and eventually became a decisive factor in the British decision to abolish the institution (Patterson, 1967: ch. 9; 1970). That tradition of revolt persisted thereafter, especially in the peasant revolt of 1865 and the plantation riots of the 1930s. Now sadly, with the British gone, the island's tradition of rebellious violence and freedom-loving disdain for authority has become a serpent biting its own tail.

Christianity came with the non-conformists who fought against slavery in Britain while its missionaries brought the gospel to the slaves and greatly assisted them in the formation of their post-emancipation peasant communities. Jamaicans took to the faith with a vengeance. One trivial statistic indicates the depth of Christian religiosity in the island: *The Guinness Book of Records* lists it as the country with the greatest number of churches per square-mile in the world. This is the world in which I grew up, saturated on every corner of every village and town and city block with every conceivable version of Christianity, in addition to an abundance of syncretic Afro-Christian cults. The Anglican church holds its own against all, and indeed thrives here more than in Britain.

I mention all this because, for me, Anglicanism was the path to civilization and intellectual introspection. Leaving the bush for the city was mediated by my Anglican grammar school with its daily chapel and Sunday services. My headmaster and Latin master also happened to be the Anglican Suffragan Bishop of Kingston. I was taught to think in English and Latin by a compact, austere brown man awesomely attired in a purple robe, whose Bishop's ring we all yearned to touch.

Slavery and its aftermath, colonial society; freedom; Christianity: the need to understand these has been my motivating force. In the simplest terms, what I eventually discovered was that they were not contingently and disturbingly linked—as a provincial focus on Jamaica would suggest—but were intimately and necessarily related both historically and conceptually.

Here, in brief is what thirty years of historical and sociological scholarship has taught me: without slavery, no genesis of freedom; without the slavery-freedom dialectic, no understanding of Pauline Christianity; without Pauline Christianity, no tradition of freedom in the West. Without the sometimes perverse, always problematic, often transcending interaction of slavery, freedom and Christianity, there would have been no Western civilization as we know it.

Is this to exalt slavery? Not at all. Rather, it is to recognize one of the central truths of Christianity, and of the civilization it fashioned: that out of evil and the greatest suffering often comes the greatest good. Isn't that what the Cross is all about?

III. Paul, Onesimus, and the Ethics of Slavery

More than one of the contributors addressed the dilemma of many Afro-American Christians faced with the fact that Paul's writings appeared to sanction slavery and were blatantly used by pro-slavery advocates in their moral defense of the system. I was once inclined to see this entire debate as a spent issue, meaningful mainly in terms of the polemics of the abolitionist struggle. However, it appears that the question is still alive among many Bible scholars, and is of relevance today to the degree that it casts light on Paul's social morality and political orientation.

The truth of the matter is that Paul neither defended nor condemned the system of slavery, for the simple reason that in the first-century Roman imperial world in which he lived the abolition of slavery was intellectually inconceivable, and socially, politically and economically impossible. A critical three-fold distinction casts badly needed light on the matter: that between slaves, the institution of slavery, and slave society.

Slaves are those real, individual persons who are held in the condition of slavery where the institution exists. At any given moment in any given society, there existed a range of attitudes toward them, as to their treatment, circumstances and opportunities for mobility out of slavery, that is, manumission. Slavery, the institution which sanctioned the keeping of slaves, was a coercively maintained relation of total domination between persons in which the slave had no independent social or legal existence and no honor to defend, because he was conceived of as a deracinated, socially dead person. This institution was worldwide, existing long before Christ and Paul, and continuing right up to present times in parts of northern Africa.

Slave society was the social system based on the institution of slavery in which slaves and slavery came to play critical, and often indispensable roles in the development and maintenance of the entire system. The vast majority of societies where slaves and the institution of slavery existed were not slave societies; there was no structural dependence on the institution and slaves were often a drain on resources. Slave society was relatively uncommon in human history—though not as rare as Moses Finley and Keith Hopkins thought—so much so that it is possible to list all known cases (Patterson, 1982: Appendix 2). Indeed, it is very likely that slave society emerged for the first time in world history in the ancient Greek world, particularly Athens, over the course of the sixth and early fifth centuries BCE (Patterson, 1991: chs. 4-6). A half a millennium later, it reached its highest point of development in the pre-modern world: that of Late Republican and early Imperial Rome and many of its provinces.

Now, in evaluating the moral stance of Paul or any historical figure toward slavery anywhere or at any time, we must first ascertain what room for moral judgement was open to them on each of these levels: the personal, the institutional and the systemic. My basic argument is that, up to the last quarter of the eighteenth century in Western Europe and America (and only in this part of the world) there was wide latitude in the moral space open to individuals in their personal attitudes towards slaves, but virtually no room for moral or conceptual doubt about the institution of slavery or slave society where it existed.

To illustrate what I mean with a modern example, let us take the case of the working poor in contemporary, super-abundant American society. In this wealthiest economy in the history of the world, millions of persons work long, back-breaking hours at two and sometimes three jobs, yet are unable to earn enough to pull themselves and their families out of poverty. There are three levels at which we confront their situation. First, we interact with the working poor daily as persons: they are the janitors who clean our offices, the workers who flip our hamburgers or check out our groceries, and for many middle class persons, the people who clean our homes. People vary in their moral attitudes toward the poor on this purely personal level. Some of us consider their condition a great misfortune and are deeply sympathetic. We do not blame them for their condition and might contribute to charity to help them. Our main moral stance here is to encourage the means of social mobility out of poverty through better educational facilities; possibly better working conditions, and so on. Nonetheless, we continue to buy the hamburgers or support the supermarkets or maintenance firms that pay them wages that keep them in poverty. In other words, while strongly sympathetic to the poor and supportive of means to enable poor persons to move out of (to be manumitted from) poverty, we offer no remedy for, and cannot even conceive of the abolition of the institution of poverty. Nor can we conceive of doing away with the capitalist system in which the institution of poverty is located, in spite of our personal and possibly even moral misgivings about the degree of poverty and inequality.

Note that agreement about poverty on the institutional and systemic levels need not imply agreement on the personal level. Thus, two persons may fully agree that nothing can or should be done about the direct abolition of poverty as an institution since this entails an assault on the market for wages, which is a foundation principle of the capitalist system. However, one of them may view poverty as a grave misfortune and a social evil for which the poor person is not responsible; hence the moral and socio-political necessity to promote individual mobility from poverty, even if nothing is done about the institution of poverty and the class system. The other, more conservative individual, however, may blame the poor for their impoverishment and may take a moral stance of harsh condemnation, not of poverty, but of the poor for their failures.

Now I think all this is directly analogous to the situation that Paul and the early Christians found themselves in, except that the social system in which they lived, and which all persons took for granted, was the large-scale slave society of imperial Rome. The kind of relatively advanced economic system which Rome had was simply not possible without slaves; nor, for that matter, was the smaller, but still relatively advanced urban socio-economic system of late fifth and fourth century Athens. The only known alternatives in the Western and Middle Eastern worlds were all more primitive social systems. Indeed, with the decline of Rome, it was precisely to these more primitive socio-economic systems that the western world returned (see Brown). The Islamic World that was to emerge a couple centuries later was to move far ahead of the West precisely because of its reliance on slavery for conquest and administration. In the West, until the emergence of agrarian capitalism in the seventeenth century, almost every attempt to escape from primitive agrarian production and to develop more productive economies entailed a return to large scale slavery: Merovingian France; Visigothic and late thirteenth century Spain; tenth century France and central Europe; eleventh century England; and the late Medieval city states, especially in Italy (see Duby; Dockes; Bonassie). What is more, agrarian capitalism did not displace slavery, but returned to the latifundia system, now known as plantations, and took it to even more complex levels of development. Only with the emergence of the industrial phase of capitalism was there an alternate economic system more advanced and profitable than a well managed plantation slave regime.[2]

In an important paper, the political scientist Ethan A. Nadelmann has demonstrated that the abolition of internationally accepted practices such as slavery, piracy, counterfeiting of national currencies and the like, are only possible when a "global prohibition regime" emerges, grounded in "the political influence of domestic and transnational moral entrepreneurs as well as that of powerful individual advocates within the government" (483). Such regimes had to await the dominance of most of the world by Europe and the acceptance by elite opinion that the activity in question worked against their interests *and* that there were clear alternatives to it. Such regimes did not exist before the late eighteenth century. And, Nadelmann adds: "Just as few people during the eighteenth century could have imagined the emergence of a global antislavery regime, few in the nineteenth century could have envisioned a global ban on ivory sales. Similarly, few in this century can imagine that activities which are entirely legitimate today may evolve into targets of global prohibition regimes" (523).

It is clearly preposterous then, to criticize Paul for not calling for the abolition of slavery, or for taking the Roman imperial slave system for granted. However, one can morally evaluate Paul in regard to the first level of confrontation with slavery: that of his face-to-face dealings with slaves of his time, because here there was a wide moral space within which he and his contemporaries ranged. And here the evidence points overwhelmingly to the fact that Paul was a humane, caring soul in regard to slaves and their plight. Like many humane persons of his day, he clearly considered the condition of slavery a great misfortune and a personal tragedy. And we may reasonably surmise that he was strongly sympathetic to the provision of all legal means for the manumission of slaves. It would have been not only immoral but downright stupid of him not to, given the fact that the most important persons in his congregations were manumitted slaves for whom freedom had been the defining experience in their lives.

The letter to Philemon makes all this quite clear and it is hard to imagine how it could be read in any other terms (citations are from RSV). Paul, it should not be forgotten, was risking his life even writing this letter. Roman law was harsh on anyone who harbored runaway slaves. Paul was already under house arrest in Rome when he wrote it. There was a high chance that it could have been intercepted, and had it been, its contents would have been legally damning since in it Paul admitted that he had not only been served by

---

[2] The view that plantation slavery was inherently unprofitable and inconsistent with capitalism, held by the classical economists such as Adam Smith, and by many prominent modern Marxist historians such as Eugene Genovese, has now been shown to be completely wrong. See Fogel and Engerman.

Onesimus but had become a "father" to him. Even if Philemon was meant to interpret this term as a "father in Christ" or "spiritual father," there can be little doubt how a Roman magistrate would have seen it: adoption was the most complete form of manumission in Rome and to a plain-spoken Roman officer hostile to Christian language and metaphor it would have meant one thing only: that Paul had both stolen another man's slave and, as if that had not been criminal enough, illegally attempted to manumit him.

Given Paul's knowledge of Roman law, and the fact that he was experiencing its brutal whip end when he wrote the letter, it must be wondered why he would expose himself to such unnecessary risk. The most likely explanation is that he was hinting strongly to Philemon that he should manumit Onesimus. In fact, the letter is replete with such hints and speaks volumes about his compassion toward slaves. This was morally at complete variance with the typical Roman attitude toward slaves generally, but especially toward ordinary household slaves, one of which Onesimus appears to have been. To the Roman a slave was a vocal instrument, a human tool to be used for the master's benefit. Significantly, the name "Onesimus" literally means "useful" or "beneficial" and Paul, as if to express scorn at Roman inhumanity, plays upon this literal meaning not once, but twice in his short letter. He tells Philemon that his slave when formerly under his control was "useless to you," which is a strange thing to tell the owner of a vocal instrument with the name "Useful," unless what Paul meant was that no human being can be a mere useful tool. However, Paul adds that after becoming his child in faith Useful "now . . . is indeed useful to you and me."

Note too that Paul's notorious cockiness and boastfulness are in full play in this letter and are used to make an important point about the nature of freedom. He tells Philemon outright that he has the authority from Christ to command him to "do what is required." He does not say immediately what this is, but a few lines later adds that he would have preferred to keep Onesimus to help him out during his house arrest, but then adds that he wouldn't dream of doing such a thing without Philemon's "*consent* in order that your *goodness* might not be by *compulsion* but by your *own free will*." Crafty 'bro'. There is only one way to interpret this passage and it must have been as clear as day to Philemon. The essence of slavery was compulsion. Paul is saying it would have been self-contradictory on his part to compel a master to allow a slave to work for another on Christ's behalf. Philemon should do so of his own free will. If Philemon had any moral wits about him he must have immediately concluded that if Paul was so scrupulous to avoid any hint of compulsion, and so respectful of the exercise of free will, he could only hold him (Philemon) in contempt for continuing to hold another person, a child in Christ no less, under his compulsion, especially when that person could have been better serving the Apostle of the Christ they all worshiped of his own free will.

But just in case Philemon was too slow-witted to get his meaning, Paul ends with another not so subtle wordplay on Onesimus' name—"Yes, brother, I want some *benefit* from you in the Lord."—and concludes by expressing confidence that Philemon "will do even more than I say." The only thing left for Brother Philemon to do that Paul has not by now explicitly stated (though repeatedly implied) was to manumit Onesimus.

IV. Paul, Freedom and the Distortions of History

Paul's moral and social stance towards slaves, slavery and freedom constituted, however, only a small part of his engagement with the subject. As the authors of this collection persuasively demonstrate, the realities and symbolism of the dialectics of slavery and freedom were central to his theology. In *Freedom in the Making of Western Culture* (1991) I attempted to show how Paul drew upon the secular conception of freedom that prevailed in his day as a metaphoric source for his doctrine of spiritual freedom in Christ.

What was that secular conception of freedom? Briefly, what first emerged from the class and intellectual struggles between free farmers and elites, as well as slaves and non-slaves over the course of the sixth and fifth centuries in the large scale slave societies of Greece was a closely linked triad of ideas about the nature of human power.[3] We are free, first, in being liberated from the power of another over us; second, to the degree that we are able to exercise control over ourselves and others; and third, to the degree that we share in the common power of the state that rules over us. This triad emerged from the struggles over slavery. The slave relation was its prototype: negative freedom emerged from the desire of the slave to negate his social death and to be reborn into community; positive freedom reached its most perfect realization in the absolute power of the master over his slave, free to do whatever he wished with him or her, and by means of this power, his greater freedom to exercise influence and power over free persons; and civic freedom, democracy, emerged from the struggle of the free *demos* against the elite slaveholder's power and for the right to share in the collective honor and power of the free state, from which all slaves, ex-slaves and women were excluded.

By Pericles' day all classes of Athenians held to all three notes of this chordal triad, but different groups weighed each note of freedom differently. Elite Athenians, as Thucydides makes abundantly clear, favored the idea of freedom as power, clothed in the old rhetoric of *areté*—honor, dignity, and manly, aristocratic prowess (on the notion of "oligarchic" freedom among

---

[3] See Patterson, 1991: Part 2. For a more recent statement of my socio-historical theory of freedom, see Patterson, 1994.

the Athenian elite, see Raaflaub). The citizen-soldiers favored democracy and jealously guarded against any dilution of the *demos* with alien members. And negative freedom was the beloved ideal of the metics and ex-slaves. To the degree that we can extrapolate from ancient drama, negative freedom was also the cherished ideal of early Athenian women who also added the idea of familial reconciliation as the cherished goal of emancipation. Antigone's defiant assertion of her freedom against Creon and his state, was ultimately on behalf of the most fundamental natal rights of her brother, Polyneices,—to be properly buried with his kinsmen. There is no more tragic expression of the yearning for freedom as natality and the restoration of honor than the entombment alive and suicide of Antigone with her kinsmen (for my interpretation of Sophocles' *Antigone*, see Patterson, 1991: ch. 5).

Rome both inherited this tradition and independently developed it in the struggles of its own emerging slave system. The Tacitean notion that freedom died with the Republic is blatant Roman upper class propaganda which modern historians for too long uncritically accepted (Tacitus, *Annals* 1.75.1–2; however, see Yavetz and, on the late republic, Millar). What died in the sordid implosion of the Republic was the Roman upper class idea of civic freedom, the elitist democracy which every aristocrat so greedily yearned to play a leading role in, that they ended up butchering their rivals or being assassinated by them. However, freedom was alive and well in imperial Rome, especially in Paul's day: no longer civic freedom, which survived only in theory and nostalgia, but most certainly freedom as power, the most exalted of which being the freedom of the Emperor, and the negative freedom of the freedmen masses and their descendants who, by Tacitus' time—and much to his disgust—had, along with the slaves, become the demographic majority in Rome.

By spiritually introjecting the Graeco-Roman conception of freedom, Paul transformed the Palestinian religion of Christ from an increasingly conservative sect of Judaism that could easily have remained so had James, Jesus' brother, had his way, into a formidable new creed. One that not only made Jesus the object rather than the subject of Christianity, and shifted its doctrinal focus from the expressed meanings of his life to the implied symbolism of his death, but reinterpreted his death on the cross as a sacrifice of liberation. In so doing he effectively remade Christianity into a religion of freedom, the only universal faith with such a focus.

This, in turn, had major consequences for the secular history of the West and its master ideal, freedom. For the 1400 years after Paul's death, Europe and European civilization was nothing more than Christendom. Christianity fashioned European culture, in so far as there was such a thing, and continued to play a critical role in its civilization thereafter. Now all this may seem like a restatement of the obvious, but it is remarkable how many continue to deny its implications.

The most important kind of denial comes from secular historians of freedom. With the notable exception of Lord Acton, earlier historians of freedom typically began their account with ancient Greece, made some passing mention of the collapse of the ideal with the end of the Roman Republic and the rise of the imperial dictatorship, then skipped over the next 1400 years and resumed the story somewhere around the Renaissance. More recently, scholars with greater knowledge of the Middle Ages have noted important developments during these long centuries, but the overwhelming emphasis has been on secular changes such as the rise of towns and long-distance trade and the growth of elite representative bodies such as early parliaments.

What nearly all historians of freedom have in common is their tendency to view the Christian church as a hostile force in freedom's path. The Reformation looms large in this secular historiography of freedom, as is well known. However, even here the conventional position is that freedom came about largely because of the murderous nature of religious conflicts which led eventually to the revolutionary truce we have come to know as religious liberty. Once the West learned to respect the freedom of dissenters to worship as they please, it was a short step toward the acceptance of the freedom of others to hold dissenting secular views. Add to this the rise of capitalism and the modern state, throw in the English, American and French revolutions, and there you have it: the history of freedom, with an emphatic thumbs down to Christianity.

I happen to believe that this entire, anti-clerical historiography of freedom is utterly wrong and am presently completing the second of a two-volume history aimed at correcting this distortion. The cornerstone of my argument is that Christianity explains the nature, pervasiveness, intensity and continuity of freedom in the West. I follow the great historian of medieval thought, Ernst Kantorowicz, in the view that throughout the middle ages all Western thought, religious or secular, was Christian thought. More importantly for my argument, is the view that up to as late as the seventeenth century all major thought was simply secularized Christology.

In no other domain was this more true than in thought about freedom. Essentially what Christianity did was to preserve the ancient tripartite conception of freedom in its trinitarian doctrine of redemption; then, a millennium and a half later, under changed circumstances, this introjected doctrine was projected back out into the secular world, which explains both the continuity and intensity of belief in freedom. Of these secularizing Christologists, the greatest is the man often considered the most important modern philosopher of freedom, John Locke. It came as no surprise to me that the most respected contemporary interpreters of Locke are now unified in their belief that his work is best understood as applied Christian theology.

Paul's significance for the history of freedom, however, has suffered also from the distortions of his doctrine within Christianity itself. Long before New World slaveholders disfigured his views for their own purposes, Paul's doctrine had been reinterpreted in radically conservative terms. We can thank the two most influential thinkers in the post-Pauline history of Christianity for that: St. Augustine, whose views were to dominate Christian thought from late antiquity to the end of the Middle Ages; and Martin Luther, whose reformation theology both reinvigorated and adapted Augustine's conservative interpretation of Paul for modern times.

Paul, it cannot be too strenuously emphasized, was a profoundly dialectical thinker. The slightest neglect of this cardinal principle of his thinking will immediately result in distortions. Yet, this is precisely what Augustine and Luther did as they selectively read their deeply conservative ideas into his doctrine of freedom. There is no need to belabor this claim with respect to St. Augustine, as it is generally accepted that under the spell of Neo-Platonism and the ingrained dualism of his superficially discarded Manicheanism, he thoroughly and deliberately misrepresented Paul's doctrine of freedom (see Armstrong).

Although he does not explicitly state this, Augustine's dualism intellectually undergirded what the theologian and historian S. W. Sykes has called the dual or bi-focal narrative of sacrifice in Christian doctrine. From the corruption of the dialectical Paul, and later reinterpretations of the crucifixion, two stories of God were to emerge:

> ... a story of power, transcendence and judgment—and a story of weakness, immanence and forgiveness. The sacrifice, which is the death of Christ, is at once a powerful condemnation of sin and a victory over the forces of evil, and also a supreme act of humble self-identification with the powerless. From this bi-focal view springs the enormous resilience of Christian faith and its capacity for adaptation to vastly different circumstances; from it similarly springs the ambivalence in its attitude to worldly power, whether that of its own hierarchy or that of the state. (Sykes: 79)

This dualism was the legitimizing cornerstone of the class systems of medieval Europe and later conquered peoples, most notably the Indians of Latin America where a perversely articulated "Creole" Christology taught a servile, penitent, and humbled "Good Friday" Christ to the Indian masses, while reserving the triumphant Easter Christ for the Hispanic elite (see McKay; Batstone). Recently, I have argued that a similar strategy was attempted by the Southern planter class in their plantation Gospel. The Afro-

American slaves quickly saw through this distortion and not only spurned it but rapidly developed their own theology (Patterson, 1998).

But the doctrinal and racial struggle did not end here. With the withdrawal of Northern troops and the abandonment of Reconstruction and Afro-Americans by the North, a reign of terror ensued in the South in which Caucasian Southerners took the dualistic narrative to its most perverse extreme, developing a militant, triumphalist Christianity for the "White" race which found its most heinous expression in the burning cross of the KKK, while it socially and culturally redefined Afro-Americans as a humbled class of inferiors, for whom only a meek Christ of obedience was appropriate. At the slightest hint of resistance or uppity expressions of honor or demands for citizenship and the rights of natality, Afro-Americans were ritually sacrificed in lynching ceremonies often supervised by clergymen in what were manifestly human sacrifices of expulsion. These are the depths to which Christian dualism had sunk in the most Christian part of the most Christian nation of Western civilization (Patterson, 1998).

Where Augustine and his followers distorted Paul by reducing his dialectics to a spiritually and socio-politically reactionary dualism, Luther did so by excessively harmonizing the two great letters, Galatians and Romans. Thomas Mann said little that was new, though he said it brilliantly, in his celebrated "Stockholm Address," when he portrayed Luther as a person who was both boorish and tender, full of hatred yet loving, a proclaimer of evangelical freedom, yet brutally dogmatic with anyone who crossed him, and above all, a thinker who was both reactionary and revolutionary (see Loewenich). Unfortunately for the modern understanding of Paul, Luther was most reactionary and distorting in his reading of Paul's letters. As Luther himself tells us, he came to a full appreciation of Paul via Augustine. Once Luther discovered the soul-transforming meaning of justification by faith through his reading of Paul, however, it was, as he himself put it, "all over with Augustine." It is quite remarkable that Luther ranks the letter to the Romans "the most important in the New Testament, the gospel in its purest expression" (1954: Preface). Paul's theology trumps the Savior's sayings.

Herein lies a good deal of the modern misunderstanding of Paul—not, let me hasten to add, Luther's evaluation of the Letter to the Romans, which may indeed be the most sublime expression of post-Palestinian Christian doctrine, but in the slighting of the Letter to the Galatians and the outright refusal to see how it was dialectically integral to Paul's final synthesis. Although Luther claimed to have been greatly fond of Galatians, and in one of his recorded dinner conversations in 1531 affectionately referred to it as his little "Katie" (and by now we should all know the place of little Katies in the patriarchal mind), it is clear from his commentaries that he refused to take seriously the problems posed by Galatians for his interpretation of Paul. Luther's long commentary on Galatians (1979) is, indeed, something of an intellectual scandal given how thorough a Bible scholar he was and what we know he knew. It neglects not only the letter's many technical difficulties, but also its great central theme. The commentary, in fact, turns out to be simply another commentary on Romans. Themes that dominate Romans he wantonly asserts to be central to Galatians, for example, the elaborate talk about God's mercy and "excellent righteousness." Remarkably, Luther repeatedly cites Romans and hardly ever Galatians in what was supposed to be a commentary on Galatians.

My point is this: if one takes the view that Galatians and Romans are dialectically and progressively linked and that there is no understanding of Paul's final synthesis of his theology without an understanding of how it progresses from the earlier powerful, though preliminary, thesis of Galatians, any uncritical harmonization is bound to result in distortions of the meaning of both letters. From these distortions emerged the reformation theology of Luther, after which, it was all over for the progressive, dialectical Paul in modern Christianity.

V. The Transparency of Paul's Doctrine of Freedom

All over, that is, except for ordinary people not misled or ideologically misguided by their leaders or trapped in the malign spell of racist groupthink. Ordinary people in the West did not need philosophers of freedom or Reformation theologians to teach them the doctrine of freedom implicit in Pauline theology. All that was necessary—and this was Luther's great achievement—was the priesthood of all believers: exposure to Paul's doctrine in the vernacular languages and the right to interpret it for themselves. As E. P. Thompson (1963) so brilliantly demonstrated, it was Methodism, not John Locke, that converted the incipient British working classes to an awareness of the power of freedom and their rights to exercise it against the "dark, satanic mills" and their owners. And the only text that the slaves and ex-slaves of the New World, from Mississippi to Jamaica, had to read, or learn of, to legitimize the freedom that their circumstances dictated, were these letters of the Apostle to the Gentiles.

The most important, and certainly the largest and best organized of the numerous slave revolts in Jamaica was that of Daddy Sharp in 1832. It so traumatized the British slaveholder class and their representatives in Britain that the British Parliament, which had been wavering on the issue, immediately got the message and passed the Bill to emancipate all slaves in the British Empire. Daddy Sharp was a Baptist class leader, a fervent believer in the new faith that had only recently been brought to his fellow slaves by the non-conformist missionaries. Among the ex-slaves of Jamaica and their descendants his revolt became known as "the Baptist War," and its memory lives on in folk tales and song, as did his reverence for the true doctrine of Paul.[4]

Works Consulted

Armstrong, Hillary
    1967   *St. Augustine and Christian Platonism*. Villanova, Pa.: Villanova University Press.

Batstone, David
    1991   *From Conquest to Struggle: Jesus of Nazareth in Latin America*. Albany: State University of New York Press.

Bendix, Reinhard
    1960   *Max Weber: An Intellectual Portrait*. Garden City, N.Y.: Doubleday.

Billings, Dwight B., and Shaunna L. Scott
    1994   "Religion and Political Legitimation." *Annual Review of Sociology* 20: 173–201.

Bonassie, Pierre
    1985   "Suivie et extinction du régime esclavagiste dans l'Occident du haut moyen âge (IV–XIs)." *Cahiers de Civilisation médiévale* 28:307–43.

Brown, Peter
    1978   *The Making of Late Antiquity*. Cambridge, Mass.: Harvard University Press.

Dockes, Pierre
    1982   *Medieval Slavery and Liberation*. Chicago: University of Chicago Press.

Duby, George
    1974   *The Early Growth of the European Economy*. Ithaca, N.Y.: Cornell University Press.

Fogel, R., and S. Engerman
    1974   *Time On the Cross*. Vol. 1. Boston: Little Brown.

Hamilton, Malcolm B.
    1995   *The Sociology of Religion : Theoretical and Comparative Perspectives*. London and New York: Routledge.

Hart, Richard
    1980   *Slaves Who Abolished Slavery*. Kingston, Jamaica: Institute of Social and Economic Research, University of the West Indies.

---

[4] See Hart and, for a contemporary missionary's view, Woolley.

Loewenich, Walther von
    1986   *Martin Luther: The Man and His Work*. Trans. Lawrence W. Denef. Minneapolis: Augsburg.

Luther, Martin
    1954   *Commentary on the Epistle to the Romans*. Trans. J. Theodore Mueller. Grand Rapids: Zondervan.

    1979   *Commentary on Galatians*. Trans. Erasmus Middleton; ed. John Prince Fallowes. Grand Rapids: Kregel.

McKay, John
    1933   *The Other Spanish Christ*. New York: MacMillan.

Millar, Fergus
    1986   "Politics, Persuasion and the People Before the Social War (150–90)." *Journal of Roman Studies* 76:1–11.

Nadelmann, Ethan A.
    1990   "Global Prohibition Regimes: The Evolution of Norms in International Society." *International Organization* 44:479–526.

Patterson, Orlando
    1967   *The Sociology of Slavery: Jamaica, 1655–1838*. London: McGibbon & Kee.

    1970   "Slavery and Slave Revolts." *Social and Economic Studies* 19:289–325.

    1972   *Die the Long Day*. New York: Morrow.

    1982   *Slavery and Social Death: A Comparative Study*. Cambridge, Mass.: Harvard University Press.

    1991   *Freedom in the Making of Western Culture*. Vol. 1. New York: Basic.

    1994   "Freedom, Slavery and the Modern Construction of Rights." Pp. 131–78 in *Historical Change and Human Rights: The Oxford Amnesty Lectures*. Ed. Olwen Hufton. New York: Basic.

    1998   "Feast of Blood: Race, Religion and Human Sacrifice in the Postbellum South." Pp. 171–232 in *Rituals of Blood: Consequences of Slavery in Two American Centuries*. New York: Basic/Civitas.

Raaflaub, Kurt A.
    1983   "Democracy, Oligarchy, and the Concept of the 'Free' Citizen in Late Fifth-Century Athens." *Political Theory* 11:517–44.

Sykes, S. W.
    1980   "Sacrifice in the New Testament and Christian Theology." Pp. 61–83 in *Sacrifice*. Ed. M. F. C. Bourdillon. New York: Academic Press.

Thompson, E. P.
    1963   *The Making of the English Working Class*. London: Gollancz.

Weber, Max
    1952   *Ancient Judaism*. Glencoe, Ill.: Free Press.

    1963   *The Sociology of Religion*. Boston: Beacon. [Orig. 1922]

Woolley, E.
    1847   *The Land of the Free: A Brief View of Emancipation in the West Indies*. Cincinnati: Printed by C. Clark.

Wuthnow, Robert
    1987   *Meaning and Moral Order*. Berkeley: University of California Press.

Yavetz, Z.
    1969   *Plebs and Princeps*. Oxford: Oxford University Press.

PART III

Responses

READING OUR HERITAGE: A RESPONSE

Antoinette Clark Wire
San Francisco Theological Seminary

What Peter says about Paul tells us more about Peter than it does about Paul. Today no would deny this dictum. Yet we do not therefore stop talking about Paul or about our heritage more broadly, even its repellent aspects, since we seek our truth by coming to face its truth. But the question remains how to do this, especially when we are reaching way back where data is fragmentary, as well as reaching into once sacred classical and biblical worlds now threatened with neglect. Is it our task to recover the bedrock of our cultural values? Or are we working to expose the illusions that deceived us? Or is it enough to see where we have been in all its variety and ambiguity, its glory and shame, and ask how we take the next steps from here?

Each of the articles in this volume gets into the history and hermeneutics of ancient Western slavery in a different way. Perhaps this collection can be seen as early soundings in a very broad sea. The soundings are too far apart to define the scene, but they do differ methodologically and show something of what each approach can accomplish. My comments will be more substantive as I get closer to Paul's letters where I have worked, but the crucial hermeneutical issues come up in each case. I will be reading the articles as testings of different approaches as we feel our way through nostalgia and revulsion toward a sobered, and thus possibly hopeful, sense of our living heritage.

Ben Wright sets out to test whether Jews accustomed to the slave systems at the foundation of Greco-Roman society reinterpret the limited slavery in the Bible as they translate and discuss it. Though this might seem to be a promising approach because Hebrew uses a single word for the male slave and classical Greek differentiates many kinds of slavery, Wright recognizes from the beginning that later Koine tends toward synonymous use of many terms, blurring what distinctions might emerge.

Yet Wright's study of terms for slavery in the Septuagint—the Pentateuch, Former Prophets, and Later Books—then in Josephus, Philo and the Apocrypha, is valuable in itself and comes up with some interesting conundrums which Wright weighs thoughtfully. Why does the Pentateuch avoid the term *doulos*? Why does the Septuagint in general not use the feminine term *doulē*? What does it mean that "slave of God" language is not found in Greco-Roman texts BCE? But much more work needs to be done before he can conclude that the translators "not only lexically translated but culturally transformed the biblical language of slavery for those who used the texts after them" (p. 97). It would be particularly interesting to know if the "slave of God" language once translated into the terms signifying Greco-Roman slavery took on meanings of humiliation or degradation not understood in the Hebrew, and if this theological construct was or was not used to legitimate slave dehumanization among Jews. Wright's work shows that vocabulary studies need to be an integral part of broader cultural studies of changing social institutions. At the same time it indicates the contribution that word studies can make there.

Lawrence Wills's article on slavery in the ancient Western novel begins by reminding us of our hermeneutical distance from that world, living as we do where "capitalism determines the economic sphere, while democracy determines the political" (p. 114). Since both systems understand individuals as independent and equivalent agents, Wills argues that we can hardly comprehend ancient society built on the metaphysical presumption of a graduated hierarchy from the highest God down to the lowest slave. This presumption, he says, set up a tension between the ideal hierarchical order, which Wills summarizes in Schüssler Fiorenza's term "kyriarchy," and the disorders of disfigurement, disaster, illness and aging that characterize so much of experience. Slavery was taken by those with pretensions of status as emblematic of this disorder, and enslaved persons were not only seen to be lesser persons, but their very humanity was denied to confirm the humanity of others.

Wills uses MacQueen's distinction of two kinds of ancient novels to exhibit how this is done in fiction. Certain novels show the ideal of domestic virtue and aristocratic sensibility—the noble woman's beauty finally makes her enslavement incredible—whereas other novels satirize this ideal at Trimalchio's table or the ass's ritual initiation and give the reader the illusion of taking part in the world below, but always in such a way as to confirm its rank inferiority, its sub-humanity.

Wills's contribution is to show us how the ancient novel constructs a world that satisfies the class that reads, perhaps particularly in helping it deal with the fear of enslavement by fictional idealization of the free and denigration of the enslaved. Yet something is lost when Wills chooses in his opening demur "not to analyze in detail the depiction of slaves and slavery in the novel of the Greco-Roman period, but merely to make some observations that will constitute prolegomena for a hermeneutics of slavery in the novel genre" (p. 113). Now that we have the hermeneutical study I hope he will go on to the no less difficult task of deciphering what the writer assumes or betrays about ancient slavery in all the narrative detail—the tacit dimension. How is it that Chariton mentions a slave going to the city without telling his master, buying him another very valuable slave and then receiving people in his own home, while in another place slaves are chained together underground after a day at hard labor? Both romantic and satirical scenes are built from pictures in the mind's eye drawn from cultural experience that we lack and need to recover.

Wright's Hellenistic Jews and Wills's ancient novelists in their respective hermeneutics of slavery return us to the key question of how we Americans of different backgrounds see ancient slavery. Allen Callahan's research on African-American interpretations of Paul shows us one extraordinary tradition. Because of slave experience or heritage, these readers can be expected not to miss what Paul's letters imply about slavery. Although this tradition has largely accepted Paul's authorship of the household codes instructing slaves to be subordinate, Callahan finds that subordination has not been widely preached by African Americans, nor has Paul been rejected out of hand. Instead he documents for us the inventive and perceptive ways that Paul's voice of freedom has been heard and proclaimed. The dominant approach was to hear the texts that spoke the truth to African-American experience, such as Romans 8, 1 Corinthians 13 and Acts 9, where necessary using these texts to neutralize others. In this process narrative accounts were more trusted than arguments to "tell it like it is." Stories of Jesus could trump words of Paul or absorb them into a story line, and Acts could overpower Paul's letters when telling his story.

In this vein Callahan is himself to be commended for telling actual stories of Americans using texts rather than generalizing, for locating evidence of women's interpretations, and for using sculpture, novels and song lyrics rather than limiting himself to the sermon. I missed any treatment of recent womanist work on Paul. But Callahan's bold sweep did manage to include James Baldwin and Albert Cleage's outright rejection of Paul and more recent liberals' reclaiming of Paul's freedom cry by dismissing Luke's and the Pastoral writer's interpretations. So the African-American academy, pulpit, artists' loft and street scene all get heard as takes on "Brother Saul."

Callahan's conclusion may arise not strictly from the evidence given so much as from his broader knowledge, but it nonetheless shows the profundity of African-American Christian hermeneutics. Paul is not thrown on the psychologist's couch, as Callahan puts it, but is found on the road where he contends with the world's principalities and powers, guided by divine visions. This is a spirit-led figure full of prayer who could at points accommodate to a world that was passing away because his calling was to fan the flames of a new world. He found this new world in Christ's love on the cross and he called others to join him in completing Christ's sufferings and taking on the power of his resurrection. To consider the ultimate conundrum of how those sufferings and that glory are—or are not—bound together would take Callahan into Sheila Briggs and Clarice Martin and Alice Walker and Toni Morrison. From this quarter we can perhaps expect "Brother Paul II."

Richard Horsley takes up another aspect of American interpretation of ancient slavery in his revealing account of how reluctant Western scholars have been to recognize the systemic and violent nature of ancient slavery. He exposes the central place that classical civilization held in Western social self-understanding and how prone the academy was to follow Eduard Meyer and others in their apology for ancient slavery. I would suggest that Americans and Europeans were interpreting classical slavery by comparison to the experience of enslaving Africans in which we were implicated. After we could no longer justify one slavery by the other we stressed the contrast between the two and sought to rescue ancient slavery and its culture because it did not incorporate racism. Yet this only fed the romanticism concerning "our" Western culture, and even M. I. Finley's work could not wake us up until Orlando Patterson took up the comparative task again in *Slavery and Social Death*. This revealed, as Horsley has shown, that the root of slavery's evil is not racism or even economic exploitation of people as property, but the ritual dehumanization that deprives people of their natal identity in family and society, a characteristic that shaped ancient as much as modern slavery. When some were determined by Roman military defeat for death, they were understood to be without the status and rights of living beings, let alone human beings. In a society that operates socially and economically on the basis of these assumptions, even apparent benefits such as the occasional allowance of family life and the promise of manumission become means of social control of these people, as Keith Bradley and others have shown.

Horsley draws together a mass of hypotheses concerning ancient society and economy as shaped by slavery within his study of the history of Western research. Here are take-off-points for many dissertations that need to be written. For example, we get Keith Hopkins's argument that the Roman elite sent Italian peasants to the legions while confiscating their lands and farming them with the slaves that the legions brought home. Did timocracy follow enslavement or produce it? And though Horsley concedes that enslaved women have been most "hidden from history," his summary reflects this relative neglect and reminds us what a crucial factor gender was in slave experience and how much more it needs to be in the foreground of research.

But to return to the hermeneutical question, Horsley's "Slave Systems of Antiquity" above all makes us take stock of ourselves by revealing how reluctant we have been to recognize what we don't want to see. This warns us how much we may be missing when we settle for the latest consensus in classical history as an adequate "background" for our studies in early Christianity. Our study must become ancient Western history, and that as a key piece of world history, or our textual work hangs in the wind—not just the wind of literary multivalence but "every wind of doctrine." We need to rethink ourselves as people with texts that can contribute to the construction of that history and texts that will remain dependent for their significance upon how that history is being constructed.

For Christian interpreters of ancient slavery, the letters attributed to Paul are the crucial texts. They are not only the earliest Christian writings to survive, but they reflect the entry of news about Jesus into Asia Minor, Greece and Italy, pacified provinces of the Roman Empire where senatorial rule continued when Augustus took contested provinces like Syria and Egypt under his own personal military control. Jesus was a rural villager crucified by Roman soldiers in a province under such military occupation where social organization was local and traditional, and slavery was limited to large estates and urban households. He was one among many Jewish prophets killed in the mid first century to quell popular hopes of apocalyptic deliverance.

Paul, on the other hand, seems to have been raised in an educated Jewish family with Roman citizenship in Asia Minor, where Galen (49) estimated one slave for every two free adults in another major city. Paul was traditional in religion and persecuted those who hailed Jesus as Messiah until a transforming experience sent him to take the message about Jesus' death and resurrection to non-Jews. His letters were written as he tried to carry out that task and are more reliable evidence than the hagiography of the Acts of the Apostles to show the intensity with which he sought to persuade very different communities and the bitter conflicts he got into with other believers. The question is to what extent he spread apocalyptic news of liberation from Roman social structures through Christ's triumph over death, and to what extent he reinterpreted this message to change lives within a Roman kyriarchal society.

It is at least clear that Paul did not tell about what Jesus said or what Jesus did, as we see happening later in the gospels, but he joined other Hellenistic city preachers in challenging people to become God's new creation by dying and rising with Christ. After being baptized naked they "put on" Christ, a new identity that was "neither Jew nor Greek, neither slave nor free, not male and female" (Gal 3:28). The last phrase here with its change of syntax shows that the early city believers were reshaping Gen 1:27 or 5:2: "In the image of God he created him, male and female he created them." But when Paul writes Galatians the stress has shifted from Christ as an identity "not male and female" to Christ "neither Jew nor Greek." Paul's willingness to risk everything to include Gentiles as Gentiles in God's people made him take on Peter in Antioch (2:11–14) and then the Galatians who wanted to circumcise believing Gentiles (5:1–12; 6:11–13). The question remains whether Paul also stood behind equally radical social innovation for women and slaves as the confessors of this new creation had first claimed. Horsley concedes that Paul's dropping "not male and female" in his use of this baptismal confession in 1 Corinthians 12:13 shows his opposition to social changes among women in Corinth. Though Horsley recognizes that Paul pulls back on this front, he does not recognize that "neither slave nor free" also becomes little more than a vestige.

To defend Paul's stance on slavery Horsley reviews three ways that Paul speaks in his letters. In each case I do not contest Horsley's basic reading of Paul but question his claim that this provides evidence of Paul constructing a social order in opposition to Roman imperial structures.

Horsley is surely right that when Paul calls Christ "Lord" he is not presenting Christ as slaveowner of all believers, nor does Paul use enslavement as a primary metaphor for Christian faith. Yet this does not mean that "Lord" was therefore a political metaphor for Christ in opposition to Caesar, even though Paul draws on a civic meaning of the term in certain contexts. Since "Lord" translates Hebrew and Aramaic words used to address a person with respect on the one hand, and substitutes for the Tetragrammaton in the Septuagint as the name of God on the other, its valence is very broad. If Paul's usage was not heard as a blanket legitimation of the structures of slavery and yet was not a consistent assertion of a rule that replaced Caesar's as Horsley sees it, more work is needed about what its implications were for Christian understanding of existing power structures, implications that may well vary in different texts attributed to Paul and even in one passage as heard from different positions of power.

Second, Horsley's study of Philemon takes us through recent research. Is Paul commending Onesimus as a runaway slave? or as a slave who appealed to his master's friend? or as a slave sent by Philemon's church to Paul? or as an alienated brother of Philemon? And does Paul ask for amicable restoration to his master, for manumission, or for reconciliation to a physical brother? Horsley presents these recently-proposed options in a welcome critique of the traditional runaway-returned-to-master reading, and he gives a strong syntactic argument for a manumission request. Yet he seems at the end to favor Callahan's thesis of estranged physical brothers which takes the letter completely outside the realm of evidence concerning slavery, except as slavery language was used symbolically to refer to a disparaged brother (1993). Horsley is especially taken by Callahan's discovery in the same article that John Chrysostom may have originated the returned runaway hypothesis in the fourth century to depict Christianity as supportive of the social order. That Chrysostom originates this reading is of course not provable from our lack of earlier readings, and Callahan's note about Athanasius' use (1993: 368, n. 51) makes it less certain. But Callahan and now Horsley have exposed how well this reading has served ancient and modern slaveholding ideology.

As for an accurate interpretation of Philemon, the difficulty is of course Paul's indirection. Paul does not give unambiguous instructions. John M. G. Barclay (165–70) reads this as Paul's genuine doubt about what should be done. If Onesimus is freed, what about Philemon's obedient slaves, and if they also, how can this household host the church? But we have no evidence that Paul is doubting the church could function without the service of slaves. Winter argues that Paul does not speak directly about Onesimus in his opening thanksgiving because the recipients know he is with Paul and have sent him there.

But surely Paul's indirection, here and elsewhere, is best explained by the real difficulty of achieving what he is asking for, in this case apparently freedom for an enslaved person who has come into conflict with his slavemaster. Paul's emphatic negative in the clause, "receive him not as a slave, but better [or more] than a slave, as a beloved brother" makes this almost surely a request for freedom, considering Paul's penchant for an initial negative to stress his positions. Or if this is at all ambiguous, there remains Paul's concluding confidence that Philemon will do even more than he has asked.

Yet the reference to debt indicates a perceived past offense. Peter Lampe, who wrote an early and brief piece in the recent spate of articles on Philemon, offers the simplest explanation: Onesimus appeals to his master's Christian patron, Paul, due to a conflict with Philemon. Lampe provides some evidence that this was not considered flight if the purpose was to seek help in dealing with the master, and his thesis is developed further by Rapske (though he misses Lampe's point that the "debt" refers to the earlier conflict, not to theft as he leaves). Only the hypothesis of appeal to a friend can explain what otherwise would be a sheer coincidence—that Onesimus is thrown into a prison where Paul is held, or would be a foolhardy act—that Onesimus runs away to a prison, or that Paul harbors an escaping slave in prison. But the imprisonment has complicated the appeal, during which time Onesimus has helped Paul and been converted, and now Onesimus and Paul want something more than a tolerable return: freedom for Onesimus and continued support for Paul. But first they must deal with the initial conflict and its alienation, which Paul handles diplomatically, though it as likely began with an offense of the Christian master as of the unchristian slave. In any case, Paul's request of manumission for one man who has helped him is in no way a counter-cultural act.

Finally Horsley considers 1 Cor 7:21 and provides syntactic and literary evidence for the growing consensus that Paul concedes manumission. Paul inserts this reference as an exception to the general instruction he is giving that his hearers stay in the social relationships they had when called to believe. Horsley recognizes that Paul is coining this rule in response to widespread practice of sexual abstinence in the Corinthian church, calling on men and women to fulfill sexual commitments where immorality threatens by an indirect appeal to the baptismal confession, but one that reverses its social effect. If in Christ "there is neither Jew nor Greek," circumcision is "nothing," if "neither slave nor free," slavery is immaterial (yet "use [freedom]" when offered), and "if not male and female," then sexual relationships can as well be continued. Horsley, following Harrill, mentions the many other exceptions Paul has conceded throughout the chapter, which make most sense, as I have argued elsewhere (1990:72–97), if Paul is at pains to persuade women to concede sexual relations with men whom he has just depicted as threatening the community with immorality. Paul's exception for slaves able to gain freedom may show he is aware that they cannot otherwise make their own sexual decisions, as Jennifer Glancy has recently proposed.

Although Paul apparently shows more leniency with slaves seeking freedom than with women claiming the celibate lives expected for female prophecy, this does not support Horsley's thesis that Paul was thereby building "a new international society alternative to Roman imperial society . . . which he insisted stand over against the institutions of the dominant order" (p. 189). Paul allows slaves where possible to gain their freedom as a concession, just as he allows women to divorce without remarriage, and even to divorce and remarry if an unbelieving husband leaves (7:11, 15, 21). This very likely indicates that there is strong interest in these options in Corinth which Paul cannot afford to ignore. But the overall admonition is nonetheless to "stay in the calling in which you were called" (7:17–24).

It must be granted to Horsley that Paul adopts a message with strong apocalyptic roots when he begins to proclaim Jesus' death and resurrection as world-transforming events that incorporate Gentiles with Jews into God's people. At the same time we find commands of household subordination in the Pastoral epistles attributed to Paul in most of the historical length and global breath of the church. The traditional view, at least in the class of people who write about these things, has been that there is no conflict between the two, either because the triumph of Christ is yet to be consummated or because the subordination of women, slaves and children is a part of God's good order. Those Christians who experience an inescapable conflict have largely chosen with Horsley to claim that the weight of Christian witness confesses Christ risen from a death inflicted by the evil structures of this age and now alive and active by God's spirit in a world being transformed through faith into a new creation of justice and peace. We dare not see Paul less committed to this than ourselves. Yet the evidence is in fact negligible that he saw a full and free life for either women or enslaved people as an esssential part of this new creation. Perhaps the best we can do is to recognize that his calling to stand for Gentiles as God's people alongside the Jews was battle enough for one person, a battle in which he used up his life without succeeding.

But where does that leave us as we read Paul? One option is to apply Paul's devotion to our different callings and read aloud only the parts of Paul that point toward new creation today by a hermeneutic of literary freedom. I prefer as an historian to listen to the biblical witness more broadly, not only to the few writers who we then impress to speak our views, but to the multiple voices that can be reconstructed through them and their successors. So I tune in to those who first shaped the baptismal confession to say "neither slave nor free," to the enslaved in Corinth who constrained Paul to concede their right to seek freedom, and to Onesimus who risked an appeal to his master's patron and apparently won his freedom along with a new life in Christ. We see their successors buying slaves free in the early church as Horsley has documented. This is quite enough, whether or not Paul wrote letters that call for household subordination, because the witness is there and continues to be made down to the present.

In the week I was writing this my cousin's wife, Anne Thomas Clark, sent me a genealogy she has been compiling. There I read for the first time the will of my great great great great great-grandfather, Christopher Clark in 1754:

> I give to my loving son Bowling Clark four hundred acres [of land] in Hanover County [lying on the northwest side] joining the land of Mr. Thomas Carr ... ten young negros ... [two young negroes, named Nance and Robin, one horse named Spret, one gun, one feather bed and furniture, two cows and calves] my trooping arms, my great Bible and all my law books.

What do I do with such a heritage? Change my name? Hide this page and read the rest to my grandson? But what is shameful should be heard. This is family history, mine and that of others descended from those who were enslaved, and I must go through it rather than around it. Likewise Paul and the enslaved people whose lives shaped his writings are our collective family history. The shame and glory are tangled, and this "mess of pottage" is our precious heritage.

Works Consulted

Baldwin, James
    1963   *The Fire Next Time.* New York: Dial.

Barclay, John M. G.
    1991   "Paul, Philemon and the Dilemma of Christian Slave-Ownership." *NTS* 37:161–86.

Bradley, Keith R.
    1984   *Slaves and Masters in the Roman Empire: A Study in Social Control.* Brussels: Latomus; New York: Oxford University Press.

Briggs, Sheila
    1989   "Can an Enslaved God Liberate? Hermeneutical Reflections on Philippians 2:6–11." *Semeia* 47:137–53.

Callahan, Allen Dwight
    1993   "Paul's Epistle to Philemon: Toward an Alternative *Argumentum*." *HTR* 86:357–76.

Clark, Anne Thomas
    1998   Family Group Record 812: Documentation. An excerpt from the will of Christopher Clark, proved 26 May 1754 and recorded in Louisa County, VA. [The square brackets add material found in a less abbreviated transcript of the will.]

Cleage, Albert
    1968   *The Black Messiah*. New York: Sheed and Ward.

Finley, Moses I.
    1980   *Ancient Slavery and Modern Ideology*. New York: Viking.

Galen, Claudius
    1821–33   *Opera Omnia*. Volume 5. Edited by C. G. Kühn. Leipzig: C. Knobloch.

Glancy, Jennifer A.
    1998   "Obstacles to Slaves' Participation in the Corinthian Church." *JBL* 117: 481–501.

Harrill, J. A.
    1995   *The Manumission of Slaves in Early Christianity*. Tübingen: Mohr (Siebig).

Hopkins, Keith
    1978   *Conquerors and Slaves*. New York and Cambridge: Cambridge University Press.

Lampe, Peter
    1984   "Keine 'Sklavenflucht' des Onesimus." *ZNW* 76:135–37.

Martin, Clarice J.
    1990   "Womanist Interpretations in the New Testament: The Quest for Holistic and Inclusive Translation and Interpretation." *JFSR* 6:41–61.

    1991   "The Rhetorical Function of Commercial Language in Paul's Letter to Philemon (verse 18)." Pp. 321–37 in *Persuasive Artistry: Studies in New Testament Rhetoric in Honor of George A. Kennedy*. Ed. Duane F. Watson. Sheffield: Sheffield Academic Press.

Meyer Eduard
    1898   "Die Sklaverei im Altertum." Reprinted in *Kleine Schriften*. 2nd ed. Halle: Niemeyer, 1924.

Patterson, Orlando
    1982   *Slavery and Social Death: A Comparative Study*. Cambridge: Harvard University Press.

Rapske, Brian M.
    1991   "The Prisoner Paul in the Eyes of Onesimus." *ZNW* 37:187–203.

Schüssler Fiorenza, Elisabeth
    1992   *But She Said: Feminist Practices of Biblical Interpretation*. Boston: Beacon.

Winter, Sara C.
    1987   "Paul's Letter to Philemon." *NTS* 33:1–15.

Wire, Antoinette Clark
    1990   *The Corinthian Women Prophets: A Reconstruction through Paul's Rhetoric.* Minneapolis: Augsburg-Fortress.

Paul and Slavery: A Response

Stanley K. Stowers
Brown University

Richard Horsley's essay, "Paul and Slavery," lies at the heart of this rich collection of articles because it seeks nothing less than to overturn conventional ways of reading Paul on slavery. It argues for a new and more pleasing view of the apostle. He seeks to challenge the socially conservative uses to which the apostle's letters have been put. The debate which the article enters rests on three specific texts—1 Cor 7:21; Gal 3:28; Philemon—and the broader issue of whether Paul understands believers to be slaves of Christ. Against a spiritual Paul concerned about getting souls to heaven or a Paul who accommodates to the realities of the Greco-Roman world, Horsley's Paul is an apocalyptic revolutionary who wants to establish communities that follow the principle of Gal 3:28 as egalitarian counters to the Roman imperial order. I have various reactions to these proposals that could involve very many pages, but I will limit my comments to some of Horsley's arguments that I see as new and helpful and then focus on places where I take certain of the key texts and issues in a different way. I want to begin, however, with some remarks about what is at stake.

Horsley tends to write as if there were only two positions: staunch social conservatives who find a conservative Paul and social progressives who find a socially progressive Paul. But I think that he has neglected the possibility of social progressives who find a conservative Paul and who want to expose the problem of teachings that have often been used for reactionary purposes. Some of the slaves and children of slaves like those that Allen Callahan writes about who rejected Philemon or statements of Paul about slavery were of this bent. They were somehow able to affirm what they knew was morally right even though it meant denying the authority of scripture on that issue. Yet another approach would hold that Paul and his Greco-Roman culture do not so directly and easily translate into our social and political ideals. As much as we would like to have a Bible that is in our image, some aspects of those writings and their worlds are remote and even alien, truly different. Without falling into cultural relativism or condoning ancient slavery, this view asserts that historical comparison and evaluation is a much more complex and ambiguous task than any of the formulas above admit. Horsley and the other authors in the volume, I believe, face the challenge of walking a narrow path. Let me add one final point. I do not believe that our convictions that slavery and the subordination of women are evil come from or are based on the Bible. As Wittgenstein and others have taught us, these convictions are based on the way we live, on the practices that we inhabit, whatever role the Bible played in the origins of our culture's moral sense.

Horsley successfully criticizes one of the most distorting assumptions of much scholarship, namely, that one can properly distinguish the political from the religious in Greco-Roman antiquity or make the Bible apolitical. As he also points out, some have accepted the interweaving of the political and the religious for Greeks, Romans and Jews, but then used this fact as a foil. The spiritual religion of Christianity arose to correct the overly political and nationalistic religion of Judaism that had forgotten the prophet's message that religion is a matter of faith. I fully agree that Paul's scenario for the future and also for the present life of his assemblies is political-religious. The communities, as Horsley says, are "beachheads of the new age" that will replace this evil age (p. 163). The issue that I want to discuss is the character of those beachheads. Texts like 1 Cor 2:6–8 and 15:23–29 are explicitly about ruling and being ruled, the fate of the current political powers and a new political-religious order.

If we are to be honest, I think, we also must admit that the scenario is violent. The church had a difficult time accepting this apocalyptic violence as shown in its ambivalent reception of the book of Revelation. Something less like Jewish apocalyptic and more like Origen's educative redemption of the universe was embraced by many Christians who could not accept this divine violence. In spite of the church's spiritualizations, forgetfulness of the early church's apocalyptic elements, and its accommodation with the Roman Empire that created a "secular" and a spiritual division of power, the church did not forget the political dimension of the New Testament until the horrific religious wars of the sixteenth and seventeenth centuries understandably caused amnesia to set in. Until that time, the Christian life was seen as a matter of obedience that covered both obedience to God and obedience to men. Luther's two kingdoms and Calvin's view that both the church and the state were instruments of God's law, were versions of this central conviction that the Bible regulated all of human governance. Modern interpreters, however, have wrongly tried to find in Paul a view that only came with the Enlightenment. Instead of the traditional Christian idea that morals is a matter of obedience to the ordained hierarchy of human and heavenly masters, the thinkers of the Enlightenment created the idea that morality was a matter of self-governance. The apex of this radically novel doctrine was Kant's philosophy that made morality a matter of autonomy (Schneewind). It seems to me that Horsley rightly wants to bring the political back to our understanding of Paul, but still desires to hold on to the modern conception of the person as autonomous, self-governing.[1] I will return to this point in discussing Gal 3:28 and the other Pauline texts.

---

[1] To be more precise, it seems to me that Horsley's liberationist readings, especially of Gal 3:28, assume a modern idea of the individual, but he also gives a more fitting formulation

Horsley also sees Paul as an intellectual "involved in Judean scribal circles with an apocalyptic perspective" (p. 161). That Paul was an intellectual I judge to be a very important point that needs to be developed in New Testament scholarship. Horsley's angle here provides a very useful explanatory tool that places Paul in a concrete social role that makes historical sense in the early Roman empire, a role with its own kinds of power. I also heartily agree with Paul's connection to "apocalyptically" oriented Judean scribal circles. I would add that it is not helpful to then make a simple contrast of apocalypticism with hellenism, as if each were homogeneous and bounded. In fact, I find hellenism to be a significant component of apocalypticism. Furthermore I would argue that the politics of both varied much more than modern scholarship has admitted. Above all, I believe, that these are usually very unhelpful categories. We do not use hellenism in the way that the ancients did and apocalypticism is a conception created by New Testament scholars that picks features out of a heterogeneous collection of texts because they seem to have homologies in early Christian literature. As far as I can determine, there was no historical phenomenon called apocalypticism. It is a hermeneutical category in service of certain kinds of New Testament theology. There is certainly something right about describing Paul as apocalyptic and connecting his thought to stories and concepts in some of these texts, but the cost has been a failure to understand this aspect of Judean culture in a way that does not filter it through later Christian lenses.

The central thesis of the article is that Paul's apocalyptic scenario with Christ as Lord is directly counter to the imperial ideology of the Roman empire with the emperor as Lord. Paul was trying to establish "in effect, an international counter-imperial society" (p. 176). Moreover, the Roman order was the sponsor of conquest and colonial oppression, slavery and social hierarchy that Paul's work directly sought to oppose and overthrow with its egalitarian communities of the new age. I can only follow Horsley so far in this thesis. To the extent that all ruling powers belong to the present evil age, Paul sees them ultimately losing their power or being destroyed at the *telos* when a conquering Christ turns the subdued cosmos over to direct rule by God (1 Cor 15:23–29). Such scenarios are so totalizing and so dualistic that it is difficult to relate them to genuinely human programs of justice. How Paul related the injustice in the social order about him to such "apocalyptic" narratives is far from clear.

I want to make three points that qualify Horsley's thesis in broad ways before discussing the Pauline texts. First, it is difficult to precisely determine

---

when he writes that Paul, unlike ancient Stoic philosophers, "did not understand 'freedom' in a formal abstract individual sense [but as] a contingent historical shift from servitude to dehumanizing superhuman forces to obedience to God" (p. 176). One still has government by God and his agents (Christ, angels, human representatives) and not self-government. I would argue that the Stoics did not envisage freedom at all in any modern sense such as Kant's freedom of the will.

Paul's attitude toward the Roman empire and until I see a scholarship that builds a clear case about his overall stance, a certain amount of agnosticism seems to me the best attitude. The rulers of this age in 1 Cor 2:8–9 must at least include the Roman administration of Judea, but Paul only says that had the rulers understood God's mysterious plan, they would not have crucified Christ. This does not help much. It only tells us that the rulers acted out of ignorance. Even if we knew that Paul held some conventional Judean or "apocalyptic" Judean view of Rome, it would not be very helpful because there were so many and they were so variable and complex. Paul may have understood the empire not as the simple antithesis to everything good, but more ambivalently as a historical instrument of God, even if corrupt. It is well to remember that the anointed one, the savior, of second Isaiah is the Persian king, Cyrus. The history of Jewish attitudes toward foreign rule is very mixed. Some Jews, like Paul's contemporary Philo (*Legat.* 8–13), greeted the new world introduced by Augustus with accolades to match Isaiah's. But the bottom line, it seems to me, is that we just do not have the information from Pauline texts to paint the clear overall picture that Horsley does. Rather I suggest that detailed study of Paul's language on various matters may allow us to eke out good guesses about attitudes toward some elements of the imperial order. We know, for example, that he follows the theme of Augustan propaganda that depicted the age as a period of moral corruption and decline (Stowers, 1994:122–25, 52–65). But Paul does not exempt the imperial order as Philo did up to the time of Gaius. Thus he can adopt an imperial theme and then put it to his own uses. It seems to me that we will end up with a more ambiguous, but not uninteresting picture. Similarly, I have argued (Stowers, 1994) that Paul's ethical thought unlike most contemporary sources does not center on an immutable fight for self-mastery. I find this significant because Augustus had made self-mastery the central moral concept of imperial ideology and had connected it to issues of hierarchy in gender and ethnicity. Horsley's proposals about Christ as Lord and savior over against the emperor involve similar kinds of arguments. All of these proposals need to be more thoroughly investigated and much more detailed work done to situate earliest Christianity in the context of Roman rule.[2]

Second, if in our use of so-called apocalyptic literature to illuminate Paul, we must take seriously the socio-historical context and whole range of interests in that literature, then Paul will look less like a modern liberal thinker. I will give one example. Horsley follows the majority of New Testament scholars in taking "no Jew or Greek" in Gal 3:28 as eliminating ethnic difference for those who are in Christ. But this certainly does not fit any of the literature labeled as apocalyptic. He even writes (p. 168) that Judean scribes "cultivated

---

[2] A very helpful step in the right direction is Horsley, 1997.

an apocalyptic perspective in their struggle to maintain their own indigenous cultural traditions ... over against the dominant imperial culture." How is it that Paul is in any sense apocalyptic and yet wants to eliminate ethnic difference? The primary political-religious interest of most of the literature classified as apocalyptic is the Judean people, the temple and priesthood. How could Paul eliminate the significance of Judaism as it had been known, even of the temple, and still in any sense be apocalyptic? Furthermore, the enemies of the apocalyptic writers are as often other Judean groups with which they disagreed in their vision of Judaism as they are the Romans or Greeks. We must resist construing the Roman empire and Judean culture (i. e., Judaism) as two antithetical monoliths. That is to fall into a mythology of the apocalyptic literature itself. But the same writers betray their own mythology by revealing in their attacks on fellow Jewish enemies that many versions of Judean culture existed, were contested and always consisted partly of overlaps and borrowings from other cultural entities, e.g., Canaanite, Persian, Greek.

Third, if Gal 3:28 does not eliminate the significance of ethnic difference, i.e., of Judaism as it had been known, then the text does not carry the modern liberal individualistic conceptions that interpreters tend to associate with it and "no slave or free" also may not have modern abolitionist connotations. Modern thought about the person assumes an "I" centered subject construed as a true self that is a socially disengaged self. Ancient Mediterranean thought does not. Lawrence Wills, I believe, rightly stresses the hierarchy and different conception of the individual in antiquity. He also warns against supposing that our ideas of equality and individuality apply to the Roman world. The Jewish apocalyptic interpretation of Paul does not help Horsley's case as much as he thinks because that literature shares the same basic hierarchical social assumptions as the imperial ideology. The Qumran literature, for example, some of which does look for the defeat of Rome, is not egalitarian, does not liberate women, or do away with ethnic distinctions and slavery. The apocalyptic cosmos, from the masters of households to the high priest (and/or Jewish king) and from angels to the one God, is every bit as hierarchical as the world that Augustus wanted. These are different hierarchies, but they are both hierarchies deemed ordained by the divine will. Neither the imperial literature nor the Jewish writings ever question the naturalness and divine ordination of the ancient household that is the social, economic, political and religious foundation of those hierarchies, including slavery. This is a point to which I will return.

I am suggesting that Horsley's picture needs to be complicated and made messy. We scholars should resist falling into the simple dualisms of the Jewish and Christian sources. Horsley may not have made this mistake, but I would want to make his picture more ambiguous. Perhaps we could learn from the recent literature on colonialism which stresses that the colonized cannot avoid some implication in their own oppression and that the culture of colonization constitutes at least part of who they are (Comaroff and Comaroff; Bell: 81–117, 182–223). Cultural purity, like racial purity, is always a lie. Paul and Judean apocalyptic writings do not escape the interconnectedness of cultures. Horsley is far too sophisticated a scholar to fall into the "good apocalypticism, good Paul and evil empire" trap, but sometimes he seems to come close. One of the great ironies of Jewish history is that the great hellenizers of Judean culture were not the Seleucid Greeks, but the Hasmoneans who had opposed forced hellenization and championed a ideology of pure and sovereign Judaism. They won the battle against "hellenism" by remaking Judean culture along the lines of a hellenistic *politeia* with its own *paideia* (Cohen: 109–39). Similarly, as Shaye Cohen points out, most of the nineteenth and twentieth century anti-colonial movements were led by the most westernized elements of the population (Cohen: 138). Furthermore they often incorporated utterly alien features like European nationalism, western mythologies and bureaucracy into the newly liberated cultures. In colonial situations, one frequently sees indirect cultural resistance instead of outright opposition or open rebellion. Horsley, it seems to me, is suggesting just this in his discussion of Christ as Lord over against the emperor as Lord.

Horsley critiques and modifies the concept of a symbolic universe and scholars who sometimes in using that conception understand a central Pauline image to be that Christians are slaves of Christ. I agree that the idea of a symbolic universe ought to be critiqued and would push the criticism of Berger's and Luckmann's concept even further because it bears on the issues of Horsley's two articles in the volume. For all of the very important and useful aspects of their social theory, it has one insuperable flaw. Namely, it assumes a Cartesian picture of the human being. Humans are fundamentally minds in bodies whose basic "activity" is perceiving and knowing reality. The theory presupposes a unified "I" centered subject that integrates knowledge into a unified consciousness that often seems in their account to exist prior to sociality. In other words, the human mind is much like people have often conceived a god. The theory rightly attempts an account that avoids totalities like the "social structure" of functionalism and marxism, but produces another totality with its Cartesian mentalism. By totality I mean a social theory that has overarching explanatory features that are greater than the sum of the parts, human activities, and that seem to have an existence independent of people. Symbolic universe is just such a totalizing product of social mind in their theory. According to Berger and Luckmann (95), symbolic universes "... integrate different provinces of meaning and encompass the institutional order in a symbolic totality...."

I would argue that there are at least two problems with this picture that are relevant to slavery in the Roman empire. First, the idea of a totally integrated umbrella of a culture's ideas and symbols greatly exaggerates the unity and integration possible for any culture. A better description would be of a hodgepodge of often loosely linked, often conflicting and changing local domains and practices of symbolization that sometimes have a set of symbols and concepts widely perceived as highest or hegemonic. Even these latter are often contested. Take Roman religion, for example. It consisted of a set of common practices such as animal sacrifice and forms of divination together with a set of locally variable sacred times, a lay elite and a greatly variable pantheon of deities with broad agreement about the names of the deities at top of the pyramid. Beyond this, not much else connected local practice which itself was widely variable, including the characters and roles attributed to deities in the contexts of particular practices. There was no articulated common theology or institutional organization. Widely used symbols and artistic representation were subject to great indeterminacy in their interpretation. Knowledge was primarily a matter of practical skills rather than theoretical knowledge or conscious articulation. Even the imperial cult, though eventually found throughout the empire, was not centrally organized, but developed from what Greeks in the East perceived as a natural reaction that would put them in touch with the new world power (Price). Augustus and his successors certainly took advantage of these practices and produced models in art and ritual for emulation, but there was nothing comparable to orthodox Christianity where intellectuals governed an empire-wide organization that sought to produce uniformity in what people believed and did.[3] Even here variety and local practice were never controlled. Such cultural umbrellas, if one can even use this metaphor, then, are not bounded and unified wholes but rag tag accumulations, manipulations and linkings that always overlap with other cultural umbrellas such as Roman with Egyptian, Syrian and Judean. Intellectuals and leaders, of course, often claim that their cultural umbrellas are pure, bounded and unified. Paul versus the Roman empire, I believe, should be analyzed along these theoretical lines.

Second, the concept of symbolic universe places too much emphasis on distinct beliefs, concepts and symbols. This is a common mistake of intellectuals who often think that society works the way that they (mistakenly) perceive themselves. But I take as certain that human life is based on practical skills rather than ideas. Humans are actors. Thinking, believing and writing are actions with histories and social contexts (as Berger and Luckmann recognize) and not an independent foundation for action (here they are confused), rather than actions themselves. Ideas, concepts and symbols only come as components of human practices. Wittgenstein, Heidegger and many others have taught us on these points (Schatzki). Even intellectuals are intellectuals because of intellectual practices. Roman religion and politics and Pauline

---

[3] A caveat is necessary here. Augustus did cultivate a process that began during the late Republic of creating domains of universal knowledges that depended upon specialists. See the very important article by Andrew Wallace-Hadrill.

Christianity should be analyzed not as a collection of ideas or a foundation of ideas upon which institutions and actions are founded, but in terms of networks of linked practices that sometimes involve reflective thinking or symbolization. Horsley recognizes these principles in critiquing the reduction of the New Testament to ideas and theology. The concept of a Roman symbolic universe will mislead by reifying ideas and symbols apart from the myriads of local practices and the particular social contexts in which they are always found.

I am not entirely sure that what Horsley thinks is at stake is truly at stake in his criticism of Petersen, Martin and others for emphasizing the image of believers as slaves to Christ and God. I see no direct correlation between such language and the institution of chattel slavery. Horsley is surely right that the image is often a moral or other sort of metaphor that does not imply a clear idea of slavery to Christ. Ben Wright's essay, however, shows clearly that Jewish texts, including the scriptures, frequently spoke of Israel and Israelites or Judeans as slaves of God. Paul's conception of his apostleship aside, it seems to me that texts like 1 Thess 1:10; Rom 6:22, 12:10 and 14:18 do describe believers as slaves of Christ. But the image is a plastic metaphor that Paul uses in many ways and a number of these are well described by Horsley and those whom he critiques. Surely he is not denying that the Jewish and Christian God is an all powerful and demanding deity who requires absolute loyalty and obedience and who takes an intimate interest in how humans live. An unreconstructed Durkheimian would say that this god was modeled after human ideas of masters and kings. Many centuries of Christian preachers and theologians said that the rule of the true and living God was the model of every form of human-master relation. Either way, until modernity relegated God to the supernatural and religion to spirituality, and gave self-governance to humans, it seems difficult to deny that the idea of a cosmos consisting of God, Christ, various sorts of angels, demons and humans did not contribute to the legitimation of social hierarchy, even if Christianity also had some resources that could be mobilized for the cause of equality. Among these resources were texts amenable to righteous misreadings by slaves and abolitionists.

Horsley's interpretation of Paul as an opponent of slavery is based on his reading of Philemon, 1 Cor 7:21 and Gal 3:28 together with taking the last text as a baptismal formula and Paul's central teaching. He points to, if not finally follows, the interpretations of Sara Winter and Peter Lampe who argue that in going to Paul, Philemon's friend, Onesimus is not technically a fugitive slave, but nonetheless still a slave. Both scholars also see Paul as an advocate for the slave's freedom. In my view, Paul's language is so subtle and ambiguous that there will probably always be a debate about just what he was implying. Horsley then goes on to accept the bold work of Allen Callahan for whom Onesimus is not a slave at all, but Philemon's brother in the blood. Unfortunately, I am not persuaded by Callahan's valiant effort. His case rests on his reading of verse 16 where he translates *hōs*, "as though." In other words, Philemon is to take Onesimus back "as if he were no longer a slave." I do not quite understand what this would mean, but the interpretation will not work because *hōs* in itself carries no hypothetical or "as if" connotation. To say that Philemon will have Onesimus back "as a slave" means in the status of or person of a slave.

Horsley makes a good case for reading 1 Cor 7:21 as an exception to the principle of "remaining in the state in which you were called" that fits the pattern of other exceptions in chapter 7. He also rightly points to the importance of Chrysostom's comment that some in the ancient church read the statement to mean "if you can become free, become free." This shows clearly that the syntax of the verse was ambiguous for native Greek speakers. Horsley has not persuaded me that Paul clearly urges slaves to seek freedom in 7:21, but he has convinced me that this reading is possible and that the verse is extremely ambiguous even considering the context. Thus in my estimation, Philemon and 1 Cor 7:21 are ambiguous on Paul's view of whether slaves should seek or be given freedom. But even if one does read them in a liberationist fashion, they give no reason to suppose that Paul opposed or sought to overthrow the institution of slavery as such. For that, Horsley appeals to a certain understanding of Gal 3:28 and its place in the apostle's thinking. Here I have fairly strong disagreements and believe that interpreters typically make assumptions that are modern and will not work for the ancient text.

I can only make a few summary remarks about 3:28 in this context. A fuller consideration would require a close reading of chapters 3 and 4 of the letter and a study of ancient and Paul's versus modern conceptions of the human being. To begin with, we do not know that the verse was part of a baptismal formula, especially a pre-Pauline formula. What we do know is that Paul understands (1 Cor 12:13; Gal 3:28) a central meaning of baptism to be the creation of a unity "in Christ" that includes Judean/Greek, slave/free, and in Galatians, also male/female. 1 Cor 7:17–24, like 12:13, contains Judean/Greek and slave/free, omitting male/female. Of the three texts, only 3:28 is easily amenable to a modern egalitarian reading. In 1 Cor 7:17–23, the argument's explicit point is that believers ought to stay in the status which they had when they came to Christ. Even if one follows Horsley in construing slaves taking opportunities for freedom as marking an exception, it remains an exception to the rule of difference and hierarchy. The context in chapter 12 strongly emphasizes difference and hierarchical unity with the image of the body and its parts of lesser and greater honor and an ordered list of "offices" in the assembly. Surely the sense of 12:13 is that whether one is of the upper orders, Judean and free, or the subordinate, Greek and slave, all have drunk of the one spirit and are thus united in the body. Unity here does not seem to deny hierarchy, even in the assembly. Indeed, appeal to interdependent hierarchy is the ubiquitous ancient Mediterranean and Medieval European way of conceiving any sort of social unity. Unity in antiquity almost never implied equality.

Those who have taken Gal 3:28 as a proclamation of equality have been unclear about what this means and have tended to assume that our modern conceptions are unproblematic. A large range of modern discourse about equality breaks down into at least two distinct concepts. The first is the idea that humans have some fundamental capacity, say as moral agents, in which they are all equal. A second conception is that of a not yet ever realized social-economic program that would somehow give all people the same power, status and economic benefits and make this arrangement unchanging. Throughout the history of the West, the first has been extremely common and was not thought to conflict with social hierarchy. Paul is unlikely to have held a post-Enlightenment conception of equality. He is likely to have held some version of the first view, e.g., all humans have the same capacity for obedience to God. As Horsley rightly sees, his ideal is not based on the way humans now are, but on the future that God is working out in history.

Perhaps the most popular way to interpret 3:28 in recent years has been in light of a myth of original human unity, a heavenly undivided human or androgyne versus a divided and imperfect earthly human (Meeks; MacDonald). From Paul's references to the creation accounts in 1 Corinthians 11 and 15, it seems unlikely that he read Genesis in this way. He does, however, suppose a kind of original unity and an ontological hierarchy. Paul's argument in 11:3–10 seems to be that man was created first in the image of God. Woman was created "out of" man and bears the reflection of man and not directly the image of God. Moreover, the ever difficult verse 10 seems to claim that woman was created not directly by God but by angels, just as the law was given by angels in Gal 3:19–20 and signifies mediation rather than the direct work of God (BeDuhn). In other words, the cosmic and social chain of hierarchy and command looks like the expanded cosmology seen, for example, in later Platonism. Paul did not, like the author of the Gospel of John, read "let us make man" of Gen 1:26 as referring to Christ, but may have seen in the plural a reference to angels, with the creation of woman allotted wholly to them. Christ plays not a cosmogonic role in Paul's letters, but one related to the new creation. This current order of creation groans until the time that those in Christ receive full adoption as sons of God. Those in Christ now suffer with creation having only the first fruits of the Spirit, not yet immortal bodies (Rom 8:18–23). Paul never treats this future state as a return to a lost perfection, but as a long ordained new and final stage pioneered by Christ, the archetype of the new humanity. But Paul with much tension, in *ad hoc* statements about specific applications, often insists that the current hierarchy, even if ministered imperfectly by angels, is still in effect (e.g., 1 Corinthians 7; 11:1–16; Rom 13:1–7).

Paul did not trace the origin of the nations or slavery back to the order of creation. Slavery, like the origin of human division into many nations formed around false gods, he may have attributed to historical degeneration and a concession by God, based on his reading of Genesis 1–10.[4] The three texts (Gal 3:28; 1 Cor 7:17–24, 12:13) do not evoke some primeval human unity signified in the original creation, but the new unity of those who are sons of God in Christ. Although Paul's idea of man originally created as a unity and woman as a secondary division may possibly lie in the distant background of the male/female duality of 3:28, his concept of God's impartiality is its immediate context. The language of God justifying the gentiles has its sense in this concept. The verse belongs to a heated argument that tries to convince gentile followers of Christ in Galatia that they do not need to keep the Judean law or parts of it in order to be in Christ. Indeed, if they do keep the law, they are obliged to keep it all and become Judeans (5:3). If they did follow the law, they would be rejecting what God has given the gentiles as a free gift as gentiles. Chapter 3 argues that the gentiles in Galatia by being in Christ, the offspring of Abraham, enter the lineage of Abraham by adoption and thus become heirs to the gift of the spirit. This fulfills "the gospel preached beforehand to Abraham that in your seed (Christ) all the gentiles will be blessed" (3:8). The lineages of Abraham now potentially include all humans. Thus Paul explains that being baptized into Christ, they were united in him without consideration of preferences based on what we call social distinctions. The point relevant to Paul's argument being that they did not need to become Judeans to be in Christ (or of a certain gender or slave/free status). It was not relevant and they should not think that it is now relevant by being circumcised. In all likelihood, it never occurred to Paul that anyone else besides these gentiles in Galatia would ever read this argument.

In Romans, he addresses the "why." Why did God treat the other nations (and by analogy slaves and lower social classes) so graciously? God ultimately rules the world and he is an impartial ruler. There is a major unstated assumption here that forms the basis for Gal 3:28 that individuals from all peoples, sexes and social classes in principle have the same capacity for obedience and perfection by the Spirit. So, for example, in Rom 10:11–13 one can see how Paul might have derived his idea of the unity of all in Christ from his Christological reading of scripture: "For scripture says, '*Every one* who is loyal to him will not be put to shame.' For there is no distinction between Judean and Greek. He is the same Lord of all who bestows riches on all who call upon him. For '*Every one* who calls upon the name of the Lord will be saved'." Although the contexts of Isa 28:16 and Joel 2:32 do not warrant the ideas,

---

[4] Unlike the temporary gentile pedagogy under the law in Galatians, Paul never says anything about slavery being temporary, although he had opportunity in Philemon and 1 Corinthians where slavery is discussed.

because of the "every one" in both verses, Paul finds the notions of universal vindication of all humans who are loyal to Christ based on the principle that there is one God who is the sovereign of all people and a just and impartial judge. The notion of impartiality occurs explicitly only once in Galatians. In 2:6, Paul puts forth himself as an example of one who followed God's way of "not showing partiality" by refusing to treat preferentially those who held authority in the community of believers in Jerusalem. I would argue that Paul's example in chapters one and two establish the principles for the arguments of three and four.

Our tendency as modern Americans or Europeans is to fix on "there is no distinction between Judean and Greek" just as with "there is no" in Gal 3:28 and assume the modern romantic true self that is supposed to be beyond anything social or cultural. "Do not treat me as an American, a woman, a white southerner, but as just a person." Our assumption is that all of these social attributes are superficial and that to get at the truest deepest me one must peel away the socially imposed roles. But in ancient Mediterranean thought if you peeled away the roles and attributes you would find nothing. Even in Greek philosophy where there is the idea of a true self that can be analytically distinguished from social attributes, the philosophers assume that the socialized capacities and roles are the raw material for the improved habits of relating to self and other that could come about through reflective discussion (Gill: 240–455). The self is constituted in social interaction. Paul's letters evince a similar focusing of the self and relativizing of roles, but not the modern idea that there is a true universal self trapped behind the roles (Stowers, forthcoming). Thus I would argue that Paul cannot imagine a person who has no ethnic or gender attributes, even if these are leveled and relativized by attaining the mind of Christ.

Note that slavery is somewhat different from gender and ethnicity. God called Abraham and began to create a people after his will. He created man and woman with the help of angels. But Paul gives us few clues about the origins of slavery. Paul's scriptures certainly gave him resources for thinking slavery to be allowed by God. It seems to me that those who have seen Paul as an opponent of slavery have not come to terms with the scripture that Paul held as authoritative. Horsley emphasizes that Paul can appeal to the model of liberation from bondage in Egypt. It would be wonderful if Paul had said to Philemon or in 1 Corinthians 7, "Christ has freed us from our Egyptian bondage; masters free your slaves and treat them as equals," but he did not. Horsley tries to downplay slavery in the Hebrew Bible, but I disagree. Ben Wright's article, I believe, shows that slavery was significant in Israelite thought, even if the essay fails to emphasize that the Biblical legislation is utopian law in a narrative context and that there is little evidence of its peculiar features ever having been practiced. Slavery is pervasive, brutal and sanctioned by God in Paul's "Bible." True, Israelites were discouraged from owning other Israelites in some texts, but there are also provisions for making a fellow into a slave, even if not permanent chattel. In Lev 25:44–46, Israelites are told by God to buy slaves from the peoples round about them that they can possess along with the descendents of the slaves forever. War is another approved means for acquiring slaves (Deut 20:10–18), although this means is restricted to women and children because all captured men are to be killed. Gen 9:24–27 curses one third of humans to slavery in a decree that the narrative will later use to justify conquest and ethnic cleansing. My guess is that Paul probably read these texts as temporary concessions that belonged to the old age, but that would not be abolished until the age to come.

Gal 3:28 seems to mean that all of those in Christ regardless of ethnicity, gender or social status have the Spirit and its benefits granted in the current age. It does not, I think, mean that ethnicity or the sexes or social status has been eliminated, even if the importance of such roles has been relativized because the form of this world is passing away. Only modernity has entertained the idea of an asocial, disengaged self. Even Jesus Christ is a Judean, a man and free. If Paul's idea was, for example, that Christ would lead humans to become angelic beings, then it is in virtue of becoming non-human that one could imagine a self that has no social attributes. But even if this were a true account of Paul's view, it would only happen in a heavenly future, and not this order of creation. I agree with Horsley that both the order that Paul wanted for his assemblies and that he imagined would take place with Christ's return is political and not spiritual. It is only spiritual in the sense of being empowered by God's spirit, but it certainly involved power, a hierarchy of governance and social relations.

If Gal 3:28 does not contain the modern romantic notion of an asocial core self, then it might contain some more concrete notion of equality. Absolute equality would be complete sameness of individuals and their relations. Ordinarily equality means sameness in some respect. A modern version of equality uses the notion of self-governing agents who are the subject of legal, economic and political rights regardless of social roles and statuses. In Greco-Roman antiquity there was a widespread idea of the equality among peers of a certain class of persons over against other classes. In classical Athens, for example, all citizens were in theory to be equal in terms of legal and political status in the city. There was also a similar conception of the equality among members of the Roman senatorial order or equestrian order. The Pauline argument concludes that Judean/Greek, male/female and slave/free all have been adopted into the Abrahamic lineage and are sons of God with equal rights upon the analogy of sons in a family. But this does not mean that Paul envisaged the end of these hierarchies in this age. In the new family, Christ will be the "first born of many brothers" (Rom 8:29). In this context in Romans, sonship is a future event of which those in Christ now only have a taste through the Spirit (8:23). All descendants of Abraham, as Judeans, are sons of

God (Rom 9:4) rather than godless gentiles, but with no thought of eliminating slavery, social classes, gender or, of course, ethnicity. So it comes as no surprise that this is exactly how Paul seems to treat issues regarding women, ethnicity and slavery. He relativizes the social roles in relation to Christ, but does not eliminate them. Judeans are not to seek to reverse circumcision or gentiles to become Judeans, women to forget their veils and places, but these identities take second place to serving the new cause of Christ.

Thus I agree with Horsley that Paul is opposed to the order of the current age including the political and social order, but his letters do not provide a clear social and political critique and a plan for a new order except in terms that are too mythic to be practical for the reform of human social and political communities An apocalyptic mythology makes the current order doomed and provides hope for a band of true believers. It does not reform society. The weight of reform falls upon us with our many resources from modernity without very much help, I fear, from the Bible. I also agree that the social-religious-political experiments that were Paul's assemblies might have provided a space for serious social play and a loosening of roles and statuses. But room for play and loosening do not mean an articulated social ideal. Rather, Paul's focus on the unitary goal of Christ made all other values relative (Stowers, forthcoming).

Scholars in the Augustinian traditions of western Christianity often overlook the most powerful way in which Paul indirectly articulated a social ideal, namely in the Pauline virtues. Greek and Roman traditions often thought of virtues as the qualities of relating to self and others in a social-political-religious community. The concept of virtues answered the question, what qualities do I need to live my life so as to play my part well in the kind of community that is the ideal? The Pauline virtues ought to be analyzed along these lines and compared to others like the virtues sanctioned by the new order wrought by the emperor Augustus. Perhaps here we might learn something useful and discover an implicit social order.

But there is, I believe, another sense in which Paul's writings attack slavery and the subordination of women. The radical implications of certain advice to his communities are largely unintended consequences. The most radical of these is his failure to support marriage and the practices maintaining intergenerational continuity. These were absolutely central to ancient Mediterranean society. Ancient religion whether Greek, Roman, Egyptian or Judean was largely about the gifts of land and womb given by the gods so as to sanction particular ethnically organized kinship groups beginning with the household. For Paul to say that he would prefer that believers follow his example and not marry is to strike at the foundation of ancient society, the household itself. The social-political implications become apparent when one understands the social-moral organization of the ancient Mediterranean household. The household was where nearly all economic activity took place.

It was conceived as a collection of human and non-human property and the control that belonged to the *kyrios*. The goal of the household was the leisure of the master; leisure not in the modern sense, but in the ancient sense of the elective (i.e., free or unconstrained) activity of culture-religion-politics. Most activity in the latter necessarily hyphenated areas was the domain of free men, i.e., masters (*kyrioi*) and soon-to-be masters. This cultural-religious-political order rested almost entirely upon the labor of women, children and slaves of various sorts. The Gospel of Luke even has Jesus and the disciples supported by a group of women (8:2–3). Paul radically breaks the mold by insisting on working with his hands. The ideal of the household economy, of course, was achieved in various degrees. The very poorest Greek or Judean farmer or artisan might have no slaves. But to the extent that the master participated in the leader-ship of the local community, public religious practices, educational activities and so on, it was because the women, children, apprentices, widowed or orphaned relatives taken in and others labored to provide the household's space for those leisure activities. Slavery, however, was pervasive and households who were too poor to own slaves wanted to own them and would acquire them if their situations improved. Paul's attack on slavery and the abuse of women and children came not through any doctrine of social equality or program of liberation or any intentional plan, but through refusing to marry and thus form a traditional household and by insisting on living by his own labor. This model of Paul, the ideal ascetic, was followed by many thousands of later Christians and struck at the very foundation of Greco-Roman society. Thus even if Paul at some time owned slaves, the model life that he left in his letters structurally attacked slavery by attacking its social basis, the household, and its continuity through inheritance from master to master.

I make one last point for the sake of perspective. Ironically the only Christian writer of antiquity who wanted to abolish slavery and may have actually tried to effect a fully egalitarian community was not the canonical Paul, but the despised "Carpocratean," Epiphanes.[5] Epiphanes in his work, *On Justice*, drew on Paul, especially regarding the law, but probably also Gal 3:28. He also did away with marriage and the traditional family explicitly because they instituted injustice and inequality. But he is likely to have also drawn on the *Politeia* of Zeno, the founder of Stoicism, which also called for complete equality and an end to slavery (Erskine; Dawson: 264–76). Because only small fragments of the work remain, scholars debate whether Zeno envisioned a practical program or an ideal society. It is, however, now widely agreed among experts on Greek philosophy that Hellenistic philosophy was not individualistic and that important strains of Greek philosophy sought the

---

[5] According to Clement of Alexandria, Carpocrates was the father of Epiphanes. The sources are convienently collected in Smith.

actual reform of society and the establishment of ideal societies. So Paul was one inspiration for the one Christian thinker and leader in antiquity who wanted to abolish slavery and indeed Paul himself may have been influenced by some of these philosophical currents (Engberg-Pedersen). So also, as Horsley and this volume show, Paul (read in modern categories?) has also been an authority for a truly just vision of society that would allow no room for slavery. The debate will go on as to whether this is the historical Paul or a righteous misreading.

Works Consulted

BeDuhn, Jason David
    1999   "'Because of the Angels': Unveiling Paul's Anthropology in 1 Corinthians 11." *JBL* 118:295–320.

Bell, Catherine
    1992   *Ritual Theory, Ritual Practice*. New York: Oxford University Press.

Berger, Peter and Luckmann, Thomas
    1966   *The Social Construction of Reality*. Garden City, N.Y.: Doubleday.

Callahan, Allen Dwight
    1997   *Embassy of Onesimus*. Valley Forge, Pa.: Trinity Press International.

Cohen, Shaye J. D.
    1999   *The Beginnings of Jewishness*. Berkeley: University of California Press.

Comaroff, John and Jean Comaroff
    1992   *Ethnography and the Historical Imagination*. Boulder, Colo.: Westview.

Dawson, Doyne
    1992   *Cities of the Gods: Communist Utopias in Greek Thought*. New York: Oxford University Press.

Engberg-Pedersen, Troels
    Forthcoming   *Paul and the Stoics: An Essay in Interpretation*. Edinburgh: T&T Clark.

Erskine, Andrew
    1990   *The Hellenistic Stoa: Political Thought and Action*. Princeton: Princeton University Press.

Gill, Christopher
    1996   *Personality in Greek Epic, Tragedy, and Philosophy: The Self in Dialogue*. Oxford: Oxford University Press.

Horsley, Richard A., ed.
    1997   *Paul and Empire: Religion and Power in Roman Imperial Society*. Harrisburg, Pennsylvania: Trinity Press International.

Lampe, Peter
    1985   "Keine Sklavenflucht des Onesimus." *ZNW* 76:135–37.

MacDonald, Dennis Ronald
    1987   *There is No Male and Female: The Fate of a Dominical Saying*. Harvard Dissertations in Religion. Philadelphia: Fortress.

Meeks, Wayne A.
    1974   "The Image of the Androgyne: Some Uses of a Symbol in Earliest Christianity." *HR* 13:165–208.

Price, S. R. F.
    1984   *Rituals and Power: The Roman Imperial Cult in Asia Minor*. Cambridge: Cambridge University Press.

Schatzki, Theodore
    1996   *Social Practices: A Wittgensteinian Approach to Human Activity and the Social*. Cambridge: Cambridge University Press.

Schneewind, J. B.
    1998   *The Invention of Autonomy: A History of Modern Moral Philosophy*. Cambridge: Cambridge University Press.

Smith, Morton
    1973   *Clement of Alexandria and a Secret Gospel of Mark*. Cambridge, Mass.: Harvard University Press.

Stowers, Stanley
    1994   *A Rereading of Romans: Justice, Jews and Gentiles*. New Haven: Yale University Press.

    Forthcoming   "Does Pauline Christianity Resemble a Hellenistic Philosophy?" In *Paul Beyond the Hellenism/Judaism Divide*. Ed. Troels Engberg-Pedersen.

Wallace-Hadrill, Andrew
    1997   "*Mutatio morum*: The Idea of a Cultural Revolution." Pp. 3–22 in *The Roman Cultural Revolution*. Ed. T. Habinek and A. Schiesaro. Cambridge: Cambridge University Press.

Winter, Sara
    1987   "Paul's Letter to Philemon." *NTS* 33:1–15.

www.ingramcontent.com/pod-product-compliance
Lightning Source LLC
Chambersburg PA
CBHW030523230426
43665CB00010B/746